LAND of THE SOUTH

LAND of THE SOUTH

James W. Clay

Paul D. Escott

Douglas M. Orr, Jr.

Alfred W. Stuart

Oxmoor
House.

© 1989 by Oxmoor House, Inc.
Book Division of Southern Progress Corporation
P. O. Box 2463, Birmingham, Alabama 35201

All rights reserved. No part of this book may be reproduced in any form or by any means without the prior written permission of the publisher, excepting brief quotations in connection with reviews written specifically for inclusion in magazines or newspapers.

Library of Congress Catalog Number: 84-62443
ISBN: 0-8487-0547-5
Manufactured in the United States
First Edition

Executive Editor: Candace N. Conard
Production Manager: Jerry Higdon
Associate Production Manager: Rick Litton
Art Director: Bob Nance

Land of the South

Editor: Cecilia C. Robinson
Editorial Assistants: Margaret Allen Northen, Pam Hall,
    Susan Cheatham
Designer: Earl Freedle
Production Assistant: Theresa L. Beste

For the University of North Carolina at Charlotte:
Staff Cartographer: Jeff Simpson
Cartographic Assistants: Gary Addington, Carla Jean Alman,
    Miles Champion, Kelly Culpepper, Hope Julian Craven,
    Jackie Johnson McKeon, Antonia Gomez Patten, Kevin
    Porterfield, Thomas A. Roff, Sarah Park Stuart

To subscribe to *Southern Living* magazine, write to *Southern Living*®, P. O. Box C-119, Birmingham, Alabama 35283.

CONTENTS

ACKNOWLEDGMENTS

This book is intended for anyone interested in the relationships between the land of the South and the people who live on it. It is a compelling story, and we have sought to make it clear to the lay reader as well as to the academician. The text is based on a wealth of scholarly research, but it is presented in nontechnical and jargon-free language. Colorful graphics are used to illustrate and amplify the various themes. Through this approach, we hope to fill a void between the coffee-table book and a reference book.

This nontechnical approach to complicated subjects has emerged over the years as some of us saw the need to provide substantive information to a broad population about the area in which they live. The first major product was a portrayal of the larger Charlotte region, the *Metrolina Atlas,* published in 1972. A similar approach was followed in *North Carolina Atlas: Portrait of a Changing Southern State* (1975) and in a series of Charlotte atlases, the most recent published in 1987. In between those, the North Carolina Department of Commerce saw the need to display the state's urban areas and commissioned several of us to produce a series of atlases on eight urban regions. All of these books have proven to be useful to public officials, business executives, editorial writers, the general public, and a generation of school students.

Throughout this time, we became increasingly aware that much of the change occurring in North Carolina was part of a bigger story, the dramatic economic and population growth of the entire South. Consequently, the idea of an atlas-style treatment of the South grew in our minds, and we began to seek support for such a project. During the course of this search we came to know John Shelton Reed, widely published student of the South and a sociologist at UNC Chapel Hill. John subsequently mentioned us and our ambition to John Logue, Creative Director of *Southern Living®*, who, in turn, encouraged us to present our idea for Oxmoor House's consideration. The rest, as they say, is history, but we remain grateful to John Shelton Reed for speaking for us and to John Logue and Oxmoor House for their generous and patient support. We hope that this book justifies for them their leap of imagination in backing us.

This is not a work of original research so much as an attempt to present information from a vast array of studies and accounts. We gratefully acknowledge the intellectual treasure that scholars, authors, and early settlers left for us to use. Often our largest problem was deciding what not to include from that wealth of studies and information.

Doing the research for and writing this book was a major task in itself, made possible only through the help of a dedicated pair of editorial assistants, Carol Rhea and Cheryl Ramsaur Roberts. They were models of persistence, thoroughness, and diplomacy. Cheryl came along just as Carol was leaving to take a new job. Without Cheryl's patient labors, this book would not be ready to publish yet.

On top of the writing, however, there was the labor of producing the numerous original maps and charts that illumine the text. They were created in the Cartography Laboratory of the UNC Charlotte Department of Geography and Earth Sciences. Funding for this was provided by Oxmoor House through the UNC Charlotte Urban Institute. Mary Dawn Bailey and Bill McCoy provided administrative support for the project.

Jeff Simpson, Staff Cartographer, was the creative force behind the design of many of the graphics, and Gary Addington kept the work flowing through the darkrooms. A small army of cartographic assistants, listed on the copyright page, worked diligently to construct the maps and graphs. At times they must have felt that their task was endless, but we hope that what they see in this book justifies their labors.

Our colleagues within the Department of Geography and Earth Sciences also have our thanks for helping in a myriad of ways: discussing specific concepts, providing reference materials, and being patient when we were preoccupied with working on the book.

A highly capable group of secretaries provided clerical assistance throughout the nearly six years it took to complete this project. Becky Guy was the only one to see it from beginning to end, but we also thank Joy Stewart, Anne Roberts, Dori Thurman, Mary Skidmore, Marsha Armes, and Scotty Williams.

We also want to acknowledge the meticulous and patient editing of Cecilia Robinson. Mistakes, inconsistencies, contradictions, and omissions creep into a complicated work like this, but Cecilia caught most, if not all, of them. Any that remain are the responsibility of the authors, not Cecilia and the editorial staff at Oxmoor House. We hope that our readers will focus on what is interesting and correct and be tolerant if they find something displeasing.

Finally, we thank our families for understanding and support, especially our children, who are of the next generation to live in the Land of the South.

James W. Clay

Paul D. Escott

Douglas M. Orr, Jr.

Alfred W. Stuart

The University of North Carolina at Charlotte

PREFACE

As our world becomes more and more complex, we continually search for the means to understand and control the environment. In this quest, especially in our highly technological society, we sometimes lose sight of the important relationships between ourselves and the land on which we depend for our very livelihood.

In a sense, the South is a stage, complete with richly diverse and picturesque sets, on which the human story is played out. *Land of the South* begins with the region's geologic history, then proceeds to the early Indian impact, European entry and settlement, the retardation effects of war and racial separation, and finally the present-day Sunbelt phenomena of population immigration and urbanization.

The introductory chapter of the *Land of the South* addresses the age-old questions of what and where is the South, and what of this land, always of great promise and on the edge of transition. Chapters 2 and 3, "Land of the South" and "People for the Land," present an overview of the physical and human character of the South as it has evolved.

This book's basic framework, however, focuses on the land-people drama in the geographic dimension. Consequently, chapters 4 through 16, in which the authors subdivide the South into eleven regions, form the heart of the book. From the Chesapeake Bay to the Dry Margin, every one of these regions has played a unique role in the development of the South in addition to supplying a distinctive local history. These eleven regional chapters are grouped under two larger headings, "The Lowland South" and "The Upland

The Natural Regions of the South

South." The book's last chapter, "The Land and the Future," is a perspective on the manner in which the South's future is evolving within an increasingly dynamic national and international context.

The South can best be understood as a visual experience, so the text is complemented by a variety of color photographs, maps, graphs, and charts. These graphics aid in capturing the diversity of the Southern people and their land and are particularly helpful in highlighting subject matter discussed in the text and depicting patterns in time and space.

The *Land of the South* is not meant to be all inclusive; an in-depth account of the Blue Ridge geologic uplifting or of the Civil War experience should be looked for elsewhere. But the story that follows graphically depicts a complex physical environment that has had an unending pattern of human interrelationships. The rich history of the South's land and its people can serve as a kind of universal experience. Perhaps it will aid us in gaining a better understanding of where we have been and where we might be headed as custodians of the physical environment and, in the words of the late Adlai Stevenson, as "we travel together, passengers on a little space ship, dependent on its vulnerable reserves of air and soil; . . . preserved from annihilation only by the care, the work, and I will say the love we give our fragile craft."[1]

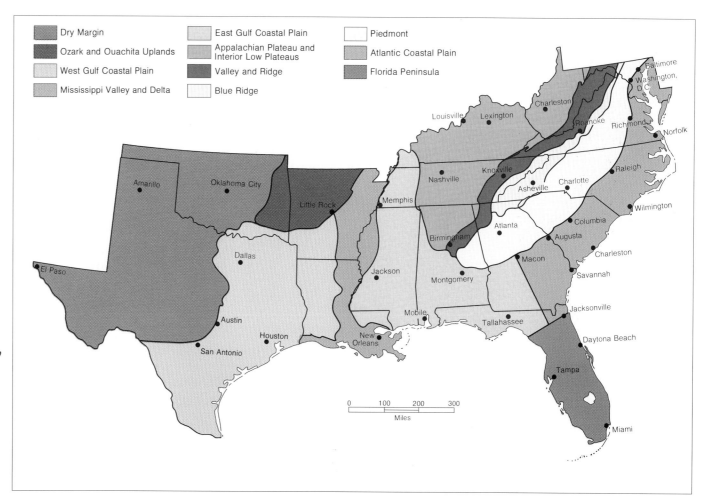

Dry Margin	East Gulf Coastal Plain	Piedmont
Ozark and Ouachita Uplands	Appalachian Plateau and Interior Low Plateaus	Atlantic Coastal Plain
West Gulf Coastal Plain	Valley and Ridge	Florida Peninsula
Mississippi Valley and Delta	Blue Ridge	

PART I OVERVIEW

1 INTRODUCTION

What is the South? Is there one? Or is the Southern section of the United States more myth than substance? . . . Surely there lurks somewhere a South, a tangible, knowable, living South, with traditions and meanings and ideals to serve the present and future as well as the past.

FRANK E. VANDIVER
The Idea of the South

The South, one might say, is a tree with many age rings, with its limbs and trunk bent and twisted by all the winds of the years, but with its tap root in the Old South.

WILBUR JOSEPH CASH
The Mind of the South

The American South embraces a broad spectrum of the North American continent, from the Atlantic and Gulf coastal plains inland and upward through the great Appalachian system and the Ouachita Mountains. A closer look at this spectrum reveals the South to be a mosaic of smaller physical provinces that formed the background for the unfolding human drama.

Few regions of the world have witnessed as richly filled chapters of human endeavor in juxtaposition with the physical environment as has the South. The land has been part of a continuing series of vignettes with widely varying hues: the first Southerners, with their centers of the highly developed Indian civilization; the European pioneers, who established the coastal toeholds and trekked through river basins and high mountain passes; the development of a distinctive plantation economy, which led to the enslavement of a large black population; the devastating war fought to preserve that economy; the South's bitter defeat and the empty promises of a reconstruction; and the belated emergence of a New South, with all its opportunities as well as new problems.

A common thread throughout this story is the affinity of the people for the land. It is an enduring closeness, this feel for the soil, the seasons, and the numerous settings. Many explanations have been advanced for the conspicuous role of the physical environment in the life of the South. Certainly, the diverse and striking nature of the land is one factor. The long growing season, abundant rainfall, and good soils strengthened the agrarian culture. And the delayed development of major manufacturing and urban centers helped to maintain a rural landscape of farms and small villages and towns. The consequence is a strong sense of place, a smaller scale of things, and a love of the land.

This trait of close kinship with the land and "getting back to the soil" has sometimes been expressed as a reaction against a New South of industrialization and cityscapes. In 1930, a group of 12 Southern writers, the self-styled Nashville Agrarians, delivered a treatise entitled *I'll Take My Stand*. It called for the South to reject the lure of an urban society and return to the fundamental values of an agrarian and rural life. At that time the Southern states were still overwhelmingly rural, but the warning was already being sounded. The Agrarians, however idealistically and romantically, were echoing a deeply felt preference of an earlier Southern statesman and farmer, Thomas Jefferson, who contended that a rural society represented the best values not only of Southern tradition but of civilization in general.

Other peoples in various parts of the globe have experienced a close relationship to land and nature. Nevertheless, there is little question that this kinship is a major characteristic in defining the South as a region and people, and it must be interpreted to fully understand the South.

*The land of the South
is a mosaic of many expressions.*

WHAT IS THE SOUTH?

The search for a theme or a set of criteria to define the South has been an ongoing task of Southern scholarship, journalism, and popular discussion, both within and outside the region. It seems the South has always been the most talked about, defined, and re-defined section of the country. It is distinctive in the United States as a place apart, a region that is, in a way, a "history without a country." Indeed, its past is filled with many histories flavored by myth and reality, and objective criteria do not come easily.

It has often been noted that few regions of the world have bred so great a cast of characters and variety of subcultures as has the South. Josephus Daniels, newspaper editor and historian, once described Southerners as "a mythological people, created half out of dreams and half out of slander, who live in a still-legendary land."

There are, in fact, many different Souths and Southerners. A cursory browsing of most libraries reveals a diversity of book titles about the region describing the South as "new," "old," "everlasting," "changing," "sunny," "romantic," "solid," and "not so solid," adding spice to the variety as well as to the mythmaking. Historian George Tindall notes that the main burden of Southern mythology resides in two images born of the internal conflict of the nineteenth century: the romantic myth of gentility on the one hand and the abolitionist myth of barbarism on the other—a sunny South versus a tragic South, or in contemporary vernacular, *Gone with the Wind* versus *Roots*. More recently, there has been a journalistic tendency to define the South in terms of "Southern-fried chic," with the hallmarks including pickup trucks, good old boys, and grits.

Historian Ulrich Phillips contended that the focal theme of Southern history has been one of race, with its history of divisiveness, prejudice, and conflict, but this attempts to simplify a multifaceted story. More realistically, the South is a region and a people that share a common historical and cultural experience.

WHERE IS THE SOUTH?

The search for the Southern identity extends to the question of geography. Is there a definable piece of the North American continent that is the "Land of the South," or is the South "a geography of the spirit?"

Many boundaries have been drawn for the South, but no universally agreed-upon physical place has been established. Just as the historian looks for a theme and a pattern over the course of time, the geographer's craft includes regional delimitation, stemming from a regional concept based on appropriate criteria. The concept for the South, of course, must be strong enough to transcend the considerable number of subregions that exist throughout the area. Within the single state of North Carolina, for example, there are three distinct subregions: the Atlantic Coastal Plain, with its Deep South heritage of plantation agriculture and tenant farming; the urban-industrial midlands called the Piedmont; and the western Appalachian Mountains, with their unique history and geology. Florida offers just as sharp internal contrasts: the northern panhandle reflects a kinship with south Georgia or Alabama, and the peninsula creates a Sunbelt mosaic of retirement communities, exploding urbanization, Disney World, and Latin America. There is even a South that exists in the North and Midwest, including Southern blacks in Brooklyn's Bedford-Stuyvesant area and Appalachian immigrants in the mills of Chicago and Cincinnati and on the assembly lines of Detroit.

By what measures are the boundaries around a contiguous South to be drawn? The guideposts for the Old South would run along the lines of mules, magnolias, and mockingbirds. Howard Odum, in his classic 1936 book, *Southern Regions,* developed over 700 items that characterize the South, including such disparate criteria as climate, black population, ruralism, individualism, good songs, and moonshiners. Writer Fred Powledge, after an odyssey through the region, reflected that the South is anywhere restaurants serve grits in the morning, and the Deep South is where they bring the grits without asking. While criteria can be detailed endlessly, if one accepts the idea of a common historical and cultural experience and, stemming from that, a conspicuous regional consciousness, perhaps acceptable boundaries come into focus. In other words, in what areas (or states) do people think of themselves as Southerners?

In regions throughout the world, there is a core area where regional traits and consciousness have their most intense expression. For the South, this area is usually considered the Old or Deep South. Perhaps it could just as well be referred to as Dixie. Sociologist John Shelton Reed observed that "Dixie" is a purer or meaner term than "Southern," and he conducted an experiment to define a core area as well as a total Southern region by the relative frequency of those terms in telephone directory listings of companies. His Old South or Dixie extended in a belt from the Carolinas' Atlantic Coastal Plain through Mississippi.

Regionalism does have a kind of ripple effect in that regional feeling is strongest in the core area and then subsides as one moves out from the epicenter.

But there are aberrations in this geographic symmetry because, as it has often been pointed out, Dixie is as much a matter of attitude as latitude. The key consideration is where to draw a boundary that encloses the South. The original Mason-Dixon Line could serve as the northernmost boundary, but it is generally forgotten and of little relevance today.

The most accurate boundaries would tend to ignore state lines. For example, southern Ohio, Indiana, and Illinois have strong Southern features. East Texas is Gulf Coast Southern, while west Texas (west of the Balcones Escarpment) is Southwestern. Southeastern Oklahoma, which shares with Arkansas the Ouachita Mountains, is Southern as well. Geographer Wilbur Zelinsky has developed a "Southern Cultural Area" that encompasses just such a region (FIGURE 1.1B). This approach no doubt gives the most precise boundaries of the South. And yet, however diverse each state may be in its internal divisions, a state does have a unique historical and cultural experience of its own that figures into the legacies and destinies of the larger region. For that reason (as well as the pragmatic consideration that data accumulation is often on a state-by-state basis), state lines will be maintained in this book's Southern delimitation.

Perhaps the most frequently used grouping of Southern states, at least from a historical perspective, is the original Confederacy, which includes Alabama, Arkansas, Florida, Georgia, Louisiana, Mississippi, North Carolina, South Carolina, Texas, Tennessee, and Virginia (FIGURE 1.1A). Howard Odum's *Southern Regions* also counted 11 states but substituted Kentucky for Texas. In 1985, the South's major economic development organization, the Southern Growth Policies Board, encompassed Odum's 11 states plus Texas

(which has subsequently withdrawn) and Oklahoma (FIGURE 1.1C). At one time or another it also listed Maryland and West Virginia. Finally, the Bureau of the Census includes all of the above mentioned plus

Delaware and the District of Columbia (FIGURE 1.1D), while the Southern Governors Association adheres to the census delimitation of states but adds the territories of Puerto Rico and the Virgin Islands.

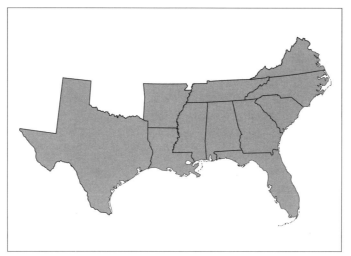

FIGURE 1.1A *The Confederate South*

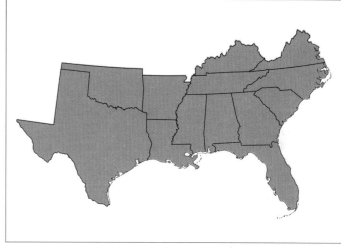

FIGURE 1.1C *The Southern Growth Policies Board's South, 1985*

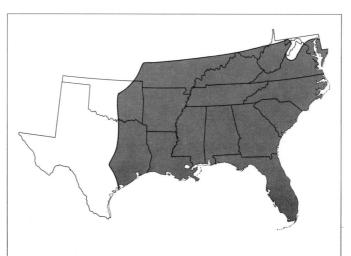

FIGURE 1.1B *Wilbur Zelinsky's Southern Cultural Area*

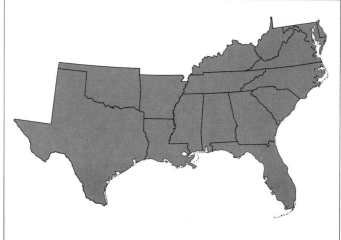

FIGURE 1.1D *The U.S. Census South*

2 LAND OF THE SOUTH

EVOLUTION OF THE LAND

The land of the South is the product of global forces that have been operating for billions of years. These forces are enormously powerful, yet they work with excruciating slowness. Basic to this process are the still incompletely understood natural mechanisms for forming and rearranging the very continents themselves. The crust of the earth has had a dynamic history during which continents have emerged, moved, collided, separated, and moved on. These movements and associated events in the surrounding ocean basins have created both the great mountain systems and the broad plains of the earth. Along with episodes of mountain building, the less dramatic but equally powerful forces of erosion and deposition, products of gravity and climatic conditions, slowly modified the new landscape by tearing down mountains and turning rock into soil.

The predecessor of today's continent of North America took shape at least several billion years ago. It was a broad platform, the core of the present continent. Most of the present South was ocean floor. By about 570 million years ago, much of the southeastern edge of the contemporary continent was comprised of troughs or elongated depressions in the ocean floor in which great thicknesses of sand, mud, and organic remains were deposited. Sometimes thousands of feet thick, these layers slowly sunk into the earth's crust. A belt through central Maryland, Virginia, western North Carolina, northern Georgia, central Alabama, southern Mississippi, Louisiana, and along the Gulf Coast of Texas was the site of a deep trough with volcanic islands scattered throughout it. Immediately west, from Virginia to Alabama, was a shallower trough. The climate was tropical, and coral reefs were characteristic of this shallow marine environment. The sea covered the continental interior west of this trough, again leaving behind layers of limestone, shale, and sandstone. With time and earth movements, these layers hardened and were lifted up out of the sea floor.

Geologic Time Scale

Millions of years ago	Era	Period		Epoch
0				
1	Cenozoic	Quaternary		Recent or Holocene
2				Pleistocene
3				
4			Upper	Pliocene
5				
6				
7		Tertiary		Miocene
8				
9				
10				
20				
30				Oligocene
40			Lower	Eocene
50				
60				Paleocene
70				
80		Cretaceous		
90	Mesozoic			
100				
		Jurassic		
200		Triassic		
		Permian		
300		Carboniferous — Pennsylvanian / Mississippian		
		Devonian		
400	Paleozoic	Silurian		
		Ordovician		
500		Cambrian		
600				
700				
800		Younger		
900	Precambrian			
1000				
2000		Older		
3000				

TABLE 2.1 *Geologic Time Scale*

The thick layers of sediments formed a veneer on top of the ancient low platform of the continent. Meantime, great events were beginning to occur to the east of ancestral North America. Most notably, the supercontinent of Gondwanaland, containing primary elements of ancient Africa, South America, Antarctica, and Australia, was on the move.

Close examination of the map of ancestral North America reveals that an important segment of the coastal area was missing (FIGURE 2.1). Eastern

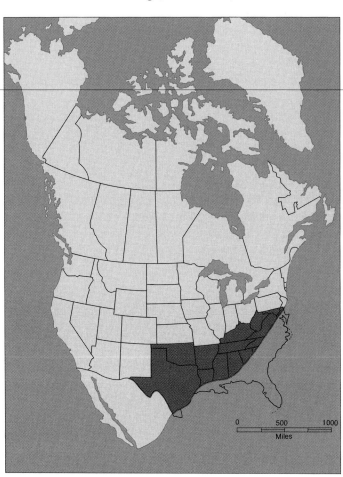

FIGURE 2.1 *Ancient Coastline of the South*

Ancestral North America, about 570 million years ago. The present coastline is sketched in to show how much of the eastern margin was missing at that time. The remainder of the North American coastline, north of Mexico, is shown as it is today.

Mountains, are now classified as *metamorphic* (changed form), since they reflect an earlier existence as sandstone, shale, and limestone, respectively—the kinds of rocks that presently underlie the surface to the west.

East of the present Blue Ridge Mountains, the collision of ancestral North America with Gondwanaland created an even more massive upheaval that produced a major mountain range, of which the current Piedmont is a radically diminished remnant (FIGURE 2.3).

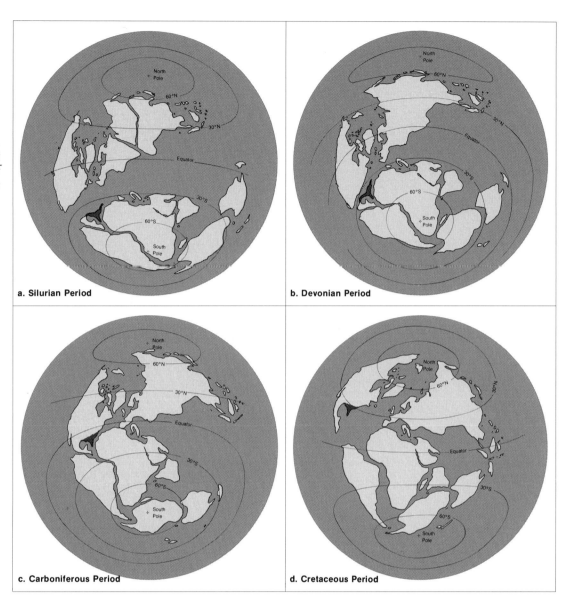

FIGURE 2.2
Continental Drift and the Completion of the Land of the South
A. **Silurian period** (395–435 million years ago). Note the fragment that includes Florida, part of the Atlantic Coast, and the Gulf of Mexico just off the coast of Africa.
B. **Devonian period** (345–395 million years ago). North America has moved close to Africa and South America.
C. **Carboniferous period** (293–345 million years ago). The Florida fragment has been sutured to the coast, and North America is taking on its present shape.
D. **Cretaceous period** (65–136 million years ago). The continents have been pulling apart since the Carboniferous period, and North America has reached its current location.

a. Silurian Period

b. Devonian Period

c. Carboniferous Period

d. Cretaceous Period

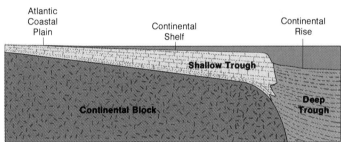

450 million years ago
Cross section of coastal margin prior to the breakup of Gondwanaland

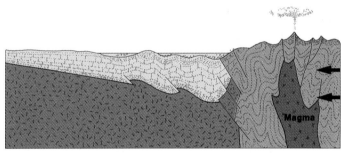

300 million years ago
Mountain building associated with crustal movements pushing in from the east

Virginia, most of the Carolinas, and huge chunks of Georgia, Alabama, and Mississippi were not there. Florida did not show at all. A similar examination of FIGURE 2.2 shows that the missing segment, along with the entire western rim of the Gulf of Mexico, was a part of Gondwanaland, which was near the South Pole at the beginning of the Silurian period (about 435 million years ago). Movement apparently began about that time, and the space between ancestral North America and Gondwanaland began to close. Sometime between 300 and 350 million years ago, the two landmasses collided with a slow, grinding majesty of inconceivable power.

The crushing force of the continents' collision bent and broke the old marine sediments that covered the eastern part of ancestral North America. Evidence of this still exists in the contorted strata of the eastern Appalachians, whose rocks were also changed radically by the heat and pressure of the collision. In the western part of the Appalachian system, the folding and faulting were less severe and gradually played out, leaving the original horizontal layering of the sedimentary rocks almost intact. Similarly, the intense heat and pressure that transformed the rocks in the east also diminished to the west, leaving the western rocks in a much less altered condition. Rocks such as quartzite, slate, and marble in the eastern Appalachians, particularly in the Blue Ridge and Great Smoky

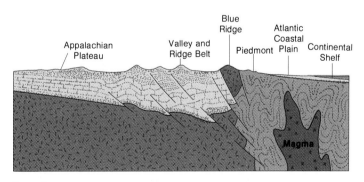

Present
A much-eroded remnant of earlier landforms

FIGURE 2.3 *Cross Section of Major Geologic Episodes in the Formation of the Land of the South*

The processes that caused the collision began to reverse by about 200 million years ago, and Gondwanaland pulled away from North America, forming the Atlantic Ocean basin in the process. During the pullback, however, the missing piece of North America was left behind, having been sutured to the Atlantic Coast of ancestral North America.

In the millions of years following these awesome events, erosion attacked the great mountain chain along the East Coast and the various lesser ridges that had been thrust up by the collision to the west. Enormous quantities of weathered rock were carried out to sea to be laid down on the ocean floor.

By about 136 million years ago, the mountains east of the current Blue Ridge were so lowered that it was possible for the oceans to invade the interior along the coast. As the waters lapped up on the rocks of the Piedmont, layers of sand, clay, and lime mud were again laid down on the sea floor. Sand dunes were created along the shores of this new coastal margin. This marine invasion not only affected the Piedmont along the Atlantic Coast but also covered a broad rim around the Gulf Coast as well, reaching far into the interior of North America along the present course of the Mississippi River.

The oceanic invasion waxed and waned over the next millions of years, but a general retreat was underway (FIGURE 2.4). By 25 million years ago, a large area was dry land again, especially from Alabama into eastern Texas. By the Pleistocene period, which began less than two million years ago, the flooded area was small, confined to strips in eastern Maryland, Virginia, and North Carolina; eastern Georgia and Florida; and the Gulf Coast west of Alabama. This last episode of oceanic flooding was associated with the great ice sheets that invaded northern North America during the Pleistocene period. As the glaciers grew, the sea level fell, only to rise again as the glaciers melted. This episode of fluctuating sea level ended about 10,000 years ago, as the latest glacier surge also ended. Thus, the coast as it is now known emerged only recently.

The layers of sand, clay, and lime mud that were laid down during these episodes of oceanic invasion make up the coastal plain area of the contemporary

FIGURE 2.4 *Oceanic Invasion of the South*

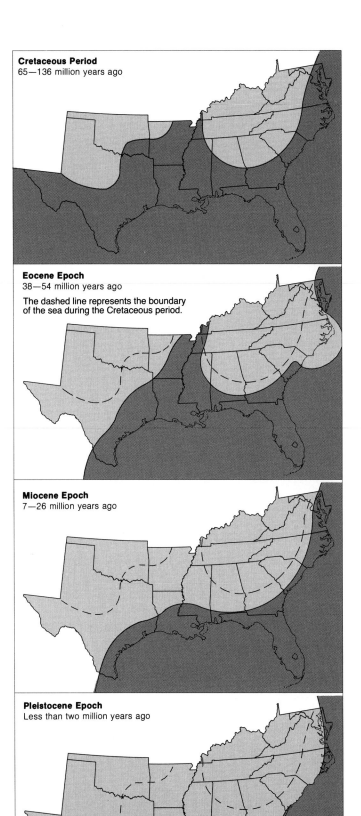

Cretaceous Period
65—136 million years ago

Eocene Epoch
38—54 million years ago
The dashed line represents the boundary
of the sea during the Cretaceous period.

Miocene Epoch
7—26 million years ago

Pleistocene Epoch
Less than two million years ago

South. These recent sediments represent a veneer on top of the underlying harder rocks. The Sandhills of the Carolinas are the old sand dunes that mark the innermost coastal line. The fall line is the zone along this old coast where the hard rocks of the Piedmont reemerge at the surface. The term *fall line* is very descriptive because it is here that the crystalline rocks give rise to rapids or falls in streams that cross them, ending navigability. East of the fall line, rivers can easily erode their channels through the softer coastal plain sediments. The fall line is not present inland along the Gulf coastal plain because the crystalline rocks of the Piedmont do not occur there. Instead, the transition is from the coastal plain sediments to older, harder sedimentary rocks that covered the interior platform of North America.

The Pleistocene ice sheets never reached the South, but the region was affected by them in a variety of ways. One effect, as noted, was the rising and falling of the sea level. Another was the rearrangement of river channels, causing the predecessors of the Ohio and Mississippi river systems to be relocated southward. The current New and Kanawha rivers that flow through North Carolina, Virginia, and West Virginia are tributaries of the ancient Teays River that preceded the Ohio River and which flowed originally across Ohio, Indiana, and Illinois (see "Teays—The Lost River" in chapter 14 on page 167).

As the ice melted, the water gorged the rivers that drained southward, especially the Mississippi. Northeastern rivers, principally the St. Lawrence, were dammed by the ice for a time, greatly increasing the load of water and sediment in those rivers that remained open. Today, the Mississippi flows across a broad floodplain in a valley that is underlain by these Ice Age sediments. Since the Ice Age, the river has cut its channel deeply into layers of these glacially derived materials, some of which now form bluffs several hundred feet above the present river.

The preceding discussion was simply background explanation for the geologic framework of the contemporary South. To the casual eye, the surface geology is hidden by vegetation, soil, and the works of man. Rarely is the bedrock visible at the surface to represent the greater mass that lies underneath. FIGURES 2.5A and 2.5B portray the underlying geology as if it were not obscured from view.

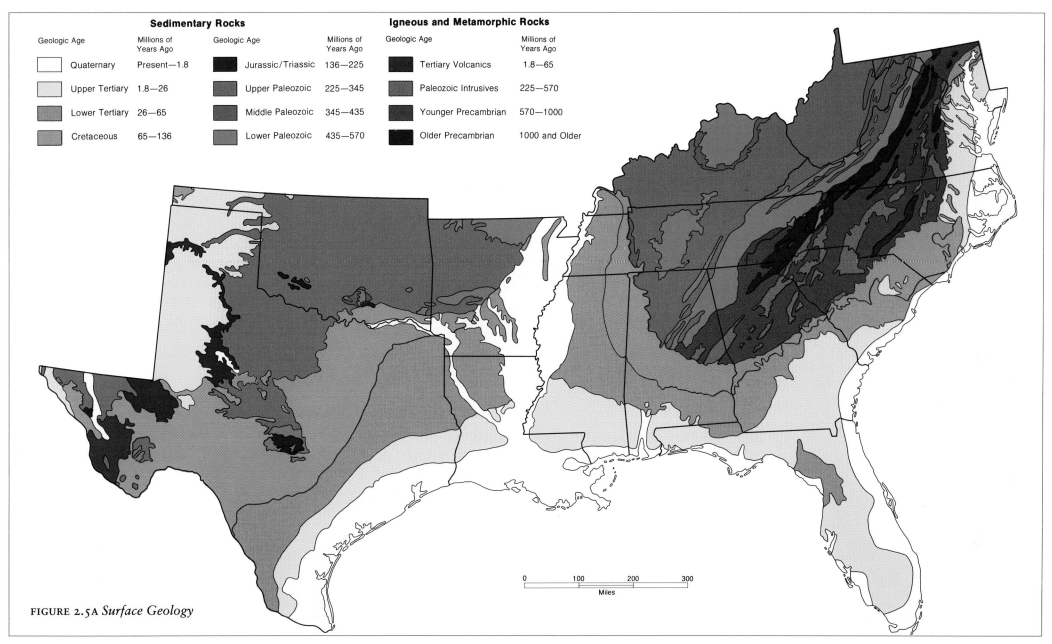

Sedimentary Rocks

Geologic Age	Millions of Years Ago	Geologic Age	Millions of Years Ago
Quaternary	Present—1.8	Jurassic/Triassic	136—225
Upper Tertiary	1.8—26	Upper Paleozoic	225—345
Lower Tertiary	26—65	Middle Paleozoic	345—435
Cretaceous	65—136	Lower Paleozoic	435—570

Igneous and Metamorphic Rocks

Geologic Age	Millions of Years Ago
Tertiary Volcanics	1.8—65
Paleozoic Intrusives	225—570
Younger Precambrian	570—1000
Older Precambrian	1000 and Older

FIGURE 2.5A *Surface Geology*

0   100   200   300
Miles

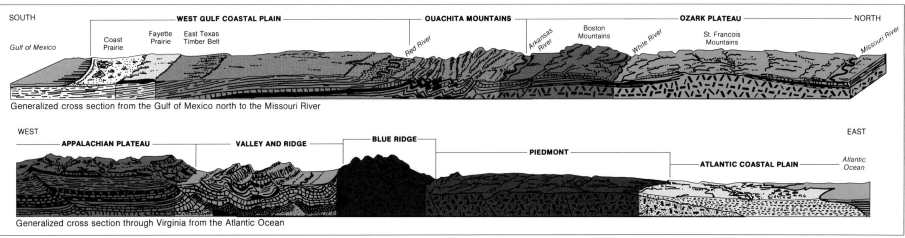

FIGURE 2.5B
Schematic Cross Sections
These cross sections are intended to illustrate the various geologic and physiographic areas in general terms only, rather than matching precisely the surface geology shown in FIGURE 2.5A.

SOUTH — **WEST GULF COASTAL PLAIN** — **OUACHITA MOUNTAINS** — **OZARK PLATEAU** — NORTH

Gulf of Mexico — Coast Prairie — Fayette Prairie — East Texas Timber Belt — Red River — Arkansas River — Boston Mountains — White River — St. Francois Mountains — Missouri River

Generalized cross section from the Gulf of Mexico north to the Missouri River

WEST — **APPALACHIAN PLATEAU** — **VALLEY AND RIDGE** — **BLUE RIDGE** — **PIEDMONT** — **ATLANTIC COASTAL PLAIN** — Atlantic Ocean — EAST

Generalized cross section through Virginia from the Atlantic Ocean

The shadings of yellow identify the unconsolidated sediments that were left by the various geologically recent invasions of the sea. Appearing in dark brown are the badly deformed (metamorphic) and deeply eroded rocks of the Piedmont area. Interspersed with the metamorphic rock are areas where materials were implanted in *igneous* (molten) form, either onto the surface through volcanoes or as subsurface injections. In some cases, the latter were subsequently exposed to the surface as erosion removed the covering layers.

The small, dark green areas on the Piedmont represent remnants of an episode that occurred about 220 to 225 million years ago. At that time, faulting created basins in the surface of the Piedmont, which were filled with sand, gravel, and silt along with occasional volcanic mountains. These Triassic basins collectively make up about five percent of the total area of the Piedmont.

Most of the ancient metamorphic and igneous rocks of the Piedmont and the Blue Ridge Mountains occur in areas of geologically "middle-aged" rocks (several hundred million years old) that still reveal their sedimentary origins. The long strip that parallels the mountains is somewhat older than the rocks immediately to the west. At some point in the past, the relatively horizontal layers of rock that make up middle Tennessee and most of Kentucky were arched enough to allow water to erode through the surface layers and expose the underlying limestone. This process formed the Nashville and Lexington basins, both known for their rich soils derived from the limestone rocks.

The westernmost part of Texas was affected by the forces, including strong volcanic activity, that created the Rocky Mountain system. In northwest Texas, a deep invasion of the sea was accompanied by the deposition in that sea of layers of sand, gravel, and other materials that washed off adjacent mountains to the west.

LANDFORM REGIONS

The long geologic history of North America has left the South with a varied landscape. Most of it is composed of plains, and truly high mountains are not present. However, the Appalachian Mountains have been a major factor in the history of the region, even though only a few of the peaks exceed 6,000 feet in elevation. The variety of landforms is a complex pattern to the traveler, but they can be organized into landform groups or regions of relatively homogeneous character. These regions form two broad landform categories: the Lowland South and the Upland South.

Lowland South

By far the most extensive area in the South is the coastal plain that extends from eastern Maryland in a great arc all the way westward to the Mexican border and beyond. It is less than 100 miles across in Maryland, widens to as much as 150 miles in North Carolina, then spreads to encompass all of Florida, reaches its maximum width of over 500 miles in the valley of the Mississippi River, and finally remains no less than 150 miles in width through Texas. The plain is a land of geologically young sediments that rises slowly away from the coast, and many rivers enter it from the higher interior. The Atlantic Coastal Plain, Florida Peninsula, East and West Gulf Coastal Plains, and Mississippi Valley and Delta make up the Lowland South (FIGURE 2.6).

Upland South

The term *upland* refers to a variety of features including mountains, hills, plateaus, and elevated plains. They occupy most of the northern rim of the South, especially the northeastern and western parts. The most famous portion is the Appalachian system, which has four major subdivisions: the Piedmont plateau, the Blue Ridge system, the Valley and Ridge corridor, and the broad Appalachian and Interior Low Plateaus.

Across the Mississippi Valley are the twin hill areas of the Ozarks and Ouachitas. West Texas and Oklahoma contain the southern part of the extensive High Plains that cover much of the interior of North America. This region also marks a climatic transition from the humid South to the dry Southwest. Dryness is even more notable in a fragment of the Basin and Range area in Southwest Texas. The Dry Margin, Ozark and Ouachita Uplands, Appalachian Plateau and Interior Low Plateaus, Valley and Ridge, Blue Ridge, and Piedmont constitute the Upland South (FIGURE 2.6).

FIGURE 2.6 *Landform Regions of the South*

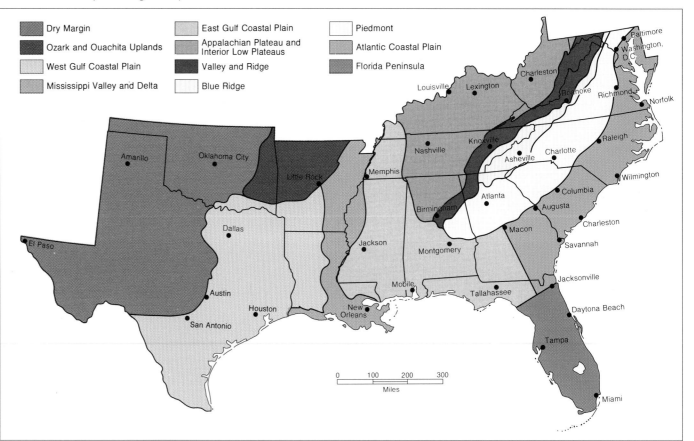

WEATHER AND CLIMATE

The daily weather and long-term climate of the South are determined basically by latitude, which controls the amount of sun energy that is received, and proximity to the oceans that supply most of the atmosphere's moisture. The land modifies this moisture supply when mountain barriers interfere with air movement or when large land areas isolate a region from ocean areas.

The influences of these conditions are best understood in terms of great masses of air that form in certain locations and move across the earth's surface (FIGURE 2.7). They bring with them the characteristics of the area in which they originated. Their movements appear to be controlled by the jet stream, a current of air flowing from west to east at velocities sometimes exceeding 200 miles per hour. The jet stream is typically 30,000 feet or more above the earth's surface, and it drags along air masses beneath it. Occasional wavelike movements in the jet stream cause air masses to penetrate farther north or south than usual.

As their name implies, the maritime tropical air masses that generate over the Atlantic and Caribbean oceans and the Gulf of Mexico are warm and moist. When they invade the South, they produce warm or hot weather with high humidity, some cloudiness, and the ubiquitous afternoon thunderstorms of summer. By contrast, the Arctic air masses that originate in northwest Canada are relatively cool and dry. In wintertime, they bring frigid air deep into the South because of the lack of mountain masses to block their southeastward thrust. Only the Appalachian Mountains are large enough to impede the invasion of these Arctic air masses.

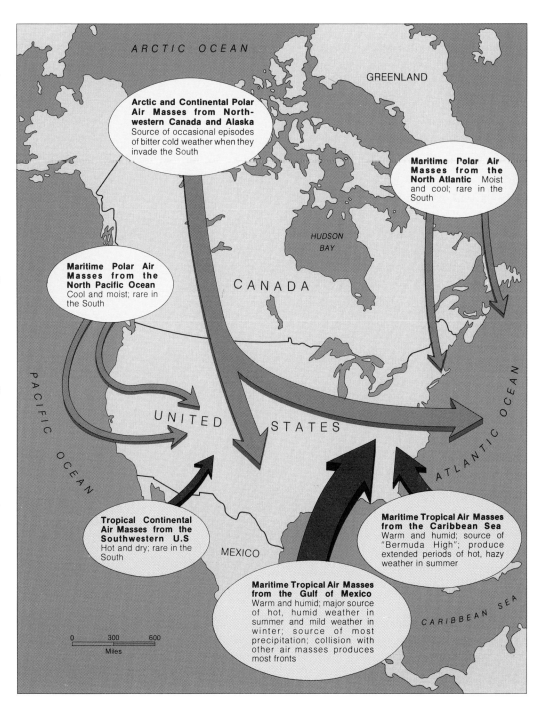

FIGURE 2.7
North American Air Mass Source Regions

FIGURE 2.8A
Typical Mid-Latitude Cyclone

The cyclonic storm is an air mass with relatively low atmospheric pressure at its center. Winds in the northern hemisphere flow into the center in a counterclockwise direction. Precipitation occurs in the center as the converging air rises and cools. It also occurs along fronts, lines where warm and cold air portions of the storm contact each other. Uplifting air associated with the front sometimes triggers thunderstorms and tornadoes. The storm path is the route followed by the moving system.

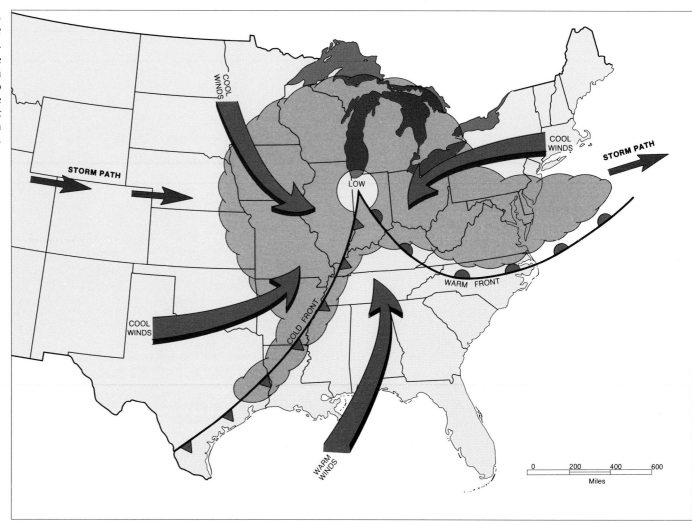

The passage of air masses affects weather in another important way when two unlike masses collide to form weather fronts, which are zones of contact between sharply contrasting bodies of air. The land areas of the South are battlegrounds over which invading air masses move and regularly collide. These collisions typically cause the warmer air along the front to be lifted (FIGURE 2.8B). Precipitation (rain, snow, or sleet) often results from the cooling that occurs as the air is lifted (FIGURE 2.8C).

As the contrasting air masses collide, they not only produce weather fronts (contact zones) but also form large swirls of air known as mid-latitude cyclones. These are associated with broad cloudy areas and precipitation, especially inside cyclonic storms (FIGURE 2.8A). Extended periods of rain or snow are almost always products of cyclonic storms. More severe thunderstorms and tornadoes may develop near the fronts themselves when conditions are conducive for rapid updrafts of very humid air, especially when fronts separate strongly contrasting air masses. On the television news weather maps, the cyclonic storms are shown with Low (L) in the middle and one or more fronts radiating as lines from the L to the edges. Cyclonic storms are often hundreds of miles across and can move as fast as 30 to 40 miles per hour.

The hurricane is a more violent cousin of the mid-latitude cyclone that forms over warm oceanic areas. It is much more compact and lacks fronts because its high velocity winds mix the air more thoroughly. While more dangerous and dramatic than cyclones, hurricanes are fewer in number and contribute far less to total precipitation and air movement than do the cyclones.

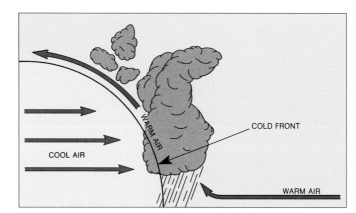

FIGURE 2.8B *Typical Cold Front*

The cold front is the line of contact between warm and cool air masses within the storm. As the cool air pushes against the warm air, the less dense warm air is thrust upwards. The resultant cooling causes air to hold less moisture. Condensation occurs, forming clouds that in turn often yield heavy precipitation of short duration.

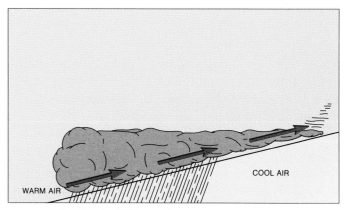

FIGURE 2.8C *Typical Warm Front*

The warm front develops where warm air pushes up over a mass of heavier cool air. Since warm air has a lower density, its push is not as strong, resulting in a gentle ascent along the front. The slow ascent yields light precipitation that can last for several days.

The movements of air masses, storms, and fronts produce the characteristics of daily and seasonal weather. Precipitation and air temperature are the most familiar elements. In general, the South is characterized by warm weather (FIGURE 2.9) with long, hot summers and mild winters. In most areas rainfall is abundant and distributed evenly throughout the year (FIGURE 2.10). The heat of summer distinguishes the region, even in literature and drama, but equally important to residents are the other distinct seasons of the year. Autumn and spring are beautiful rewards for the sticky heat of summer, and winter is a refreshing, cool period that only occasionally brings freezing weather or snow.

Actually, the heat of the Southern summer is often exaggerated. Large areas of the Midwest have hotter summers than do parts of the South (FIGURE 2.11). Atlanta, for example, averages fewer hours with temperatures above 80°F than does Sioux Falls, South Dakota. Higher humidity levels in Atlanta create greater discomfort, however.

Thunderstorms average one every six to ten days and so are fairly common in the South, especially north of the Gulf of Mexico. The Gulf provides the moisture that is essential to the formation of such storms (FIGURE 2.12). Thunderstorms are also somewhat more frequent over the Piedmont of the Carolinas, but the heaviest concentration is over Florida and the Mississippi River Delta. In those areas, thunderstorms average one every four to five days.

These thunderstorms are important contributors of overall rainfall in the South, where total precipitation averages at least 35 inches per year, except in western Texas and Oklahoma. Many areas receive 50 inches or more, especially along the Gulf Coast and Florida, but the highest totals are recorded along the western slopes of the Great Smoky Mountains, where the high elevations cause air masses to yield moisture as they rise to cross the mountains.

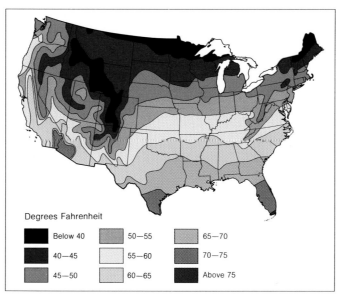

FIGURE 2.9 *Average Annual Air Temperatures*

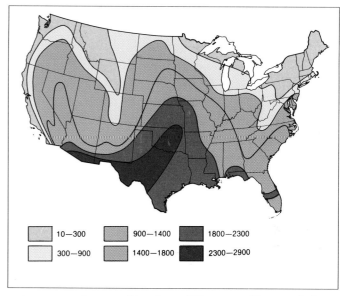

FIGURE 2.11 *Average Number of Hours per Year with Air Temperatures over 80°F*

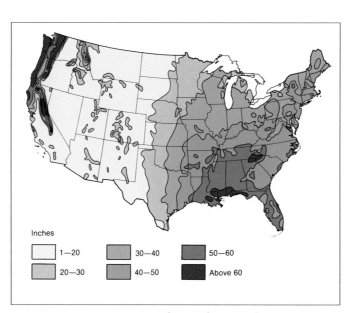

FIGURE 2.10 *Average Annual Distribution of Precipitation*

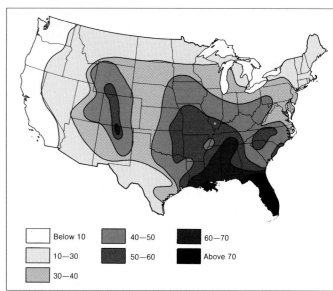

FIGURE 2.12 *Average Annual Number of Days with Thunderstorms*

Most precipitation in the South is in the form of rain; snowfall is light. Along the Gulf Coast and in Florida, snow is a rare event. South of Tennessee it averages less than five inches per year, and many years are without snowfall at all. In the upper South, snowfall is more common, especially in the higher elevations of the Great Smoky and Blue Ridge mountains (FIGURE 2.13).

A useful way to generalize about the weather of the South and to compare it in practical terms with other regions is to look at relationships between moisture and temperature. FIGURE 2.14, for example, relates mean annual precipitation with mean annual temperature for a variety of cities. Most of the Southern cities show up as warm and wet. Those along the coast and farther South are highest in these respects, whereas the more northerly and inland cities are cooler and drier. The more westerly parts of the South receive significantly less precipitation. The influence of elevation is seen in the lower temperature levels of Asheville and Roanoke.

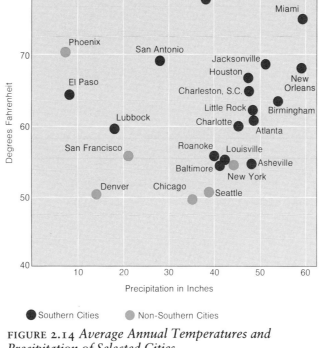

FIGURE 2.14 *Average Annual Temperatures and Precipitation of Selected Cities*

In this chart, the Southern cities are distinguished mainly on the basis of higher average warm-season temperatures, and the more southerly ones have higher precipitation as well. The mountain cities of the South resemble some of the non-Southern cities.

For comparison, a sample of non-Southern cities shows that they are distinguished by lower temperatures in the eastern United States and lower precipitation as well in the West, except for humid Seattle.

The pattern is similar for the summer season when temperature is compared with the relative humidity of the air (FIGURE 2.15). The latter is a measure not just of moisture but also of the air's ability to cool by evaporating moisture from the skin and other surfaces. "It ain't the heat but the humidity," although a cliche, is true. Almost all of the South is warm and humid, but so are New York and San Francisco.

Still another useful way of interpreting climatic conditions is the *degree day* concept. The number of heating degree days is calculated by subtracting the daily average temperature from 65°F. If, for example, the average was 50°F on a given day, then 15 degree days would be recorded. A daily average temperature of 60°F would give a value of 5 degree days. The annual number of heating degree days is then determined by adding up these negative departures

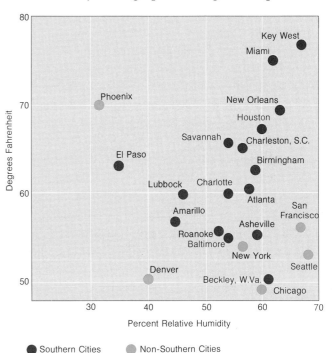

FIGURE 2.15 *Average Annual Temperatures and Relative Humidity of Selected Cities*

This chart relates average warm-season temperatures with mid-day humidity for a selection of Southern and non-Southern cities. Notice that New York and San Francisco are not unlike a number of Southern cities in this respect. The Gulf Coast tropical Southern cities stand out with high humidities associated with their higher temperatures.

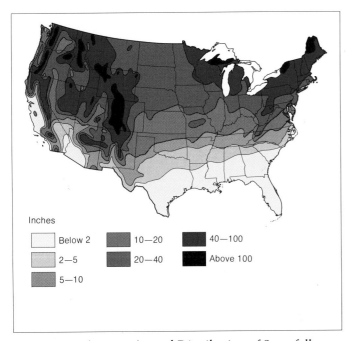

FIGURE 2.13 *Average Annual Distribution of Snowfall*

A Southern rarity: snow on a cotton field in the Piedmont, North Carolina

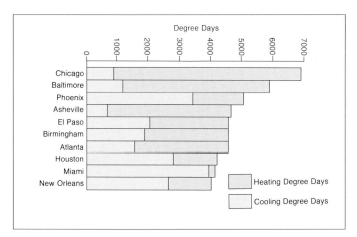

FIGURE 2.16 *Heating and Cooling Degree Days of Selected Cities*

from the 65°F standard for every day in the year. Cooling degree days are calculated in the same manner, except that they represent the extent to which the daily average is higher than 65°F. Heating degree days relate directly to energy consumption necessary for space heating, while cooling degree days give a general indication of air-conditioning requirements.

As FIGURE 2.16 shows, the number of cooling degree days tends to be high in the South, while the number of heating degree days is low. The combination, which expresses total annual heating and cooling energy needs, shows that many areas of the South compare favorably with most other parts of the United States. Low totals in heating degree days more than compensate for the extended heat of summer, at least in maintaining comfortable conditions inside a building. Conversely, high heating requirements in the interior of the United States more than offset relatively low cooling requirements.

The introduction of the air conditioner was an important stimulus in the recent growth of cities and businesses in the South. Its increasing use throughout the region has served to reduce one of the South's most severe environmental handicaps.

Climate Regions

Scientists use temperature and moisture conditions

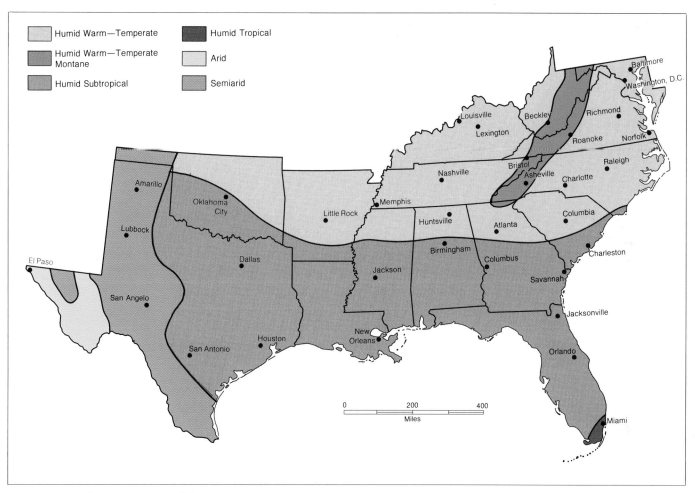

FIGURE 2.17 *Climate Regions of the South*

to delineate broad regions in which long-term weather conditions are similar. While the South is a generally warm and humid region, significant internal variations do exist. These differences are important for farming, gardening, recreation, and many businesses.

FIGURE 2.17 shows the distribution of six types of climates that characterize the South. The Humid Subtropical and Humid Warm–Temperate types dominate the region; these two, in fact, tend to distinguish in weather terms between the Deep South and the somewhat cooler upper South. Weather statistics in TABLE 2.2 are for representative cities in each area. Average temperatures for both the coldest and warmest

months are similar throughout except in the Humid Tropical, where winters are warmer and summers are hotter. These similarities largely disappear, however, when the regions are compared with respect to the number of days hotter than 90°F or colder than 32°F. The Humid Subtropical and Arid areas are the warmest, and Montane is the coldest. The Humid Tropical areas have mild summers; they are distinguished mostly by mild winters. Some of the Semiarid and Arid locations are both hot and cold because their low humidity and cloud cover permit temperature extremes to occur in all seasons.

TABLE 2.2 *Weather Conditions in Major Climate Regions of the South*

REGION City	Avg. Temp. (°F)		Avg. Annual (In.)		Avg. No. Days With Temperature		Avg. Number of Degree Days		% of Possible Sunshine	Avg. % Relative Humidity At Midday	
	Jan.	July	Precipitation	Snowfall*	Above 90°	Below 32°	Heating	Cooling			
HUMID TROPICAL											
Key West, Florida	70.0	83.8	37.99	0.0	43	0	64	4888	76	67	Humid Tropical climates are permanently frost-free. There is ample precipitation, and hot summers are followed by warm winters.
Miami, Florida	67.2	82.2	58.93	0.0	30	RARE	206	4038	67	62	
HUMID SUBTROPICAL											
Birmingham, Alabama	45.2	80.0	53.43	1.1	43	61	2844	1928	58	58	Humid Subtropical climates are found in areas with abundant precipitation, ranging from over 70 inches per year along their more southerly boundaries to nearly 50 inches along their northward margins. They are climates that normally have sufficient water available in all seasons to support plant growth. Summers are long and hot, while winters are mild. Snowfall is rare and seldom remains on the ground for more than a few days.
Charleston, South Carolina	50.0	81.1	48.68	.6	48	36	2146	2078	65	56	
Houston, Texas	50.4	82.4	46.92	.4	88	27	1434	2889	57	60	
Jacksonville, Florida	54.7	80.4	51.54	TRACE	82	14	1327	2596	61	55	
New Orleans, Louisiana	53.8	82.3	59.35	.2	68	13	1465	2706	59	63	
San Antonio, Texas	51.9	84.0	27.80	.5	111	22	1570	2994	61	55	
Savannah, Georgia	51.6	81.4	48.34	.4	58	36	1952	2317	62	54	
HUMID WARM–TEMPERATE											
Atlanta, Georgia	43.2	78.4	48.55	1.5	22	60	3095	1589	61	57	Humid Warm–Temperate climates are associated with large land areas. Their annual precipitation is modest (40 to 50 inches) but sufficient to meet the needs of a variety of plants in most years. Summers tend to be hot and humid, similar to those in the Humid Subtropical areas. A stronger contrast exists between Humid Warm–Temperate and Humid Subtropical in the winters, which are significantly cooler in Humid Warm–Temperate areas.
Baltimore, Maryland	32.6	76.8	41.49	21.7	31	99	4729	1108	57	54	
Charlotte, North Carolina	41.8	78.7	44.95	5.4	33	71	3218	1596	66	54	
Little Rock, Arkansas	41.5	81.4	48.26	5.4	71	63	3354	1925	N/A**	57	
Louisville, Kentucky	34.4	78.3	42.91	18.3	26	92	4640	1268	57	59	
Memphis, Tennessee	41.1	81.2	48.77	5.5	65	59	3227	2029	65	57	
Richmond, Virginia	37.6	77.6	43.65	13.9	42	86	3939	1353	61	53	
HUMID WARM–TEMPERATE MONTANE											
Asheville, North Carolina	35.8	72.8	48.15	17.8	6	104	4237	672	61	59	Humid Warm–Temperate Montane climates are found in higher altitude areas within the Humid Warm–Temperate climate region. Summers tend to be mild due to the higher elevations. Winter temperatures are likewise lower than in adjacent lowlands. The frequent passage of cyclonic storms in the winter provides snowfall that can accumulate on the ground for several months.
Beckley, West Virginia	30.4	69.3	42.65	56.8	RARE	114	5615	490	N/A	60	
Bristol, Tennessee	36.1	74.9	41.33	15.8	13	96	4306	1107	N/A	57	
Roanoke, Virginia	36.1	76.0	39.97	24.6	23	92	4307	1030	N/A	52	
SEMIARID											
Amarillo, Texas	36.4	77.9	20.44	14.6	64	108	4183	1433	73	44	Semiarid climates are transitional types lying between humid lands to the east and arid regions to the west. Precipitation is insufficient for most plants and normally totals between 10 and 25 inches per year. Winters are generally mild, but occasionally these areas may experience short, severe winter storms.
Lubbock, Texas	38.7	79.5	17.68	9.7	78	98	3545	1647	75	46	
San Angelo, Texas	45.6	83.7	20.37	3.2	109	52	2240	2702	N/A	48	
ARID											
El Paso, Texas	44.7	81.9	8.5	4.6	104	63	2678	2098	83	35	Arid climates feature very low moisture. Lack of an insulating cloud cover fosters dramatic daily temperature changes.

*Snow is reported in the actual number of inches of snowfall. To relate its water equivalence to general precipitation, it is usually assumed that an inch of melted snow will yield one-tenth inch of water. **N/A indicates data not available.

RIVERS

The South contains one of the world's great river systems, the mighty Mississippi, which discharges an incredible 4.6 million gallons of water into the Gulf of Mexico every second, or almost 400 billion gallons per day. This great river dwarfs all others in the region, and the other large rivers—the Tennessee, Arkansas, Red, and Cumberland—are tributaries of the "Father of Waters." The other rivers of the South are relatively small, with only the Tombigbee, Alabama, and Apalachicola rivers averaging flows of at least 150,000 gallons per second.

The Mississippi River is so large because it drains an enormous basin that encompasses virtually the entire interior of the United States (FIGURE 2.18). Along the East Coast, the Appalachian Mountains prevent

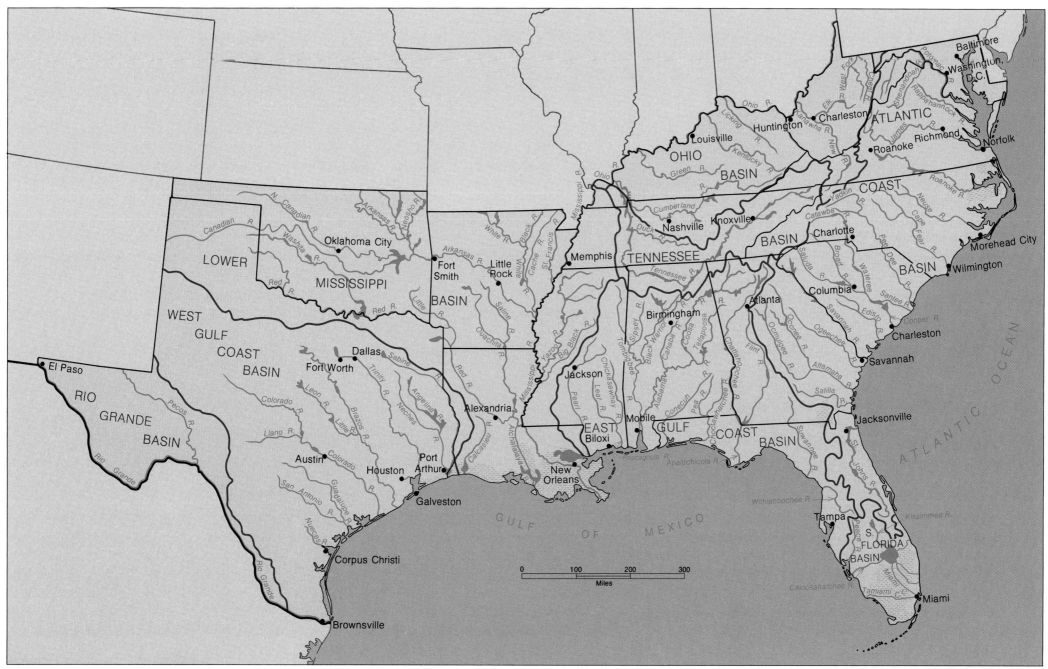

FIGURE 2.18 *Rivers of the South*

the formation of a unified drainage basin. Consequently, these well-watered mountains are the source of a host of smaller rivers that flow a few hundred miles southeastward into the Atlantic Ocean. These South Atlantic rivers have fairly steep courses; the resulting rapid flow carves narrow valleys into the Piedmont as they flow out of the mountains. Such narrow valleys were easy for settlers to cross as they moved down the Piedmont. Furthermore, they provided good waterpower sites for early textile mills and, later, for the generation of electricity. What they did not provide, though, was water transportation into the interior, since generally they were navigable only as they flowed across the coastal plain.

By contrast, the Mississippi River system historically served as a highway into the interior of North America. The settlement and development of that vast interior was accelerated by the presence of a great navigable waterway. Rivers, canals, and intracoastal waterways today continue to be important transportation corridors in the South (FIGURE 2.19).

FIGURE 2.19 *Navigable Inland Waterways of the South*

SOILS

Soils are a reflection of an area's climate, slope and drainage, underlying rock type, and vegetation. Together, these natural features control the evolutionary process of soil formation. Given sufficient time, a soil's color, texture, structure, pH, and other attributes will evolve in a manner consistent with its environment. In the South, the natural environment varies greatly from place to place, causing corresponding changes in the soil.

In turn, this diversity of soil type directly affects human culture. Because of a traditional emphasis on agriculture, the South's prosperity, land use, and settlement patterns have all been influenced greatly by the nature and internal variation of the soil.

The seven major types of soils in the South are shown in FIGURE 2.20.

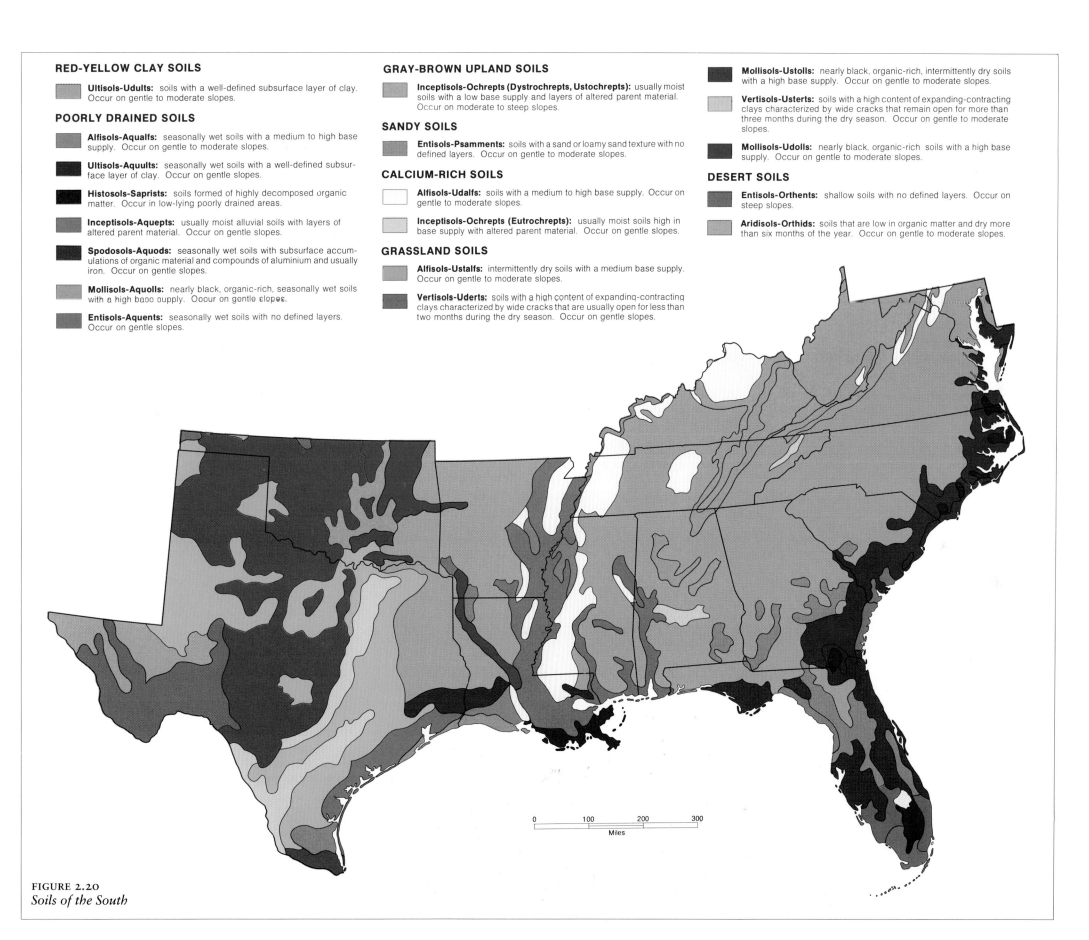

RED-YELLOW CLAY SOILS

Ultisols-Udults: soils with a well-defined subsurface layer of clay. Occur on gentle to moderate slopes.

POORLY DRAINED SOILS

Alfisols-Aqualfs: seasonally wet soils with a medium to high base supply. Occur on gentle to moderate slopes.

Ultisols-Aquults: seasonally wet soils with a well-defined subsurface layer of clay. Occur on gentle slopes.

Histosols-Saprists: soils formed of highly decomposed organic matter. Occur in low-lying poorly drained areas.

Inceptisols-Aquepts: usually moist alluvial soils with layers of altered parent material. Occur on gentle slopes.

Spodosols-Aquods: seasonally wet soils with subsurface accumulations of organic material and compounds of aluminium and usually iron. Occur on gentle slopes.

Mollisols-Aquolls: nearly black, organic-rich, seasonally wet soils with a high base supply. Occur on gentle slopes.

Entisols-Aquents: seasonally wet soils with no defined layers. Occur on gentle slopes.

GRAY-BROWN UPLAND SOILS

Inceptisols-Ochrepts (Dystrochrepts, Ustochrepts): usually moist soils with a low base supply and layers of altered parent material. Occur on moderate to steep slopes.

SANDY SOILS

Entisols-Psamments: soils with a sand or loamy sand texture with no defined layers. Occur on gentle to moderate slopes.

CALCIUM-RICH SOILS

Alfisols-Udalfs: soils with a medium to high base supply. Occur on gentle to moderate slopes.

Inceptisols-Ochrepts (Eutrochrepts): usually moist soils high in base supply with altered parent material. Occur on gentle slopes.

GRASSLAND SOILS

Alfisols-Ustalfs: intermittently dry soils with a medium base supply. Occur on gentle to moderate slopes.

Vertisols-Uderts: soils with a high content of expanding-contracting clays characterized by wide cracks that are usually open for less than two months during the dry season. Occur on gentle slopes.

Mollisols-Ustolls: nearly black, organic-rich, intermittently dry soils with a high base supply. Occur on gentle to moderate slopes.

Vertisols-Usterts: soils with a high content of expanding-contracting clays characterized by wide cracks that remain open for more than three months during the dry season. Occur on gentle to moderate slopes.

Mollisols-Udolls: nearly black, organic-rich soils with a high base supply. Occur on gentle to moderate slopes.

DESERT SOILS

Entisols-Orthents: shallow soils with no defined layers. Occur on steep slopes.

Aridisols-Orthids: soils that are low in organic matter and dry more than six months of the year. Occur on gentle to moderate slopes.

FIGURE 2.20
Soils of the South

Red-Yellow Clay Soils

The warm, moist climate that characterizes much of the South is largely responsible for the distinctive red-yellow clay soils that cover the Piedmont, Blue Ridge, and much of the coastal plain. The warm climate, with its lack of a severe winter season, permits a sustained bacterial action that destroys dead vegetation as rapidly as it is produced. Under these conditions, little humus accumulates in the soil. In the absence of humic acids, iron oxides in the underlying rocks are insoluble and accumulate in the soil as red and yellow clays. Meanwhile, the warm rains rob the soil of its base minerals (such as calcium, phosphorus, potassium, and magnesium) and its silica by carrying these mineral elements to the water table through a process called *leaching*. The resulting red-yellow soil is low in organic content (and thus nitrogen), acidic, clayey in texture, and low in fertility. These soils are commonly called *red-yellow podzolics*. More technical literature refers to them as varieties of *ultisols-udults*.

This Southern soil provides excellent support for forests, which were truly magnificent when European settlers arrived. Unlike most cultivated crops, trees seem to do well in acid soils and do not suffer from the shortage of base minerals and nitrogen. However, these soils are quite deficient for support of field crops. It must have been a considerable disappointment to the European settlers to discover that the land supporting such forests was so poor for the cultivation of ordinary crops. This deficiency and its remedy were noted early in the nineteenth century by Edmund Ruffin. Ruffin had inherited a Tidewater Virginia farm at a time when the local farmers were practicing a form of shifting agriculture. The red-yellow soils had formed from underlying sandstone and shale and were low in base minerals. With cultivation, those minerals were rapidly depleted; thus, it was common for farmers to grow tobacco for a few years, then abandon the land and move farther west.

Ruffin was determined to remain on his farm, and he set out to discover a countermeasure. Good European agricultural practices, such as adding manure, produced little result in the red-yellow clay soil because of its high acidity. Ruffin took local marl, a calcium-rich rock, and put a portion of it in his land,

Red-yellow clay soil (ultisol) in western Arkansas

Red-yellow clay soil (ultisol) in the Piedmont, North Carolina

thereby enhancing the basic quality of the soil. The results were incredible: yields increased by 40 percent. Though best known for supposedly firing the first shot against Fort Sumter and thus starting the Civil War, Edmund Ruffin's major contribution to the South was his book, *An Essay on Calcareous Manures*. The findings set forth in this book, drawn chiefly from Ruffin's experiences on his Tidewater farm, ushered in a new era of productivity for the abandoned red-yellow soils.

Today, with modern farm management practices of liming and fertilizing, pasture and cultivated field crops do quite well in this commonplace soil. This is indeed fortunate, for it covers the vast majority of Southern lands.

Poorly Drained Soils

Much of the outer portion of the Atlantic and Gulf coastal plains and floodplains along mature rivers are poorly drained and characterized by a shallow water table, contributing to the evolution of a variety of complex soils shown in FIGURE 2.20. In this environment, a gray-, blue-, or black-colored soil evolves. Where organic matter accumulates in abundance without decomposing, the soil is known as peat, muck, or organic soil. In other instances, the organic matter is incorporated into the soil. Along the outer coastal plain, a layer of deoxidized iron compounds called a *gley* layer generally develops as a result of oxygen deficiency. The material is sticky, compact, without structure, very acid, and bluish gray in color.

Without artificial drainage, these soils are primarily useful only for pasture, rice cultivation, or woodland. However, many are quite productive when drained, fertilized, and limed. Drainage has long been a common practice. Years before the American Revolution, George Washington, then a land surveyor, laid out routes for draining large acreages along the North Carolina–Virginia border. Drainage of the land causes the water table to fall, permitting shallow-rooted crop

Poorly drained soil (spodisol) in eastern North Carolina

cultivation. Today, land drainage continues as new lands are opened for cultivation.

Along the nearly level, broad floodplains of the Mississippi and other major rivers of the South, deep layers of river-transported sediments have been deposited. As the rivers successively flooded and receded, silt, sand, and clay were laid down. The resulting floodplain soil is gray brown in color, slightly acid, and moderately high in organic content. The floodplains became prized agricultural land, but that of the broad Mississippi was avoided by early settlers for fear of floods. After the construction of protective levees in the 1840s, however, the Mississippi Delta was transformed into one of the South's great agricultural regions. It was along this fertile river bottom as well as along the Tennessee River and in the Black Belt that the large plantation system became the most entrenched (some floodplain soil areas are too small to be shown clearly on FIGURE 2.20).

As flood control structures were built, however, the annual replenishment of soil was lost. In this warm, moist climate, the original humus of the soil is quickly depleted and the mineral bases lost by leaching. Thus, just as with the red-yellow soils, the floodplain soils increasingly will require liming and fertilizer for best results. Still, with good management, yields from the cultivation of cotton, soybean, wheat, corn, alfalfa, rice, and sugarcane are outstanding.

Coastal plain soil in eastern North Carolina

Gray-Brown Upland Soils

In the Appalachian Plateau, portions of the adjacent Valley and Ridge province, and central Oklahoma, lower temperatures retard bacterial activity, permitting a greater accumulation of humus. This accumulation is evident in the gray-brown color of the surface soil. The underlying rocks are generally sandstone and shale, and in the moist climate, base minerals are removed because they leach much faster than they can be replenished. Thus, these gray-brown soils are usually quite acid and deficient in calcium, phosphorous, potassium, and other bases. Because much of the area has a rugged topography, soils also suffer from erosion and are often shallow. The resulting soil is low in native fertility. While it responds well to treatment, the lack of large level areas and the isolation of these regions discourage such effort. Soil scientists call these soils *ochrepts* of the *inceptisols* order.

The low agricultural productivity of the Appalachian Plateau led to its initial rejection by pioneers moving into Tennessee and Kentucky. However, when the productive lands to the east and west became less available, the area was gradually settled and much of it cleared. Because of low yields and steep slopes, the cleared land was soon abandoned, and today most farming is restricted to isolated valley areas.

The area's economy is rooted more in the extraction of its mineral and timber resources than in agriculture. The topography and thin acid soils support a lush forest cover, and the timber industry has been a mainstay of many generations. Those families not associated with timbering are likely to depend on the extensive coal mining industry. Throughout much of the area, seams of coal are interspersed between the layers of shale and sandstone.

Gray-brown upland soil in West Virginia

Gray-brown soil in Beckley, West Virginia

Sandy Soils

Areas of sandy soils scattered along the inner coastal plain of both Carolinas, Georgia, Alabama, Texas, and Florida are classified as *entisols* (*psamments* variety or suborder). These soils are characterized by the absence of defined layers, except for a thin plow level. They have evolved from young-parent sandy material such as levees, old beaches, and sand dunes.

The soil has a grayish brown surface, contains very little clay, and tends to be acidic. For most cultivated crops, these soils need considerable fertilizer and lime. However, because they are well drained and warm rapidly, they provide excellent sites for citrus. Further, they respond well to urban development, for they provide an excellent medium for septic fields and present few problems as building sites. Care is advisable when the vegetation cover is removed or disturbed because these soils are vulnerable to wind erosion.

Sandy soil in Weymouth Woods State Park, North Carolina

Calcium-Rich Soils

Areas underlain with calcium-rich rocks like limestone generally have dark-colored, basic, very fertile soils. While bases in the soil are removed by leaching, they are continually replenished by the decomposition of underlying basic rocks. The resulting high fertility supports a tall grass cover that returns both organic material and bases to the soil, further increasing productivity. The productivity remains high with only a minimum application of fertilizer and lime.

More technical publications refer to these soils as *udalfs* of the *alfisols* order and *ochrepts* of the *inceptisols* order. While scattered throughout much of the South, they are concentrated in six areas. In each location, they have dramatically affected the natural and cultural landscape and sometimes have had a commanding role in settlement patterns.

Three of these areas are located in the Upland South. They are the Nashville Basin, the Kentucky Bluegrass region around Lexington, and the limestone valleys of the Valley and Ridge province. They all evolved in low-lying basins and valleys produced by the erosion of sandstone caprocks and subsequent weathering and erosion of the underlying softer limestone. Settlers, strongly attracted to these fertile lands, took possession of the Great Valley in the mid-eighteenth century. Soon thereafter, they were drawn westward through the Cumberland Gap to the "promised land" of the Kentucky Bluegrass region and into the Nashville Basin.

A fourth area is the treeless Black Belt, a calcium-rich belt running across central Alabama. Its basic black soil, as fertile as any in the South, supported magnificent plantations in earlier times.

A fifth area is the north-south 40-mile strip of wind-deposited material called *loess* along the east bank of the Mississippi River from southern Kentucky to southern Louisiana. The calcium-rich loess was laid down during one of North America's interglacial periods, and this area was so fertile that early cotton planters sought land there despite its rough character.

The calcium-rich soils of the West Gulf Coastal Plain, such as the Blackland Prairie, have also been included in the grassland soils classification.

Calcium-rich soil in Potomac Valley, West Virginia

Grassland Soils

Another group of soils evolved in the Southern grasslands of Texas and Oklahoma. While many of the soils evolved from calcareous rocks, the basic character is also influenced by a drier climate and a grass vegetation cover. In this semiarid climate, leaching of mineral bases is limited. Further, the decay of the grass cover and its roots restores bases to the soils much more efficiently than does forest decay; thus, bases are replenished as rapidly as they are lost. Decay of organic material is moderated by the dry climate, allowing humus to accumulate in the soils, which take on a reddish to black color.

Soils that form under tall prairie grassland have traditionally been labeled prairie soils or black earths and those associated with short grass, chestnut or steppe soils. Soils scientists refer to them as *ustolls* of the *mollisols* order if a dark surface mineral layer is present, *ustalfs* of the *alfisols* order if a dark mineral layer is not present, and *vertisols* (*uderts* or *usterts*) if the soil has deep, wide cracks during the year.

These soils are very fertile when moist, but frequent droughts in these areas may limit agriculture. Land use varies with the availability of water.

Small areas of grassland soils are also found in humid parts of the South. FIGURE 2.20 shows areas in Mississippi, Arkansas, and Louisiana.

Grassland soil (vertisol) in Texas

Desert Soils

Desert soils of the South are found largely in Texas and in small areas of Oklahoma. Vegetation is sparse, causing a deficiency in organic matter and a corresponding grayish or reddish color. Weathering of the soil in an arid climate is slow, and the soils are generally thin. Desert soils are of two types: *orthents* of the *entisols* order and *orthids* of the *aridisols* order.

The major agricultural problem is lack of moisture. In those areas where water is available for irrigation and soils are fine textured, farming prospers. Along floodplains such as the Rio Grande, where alluvial soil occurs and moisture is available for irrigation, productivity is excellent and a wide range of crops is grown.

Red desert soil (aridisol) in the Southwest

VEGETATION AND ANIMALS OF THE SOUTH

Plants and animals have long provided the South with important resources. While the early Southern economy was more dependent on them than is today's, they remain important to the South's economy as well as quality of life. The distribution of plants and animals gives the South some of its most interesting internal variation.

Geographical diversity in the type and number of plants and animals is, in turn, largely a result of the differences in climate, soil, drainage, and relief discussed previously. The South can be subdivided into the seven vegetation zones shown in FIGURE 2.21.

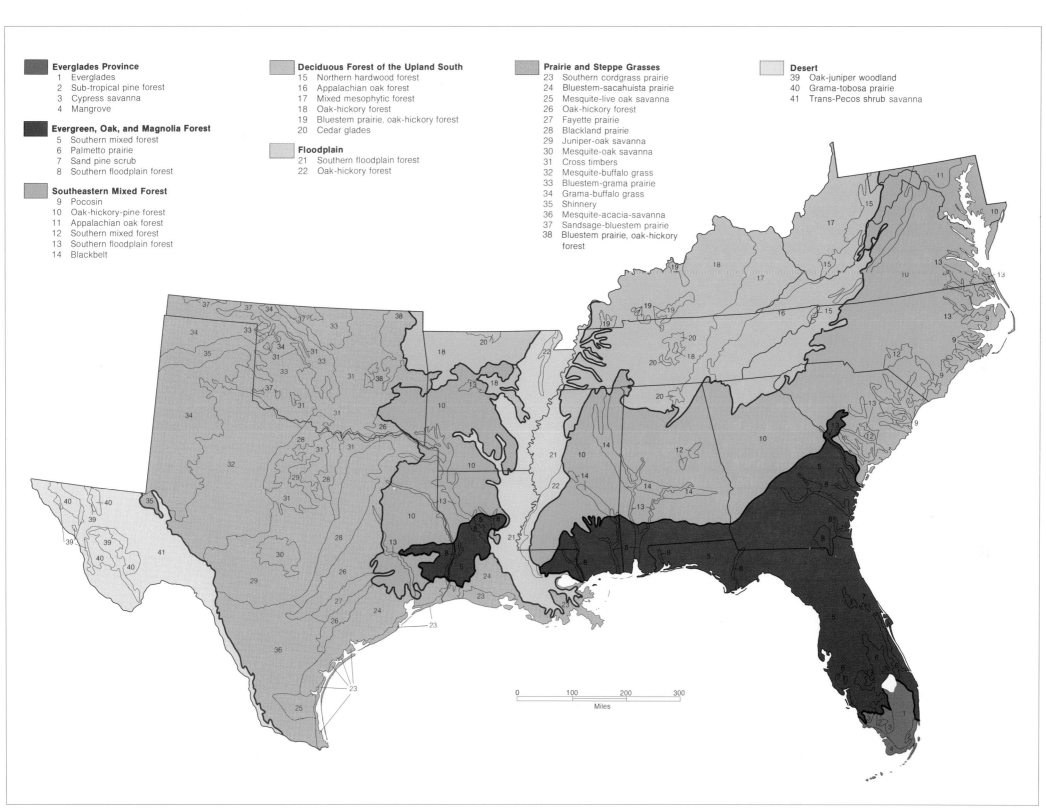

Everglades Province
1 Everglades
2 Sub-tropical pine forest
3 Cypress savanna
4 Mangrove

Evergreen, Oak, and Magnolia Forest
5 Southern mixed forest
6 Palmetto prairie
7 Sand pine scrub
8 Southern floodplain forest

Southeastern Mixed Forest
9 Pocosin
10 Oak-hickory-pine forest
11 Appalachian oak forest
12 Southern mixed forest
13 Southern floodplain forest
14 Blackbelt

Deciduous Forest of the Upland South
15 Northern hardwood forest
16 Appalachian oak forest
17 Mixed mesophytic forest
18 Oak-hickory forest
19 Bluestem prairie, oak-hickory forest
20 Cedar glades

Floodplain
21 Southern floodplain forest
22 Oak-hickory forest

Prairie and Steppe Grasses
23 Southern cordgrass prairie
24 Bluestem-sacahuista prairie
25 Mesquite-live oak savanna
26 Oak-hickory forest
27 Fayette prairie
28 Blackland prairie
29 Juniper-oak savanna
30 Mesquite-oak savanna
31 Cross timbers
32 Mesquite-buffalo grass
33 Bluestem-grama prairie
34 Grama-buffalo grass
35 Shinnery
36 Mesquite-acacia-savanna
37 Sandsage-bluestem prairie
38 Bluestem prairie, oak-hickory forest

Desert
39 Oak-juniper woodland
40 Grama-tobosa prairie
41 Trans-Pecos shrub savanna

0   100   200   300
Miles

FIGURE 2.21 *Vegetation and Life Zones of the South*

Everglades Province

The tropical wet and dry climate of southern Florida has produced some three distinctive forests and one of the world's largest freshwater marshes, the Florida Everglades.

Along the western edge of the Everglades lies the Big Cypress Swamp. Here, trees reach heights of 170 feet and diameters of 15 feet. The trees are well adapted to the shallow water table, and often their roots stand in water at least part of the time. The wood from the tree is valuable because of its unusual durability. Even when exposed to extreme climatic elements, the wood seems to last forever. The cypress tree is unusual in that it is a deciduous conifer; that is, unlike the typical conifer, it loses its yellow-green needles in the fall in the same way a broadleaf oak or hickory tree does.

On the southern coast of Florida, the mangrove forest is widespread and prominent. Here, trees reach heights of 80 feet or more, and their roots extend vertically like stilts from the trunk and limbs to anchor them firmly in the ground. The tangle of their roots blocks tidal currents and allows organic debris to settle from the water. This, together with falling leaves and bird droppings, builds up the underlying soil to high-tide level. These trees also serve to protect the coast and inland area from the ravages of hurricanes. The tree is a broadleaf evergreen and so sheds its leaves gradually throughout the year, providing a steady supply of food for the manatee, a fast-disappearing mammal.

The mangrove and other broadleaf evergreens have crooked trunks and hard, heavy wood. They provide dense shade and house numerous *epiphytes* (parasitic air plants such as the orchid). The bumbo, strangler fig, West Indian mahogany, royal palm, and thatch palm are also typical trees of this environment.

A third forest, a subtropical pine forest, is found along the southeast coast and adjacent to the Big Cypress Swamp.

The dominant vegetation type in the Everglades province is not a forest but an open marsh covered by tall sawgrass. Within the grasses are floating land-masses called *hammocks*. It is this freshwater marsh, which covers more than one-half of southern Florida, for which the term Everglades is most typically reserved.

Mangrove waterway in south Florida

Hammocks in the Florida Everglades

This unique habitat produces food and shelter for a vast array of wildlife. Mammals include the panther, black bear, mountain lion, and occasionally white-tailed deer. Numerous species of birds thrive. Snakes include the rough green, rat, and coral. But it is the American alligator, a well-known resident, that more than any other animal symbolizes this wild area. Finally, the hot-damp environment encourages an abundance of insects.

This precious natural area is environmentally sensitive. Even a slight change in the subsurface water level alters the habitat and fauna markedly. Because of excessive drainage, many species of birds that inhabit the area, such as the great blue heron, already are threatened.

Evergreen, Oak, and Magnolia Forest

The warm, moist environment of central and northern Florida, southern Georgia, coastal Alabama and Mississippi, eastern and western Louisiana, and a portion of east Texas was covered by an impressive broadleaf evergreen forest when Europeans first viewed the landscape. The romantic beauty of the South is still closely linked with two of these trees: the live oak, with its huge branches and their deep shade; and the magnolia, with its shiny leaves and frosty white blossoms. Laurels, with an associated dense undergrowth, and epiphytes such as Spanish moss are also common in this forest. Where the soil is sandy or drainage is poor, vegetation is quite different. Sandy soils tend to be associated with stands of loblolly and slash pines, while the bald cypress dominates the swampy habitats. Today, most of the virgin forest has been timbered or burned, and large areas are second-growth pine forest.

As elsewhere, wildlife has adjusted to the setting. The white-tailed deer, the only large indigenous mammal here, ranges over most of the South and has been the prime game animal since man first occupied the area. Hunted for meat and its hide, the deer was the chief prey of Indians and the main staple for early European colonists. In pre-Columbian time, millions roamed the South, and the herds contained a dozen or more subspecies.

Common small mammals inhabiting the forests include the raccoon, opossum, tree squirrel, rabbit, and various rodents. The wild turkey and the bobwhite

Spanish moss in the Atlantic Coastal Plain

Live oaks in the South Carolina coastal plain

continue to be the principal game birds, but other birds are numerous. Reptiles are common, particularly in the swamp areas. The alligator has a dramatic presence and has long been hunted for its hide.

Southeastern Mixed Forest

The Atlantic Coastal Plain and the adjacent Piedmont are forested areas of diversity consisting of medium-tall to tall broadleaf deciduous and needleleaf evergreen trees. The most common evergreens include loblolly, shortleaf, and Southern yellow pines. Unless they are maintained by fire and cutting, these evergreens will be succeeded by such common deciduous trees as oak, hickory, sweet gum, black gum, red maple, and elm. In poorly drained coastal areas, gums and cypress dominate, and in the undrained depressions, upland bogs or *pocosins* occur.

The forest has always provided the population with major resources. During the colonial period, trees were the universal building material. They provided ship timbers and naval stores. An array of forest products served early settlers with fuel, dyestuff, soap, and building materials. In the Carolinas, the early naval stores industry was especially important. The labor-intensive production of turpentine, tar, and resin helped to concentrate a large number of slaves in the Carolinas' seaboard counties.

This virgin Southern forest once teemed with wildlife. Early settlers reported an abundance of deer, buffalo, bears, and other animals—70-pound turkeys and dense flocks of ducks that shut out the sunlight as they passed overhead. Streams swarmed with fish so large that ordinary nets would not hold them and in such numbers that a horse could not wade across a river where the fish were running. Sturgeon 12 feet long were killed with axes, and oysters 13 inches across were seen along the coast.

The wild turkey, beaver, and white-tailed deer played important roles in early Southern history. While the wild turkey successfully evaded natural predators, it was easy prey for man and became a major game animal for early European colonists. Hunters learned that the bird was alert, suspicious, and quick, but easily confused. While traveling in the Carolinas in 1700, John Lawson and his companions saw flocks "containing several hundreds in a Gang"

and ate so much of the bird that they became "cloy'd with Turkeys" and gratefully ate "a Possum" for variety.[1] The beaver was also widespread and abundant in the early colonial period, but along with the deer it was hunted to near-extinction. In the early days, corn had been the Indian product most in demand among the settlers. But as the danger of starvation lessened, the focus shifted to deerskin and furs. The Southern fur trade flourished, and trade in leather was even more important as deerskin became a lucrative supplement to tobacco as a colonial export. During the mid-eighteenth century, more than 200,000 pounds of skins were exported annually from Georgia alone.

Today, although the numbers are greatly reduced, these game animals continue to provide prey for the Southern hunter. The gray squirrel, cottontail rabbit, raccoon, and fox are common, and more than 20 species of breeding birds nest in the mature forest.

Deciduous Forest of the Upland South

The higher elevations and higher latitude of the South, specifically the Appalachians and the Ozark and Ouachita Uplands, are covered with a deciduous broadleaf forest. This forest is so varied that in the coves alone more varieties of trees grow than in all of Europe.

The tall trees provide a dense and continuous canopy in the summer and were once so thick and deep that, according to an early traveler, a squirrel could travel from the Atlantic to the Mississippi without touching ground. That was, of course, an exaggeration, because the Indians practiced widespread burning to support their agriculture and hunting. Still, it conveys the vastness of the early Southern forest. It was truly one of the world's magnificent forests. Although much of its original grandeur has been lost to timbering and fire, second- and third-generation growth stands provide breathtaking beauty, and there remain a few areas of protected virgin forest.

The most numerous tree in the coves is the yellow poplar, and oak dominates southern slopes and drier mountains. The chestnut once shared the land with the oak, but it was killed off by a blight in the early twentieth century and has not yet recovered. Other common deciduous trees include the beech, walnut, maple, elm, and ash.

The conifer is represented in the Southern Appalachians by the red spruce and Fraser fir, and in areas where the original forest has been cleared, by pines that develop as second growth. In the late nineteenth and early twentieth centuries, timbering was the economic mainstay in many parts of this mountainous area.

The wildlife is similar to that found in the mixed forest of the coastal plain and Piedmont. The deer, raccoon, and gray squirrel are all common, and the black bear and bobcat are other important mammals.

A southeastern mixed forest in the Piedmont, North Carolina

A Highland forest in the Blue Ridge Mountains

Floodplain

Floodplain vegetation and wildlife are so varied that generalization is difficult. The habitat varies with water level and drainage conditions and ranges from predominantly terrestrial to aquatic.

The southern floodplain forest, shown in FIGURE 2.21, is poorly drained and has five subtypes. In the poorly drained and wet areas, the *cottonwood-willow* forest dominates. The *sugarberry-elm-sweet gum* forest occurs in areas better drained but still rather wet, where the water table is shallow. In swamp areas, *cypress* forests often take possession. The cypress trees range from 80 to 120 feet in height and up to six feet in diameter. In well-drained areas, *oak-hickory* and *tulip-oak* forests dominate.

The swamp rabbit, opossum, and raccoon are common. Gray squirrels are present, and early travelers saw deer and bison coming to the river to drink. There are numerous small aquatic animals and interesting birds. Cormorants, water turkeys, great blue herons, and egrets, for example, nest in the cypress swamps.

Cypress forest near Caddo Lake, east Texas

Prairie and Steppe Grasses

The extensive grasslands of North America were a unique experience for the European settlers. In all of western Europe there was nothing similar. The early explorers named them *prairie* from the French for grassland. Extending from Mexico through west Texas into Oklahoma and north into Canada, these grasslands are among the world's largest.

The height and type of grass varies directly with availability of moisture. Annual precipitation drops dramatically from about 40 inches on the eastern boundary in eastern Texas to less than 10 inches in the westernmost part of the grasslands. Today, many writers refer to the tall grass in the moist eastern section as prairie grass and to the shorter grasses in the drier west as steppe grass. Together they make up the Great Plains.

Along the eastern portions, the tall prairie grasses are sometimes intermingled with groves or strips of deciduous trees, forming a type of parkland. This alternation results largely from soil influence and slope exposure. Trees are found most commonly on north-facing slopes and near streams. On limestone soils, grasses are the dominant plant and form a continuous cover, flowering in late spring or early summer. Tall grasses become more and more mixed with short grasses in drier habitats. While a number of grass types are present, little bluestem is the most prevalent. In the intermingled upland forests, oak and hickory are the most common trees.

West of this parkland prairie, in Oklahoma, the trees dwindle and the landscape becomes a sea of tall and mixed grasses. The most distinctive type is again the little bluestem. Left undisturbed, these grasses will reach heights of six feet. However, because of the high fertility of the soils, most of the grassland here has given way to the plow.

While the underlying soils are among the world's most productive, the dense grasses are deeply rooted and form a sod cover that is very difficult to break. This tough sod delayed settlement until John Deere introduced the heavy steel plow.

A prairie grassland in Texas

The area west of the prairie parkland in Texas can be best characterized as a prairie brushland, a place of arid grasslands where shrubs and low trees grow singly or in bunches. There are three distinct sections: On the plains of northwest Texas, bluestem, buffalo, and grama grasses are intermingled with mesquite; on the Edwards Plateau, oak and juniper trees are scattered among the grasses and mesquite; and in southwest Texas, mesquite and acacia dominate.

Northwest Texas and Oklahoma are characterized by steppe or short-grass prairie vegetation. Rainfall is scant, and the short grasses are shallow rooted. Below the roots is a permanent dry zone. Principal species include such sod formers as blue grama and buffalo grass. Much of this natural cover was destroyed by man's cultivation and overgrazing. The area was then subjected to an extended drought and subsequent wind erosion, which led to the famous dust bowl of the 1930s. Slowly, the area is recovering from abuse.

A belt of bluestem-sacahuista and southern cordgrass prairie extends from Corpus Christi to the Mississippi Delta. This coastal prairie appears not to be a climatic climax under present conditions, as rainfall is more than adequate to support an evergreen, oak, and magnolia forest.

The grasslands provide an extremely favorable environment for grazing mammals. When early settlers arrived, this was the land of the bison or buffalo. Herds of a million or more roamed the prairies, and it has been estimated that at one time the North American grasslands supported as many as 60 million bison. The bison, of course, was hunted to near extinction and in a very short period disappeared from the natural landscape.

When the bison reached their peak, the pronghorn antelope were almost equal in number and thrived in all types of grasslands. Unlike the bison, however, the pronghorn survived and are still seen on the prairies. Another large mammal, the deer, also remains widespread. Today much of the grassland is farmed and utilized by ranches as pasture for livestock, which compete with wildlife for land.

Mesquite in west Texas

Smaller animals are widespread and numerous, including the black-tailed jackrabbit, cottontail rabbit, prairie dog, ground squirrel, gopher, and mouse. These grazing mammals serve as prey for the badger, kit fox, ferret, wolf, coyote, and hawk.

Birds also have a significant presence. Unique to the grasslands, the prairie chicken, burrowing owl, and sage grouse spend their entire lives on the open plains.

An intriguing and relatively recent immigrant from Mexico, the armadillo, has extended its range across the southern part of the South. It cannot tolerate freezing temperatures, though, and is not expected to expand its range above the frost line. *Armadillo* is a Spanish word that translates "little armed one," a very descriptive name. It feeds largely on insects, grubs, and worms. Man is its principal enemy, as many armadillos are killed for their tasty meat and their armor, which is made into baskets and curios. The animals are excellent diggers, heavy for their volume, fast, and nearsighted. A female armadillo gives birth to four young at a time, and they are identical—even to the number of hairs on their undersides.

Desert

In southwestern Texas, the climate is distinctively arid, and the thorny shrub vegetation reflects this dryness. In many areas, short acacia grass grows alongside the shrubs. Other common plants include the creosote bush, juniper, and piñon pine, which dominates in large areas. In isolated mountains, oak-juniper woodland and pines are found.

Although a seemingly bleak environment, the area supports a rich array of wildlife. Pronghorn antelope, mule deer, and white-tailed deer are the most common large mammals. The rabbit, kangaroo rat, and wood rat all compete successfully with the larger mammals for the limited grasses. The coyote, bobcat, and golden eagle are common predators, and the quail is the most distinctive game bird.

Pronghorn antelopes in the desert of southwest Texas

3 PEOPLE FOR THE LAND

For thousands of years people have felt the lure of the Southern land. It has attracted many different races and cultures who came in successive waves of migration. Every group that poured into the South responded to the land and left physical changes and cultural influences that remain part of the South.

The first Southerners were men and women from Asia whom the Europeans, optimistic but mistaken in their geography, called Indians. Much of their history is shrouded in mystery, but their hold on the Southern imagination has always been strong. Since the Indians did not create written records, scholars have had to reconstruct their history, using archaeology to create islands of knowledge in a vast sea of ignorance. Such scholarship is a slow process of piecing together bits of information and framing interpretations that fit the data. The discovery of early Indian history is still going on, but some facts seem fairly clear.

The ancestors of the Indians crossed from Asia into North America near the present-day Bering Strait (FIGURE 3.1). They came over a bridge of ice and land left bare by lower seas of that time, and slowly they spread down into the continent. Moving in a southeasterly direction, some of these people probably reached Central and South America. Archaeologists have found human artifacts of great age in caves from Alaska to Pennsylvania to Peru. Their methods of dating these artifacts agree: some human beings were in the New World as long as 40,000 to 50,000 years ago.

About 30,000 years ago, however, there began another advance of the Ice Age that lasted 10,000 to 15,000 years. Research shows that layers of pollen

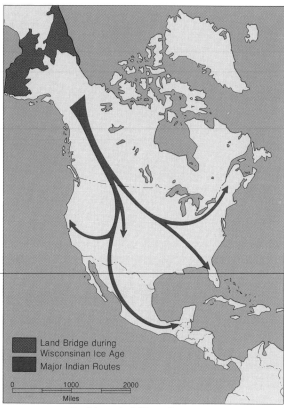

FIGURE 3.1 *Prehistoric Migration*

now buried deep in the soil become very thin during the period corresponding to this cold spell, and it seems clear that environmental conditions would not have encouraged further migration. Populations of Indians in the New World at that time may have declined under the influence of the harsh conditions.

But then, approximately 15,000 years ago, there was a dramatic change in climate. The temperature rose, glaciers retreated, and the productivity of the land increased. With improved conditions and more abundant vegetation, most experts believe migration resumed. A theory recently proposed by a team of scholars suggests that there were three major migrations. Professors Joseph Greenberg of Stanford University, Steven Zegura of the University of Arizona, and Christy Turner of Arizona State University believe that people left Siberia or eastern Asia in three major groupings between 15,000 and 4,000 years ago.

Using their diverse skills in languages, genetics, and anthropology, these scholars identified striking similarities in blood types, languages, and dental traits among the many tribes of modern Indians. For example, several hundred Indian languages begin the first-person pronoun "I" with the *n* sound, and the geographical distribution of these languages matches the distribution of different blood types. Dental traits, such as how often molars occur with two versus three roots, not only confirm the pattern but point toward certain regions of Asia as possible points of origin. According to their theory, those who came first made their way farthest south. Later waves of migrants probably chose to occupy available land rather than push through established cultures, and thus, over time, they tended to end up farther north. Indians were inhabiting the South at least 10,000 years ago.

These earthen structures at Moundville, Alabama, bear witness to the Indian presence in the South long before the arrival of Europeans.

THE INDIANS

Before Europeans arrived, Indian ways of life evolved in the direction of settled agricultural societies. The earliest *tradition*, or broad way of life practiced by different cultural groups of Indians, probably relied on the nomadic hunting of big game. A later Archaic tradition brought village life and increased use of fishing and food-gathering. The Woodland tradition, which endured from roughly 1000 B.C. to A.D. 700, embraced cultures that practiced agriculture, traded with distant peoples, and built striking burial mounds. The Mississippian tradition that followed included most of the tribes present at the time of European settlement. Cultures in the Mississippian tradition erected many temple mounds and practiced a more intensive agriculture. Corn and beans, planted with digging sticks in the soft soil of river floodplains, were the mainstays of their diet.

The thoughts and beliefs of these peoples are largely lost to us, but their temple and burial mounds endure (FIGURE 3.2). These impressive structures testify to the fact that certain religious or cultural beliefs must have had great importance in Indian lives. Years of tiring labor went into the creation of the mounds. Numerous examples of them remain throughout the South today.

In northeast Louisiana an immense mound rises 70 feet above the ground and stretches 640 feet from north to south. The Indians who built up this mound by carrying thousands of baskets full of earth were probably the first mound builders in North America. They are called the Poverty Point culture, their name borrowed from the site, which is known as Poverty Point. They were part of the Woodland tradition and flourished in Louisiana from about 1300 to 200 B.C. These people laid out near the mound a village two-thirds of a mile in diameter, with six concentric ridges repeating the shape of an octagon and aisles radiating from the center. Impressive as their achievement was, later mound builders may have been even more advanced.

The so-called Adena culture developed in the Ohio River Valley and spread into West Virginia and as far east as the Chesapeake Bay. Shortly after 1000 B.C., the Indians of this culture began to build burial mounds. One of the few that was not looted over time survived in West Virginia. Named the Cresap mound, it contained at least 54 Indian dead. In nearby Moundsville, West Virginia, the Grave Creek mound stands 70 feet high.

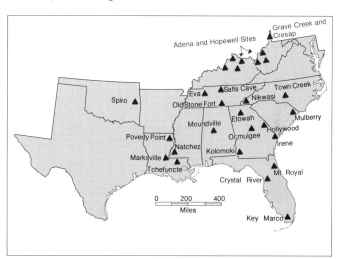

FIGURE 3.2 *Selected Temple and Burial Mound Sites in the South*

Another culture in the Woodland tradition developed in the lower Mississippi Valley and along the Gulf Coast. Called (appropriately enough) the Gulf culture, remnants of this social group maintained their way of life until the Europeans came. Small cymbals of copper and iron adorned their bodies and appear in European drawings. Gulf cultures in southern Florida planted no crops but relied on fishing and food-gathering. Indians in this culture built mounds in southern Florida and a complex of temple and burial mounds at Kolomoki in southern Georgia. The Kolomoki site covers 300 acres and has yielded many pottery sculptures.

The Mississippian tradition, with its more intensive riverine agriculture, began to rise around A.D. 700. In time it spread through most of the South, except for southern Florida (FIGURE 3.3). The Mississippian peoples were the greatest mound builders of all, creating the famous Cahokia, Illinois, site where an estimated 38,000 people lived. Mississippian mounds are characteristically flat on top with sloping sides. They resemble truncated pyramids and are found at many sites throughout the South. Typically they are on or near the old riverbeds, where the best soil for Indian agriculture was found; often a wooden palisade surrounded the site.

Ceremony became intensely important to some cultures in the Mississippian tradition, and experts refer to evidence of shared symbolism as the Southern Cult. Some of the finest works of Indian art have come from such Southern Cult sites as the Etowah mounds in northern Georgia and the Spiro mounds in Oklahoma. The Green Corn Ceremony that Europeans witnessed among the Creeks and Cherokees in the 1700s may have represented a continuation of part of the Southern Cult ceremonies. In a ritual of renewal, the Creeks smashed old pots and started new fires to welcome a new year.

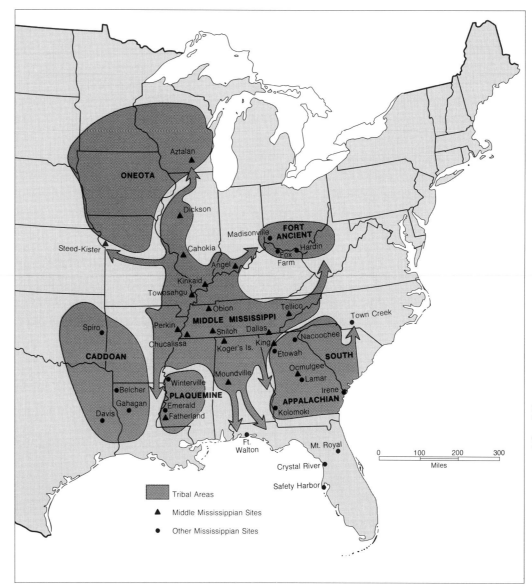

FIGURE 3.3
The Spreading Influence of the Mississippian Tradition

The accounts of those European travelers who saw the last era of the Mississippian tradition fill in the picture of a rich Indian culture. When Hernando de Soto's chroniclers visited present-day South Carolina early in a long journey that took them north to the Blue Ridge and west of the Mississippi, they were struck by the numerous houses, large ceremonial mounds, and temples near the residence of one Indian queen. Although the English colonists who came later tended to dismiss the Indians of the South as savages, such criticism revealed ignorance and fear more than knowledge. The Indian cultures represented a substantial human achievement.

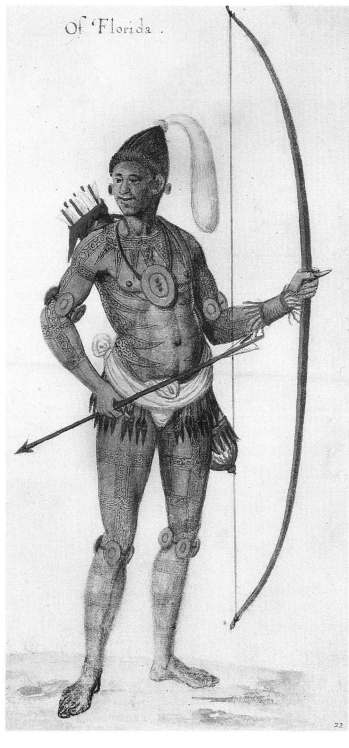

John White, an English artist, accompanied the 1585 expedition to "Virginia" that was organized by Sir Walter Raleigh. White also served as governor in 1587 of the ill-fated Lost Colony. This figure, an Eastern Timucua Indian from the St. Johns River area of Florida, is John White's work but was copied from Jacques Le Moyne de Morgues, who had accompanied a French expedition to Florida in 1563–1565.

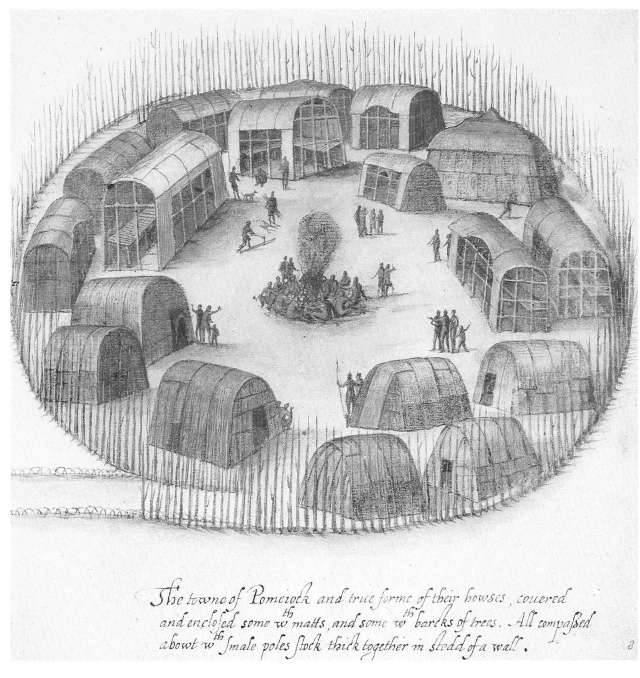

The towne of Pomeiock and true forme of their howses, couered and enclosed some with matts, and some with barcks of trees. All compassed abowt with smale poles stuck thick together in stedd of a wall.

The palisaded town of Pomeioc, which was just southwest of today's Mattamuskeet Lake in North Carolina. John White exaggerated the space between the poles to allow a clearer view of the village.

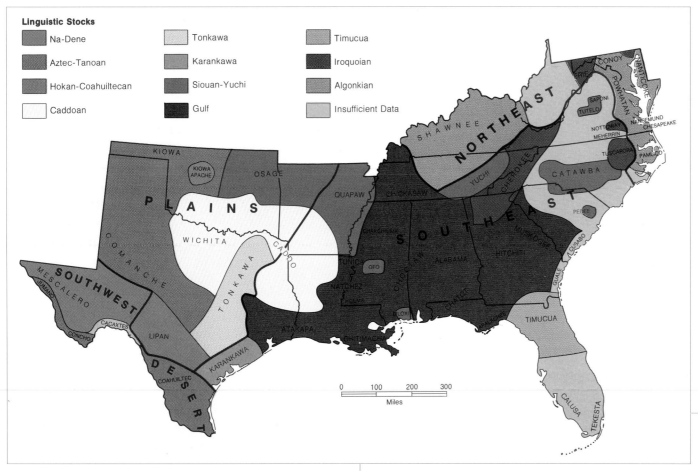

Although most Southern Indians were in the Mississippian tradition, their use of the Southern land was not uniform. This was notable in the Indians' sources of food. Different tribes had different practices, and the Indians' technology and ways of life fit certain parts of the South better than others (FIGURE 3.5). Six patterns of obtaining food from the land prevailed: 1) agriculture as the primary food source; 2) hunting, occasionally supplemented by food-gathering; 3) coastal agriculture mixed with fishing and food-gathering; 4) fishing, with the complete absence of agriculture in some coastal areas; 5) balanced use of native plants and game; and 6) total reliance on native plants.

FIGURE 3.5 *Primary Food Sources of Indians*

FIGURE 3.4 *Major Early Indian Tribes*

In addition to the location of major tribes and their linguistic stocks, this map shows the approximate boundaries between "culture areas." Tribes in one culture area, such as the SOUTH-EAST, shared basic patterns of activity that distinguished them from tribes in a different culture area, such as the PLAINS.

The South of the nineteenth century would be overwhelmingly rural, but the Indians of the Mississippian tradition had so many towns that, according to one scholar, "it is improper to refer to a rural South until after Europeans arrived."[1] These town-dwelling Indians spoke many different languages and organized themselves into several different political alliances. Both their expressive symbolic art and successful agricultural economies testified to a well-developed culture. In fact, according to expert Charles Hudson, the South's Indians possessed the richest culture of any of the native people north of Mexico (FIGURE 3.4).

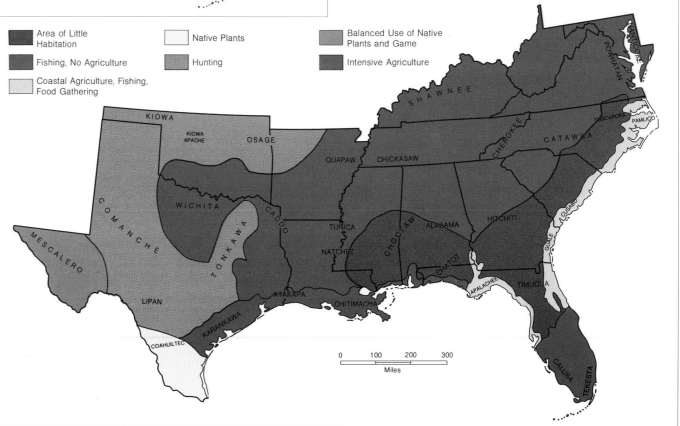

Early Spanish Explorers

Dreams of gold brought early explorers to the South. These dreams, which gripped men like a fever, led thousands into hardship, disappointment, and death. But they had an initial basis in fact.

The Spanish conquistadors Hernán Cortés and Francisco Pizarro found vast treasures of silver and gold in Mexico and Peru—perhaps the lands of the South held greater riches! Pánfilo de Narváez and his followers were among the first to take up the quest. Landing at Tampa Bay in 1528, Narváez took 300 men and moved north in search of wealthy cities that the Indians willingly described. After months of false hopes, 242 survivors embarked on crude boats to try to reach Mexico. After capsizing near the Mississippi River and wrecking on Galveston Island, only four men survived to reach Mexico City. They were led by Álvar Núñez Cabeza de Vaca, who had gained a reputation among the Indians as a healer.

Cabeza de Vaca knew the truth, but his countrymen preferred to listen to fanciful yarns from Indians who told the white men what they wanted to hear.

Eventually Cabeza de Vaca too succumbed to the demand for encouraging news and in 1537 gave his countrymen to understand that the South was the richest country in the world.

Pandemonium ensued, with wealthy Spanish noblemen selling their estates to buy places on an expedition headed by Hernando de Soto. With 600 soldiers and extensive equipment, he landed at Tampa Bay in 1539. Four years of danger, hunger, and death followed as de Soto's expedition wandered far and wide over the American wilderness. De Soto battled Indians and mutiny before he died in 1542 on the banks of the Mississippi River. His men then heard of Spaniards to the west—probably the fruitless march of Francisco Vásquez de Coronado into the Southwest in search of riches. They headed west but, making no contact, returned to the river and sailed south for Mexico. These expeditions left useful descriptions of Indian culture but found no gold. Thereafter, Spanish presence in the South was mainly in the person of friars, who came to Christianize the Indians.

In the interior part of most of the coastal plain where longleaf pine forests stood, settlement by native Americans was virtually nonexistent. In 1528, Indians near the town of Apalachen in northern Florida told the Spanish explorer Álvar Núñez Cabeza de Vaca that in the interior ahead the people "were less numerous and poorer, the land little occupied, and the inhabitants much scattered."[2] The dense forests and unpopulated places thus described bedeviled de Soto 11 years later; more than once his men almost ran out of food as they marched through uninhabited and uncultivated land.

Indians told the Spaniards that this region was one of little food because its physical characteristics did not suit their form of agriculture. The Indians planted in easily worked, well-drained riverine soils, but the sluggish streams of the coastal plain created many swamps and marshes that the Indians could not drain. The less fertile soils of the nearby pine barrens also failed to offer the Indians good support, and there were fewer animal and plant resources available on the inner coastal plain than in other regions.

Along the coast, deer and other animals were more abundant, and acorns, hickory nuts, persimmons, grapes, and black cherries supplied substantial food in the fall. In addition, blueberries and blackberries were available in the spring. Agriculture was important for most of the eastern coastal tribes, especially near the Apalachicola River in western Florida; by allowing their fields to lie fallow in sequence, the Apalachee Indians could remain in permanent villages. Along the Atlantic, however, patches of tillable soil were smaller, and the low water-holding capacity of these sandy soils meant that plants had to be more widely spaced. As a result, tribes such as the Guale had to move to new fields and repeatedly shift their residences.

In southern Florida, agriculture was unimportant to the Indians, partly because the surviving Gulf culture was less oriented to farming but also because wild food, particularly fish and shellfish, was abundant.

Routes of Early Spanish Explorers in the South

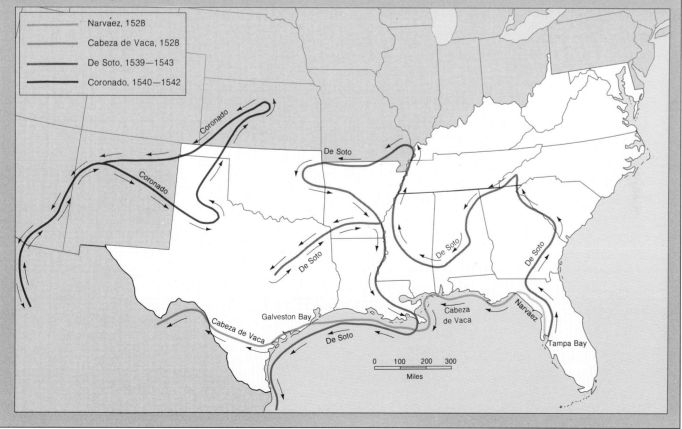

——	Narváez, 1528
——	Cabeza de Vaca, 1528
——	De Soto, 1539—1543
——	Coronado, 1540—1542

In this composite drawing, John White showed Indian methods of fishing both by day and by night (note the fire in the canoe). These waters were probably off the coast of North Carolina.

Large refuse heaps composed of shells are found throughout the Calusa Indian area; one pile of discarded shells is 12 to 15 feet deep and measures 1,700 by 1,900 feet. Shellfish and other marine animals provided most of the Indians' nutrition; fish and mammals were the primary sources of fat, with little vegetable oil being obtained from plants. Similarly, west of the Apalachicola River there is no evidence of coastal agriculture, and if Indians planted there at all, they relied on the harvest very little.

The only other Southern Indians to share that pattern were the hunting tribes located in Texas. Elsewhere, the cultures of the South's Indians typically centered on farming. Tribes that lived in the Piedmont Highlands, the Appalachian Plateau, the Great Valley, and the Mississippi Valley relied heavily on agriculture, which probably accounted for over half of their food. These tribes hunted deer and other animals and gathered wild plants, nuts, and berries, but the mainstays of their diet were maize (corn) and beans, both of which they cultivated continuously. Their fields in the Piedmont and Mississippi Valley were well drained yet close to rivers and occasionally enriched by flooding. Because corn and beans complement each other, probably no fallowing was required to maintain the fertility of the soil. This successful use of the land's resources permitted permanent settlements that were the most densely populated in the region.

The Indians did not just passively use the land; they also actively changed it. Seeing that deer liked to graze in open meadows, they burned the forest to clear parts of it. Burning also removed underbrush, made chestnuts and acorns easier to find, and probably increased the populations of deer and turkeys. In addition, Indians used fire to drive game in hunting and burned their agricultural fields before planting. All these actions interrupted the forest cover, particularly in the Piedmont, and created possibilities for new plants to establish themselves.

Overall, the Indians' relation to the land was a successful one until Europeans came. The Europeans, simply by coming, changed the environment in a very significant way: they brought diseases for which the Indian populations had not acquired immunities. Depopulation was often the consequence, and early English settlers frequently noted that smallpox and other diseases ravaged the Indian tribes. But it seems likely that the fatal effects of contact with Europeans were substantially greater than those described by the English.

More than a hundred years elapsed between the arrival of Spanish explorers or other Europeans and the establishment of thriving English settlements whose people began to comment on the Indian populations. In that long interim, European diseases could have afflicted the Indians; probably they did. Data are almost nonexistent and estimates vary, but it is clear that in Mexico, South America, and the Caribbean, large-scale devastation of native peoples took place. Applying the same ratios of depopulation to North America results in an increasing estimate of the original Indian population. All experts agree that before European settlement, the South's Indians were the most thickly settled group in North America. Undoubtedly their population numbered several hundred thousand, probably one to two million; even larger estimates are conceivable. But by 1700, their numbers dwindled to fewer than 200,000. Disease quickly put European immigrants in a position to dominate the land of the South.

EUROPEANS AND AFRICANS

When the British came to Virginia, they spread out their settlements and hugged the waterways. Discovering with regret that gold was not lying about, the first Englishmen reluctantly began to search for a staple crop that could fetch gold through export. When they found tobacco, a crop grown by the Indians, they entered into social and cultural patterns that would shape the South for generations.

Tobacco made money from the land, but it also took essential nutrients from the soil at a rapid rate. Therefore, tobacco planters had to till new fields every few years. And, of course, the ambitious among them planted as much land as they could in order to harvest the largest possible crop. Since boats offered the easiest means of transporting tobacco to the oceangoing ships that would take it to European markets, Virginia's first tobacco growers cleared far-reaching fields stretching alongside the water. The houses of individual planters were widely separated because the population spread out along the waterways rather than concentrate in large towns (FIGURE 3.6).

The plantation system for rice in South Carolina also tended to disperse people on large landholdings, and a pattern of low population density was set. The South became rural, and a rural type of society began to influence the Southern way of life. Family was the center of personal experience. Generous hospitality came naturally to people who were eager for human contact and social stimulation. Institutions such as churches, schools, and civic or cultural organizations got a slow start because they required concentrations of people. Southerners became independent people who typically lived close to the land.

The emphasis on export crops that needed a great deal of human labor had additional important effects. By 1700, the white indentured servants had almost stopped coming to Virginia, and the planters began to rely on the purchase of African slaves as laborers. To control this unfree labor force, Virginians structured their laws and society to support the slave system. Other Southerners followed Virginia's example and began investing profits in slaves.

After 1700, a swelling stream of African slaves was brought to the South and entered into its life, affecting and influencing its culture. By the middle of the eighteenth century, the black population was growing rapidly from both imports and the natural increase of new generations born in America. An Afro-American people, neither African nor English alone, began to form a coherent culture. And that culture, in ways as diverse as inflections in the Southern accent or musical instruments such as the banjo (Thomas Jefferson referred to it as the "banjar"), contributed to the development of Southern society.

Well into the eighteenth century, that society remained very close to the coast. Virginia's planters relied on coastal rivers and the Chesapeake Bay for transportation, and rice growers in South Carolina depended on the Low Country rivers to flood their water-loving crop. Charleston quickly became a natural terminus and focus for activity. The Sea Islands looked to Charleston as their port, and the Ashley and Cooper rivers also bore the products of Low Country plantations to Charleston's fine harbor. During the hot, malarial summer months, planters loved to escape from their plantations and enjoy the city's social life and sea breezes. Thus, Charleston emerged as the largest and most impressive of the Atlantic Coast's colonial cities.

Gradually the boundaries of settlement began to grow (FIGURES 3.7A and 3.7B). European immigrants—Scotch-Irish, German, Scottish, and English settlers, along with a sprinkling of other nationalities—came in large numbers. Initially they spread slowly inland from the coast, filling up established settlements and

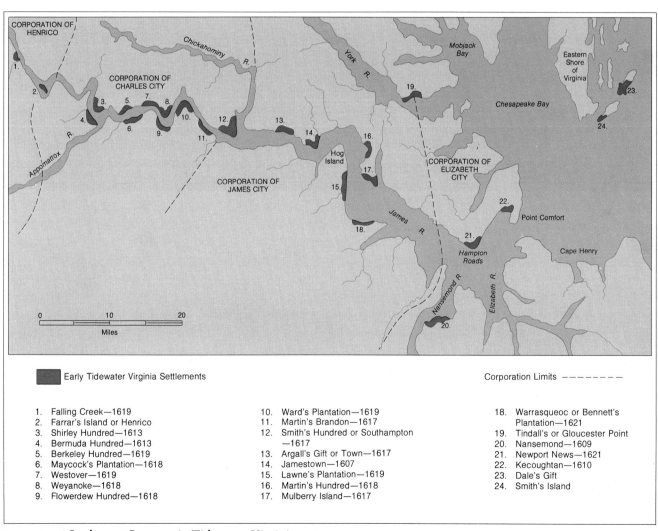

Early Tidewater Virginia Settlements — Corporation Limits - - - - - - -

1. Falling Creek—1619	10. Ward's Plantation—1619	18. Warrasqueoc or Bennett's
2. Farrar's Island or Henrico	11. Martin's Brandon—1617	Plantation—1621
3. Shirley Hundred—1613	12. Smith's Hundred or Southampton	19. Tindall's or Gloucester Point
4. Bermuda Hundred—1613	—1617	20. Nansemond—1609
5. Berkeley Hundred—1619	13. Argall's Gift or Town—1617	21. Newport News—1621
6. Maycock's Plantation—1618	14. Jamestown—1607	22. Kecoughtan—1610
7. Westover—1619	15. Lawne's Plantation—1619	23. Dale's Gift
8. Weyanoke—1618	16. Martin's Hundred—1618	24. Smith's Island
9. Flowerdew Hundred—1618	17. Mulberry Island—1617	

FIGURE 3.6 *Settlement Patterns in Tidewater Virginia, 1622*

The Southern Plantation

The plantation was one of the South's distinctive institutions. It had a large influence on Southern history and culture, yet it was not always the self-sufficient agricultural organization that automatically comes to mind. Over the years, the plantation changed more than many people realize.

In the seventeenth century, and even the first part of the eighteenth, the Southern plantation was very different from our modern image. In Virginia, planters bought up land for tobacco, expanded along or near waterways, and started many plantations. But the typical unit was small, isolated, and often on the frontier. Masters of early tobacco plantations usually owned multiple tracts of land called *quarters*. Often separated from each other, these quarters were the living- and workplaces for small numbers of servants or slaves who raised tobacco and cleared new land for planting. Not until the later eighteenth and nineteenth centuries was the large, self-contained plantation, where scores of people lived together, typical.

Whether as a collection of small quarters or as a large farming unit, the plantation had important effects on Southern life. It reinforced the tendency of an agricultural people to spread out. Planters strove to bring as much land under cultivation as possible, so people lived on the land rather than in towns and villages. A dispersed population naturally meant fewer and weaker institutions, because organizations of all kinds depend on people clustered in a mass rather than spread out. And the dispersion of Southerners across the rural landscape gave them a powerful incentive to nurture the ties of kinship, friendship, and hospitality. Visiting was the center of social life, and hospitality quickly became a famous Southern virtue.

In the nineteenth century, the special characteristics of two crops encouraged the prominence of plantations. Cotton and corn were complementary: they fit together in a work cycle that allowed the planter to grow both a market crop and a food crop for his family and work force. So, cotton and corn strengthened the tendency for the antebellum plantation to become a world unto itself. From February through November, cotton and corn needed attention, but alternately, never at the same time. The plantation's workers could sow one crop and then turn to the other, weed first one crop and then the other. At harvest, they usually finished picking the cotton before gathering the corn, whose ears had been turned down on the stalk earlier to dry. With enough labor to grow cotton, planters also could grow corn as the mainstay of the diet for men and livestock. Thus, the self-sufficient plantation developed, complete in many cases with outbuildings and craftsmen to produce almost everything needed by its residents.

Outbuildings at Middleton Place, South Carolina, where many of the items needed on the plantation were produced

then gradually reaching westward along rivers and streams. These waterways provided the first trading routes between the coast and the inland coastal plain or the Piedmont.

At this time, and for decades to follow, the different European ethnic groups lived rather separate lives. The Scotch-Irish were known for their independence and ability to withstand hard conditions, the Germans for their high standards of farming, the Scottish for their devotion to the king whom English settlers would soon be fighting. All these groups tended to settle, marry, and worship among themselves. They formed separate islands of settlement not yet absorbed into an intermingled Southern population.

In the 1740s, a large migration of settlers came into the Piedmont from a new direction, the northeast. Channeled in a southwesterly direction by the Appalachian range, thousands of Scotch-Irish and Germans from Pennsylvania poured into the southern part of the Piedmont. They were moving into North Carolina in the 1750s and into Georgia's uplands by the 1760s. The Great Philadelphia Wagon Road along which they came carried tens of thousands of passengers between 1760 and 1776. Historians have shown that this road's name was both optimistic and misleading; nevertheless, "it was the most heavily traveled road in all America and must have had more vehicles jolting along its rough and tortuous way than all other main roads put together."[3]

So steady was the flow of people along the Great Philadelphia Wagon Road that a string of towns grew up along its route to serve and sell to travelers (FIGURE 3.8). These towns were also bases from which migrants struck out into surrounding territory to settle, and as the country grew up, they became market towns for the farmers who now lived around them. Fifteen of them, including the still-familiar Hagerstown, Winchester, Staunton, Salem, Salisbury, Charlotte, Camden, and Augusta, stretched along the 700-mile route of the road from Philadelphia.

Thus, two physical features of the land—the Blue Ridge chain and the Great Valley—directly affected the pattern of settlement and development in the South. The Blue Ridge acted as a barrier to westward migration, deflecting early settlers into the Great Valley and Piedmont areas beyond. The Great Valley itself flourished as a transportation and settlement

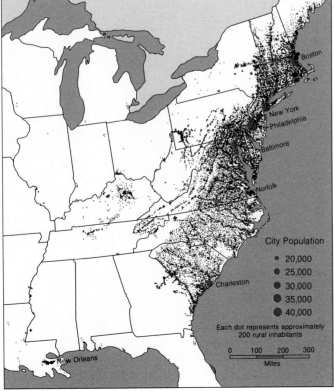

FIGURE 3.7A
*Distribution of
Non-Indian Population
in the Eastern U.S., 1720*

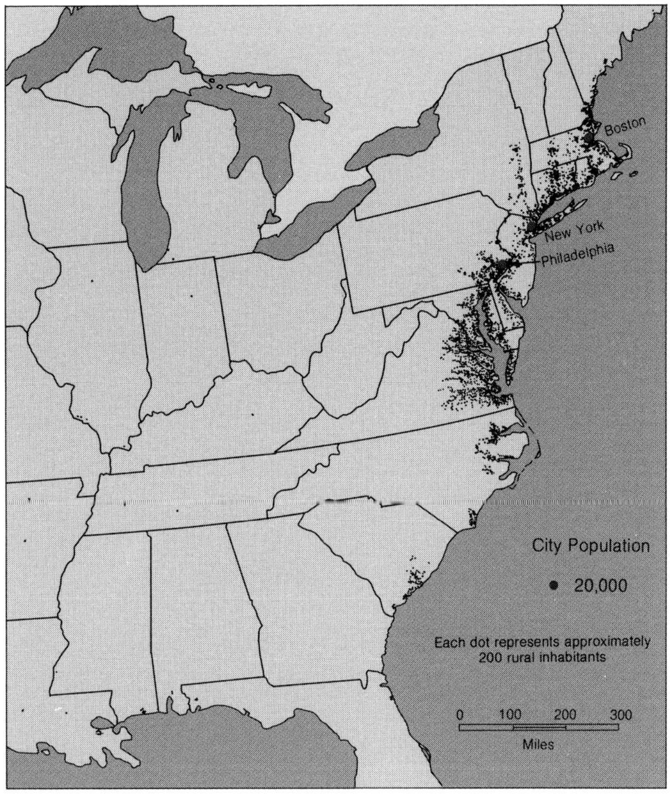

City Population

● 20,000

Each dot represents approximately
200 rural inhabitants

0 100 200 300
Miles

FIGURE 3.7B
*Distribution of
Non-Indian Population
in the Eastern U.S., 1790*

City Population

● 20,000
● 25,000
● 30,000
● 35,000
● 40,000

Each dot represents approximately
200 rural inhabitants

0 100 200 300
Miles

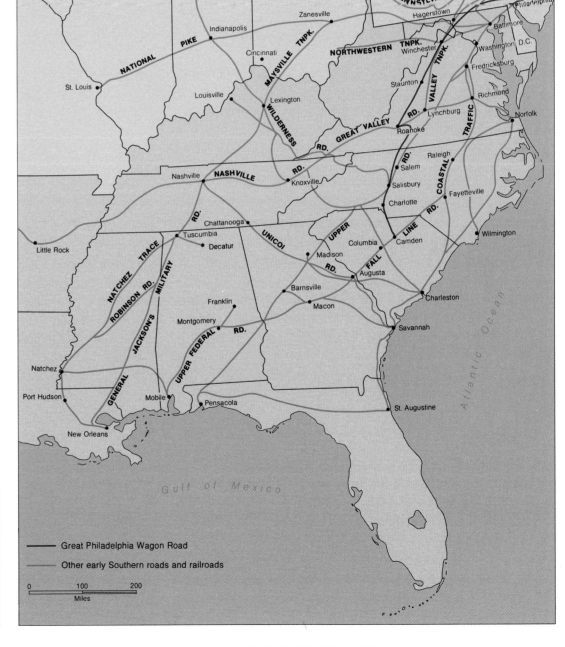

FIGURE 3.8 *Early Southern Roads*

—— Great Philadelphia Wagon Road
—— Other early Southern roads and railroads

0 100 200
Miles

corridor. It offered migrants an easy and attractive route south, and in addition to its beauty, it possessed fertile limestone-based and alluvial soils. These features convinced many travelers to put down roots and stay, instead of continuing along the road.

In 1775, Daniel Boone was surveying a new road, a path through the mountains along the present Kentucky-Virginia border. While hunting west of the mountains, Boone had found an "abundance of wild beasts of all sorts through this vast forest. The buffalo (or bison) were more frequent than I have ever seen cattle in the settlements browsing on the leaves of the cane or cropping the herbage on the extensive plains, fearless because ignorant of the violence of man."[4] Men and women would flock to such a land, he knew, if only they had a road, so he set out to locate one.

Aptly named the Wilderness Road, it made use of an opening through the mountains at the Cumberland Gap (FIGURE 3.9). This opening had served others before Europeans came to America; in earlier times, buffalo and Indians had worn a trail through the gap. The doorway originally carved by running water allowed Boone to lay out a rough trail through trees and around mountains. Before 1800, it was only roughly cleared with axes and was difficult going for anyone but horseback riders and foot travelers. But it penetrated more than 200 miles of wilderness, and its route remained almost unchanged for over a century.

Soon groups of pioneers were collecting in eastern Tennessee to make the trek together into Kentucky or the Cumberland River area of central Tennessee. People recognized that the Bluegrass country was ideal for horses—Harrodsburg, Kentucky, had a race course in 1783—but these were prime agricultural lands, too.

Over thousands of years, the action of wind and water had exposed the underlying limestone sediments in the Bluegrass area and prepared it for cultivation. As a result, the extremely fertile soils near present-day Nashville and Lexington drew settlers like a magnet. So great was the excitement over these rich lands that migration turned forest paths into virtual highways. Historian Everett Dick reports that in the 1780s, "little boards with the distance painted in black were nailed to the trees every three miles on the trail to middle Tennessee."[5]

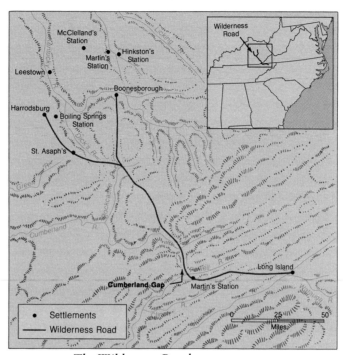

FIGURE 3.9 *The Wilderness Road*

Travelers encountered many discouragements: " . . . a turabel mountain that tried us all almost to death to get over it . . . had this creek to cross many times & very Bad Banks . . . this eaven comes a letter from Capt. Boon[e] at Caintuck of the inding [Indians] doing mischief . . . Some turns back."[6] But there seemed to be a dozen excited migrants for every one that gave up. One traveler "kept an account of the number of souls I overtook in one day going to that country [Kentucky]. . . . in riding about thirty miles, but very little faster than a waggon could drive, I overtook two hundred and twenty one. They seem absolutely infatuated by something like the old crusading spirit to the holy land."[7]

Southerners were eager to fill up the land of the South. But they were blocked from doing so first by the Appalachian range and then by the Indians that remained in Florida and the Gulf states west of Georgia. At the time of the American Revolution, only Kentucky had been settled west of the Appalachians.

Cumberland Gap, through which early settlers poured into Kentucky

Though it is easy to forget this fact when people today speak of the Old South, the Old South was actually recently settled and a new society. The first decades of the nineteenth century were full of motion and activity as migrants peopled new land.

FIGURES 3.10, 3.11, and 3.12, reprinted from a 1914 atlas, portray the rapid expansion of the Southern frontier between 1790 and 1860. The tendency for settlement patterns to be deflected by the Appalachian Mountain system is apparent, as is the dramatic westward march of the Southern people.

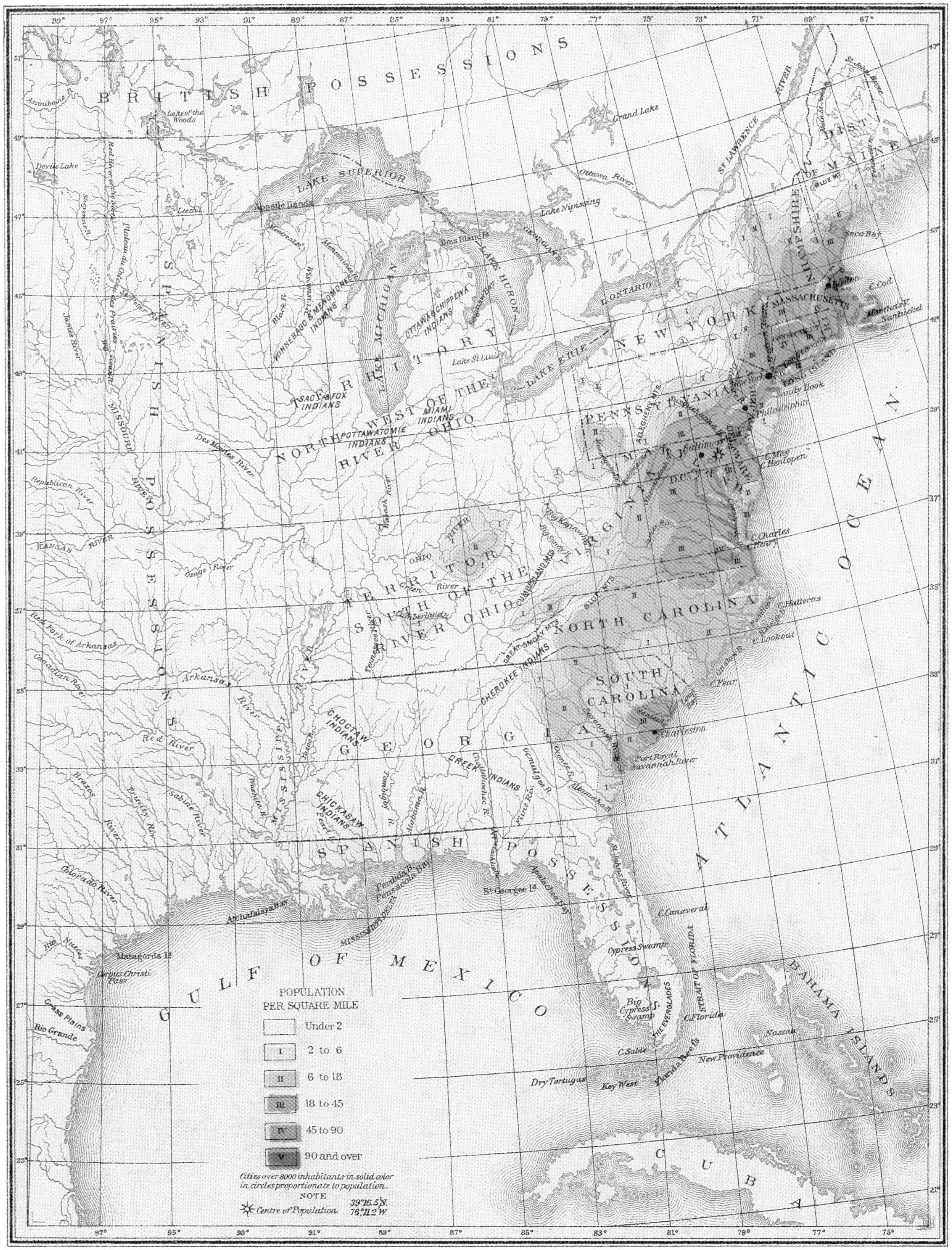

FIGURE 3.10
*Distribution of the Rural Population: 1790
(Outside of Municipalities Having
8,000 or more Inhabitants)*

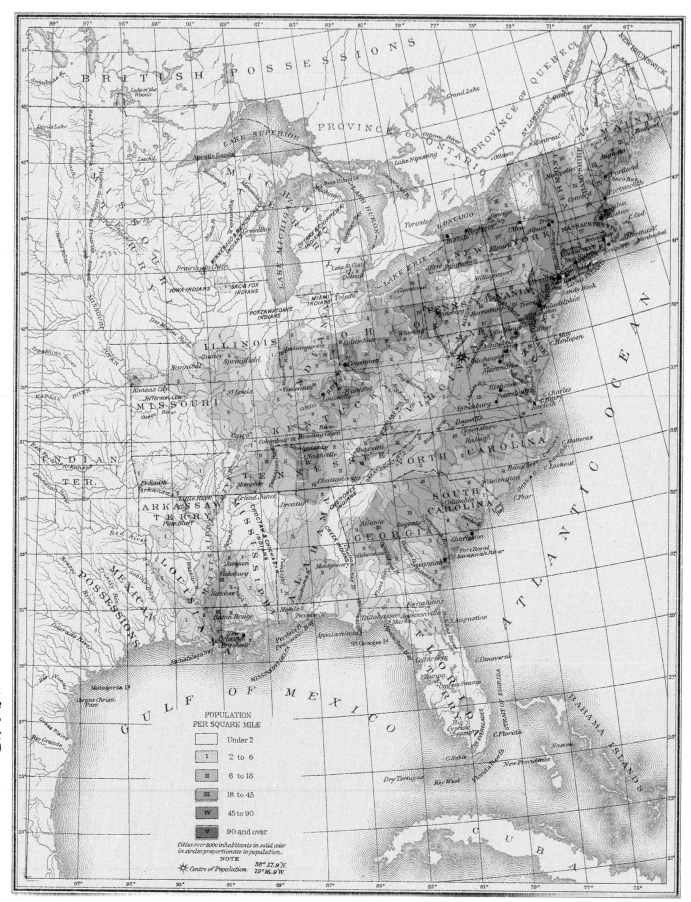

FIGURE 3.11
*Distribution of the Rural Population
East of the 100th Meridian: 1830
(Outside of Municipalities Having
8,000 or more Inhabitants)*

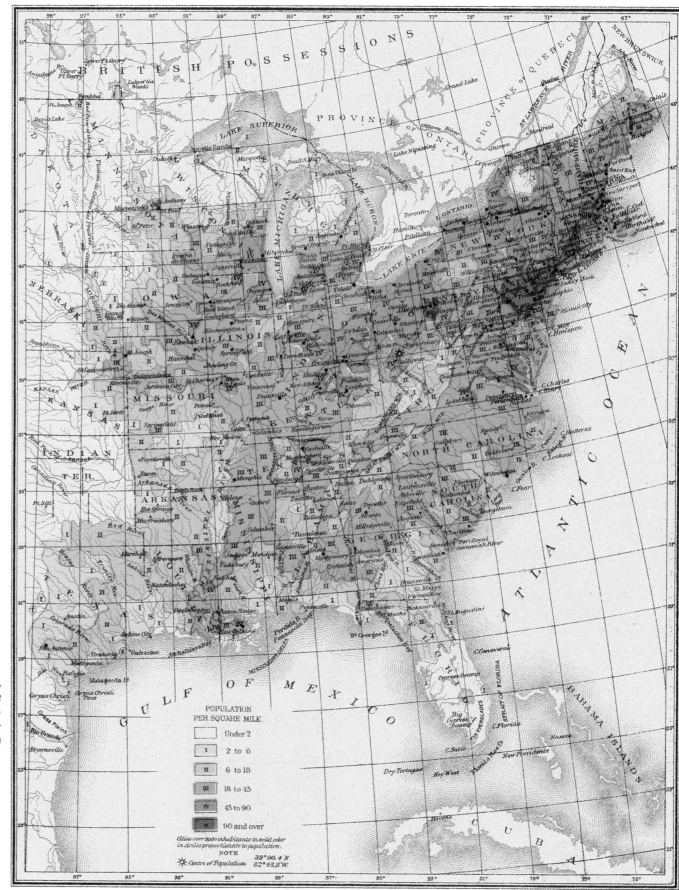

FIGURE 3.12
Distribution of the Rural Population
East of the 100th Meridian: 1860
(Outside of Municipalities Having
8,000 or more Inhabitants)

POPULATION
PER SQUARE MILE

	Under 2
I	2 to 6
II	6 to 18
III	18 to 45
IV	45 to 90
V	90 and over

Cities over 8000 inhabitants in solid color
in circles proportionate to population.
NOTE
✳ Centre of Population   39° 00. 4′ N.
82° 43. 8′ W.

INTO THE GULF PLAIN

Not until after 1800 did large numbers of settlers begin to move into Alabama or Mississippi. Indian tribes still occupied much of this territory, but the land hunger of white settlers put the Indians' lands and treaty rights in peril. The Indians lost some of their lands in 1814 and 1816 and most of the rest two decades later. Seeing that armed resistance attempted by four of the five civilized tribes (the Creeks, Choctaws, Chickasaws, and Seminoles) was futile, the Cherokees chose legal methods to try to defend their interests. In 1828, they organized themselves as an independent nation and adopted a written constitution. They appealed to the federal courts to uphold their treaty rights. Though they did not prevail in all their claims, the Cherokees did win a small victory: United States Chief Justice John Marshall, on behalf of the majority, ruled in one case that only the federal government had jurisdiction over Indian affairs. This landmark decision should have invalidated numerous state laws aimed against the Indians. But President Andrew Jackson, bent on expelling the Indians, is reported to have said: "John Marshall has rendered his decision; now let him enforce it."

Jackson's administration proceeded to remove the Indians. Forced by the federal government, most of the 75,000 Southern Indians east of the Mississippi walked the "Trail of Tears" to reservations in Oklahoma and the Great Plains (FIGURE 3.13). In the winter of 1831–1832, the Choctaws began their involuntary journey from Mississippi and Alabama; the Creeks in Alabama delayed removal until 1836, when the army forced them to leave; the Chickasaws left in 1837. Most Cherokees refused to move in 1838, but federal troops evicted about 20,000 from their homes, held them in detention camps, and then marched them under military escort to Oklahoma. Florida's Seminoles resisted removal and managed to remain in dwindling numbers deep in Florida, and a few scattered remnants of the other civilized tribes eluded the army and managed to stay in the South.

The trip west was painful for all, fatal for many. Deaths were numerous among all the tribes. Nearly one-quarter of the Cherokees died of disease and exhaustion on the Trail of Tears. Cholera afflicted the Choctaws, causing a government agent to lament that "people refused to come near us, or to sell us any

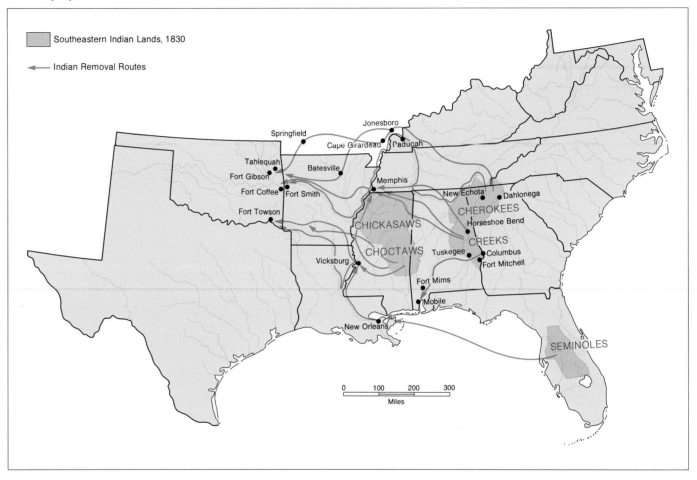

FIGURE 3.13 *Main Indian Removal Routes*

thing we wanted."[8] When Alexis de Tocqueville saw the Choctaws in Memphis, he reported "the wounded, the sick, newborn babies, and the old men on the point of death," and he could not forget the sight of those who waited to cross the Mississippi River: "Neither sob nor complaint rose from that silent assembly. Their afflictions were of long standing, and they felt them to be irremediable."[9] The effort of the five civilized tribes to live with the white settlers had ended with the Indians' eviction. There immediately began what one historian has termed "the Great Migration," as farmers and planters poured by the thousands into the beckoning lands of the Gulf plain.[10]

Only one part of the Gulf was ignored—Florida. For decades the heavy flow of people bypassed this

area, which had finally been secured from Spain in 1819. In addition to its Indian population, Florida's humid tropical and subtropical climate and poor soils discouraged settlement. Nor did Florida have an obvious staple crop before the 1850s, when it was discovered that long-staple Sea Island cotton could be grown in its interior. At mid-century, this state (which would experience booming growth in the twentieth century) had a population of less than 100,000.

But everywhere else, the settlers came enthusiastically. Two forces drew Southerners into the Gulf states across the Appalachians. One was the cotton boom, an opportunity for gaining wealth from a new export crop. Long-staple cotton, which in 1800 grew only on the warm, moist Sea Islands off Georgia and South Carolina, had been a lucrative luxury crop, but the short-staple variety was commercially useless until Eli Whitney's gin provided a means of removing the sticky seeds. Then prosperity was possible for short-staple growers all over the South.

And the demand for cotton was expanding enormously. At this moment in history, Britain was at the head of the Industrial Revolution, with textile production its leading edge. Cotton mills in industrial cities grew and grew and called for ever-greater quantities of the South's new-found bumper crop. British textiles fueled the South's prosperity, and many settlers hoped to make their fortunes by growing cotton.

The second attractive force was the lure of rich soils. West of the Appalachians, in Alabama and Mississippi, lay fabulously rich Black Belt and alluvial lands. Here the enormous Mississippi River system had deposited in its floodplain the topsoils carried off from half a continent. Through Alabama and Mississippi ran another belt of fertile black earth based on limestone sediments high in organic content. As this material settled out on the ocean floor in prehistoric times, it laid the basis for highly productive agriculture later. Wherever zones or belts of this material were exposed, the potential for farming was breathtaking.

Early travelers said the land was "like a paradise it is so good and beautiful."[11] One man admitted that his father's "description of the dark, heavy forests, the wide thick canebrakes, and the clear running river, full of fish, put me into a perfect transport."[12] The canebrakes that covered many areas were astoundingly tall and thick, standing higher than a man on horseback could reach and even attaining 30 feet in some places.

Farmers who scarcely could believe their eyes wrote home in awe to relatives and friends. According to Malcolm Rohrbough, one man who came in 1817 said the Alabama Territory had "the greatest prospect of corn and cotton I ever saw," and pointedly the man asked a friend back East, "Why will you stay . . . and work them poor stony ridges when one

half of the labor and one third of the ground heare will bring you more and not a stone nor hill in the way?"[13] The Alabama lands taken from Indians in the 1830s were presumed to be less fertile but still were so rich that one new arrival declared "that every young man should emigrate if he is poor."[14] And others agreed, for immigrants came in such numbers that "the Carolinas and Georgia seemed to be emptying themselves into the reservoirs to the west."[15]

The alluvial soils and the organically rich limestone sediments of the Black Belt were a magnet. They drew thousands of people who saw a marvelous opportunity to prosper. People became land-crazy—some couldn't wait to move into the Gulf region, and others couldn't stop moving once they had started.

A resident of the Piedmont town of Hillsborough, North Carolina, wrote in 1817: "The *Alabama Fever* rages here with great violence;" this contagious disease had already "carried off vast numbers of our citizens," and the observer confessed, "I am apprehensive if it continues to spread as it has done, it will almost depopulate the country."[16] Along the Upper Federal Road, which opened in 1811, migrants poured in from Athens, Georgia, through Columbus and Montgomery to the town of St. Stephens, north of Mobile. Others took the Natchez Trace from Nashville in search of land that "would do your heart good to look at."[17]

For some, the best land always lay just over the horizon—somewhere ahead was land that was richer, land where a person felt free, or land where other folks were not crowding in. Historian Clement Eaton notes one exhausted Southern wife declared that her husband migrated "for the mere love of moving. We have been doing so all our lives—just moving—from place to place—never resting—as soon as ever we git comfortably settled, then it is time to be off to something new."[18] An Irish traveler observed that "these frontier tamers" were "hardy, indefatigable and enterprising."[19] They endured privation and did without luxury. "It is their pride to have planted an additional

acre of cane-brake, to have won a few feet from the river, or cleared a thousand trees from the forest. . . ."[20]

By the 1830s, as these settlers filled up Alabama, they created an economic boom and a period of rising expectations known as the "flush times." The state was growing and prospering, and everyone was optimistic. There was great inflation and people "endorsed one another's notes freely and grandly," explains Eaton, because "it was regarded as an insult not to do so," and he goes on to say that a Virginian who arrived in Vicksburg in 1836 marveled at the atmosphere: "They do business in a kind of frenzy, largely on credit."[21] This frenzy affected people's lifestyles, even in the case of the rich. Many planters were so eager to clear more land, buy more slaves, and plant more cotton that they had little time for the enjoyment of material luxuries. "If you wish to see splendid poverty, come to Mississippi. If you wish to see people worth millions living as [if] they were not worth hundreds, come down here," wrote one resident.[22] A few individuals built opulent mansions, but many more lived for decades in the log cabin (possibly clapboarded or enlarged) that they had thrown up when they arrived in this fertile territory.

Despite frequent migration, many Southerners wanted to push on. Eaton records that Maria Lides's family had come from South Carolina and done well in Alabama, but nothing could tame "pa's" restless spirit. "His having such a good crop," wrote Maria, "seems to make him more anxious to move. I don't know why it is but none of them are satisfied here. I have no idea that we will stop short of red river. . . ."[23] Desperate, Maria decided to propose California as a destination because "he would be obliged to stop then for he could go no farther."[24] Her family did not reach California, but did reach Texas.

Texas already had a history of Spanish mission activity dating back to the seventeenth and eighteenth centuries. Settlement by large numbers of Americans

Mission San José y San Miguel de Aguayo was one of many early Spanish missions in what is now Texas.

Spanish Missions

Few have ever dared or endured as much in devotion to an ideal as the Spanish friars of the sixteenth, seventeenth, and eighteenth centuries. They came with the first conquistadors and immediately set about the task of learning Indian languages and winning converts to Christ.

Jesuit and Franciscan missionaries visited North America with early explorers but did not have an opportunity to establish a lasting mission in Florida until 1583. Within fifty years, the Franciscans staffed missions from the Gulf Coast to Port Royal (just north of Savannah) on the South's Atlantic Coast. In the eighteenth century, Jesuit friars working out of Mexico established missions throughout Texas and the Southwest. They succeeded earlier Franciscan missionaries whose efforts had been obliterated by Indian warfare.

Repeatedly, Roman Catholic friars perished at the hands of hostile tribes, but undaunted, other friars replaced them, rebuilt the missions, and reestablished contact. For most of the seventeenth and eighteenth centuries, these priests were the primary Spanish presence in the South, indeed in all of North America. Their devotion created a Spanish heritage in the South that is far from negligible.

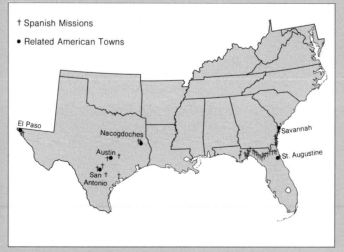

Spanish Missions

began in the 1820s. The Mexican government had encouraged immigration by American settlers, only to see the growing colony fight and win its independence in 1836. Annexed to the United States in 1846, Texas saw its population triple in the 1850s. But in the decades both before and after 1860, there was a pattern of settlement in Texas that showed the influence of two migratory streams. One consisted of people moving in from the upper South states and the other of settlers coming from the Gulf.

Migrants from the Gulf Southern states of Alabama, Georgia, Mississippi, and Louisiana had predominated in coastal areas by 1836. Farther in from the coast, people born in the upper Southern states of Tennessee, Kentucky, Missouri, and Arkansas were more numerous (FIGURE 3.14). By 1880, both groups had expanded, but the pattern had endured (FIGURE 3.15). Gulf Southerners dominated cotton-growing plantation districts in the east, and small farmers from the upper South tended to grow wheat, oats, and food crops in the middle portions of the state. Not surprisingly, these differences corresponded to differing degrees of self-sufficiency in food crops, reliance on slave labor, and even support for secession. The varying life-styles of upper and lower South were meeting in Texas.

Most settlers in Arkansas came from the upper South, though relatively few—only 435,000—had arrived by 1860. Many of these people were absorbed in the tasks of clearing land and establishing communities, and much of the state was almost a frontier until after the Civil War. But the beauty of the Ouachita Mountains attracted the attention of settlers who had been used to living in the South's uplands farther east.

Just as the land attracted and channeled Southerners' movements, it influenced their use of resources. The antebellum pioneers who poured into

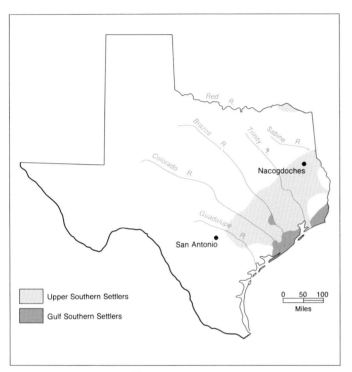

FIGURE 3.14 *Mexican Texas, 1836*

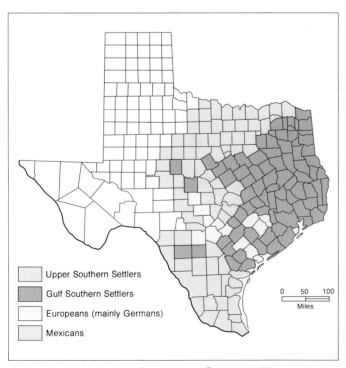

FIGURE 3.15 *Dominant Immigrant Groups in Texas, 1880*

Texas discovered that eastern counties primarily were suitable for cotton; farther west, cattle-grazing became a major agricultural activity in regions too dry for the staple crop. The most favorable areas of climate and soil for tobacco lay in Virginia, North Carolina, and Kentucky, with additional production in adjacent areas of Maryland and Tennessee. Consequently, those states became and remain the leading tobacco producers (FIGURE 3.16). Rice, with its need for abundant water, was a coastal crop important to Louisiana and the Atlantic Coast states from Wilmington, North Carolina, to the northern border of Florida. Sugarcane was also an important and profitable Southern plantation crop, but only in very warm districts. It was grown principally in Louisiana, and only minor amounts were grown elsewhere.

The physical features of the land had an even clearer influence on the location of the South's cities. Invariably, major urban centers in the early South were ports. Their harbors served the needs of trade, which was so vital to struggling colonies and later to booming export economies. Moreover, the drowned rivers of the South's Atlantic Coast provided attractive anchorages. North of the Neuse River in North Carolina and from the Santee River in South Carolina to Florida, the depression of the coastal rim created great potential for harbors. For all these reasons, such ports as Norfolk, Wilmington, Charleston, Savannah, Mobile, and New Orleans became leading cities, and they generally remained major urban centers in the South until or after the Civil War.

After the establishment of port cities, however, Southerners founded their urban places in response to geography and the needs of trade. Some towns, such as Chattanooga, grew up along the paths of wagon roads. Since rivers were the best highways before the days of modern transportation, the earliest important inland cities usually were river cities. Louisville and

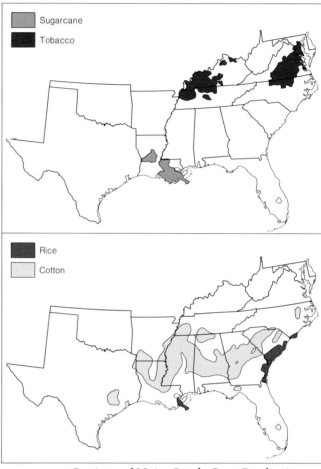

FIGURE 3.16 *Regions of Major Staple Crop Production, 1860*

Memphis collected and forwarded trade that flowed down the Ohio and Mississippi rivers. New Orleans, at the mouth of the Mississippi, continued to be (as it had been under the Spanish and French) the destination for all river-borne commerce of the Mississippi Valley. Not surprisingly, it was by far the largest of the South's cities in 1860, boasting a population of 169,000.

Along the interior edge of the coastal plain, from Virginia all the way to the Dallas–Fort Worth area in Texas, other cities grew up at the zone of transition to the Piedmont. Due to the differing geology of the Piedmont and coastal plain, rivers and streams usually encountered rapids at this point of transition, called the fall line (FIGURE 3.17). The rapids or waterfalls of the fall-line area spurred the growth of cities, because boats had to tie up to shore and unload their cargoes, which then were carted overland to quieter waters or to market.

Warehouses and shops naturally sprang up at such break-of-bulk points, and many of the Piedmont's best-known cities evolved at or near these transfer points. Richmond, Petersburg, Raleigh, Columbia, Augusta, Macon, Columbus, and Montgomery all grew up on the fall line. The large number of state capitals among them reflects the fact that transshipment points were logical sites for inland commercial and political centers.

At a later date, other cities would arise in response to new economic and technological developments. Waterpower became an important influence after the Civil War on the location of textile factories. Railroads, modern highways, airplanes, and the vigorous economic growth of the Sunbelt have created new patterns of settlement, which are discussed in the following sections on the South's subregions. But in all eras, the Southern land and people have interacted: the land setting boundaries or offering opportunities, the people making choices about use of the land. On the scale of geologic time, human cultural patterns may seem brief, but they often endure for many generations. Therefore, both man's works and nature need close attention in examining the subregions of the South.

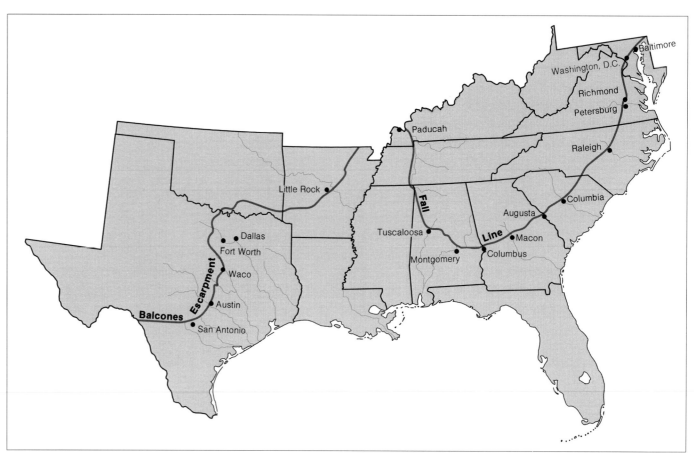

FIGURE 3.17 *Fall Line and Escarpment Cities*

Turbulent waters mark the fall line, along which many important Southern cities grew.

PART II   THE LOWLAND SOUTH

4 INTRODUCTION—*The Lowland South*

The South is more than a geographical region. For natives and visitors alike, it has always been a physical, almost sensual, experience. The South's environment is so lush and compelling that it floods one's perceptions and persists in feeling as well as in memory. History has only redoubled the South's special appeal, and as a result, rich images of the South fill the American mind.

Sights of the South linger in one's eye: Spanish moss trailing from the massive live oaks . . . the glossy green of a magnolia leaf . . . stately plantation homes . . . simple tobacco barns and unpainted share-croppers' cabins . . . narrow lanes in historic cities and courthouse squares in small towns . . . slow-moving rivers and languid bayous . . . cypress swamps and cordgrass marshes . . . the tilting gull and long-legged water birds.

Other impressions surround these images with an almost palpable atmosphere: the warmth of sun on one's skin, light that is vivid yet soft, the rustling of palm fronds and the dripping of rain, sultry weather relieved by occasional breezes, the strong perfume of flowers.

Most of these sensations come from the oldest part of the South, the Lowlands, which have influenced the South longer than any other subregion. The Atlantic portion of the Lowlands was settled first, and there the first port cities grew. There also ship captains landed African slaves and tobacco and rice plantations developed. Lowland people and institutions established deep roots in Southern society and set patterns for the future.

The coastal plain is the site of most of the South's elegant old plantations and a favorable environment for the majestic live oak. This photograph shows Oak Alley at the Magnolia Mound Plantation in Baton Rouge, Louisiana.

*The Lowland South contains many swamps
and wetlands where the cypress tree,
with its distinctive "knees," grows well.*

Nearly until the American Revolution, most Southerners continued to cling to the low coastline along the Atlantic Ocean. When settlers streamed across the Appalachian Mountains, the Lowlands of the Gulf emerged to lead the Cotton Kingdom. Plantations and slaves characterized the Lowlands before the Civil War, and the sharecropping system and furnish merchants dominated it afterwards. As the nineteenth century gave way to the twentieth, people of the Lowlands tended to hang on to old and familiar patterns, while the people in Upland areas such as the Piedmont led in change.

The Lowland South sweeps in a great arc from the estuary of Chesapeake Bay southwestward to the Gulf Coast of Texas. It forms a strip 1,800 miles long and from less than 100 to 500 miles wide. Surface elevations are low, ranging from sea level to a few hundred feet above it. The surface is flat to gently rolling, and hills are rare. Loose, unconsolidated sediments comprise the surface and combine with the gentle slopes to create the poor drainage that distinguishes so much of the Lowland South. Broad, shallow rivers; swamps, marshes, and wetlands; and thousands of narrow lakes are all reflections of this poor drainage.

The character of the land of the Lowlands was established when the coastline reached far into the current interior. Between about 65 and 136 million years ago (recent by geologic standards), the Lowlands area was inundated by oceanic invasions. These maritime expansions left behind a land that resembles the sea floor it once was. The ocean bottom sediments are as much as 10,000 feet thick in Virginia, and they thicken gradually westward, reaching as much as 30,000 feet in Texas.

The Lowlands end along the Atlantic Coast where these ocean sediments give way to the ancient crystalline rocks of the Piedmont, along the fall line. On the East Gulf Coastal Plain, the interior boundary occurs where the fall line hills (other remnants of an ancient shoreline) lap onto harder sedimentary rocks of intermediate age, younger than those on the Piedmont. Larger rivers, especially the Mississippi, were able to erode their channels through these rocks more readily, and navigability did not end so abruptly here as it did to the east. West of the Mississippi Valley the transition is more visible, marked by the abrupt Balcones Escarpment, a fault zone along which the great weight of recent maritime sediments caused the surface to fracture and sink. Behind it the Edwards Plateau of Texas forms a line of hills that loom over Fort Worth, Waco, Austin, San Antonio, and points in between.

This Southern region is an area of stereotypical Southern weather: high humidity, rare snowfall, oppressively hot summers, mild winters, and a protracted springtime. The image derives from reality, but it tends to obscure the substantial variety within the area. For example, the Florida Keys have a truly tropical climate, while in central Texas one encounters a semiarid climate that is more characteristic of the southwestern United States. Strong storms that occasionally blow through the region provide another type of climatic variety. Thunderstorms are frequent in the summer and bring large amounts of rainfall. More spectacular are tornadoes and hurricanes that, collectively, are more common in the Lowland South than in any other part of the country.

A coastline bay of the Atlantic Coastal Plain

The Lowland South also has characteristic vegetation patterns, but as with the weather, there is considerable internal diversity. Most of the area was originally covered by an evergreen pine forest, and large stands of such forest still exist. On the northern and western edges of the Lowlands, the pine forest gives way to a mixed oak-and-pine forest. Shortleaf, loblolly, longleaf, and slash pines dominate the sandy uplands, and alluvial bottomlands often contain sweet gum, tupelo, various oaks, cypress, hickories, willows, hollies, magnolia, and cedars as well as pines. Southern Florida has a more tropical forest that includes mangroves, palms, and yews. Species such as mesquite, cactus, thornbushes, and prairie grasses are found in the drier parts of the Lowlands in Texas. Marshes along the extensive coastline include Indian ricegrass, cattail, and tule in freshwater areas and spartina grass (cordgrass) in salt marshes.

THE LAND-WATER INTERFACE

The outer boundary of the Lowland South is set along the coastal margin, the land-water interface. This boundary extends for a distance of more than 1,800 miles—from Maryland's Chesapeake Bay to Texas's Padre Island, making it the longest stretch of coastline in the conterminous United States. This land-water boundary, or continental margin, should be viewed as a broad transitional zone rather than as a sharp demarcation. Here the sea penetrates inland for miles along drowned, sluggish rivers, and the continental landmass extends seaward to form submerged shallow continental shelves that reach 50 or more miles into the sea. This continental margin is particularly important because it supports a dense and rich variety of marine life, promises a wealth of mineral resources, provides critical support for trade and commerce, and is the focus of major recreational development. It is, however, a province of fragile and unique ecosystems. Caution is needed if major environmental problems are to be avoided.

One of the most important reasons for the diversity of the marine environment is the nature of the continental margin's topography. As shown in FIGURE 4.1, the ocean can be divided topographically into three parts: the *continental shelf,* which is a relatively flat, submerged platform that stretches from the shoreline to the open sea; the *continental slope,* which is a sharply inclined surface beginning at the seaward terminus of the shelf and extending to the ocean basin; and the *ocean basin,* a broad expanse which is generally below a depth of 3,000 feet.

Oceanographers and ecologists recognize the importance of topography in the distribution of marine life and classify marine environments accordingly. Ocean waters lying above the shallow continental shelf are referred to as *neritic,* and all waters seaward of the shelf are called *oceanic.* Ocean floor environments beyond the continental shelf are labeled *deep-sea environments,* while those on the continental shelf are called *littoral.* The littoral environment is subdivided into *supralittoral,* the beach area above high tide; *littoral,* the intertidal region; and *sublittoral,* the area from the low-tide line to the edge of the continental shelf (FIGURE 4.2).

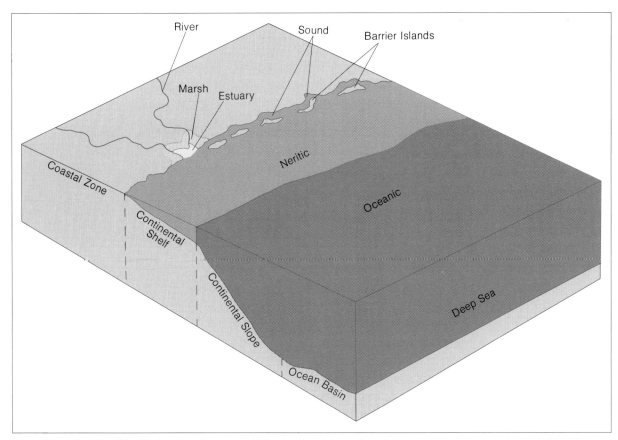

FIGURE 4.1 *Marine Environments*

The Sandy Beach

The sandy beaches of the Southern coastal fringe provide the country with its most popular recreational environment. The noisy surf, warm sand, clear breezy air, and bright sun delight visitors and residents alike. Boating, fishing, swimming, surfing, and other ocean-side activities have become passions for millions. Both Southerners and Northerners flock to the attractive beaches.

As an ecosystem, the beach area is defined as the zone that lies between the high-water mark along the coast and the shallow water along the continental shelf where waves begin to break (the surf zone). Often referred to as the open coast, this environment is characterized by the perpetual motion of both water and sand. The shoreline is steadily under attack by the surf, longshore currents, swash, and backwash. The form and configuration of beaches—sand dunes, berms, beach ridges, sandbars, and sandspits—reflect these and other natural processes.

A sandy beach in coastal North Carolina

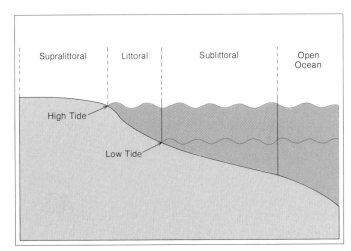

FIGURE 4.2 *Littoral Environments*

Localized features also account for four important marine environments within the Lowland South: the sandy beach zone, the estuary, the tropical coral reef, and the open sea. Of these, it is the sandy beaches and estuaries that distinguish so much of the Southern coastal fringe. The coral reefs are restricted to the shallow tropical waters of southern Florida.

The continual motion of water and sand and the resulting transitionary nature of the landscape have complicated man's occupancy as well as marine life colonization of the land areas adjacent to the beach. Real estate along beach areas has been in considerable demand and is being heavily developed in spite of the fact that many of these beach areas are geologically unstable. Residents struggle to secure the shoreline by constructing seawalls, groins, jetties, and other water-diverting structures. In some instances, these provide short-term stability, but too often the relief is momentary. Because of the attractiveness and environmental sensitivity of these beach areas, greater care is needed to protect and preserve this rich natural resource.

While sandy beaches may appear barren of life at low tide, beneath the sand, life is commonplace. The sandy shores of the Lowland South's coastline challenge marine inhabitants. There is no surface for attachment of seaweed. There are no rock crevices to give protection to worms and snails. But marine life still adapts, largely by occupying tubes within the sand or burrowing into it and feeding on particulate and suspended organic matter carried in by the moving water.

Marine life in beach areas is sharply divided by zone. The supralittoral fringe is home to the encrusting algae and lichens. Animals include the sea roach, ghost crab, beach flea, and fiddler crab. Seaward in the littoral zone, mole crabs, soft-shell clams, ghost shrimp, and other burrowing animals lie beneath the sand. Farther out, in the sublittoral region, more burrowing creatures—sand dollars, starfish, young flounder, clams, and a multitude of others—are found. Drift animals such as jellyfish may also wash ashore in numbers from time to time.

The Estuary

Estuaries are semienclosed areas where the waters of the land mix with the waters of the sea. Their uniqueness derives from their brackish water, which supports a wide variety of marine organisms and serves as a nursery for juvenile fish.

Because of a unique combination of physical features, estuaries are among the most productive ecosystems on earth (FIGURE 4.3). Located at the endpoint of rivers carrying abundant organic materials, estuaries serve as nutrient traps. As the streams approach the ocean, their velocities decrease, allowing suspended materials to settle out. This productivity is additionally enhanced by adjacent tidal marshes and swamps, whose salt-tolerant grasses are flooded daily by tides providing a huge surplus of organic matter. The collision of fresh and salt waters circulates the nutrients up and down, further enriching the waters.

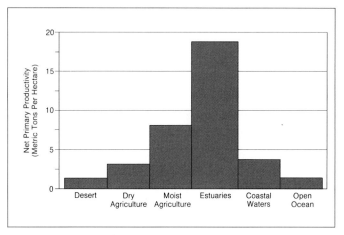

FIGURE 4.3 *Natural Productivity of Estuaries Relative to Other Environments*

Most estuaries are dominated by a few species. The constant shift in salinity, turbidity, and temperature create a complex environment that limits the number of species that can successfully adapt. However, because of the estuaries' extremely high productivity, those species that are able to adapt are usually present in large numbers and are generally salt-tolerant marine forms.

Nowhere is the interpenetration of land and water more important than in relation to seafood. The intimate mingling of sea and shore makes possible the abundance and variety of tasty fish and crustaceans. Most estuaries support such floor-dwelling marine species as crabs, lobsters, shrimp, clams, and oysters. Other estuary species include young flounder, striped mullet, menhaden, and croaker. As shown in FIGURE 4.4, there is a strong latitudinal variance in typical species. For these commercially valuable sea creatures, estuaries are more than fertile feeding grounds. Many fish and crustaceans reproduce in tidal marshes and estuaries, where the hatchlings can find both food and safety. Normally, these young animals could not survive in the ocean, where they would be eaten up by adult species, nor could they live in fresh water. But they can tolerate the brackish tidal waters that larger fish avoid, and so the marshes and estuaries function as nurseries where these juvenile animals feed and grow.

The two chief types of estuaries of the Lowland South are *drowned river valley* and *bar-built*. They are dramatically different in their surface appearances, and their differences are related to geologic conditions at the time and place of their origin (FIGURES 4.5 and 4.6).

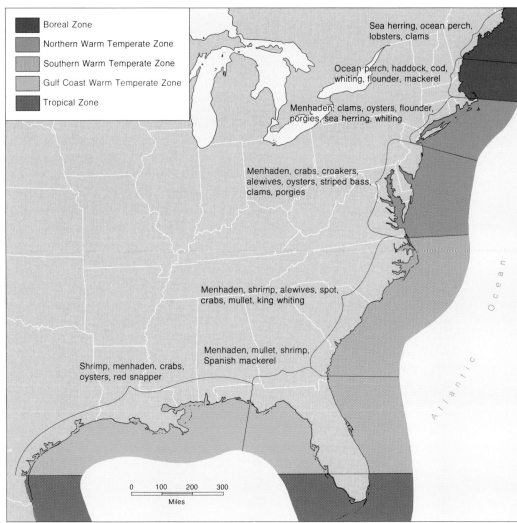

Boreal Zone
Northern Warm Temperate Zone
Southern Warm Temperate Zone
Gulf Coast Warm Temperate Zone
Tropical Zone

Sea herring, ocean perch, lobsters, clams

Ocean perch, haddock, cod, whiting, flounder, mackerel

Menhaden, clams, oysters, flounder, porgies, sea herring, whiting

Menhaden, crabs, croakers, alewives, oysters, striped bass, clams, porgies

Menhaden, shrimp, alewives, spot, crabs, mullet, king whiting

Menhaden, mullet, shrimp, Spanish mackerel

Shrimp, menhaden, crabs, oysters, red snapper

Atlantic Ocean

0   100   200   300
Miles

FIGURE 4.4 *Latitudinal Zoning of Fish and Shellfish*

Latitudinal zoning of fish along the Atlantic and Gulf coasts is illustrated by the production of some commercial fish. For each stretch of coast, the fish are listed in the order of their weight of commercial production.

FIGURE 4.5
Drowned River Valleys and Barrier Islands

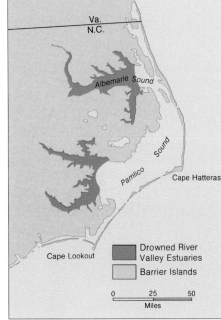

Va.
N.C.

Albemarle Sound

Pamlico Sound

Cape Hatteras

Cape Lookout

Drowned River Valley Estuaries
Barrier Islands

0   25   50
Miles

Drowned river valley estuaries result from recent submergence either from the melting of continental glaciers and the subsequent rise in sea level or from subsidence of the earth's crust. An excellent example is the world-famous Chesapeake Bay. As in similar drowned estuaries, here seawater, having a higher density, flows inward along the bottom, while fresh water from the river flows outward at the surface.

Bar-built estuaries are found in every Southern coastal state from Maryland to Texas. They lie behind the world's largest chain of barrier islands, ranging in size from small outcroppings of wave-washed, wind-blown sand to large forested islands. As shown in FIGURES 4.5, 4.6, and the barrier island illustration, these islands enclose coastal areas to form shallow lagoons. The islands are popular recreational areas, and a number have been set aside as national sea-shores, including Assateague Island, Maryland; Cape Hatteras, North Carolina; and Padre Island, Texas.

There is a theory that barrier islands are a result of rising sea levels. During the last 15,000 years, melting ice has added over 400 feet to the ocean's depth, and although the rate of increase slowed drastically about 5,000 years ago, the sea level has continued to rise about one foot per century. In fact, the sea level of the Atlantic Ocean at Charleston, South Carolina, has risen 14 inches since 1920.

This added volume of water could have created most of the South's barrier islands. According to the theory, dozens of the smaller islands once were dunes or ridges of sand along the previous coastline. As the waters slowly rose, powerful waves attacked the shore, breached some of the dunes, and steadily invaded the land behind. The rising sea thus created lagoons on the landward or lee side of the coast and left the dunes isolated as newly formed islands. A new coastline appeared with a string of small islands close offshore.

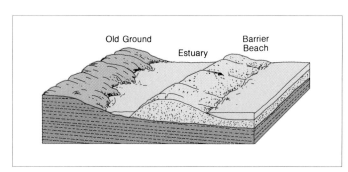

Old Ground   Barrier Beach
          Estuary

FIGURE 4.6
Bar-Built Estuary

Barrier Island Environment

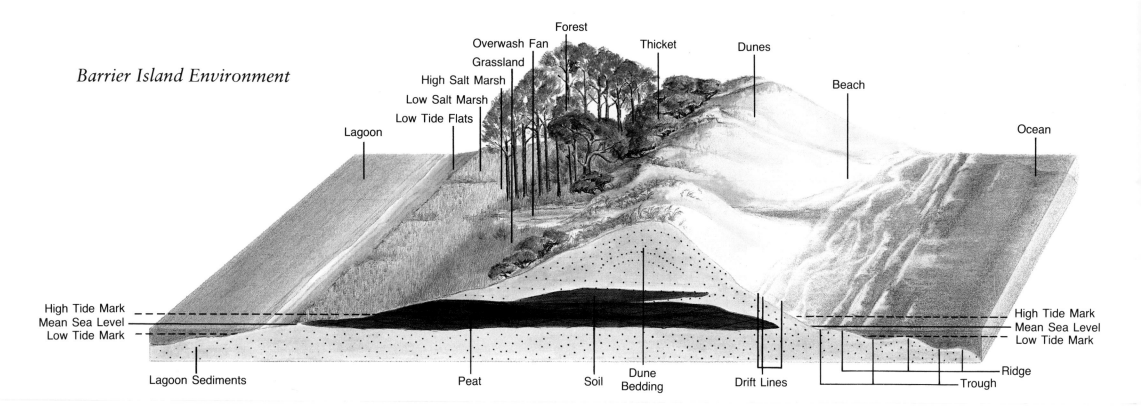

Forest

Overwash Fan

Grassland

High Salt Marsh

Low Salt Marsh

Low Tide Flats

Thicket

Dunes

Beach

Lagoon

Ocean

High Tide Mark

Mean Sea Level

Low Tide Mark

High Tide Mark

Mean Sea Level

Low Tide Mark

Lagoon Sediments

Peat

Soil

Dune Bedding

Drift Lines

Ridge

Trough

Many of these islands are thousands of years old, but they remain fragile. Their existence and location depend on the balance between available sand or sediment and the forces that move them about. People can also be a potent force, for their intervention may damage the balance of nature's forces and increase pressures on the islands. Without intervention, change is still continual at most of the islands. They migrate as the ocean rises or falls. Since the Atlantic Ocean has been rising for thousands of years, most of the small, sandy barrier islands have been retreating, or moving steadily westward with the shore (FIGURE 4.7). Where there was too little sand, or where wind and waves were too powerful, some barrier islands were covered up or drowned.

The retreating barrier islands move by rolling over themselves. Wind and waves move sand from the ocean side of the island toward the lagoon or landward side. Slowly the elements remove sand from the shore facing the ocean and deposit it on the lee side. Even more important are submarine currents, for the tides carry vast amounts of sediment. As they cut channels below sea level and between the islands, huge amounts of sand can build up the lagoon behind a barrier island. The island's migrating sand then

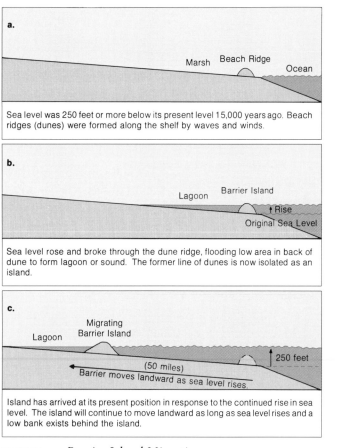

a.

Marsh   Beach Ridge

Ocean

Sea level was 250 feet or more below its present level 15,000 years ago. Beach ridges (dunes) were formed along the shelf by waves and winds.

b.

Lagoon   Barrier Island

↑ Rise

Original Sea Level

Sea level rose and broke through the dune ridge, flooding low area in back of dune to form lagoon or sound. The former line of dunes is now isolated as an island.

c.

Migrating Barrier Island

Lagoon

(50 miles)

↑ 250 feet

Barrier moves landward as sea level rises.

Island has arrived at its present position in response to the continued rise in sea level. The island will continue to move landward as long as sea level rises and a low bank exists behind the island.

FIGURE 4.7 *Barrier Island Migration*

comes to rest on top of the newly deposited material in the lagoon.

Powerful winds and waves help an island retreat by tearing down its established dunes. Strong winds can make the dunes drift despite their anchoring grasses, and storms can wash waves over the dunes. Any human activity that damages the dunes, such as driving vehicles through them or uprooting their grasses, greatly accelerates the process.

Usually waves wash over an island at some weak point in the system of dunes. Every surge of water rushing through a breach in the line of dunes carries with it a heavy load of sand. The invading waves spread out on the lee side of the dunes, depositing a fan-shaped mass of relocated sand. As the process is repeated, large amounts of sand build up, and plants then begin to establish themselves in the sediment. Thus, a new line of dunes begins to form deeper in the island as the shoreline erodes.

In this way, even migrating islands tend to maintain the topography and ecology typical of barrier islands. They rise from a rather wide ocean-side beach to a higher central plateau that may be grassy, overgrown into a thicket, or forested. Along the Atlantic Coast, frequent overwashes usually create a broad, grassy, flat area in the island's center. On the lee side, a salt marsh quickly drops below sea level. Dozens of plant species thrive in each zone of a barrier island. Salt-meadow cordgrass and sea oats play the particularly important role of anchoring sand, and the low marsh is a major site for plant and animal growth.

Human populations have always clustered near estuaries because they provide food, are navigable, support industrial activities, and are attractive recreational areas. The pressures, though, have never been as severe as they are now. The problem centers around tidal marshes, the grassy wet bands around estuaries. Since colonial times people have tried to make use of marshy areas that often appear useless to anyone not informed about marine biology. Early settlers harvested the naturally growing salt hay and cordgrass as fodder for livestock. They drove stakes (which sometimes can still be seen) into the ground and stacked the hay up on them to keep it dry at high tide. Later on, people fastened large wooden shoes to the hooves of horses and used horsepower to pull mowing machines through the marshes. In modern times, however, the major threat has come from real estate development. Growing cities look at marshes as a source of needed room for expansion. Private companies fill and build there to supply housing for those who want to live near the ocean.

No one knows how much of the original marshland has been lost because accurate surveys from the colonial period do not exist. But most knowledgeable observers agree that in some states along the Atlantic Coast, as much as one-half of the coastal salt marsh system has been destroyed. The marshes in the single state of South Carolina represent more than 25 percent of all the tidal marshland remaining along the East Coast.

The loss of seemingly useless marshes is important because these areas are, in fact, crucial to the food chain on which many commercially valuable marine animals depend. The salt hay and cordgrass that cover marshland, plus the animals that flourish there, create a tremendous amount of biological food. Only the most intensively cultivated and heavily fertilized farmlands can compare with them. Marshes are, on average, twice as productive as moist agricultural lands and several times more productive than dry agricultural areas. They are 10 times more productive than

the nearshore waters and roughly 100 times more productive than the deep ocean.

The secret to this bounty is the decomposition of each year's crop of salt hay and cordgrass. As the weather turns cold in the fall, the above-water stems of marsh grasses die and fall over on each other in clumps or piles. Bacteria and fungi begin to break down the plant fibers, and this decomposing mass becomes a rich organic soup called *detritus*.

The organic nutrients contained in detritus reach marine animals in two ways. First, as the tides flow in and out of the marshes, the salt water flushes some of the detritus out into the nearby estuaries or the ocean. There it is utilized directly by other forms of life. In an alternate route, these nutrients enter the food chain in the marsh through consumption there by small marine animals—shrimp, fish, shellfish, and crustaceans. In time many of these smaller animals are eaten by larger creatures and some eventually by man.

In seeming recognition of the organic abundance contained in tidal marshes, nature has provided for an amazing number of marine organisms to begin their lives there. All commercially harvested shrimp spend their juvenile state in marshes, eating and growing where they are safe from predators (FIGURE 4.8). In fact, approximately two-thirds of all the fish and crustaceans harvested along the East Coast live at least a part of their lives in a salt marsh or estuary. In addition, waterfowl feed on the nutrients and animals produced there.

The intrusions of man and his activities can ruin these highly productive environments. The simple dumping of spoils from dredging can kill a marsh's plants and animals and make it sterile. Discharges of sewage can poison a marsh's waters, although if they are in small quantities, the abundant microorganisms of the marsh can absorb the sewage and use it as fertilizer. Most wastes created by man, however, contain harmful chemicals. Oils, lead, industrial chemicals, and chlorinated hydrocarbons from insecticides all can kill some of the animals in the marsh. Such kills remove vital links from the food chain.

Even the discharge of purified or treated water, if it is in large quantities, can harm marsh life. Many of the juvenile sea animals, such as shrimp, that use the tidal areas as a nursery depend on brackish water. Their tolerance of fresh water, though greater than

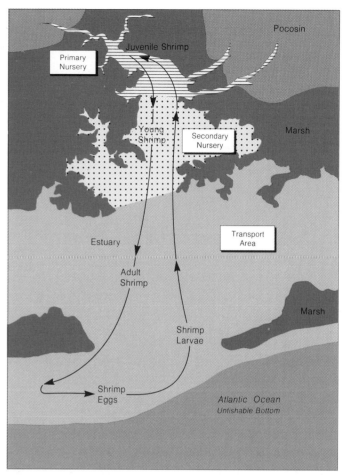

FIGURE 4.8 *Life Cycle of Commercial Shrimp in North Carolina*

that of many mature species, is limited. Too much nonsaline effluent from human settlements can kill the marsh just as surely as toxic wastes.

A somewhat different threat arises from impoundment. For example, in South Carolina there is considerable interest in impounding marshes for duck hunting or aquaculture (the harvesting of one or two species of marine animals). Nearly one-fifth of that state's tidal marshes are impounded, and many more could be so appropriated rapidly if state regulatory commissions give their approval.

The disadvantages of impoundment are two. First and most important, this process interrupts the normal flow of water, nutrients, and animal life into and out of a marsh. The contribution of nutrients that the marsh makes to the nearby estuary or ocean is reduced, and various forms of sea life find it much more difficult to use the marsh as a nursery. Thus, impoundment works against all except the species to be benefited (ducks or crabs, for instance). Second, no one knows enough to say if society is wise to exchange the natural forms of productivity for managed ones. All that is certain is that tidal marshes are a valuable resource that must be handled prudently.

The Tropical Coral Reef

In the warm, sunny, tropical waters of Florida, biological rather than geological factors are responsible for an intricate and interesting marine environment, the *coral reef*. Coral reefs are built by carbonate-secreting organisms, of which coral is the most conspicuous. Corallina red algae, foraminifera, and mollusks also contribute to building the reef. Their life cycles require shallow tropical waters, so the reefs are built underwater to a maximum depth of about 30 feet below low tide. FIGURE 4.9 illustrates one type of coral reef, the fringing reef.

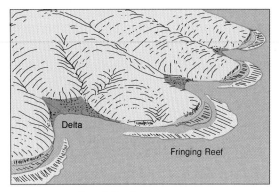

FIGURE 4.9 *Coral Reefs*

Like the estuary, the coral reef is one of the world's most productive ecosystems. Its richness results from a complex relationship between the coral and algae as well as a nutrient recharging by tidal waters. Because of this food abundance and the wide variety of habitats provided by the coral structure, thousands of different species are found here. Skin and scuba divers delight in exploring these reefs and the marine life found there.

The Open Sea

Beyond the coral reefs, estuaries, and sandy beaches lies the open sea. The neritic province, which lies above the shallow continental shelf, is by far more productive than the deep ocean. Because the shallow coastal area is the terminus for land drainage, the waters are rich in nutrients. In areas where vertical mixing or upwelling occurs, productivity is greatly enhanced. Sea life here is abundant and diverse. As illustrated by TABLE 4.1, this coastal zone (including the estuaries and coral reefs) accounts for most of the fish production of the sea.

Area	Percent of Ocean Surface Area	Annual Fish Production (millions of metric tons)
Open Ocean	90.0	1.6
Coastal Zone	9.9	120.0
Coastal Upwelling Areas	0.1	120.0
Total Annual Fish Production	100.0	241.6

TABLE 4.1 *Fish Production of the Ocean*

The northward-flowing *Gulf Stream* is another important force in shaping the South's marine environment (FIGURE 4.10). Prevailing winds are the major driving force of all surface currents. The waters begin to flow in the direction of the prevailing wind but are immediately diverted to the right (in the northern hemisphere) as the result of the *Coriolis force*, a phenomenon resulting from the earth's rotation. The combined result of the Coriolis force and wind

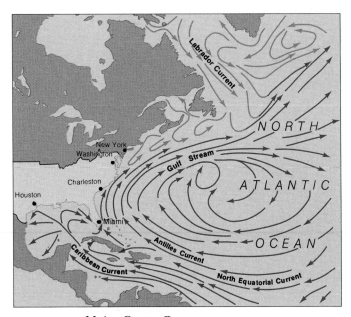

FIGURE 4.10 *Major Ocean Currents*

patterns is a system of clockwise-flowing currents in the Northern Hemisphere (counterclockwise in the Southern Hemisphere).

In the equatorial latitudes of the Atlantic Ocean, surface waters are driven by the trade winds, which generate a westward-flowing *Equatorial Current*. As this current flows westward, it is split by the landmasses of the Americas into the *South Equatorial Current* and the *North Equatorial Current*. Upon reaching the West Indies, the North Equatorial Current, in turn, splits. Part is forced northward to become the *Antilles Current,* and part turns in a more westerly direction to form the *Caribbean Current*. Meanwhile, as the *South Equatorial Current* hits the coast of Brazil, the shape of the land causes another split. Part of this current is diverted north across the equator to join the Caribbean Current. Then the Caribbean Current is driven through the Gulf of Mexico to the south of Florida, where it joins the Antilles Current to form the mighty Gulf Stream.

Here, the Gulf Stream becomes one of the greatest rivers in the sea. Its water load at this point is many times greater than all the land rivers combined. Along the coast of south Florida, the current is transporting approximately 2.3 billion tons of water per minute. It has been heated by the tropical sun for a month or more and is now warm and salty.

The Gulf Stream hugs the coastline in southern Florida and then flows northward toward Cape Hatteras, North Carolina. There it veers off to the east to form the *North Atlantic Drift* as it is driven eastward toward Europe by the prevailing *Westerlies* (winds flowing from west to east).

Along this journey, the Gulf Stream leaves its impact. The tropical waters of Florida, the mild climate of the Sea Islands, and the moderate winters of Great Britain and western Europe are among its products. The diversity and quantity of marine life have been enhanced by the warm, rich waters, and where the Gulf Stream meets the colder *Labrador Current* and an upwelling occurs, major fishing banks are produced. Up and down the coast, commercial and sport fishermen alike set out in their vessels to fish the waters of the Gulf Stream.

SUBREGIONS OF THE LOWLAND SOUTH

The geology, topography, climate, vegetation, drainage, soils, and other natural features of the Lowland South distinguish it from other parts of the South. The internal variety in these patterns also provides the basis for five subregions: the Atlantic Coastal Plain, Florida Peninsula, East Gulf Coastal Plain, Mississippi Valley and Delta, and West Gulf Coastal Plain. These are delineated in FIGURE 4.11, and the following overview explains the major characteristics of each. Chapters 5 through 9 contain more detailed discussions of the individual subregions.

Atlantic Coastal Plain

The long strip of coast that fronts on the Atlantic Ocean is the most narrow portion of the Lowland South. Ranging from the Chesapeake Bay to the middle of Georgia and northern Florida, the width of the Atlantic Coastal Plain almost everywhere is less than 200 miles from the coast and frequently less than 50 miles. It includes the first site of European settlement in the United States, and it was here that the cultivation of cotton and tobacco under a slave-based plantation system emerged in North America. The Atlantic Coastal Plain is cut by relatively short rivers that flow out of the highlands to the northwest. The coast is noted for its broad estuaries and wide beaches, which are the focus of major recreational developments. Early port cities developed around Chesapeake Bay, Hampton Roads, Wilmington, Charleston, Savannah, and a few other favored sites.

Florida Peninsula

The long Florida Peninsula is comprised of a limestone arch that is covered by a veneer of sand and gravel and dotted with lakes and swamps. It is the most tropical part of the South. Late in being developed, the peninsula is now one of the nation's fastest-growing areas. Its unique agricultural/recreational economy features citrus fruit, tourism, and retirement communities. This rapid growth is also a cause of concern for often fragile ecosystems, which many times attracted development in the first place.

East Gulf Coastal Plain

This wide belt of coastal plain extends westward from central Georgia and northern Florida to the valley and delta of the Mississippi River. It includes not only that coastal margin along the Gulf of Mexico, but also extends inland for hundreds of miles, including the southern half of Alabama and most of Mississippi and reaching far enough north to take in western portions of Tennessee and Kentucky. This is classic Deep South country, with a historic emphasis on cotton farming in the rich alluvial soils along the Mississippi or in the Black Belt of Alabama.

Mississippi Valley and Delta

This region is in many ways similar to the adjacent Gulf coastal plain areas, except for the dominating fact of the great Mississippi River. Draining a vast basin in the interior of North America, this enormous river serves as a major transportation artery that connects a huge region with the world ocean system at New Orleans. In addition, the river has created an alluvial valley of rich soils that has sustained a large part of cotton and rice cultivation in this country. Commerce along the river has given rise to other cities, including Baton Rouge, Vicksburg, and Memphis. Around the river evolved a subculture that is as distinctive as Mark Twain and New Orleans/Memphis jazz.

West Gulf Coastal Plain

The western part of the Gulf coastal plain is similar physiographically to its eastern counterpart. However, in most other ways it is quite different. It is more industrial, more dependent upon oil, bigger, drier, and more varied. It covers the western half of Louisiana, the eastern third of Texas, and a southern portion of Arkansas. The West Gulf Coastal Plain also marks the western edge of the humid South. Immediately west of it, on the Llano Estacado of Texas, the climate has an aridity that is more characteristic of the American Southwest. The megacities of Houston and Dallas–Fort Worth have evolved in this region, along with other important Texas cities such as Austin and San Antonio.

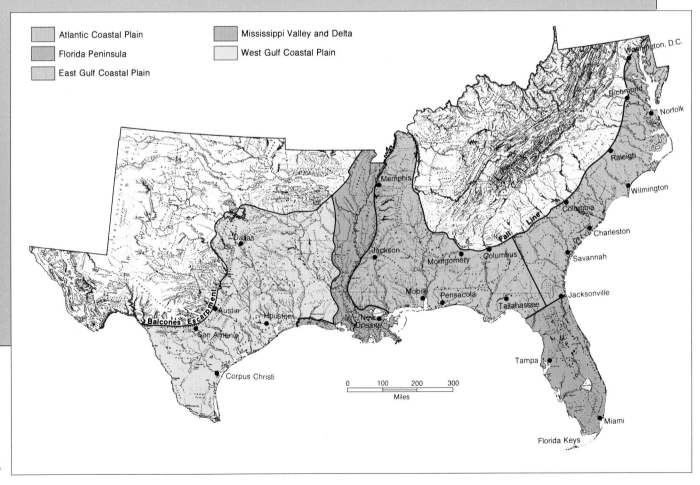

FIGURE 4.11
The Lowland South

5 THE ATLANTIC COASTAL PLAIN

The Atlantic Coastal Plain extends from the Chesapeake Bay in Maryland to southern Georgia and the northeastern tip of Florida above Jacksonville, where it is bound by the East Gulf Coastal Plain and the Florida Peninsula (FIGURE 5.1). In an east-west direction, it runs from the Atlantic coastline to the fall line. A low-lying area with little topographic relief and scant variety in climate or geology, the Atlantic Coastal Plain seems to be homogenous in many ways. Yet, upon closer examination, profound differences appear. The inner coastal plain contrasts dramatically with the poorly drained outer coastal plain, and this provides an east-west division. The north-south variation in the coastal fringe is quite pronounced. To the north, the shoreline has been deeply submerged, creating great embayments such as the Chesapeake Bay. From the Chesapeake to Cape Lookout, the submergence has been less extreme, leading to the development of a chain of barrier islands. South of Cape Lookout and into South Carolina the shoreline emerges, forming the broad sandy beaches of the Grand Strand. At the southern end, structural downwarping led to a strong drowning of the coastline, creating the Sea Islands district. People, their settlement patterns, and their economies have responded to this physical diversity in distinctive ways. Using these spatial differences, the Atlantic Coastal Plain can be organized into five subregions: the Chesapeake Bay, the Atlantic beaches, the Sea Islands district, the swamps and wetlands, and the inner coastal plain.

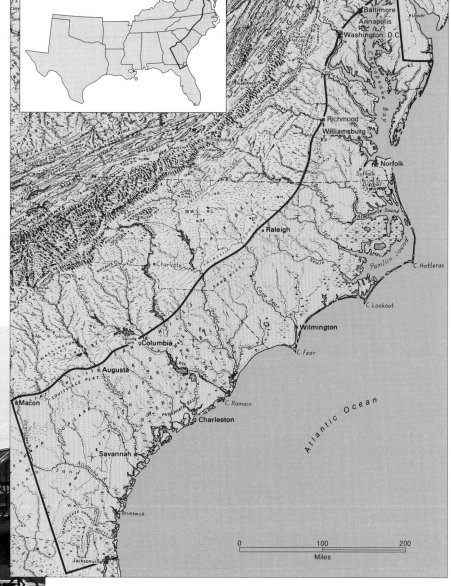

FIGURE 5.1 *The Atlantic Coastal Plain*

Mann's Harbor in
North Carolina's Albemarle Sound

THE CHESAPEAKE BAY

Ever since Captain John Smith explored and mapped the Chesapeake Bay, following the establishment of America's first permanent English settlement at Jamestown in 1607, the Chesapeake has been one of the nation's most storied, studied, and threatened bodies of water. It literally cradled a new nation on the banks of the James River and has been a distinctive barometer of the ebb and flow of human relationships with the physical environment of a newly developing land.

The Bay, as natives call it, is the continent's largest estuary. It is an immense mixing bowl into which five large rivers drain a far-flung watershed that extends north through Pennsylvania and the Finger Lakes area of New York. Into the Bay flow fresh waters from the rivers and salty waters pushed by the tides of the Atlantic, so that its salinity varies from near zero at the mouth of the Susquehanna River at the northern end to 30 parts per thousand around the Chesapeake Bay Bridge-Tunnel in the south.

As the Chesapeake extends its fingers inland, this drowned river valley becomes a meeting place where forest, field, marsh, water, and an ever-changing sky intertwine. It is little wonder that such a setting is home to some 2,700 species of creatures and a major stop on the Atlantic flyway for approximately 800,000 waterfowl.

For a long time, the Bay has served as a human habitat as well as a home for fish and fowl. John Smith's exploration map used the spelling *Chesapeack* (from an Indian word probably meaning "mother of waters"), and Smith recognized immediately the grandeur before him as he rounded Capes Charles and Henry from the Atlantic: ". . . Within is a country that may have the prerogative over the most pleasant places of Europe, Asia, Africa, or America, for large and pleasant navigable rivers, heaven and earth never agreed better to frame a place for mans habitation. . . . a faire Bay compassed but for the mouth with fruitfull and delightsome land."[1]

In later years the Bay would launch the Baltimore clipper ships, yield an immense annual fish catch, and provide a recreational haven along its shoreline. But this mixing bowl is finely balanced, and its ecosystem has been greatly threatened in recent years by the products of human habitation.

The Bay

The Chesapeake Bay had its beginnings as a well-entrenched river, scouring its way to the ocean and fed by Pleistocene glaciers to the north. Melting glaciers in the post-Pleistocene era raised ocean levels, drowned the river valley, and created the Bay as it presently exists. The old river channel is well-known to today's ship captains as they follow the 180-mile deep-water course between Baltimore and the sea.

Embayments and tributary streams of various sizes give the Chesapeake its prodigious 8,000-mile shoreline. Nineteen rivers (of which the 11 largest are shown in FIGURE 5.2) and approximately 400 smaller creeks comprise the tributary system. The western

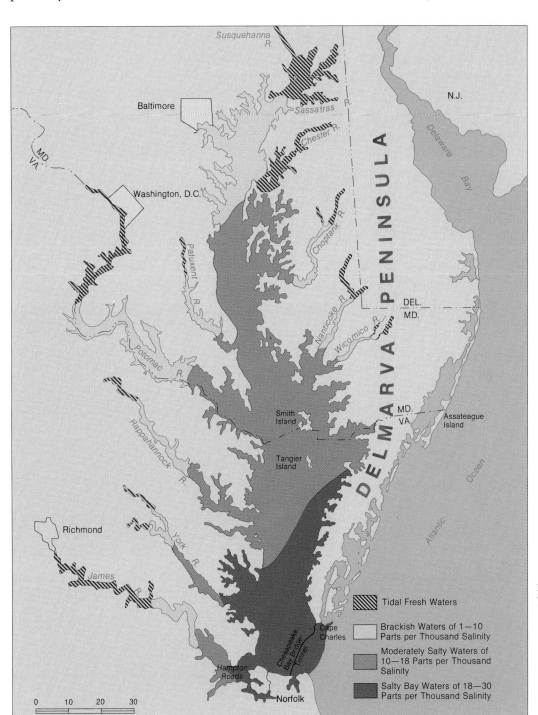

FIGURE 5.2
The Chesapeake Bay Region

shore rivers are the larger sources of the Chesapeake's fresh water, draining a watershed that extends west and north into the Appalachian Mountains. For example, five of these rivers—the Susquehanna, Potomac, James, Rappahannock, and York—comprise 90 percent of the Bay's freshwater content. The Eastern Shore rivers and streams filter through the low-lying marshland of the Delmarva Peninsula, providing an ideal haven for migratory waterfowl and a spawning ground for aquatic life.

Two major reasons for the Bay's unusually rich biological productivity are the relative shallowness of its waters and its high degree of circulation. The average depth of the Chesapeake's main stem is less than 30 feet, and for the entire system (including tidewater tributaries) it is only 20 feet. Such shallow water allows sun penetration to nourish plankton and rooted aquatic plants. Additionally, the extensive marsh areas, with the lacework of coves and shallow tidal creeks, trap nutrients and protect larvae. The Chesapeake also possesses a superlative circulation pattern, both horizontal and vertical. Its elongated north-south configuration fosters a two-layered circulation, as the lighter fresh water from the rivers flows south within the Bay's upper layers, and the heavier salt water flows north and up the Bay in its lower layers. Tides, winds, and seasons also affect the currents, and the total effect is a continuous flushing and cleansing action between estuary and ocean.

Consequently, the biological productivity of the Chesapeake mixing bowl sharply contrasts with that of an estuary such as a Norwegian fjord, with its uniformly deep and rocky character, limited circulation, and resulting biological impoverishment. That is why the Nordic fishermen have historically ventured into the stormy offshore banks of the North Sea rather than fish the protected fjords.

The Chesapeake's rich marshlands produce an estimated annual average yield of 5 tons of vegetation per acre and as high as 10 in some southern areas along the lower Eastern Shore. From the decomposition of this production comes a substantial and nourishing flow of silage filtering through the network of marsh islands. The recipient of this flow is a diverse population of aquatic life, from plankton to the larvae of fish, clams, oysters, blue crabs, jellyfish, and worms. After consuming great quantities of nutrients, the

Oystering on the Chesapeake

They call them Bay watermen, these dwindling bands of men who probe for oysters in the Chesapeake Bay in their small vessels silhouetted against the daybreak sky. Outfitted in baseball caps, blue jeans, and a range of T-shirts, jackets, or flannel shirts (depending on the weather), they are up well before dawn and work until dusk for five to six days a week. Sunday is not worked simply because the law won't permit it.

The watermen dredge oysters out of the mud 20 feet below the water surface by using hand tongs (wooden scissorlike pincers) with wire baskets at the end. "Tonging for oysters is like trying to pick up a pearl with a pair of chopsticks through a bowl of cream of tomato soup," said retired waterman Joe Valliant in the *Charlotte Observer* (12 October 1985). Mechanized oystering is banned by Maryland fishing law unless done from a sailboat called a skipjack. The purpose is to protect the diminishing oyster beds from further disruption.

It is a threatened trade, as the world-renowned Chesapeake oyster catch has dwindled from a customary 2 to 3 million bushels a year of earlier decades to a record low recently of about 375,000 bushels in Maryland. Study commissions sound ominous warnings about the future of this once-lucrative catch unless plans to clean up Bay pollution are implemented with renewed commitment.

Meanwhile, the watermen head out each morning, drawn by a free-spirited life-style that keeps them in close harmony with their special body of water, and then unload their catch dockside each evening for up to $175 on a good day. It is a livelihood that many carry on from previous generations, but it remains to be seen if their offspring will have the same inheritance.

Sunrise on Chesapeake Bay

various marshland creatures then release substantial amounts of nitrogen and phosphorus, thereby fertilizing the marshland water in a regular 24-hour pattern.

From this continuous interaction and spawning process comes a world-famous bounty of seafood. Perhaps most renowned are the Chesapeake oyster and blue crab. In dollar terms, the oysters have been the most valuable resource, while the Bay's blue crab

fishery has made the United States the leading crab-consuming nation of the world. The Chesapeake's fine mixture of fresh and salt water is also ideal for anadromous fish, those that divide their lives between spawning and growth in the estuaries and time in the saltwater sea. The striped bass, or rockfish, is most prized by sport and commercial fishermen. And the rapidly dwindling sturgeon and the periodic runs of herring have long been part of the Chesapeake fishing legend.

As an immense and complex ecological system, the Chesapeake has been a classic story of the reproductive powers of one of nature's great estuaries. Its capacity for replenishing is indeed impressive; however, it is the Bay's relationship with human habitation and production that provides the ultimate challenge to its life-support system.

Human Settlement of the Chesapeake

The Chesapeake historically has transmitted a siren call, beckoning the earliest explorers to the continent. There is evidence that Vikings came down the Atlantic seaboard as far as the Chesapeake and were awed by the Bay's abundance. Several different Indian tribes lived near its banks and fished its rich waters. Much colonial history took place in the area, as the Jamestown settlement was followed by other early sites such as Williamsburg. In the War of 1812, the British invaded through the Bay.

Two major metropolitan areas rose on the Chesapeake: Baltimore to the north and the Newport News–Norfolk–Portsmouth–Hampton complex that developed around Hampton Roads to the south. Founded in 1729, Baltimore had become the third-ranking port of the United States by 1800. Characterized as "the most Southern of the Northern ports and the most Northern of the Southern ports," Baltimore capitalized upon its strategic location and served a broad mid-Atlantic hinterland for its traffic. With good rail connections to the coal and steel areas, Baltimore's primary function became bulk handling of goods from the interior, imports of petroleum and ores, and grain exports. Meanwhile, the urban area around Hampton Roads utilized its location close to the mouth of the Chesapeake to become a major navy installation and shipbuilding center. In 1964, the 17.6-mile Chesapeake Bay Bridge-Tunnel was completed, linking the Norfolk area to the Eastern Shore capes and enhancing the area's accessibility to the urbanized northeastern corridor.

Baltimore and the Hampton Roads complex are both on the western shore, and between them is the historic community of Annapolis, the capital of Maryland. And of course the nation's capital, Washington, D.C., lies along the Potomac, adding emphasis to the highly developed and strategic nature of the Bay's western shore.

A much different world exists across the Bay—the fabled Eastern Shore, where time hangs suspended as a graceful reminder of what life once was like on the eastern seaboard. Although the Eastern Shore is changing as land values escalate, much of the area reflects a time when colonial Maryland was a region of spread-out tidewater plantations accessible only by water. The sprinkling of small islands like Tangier and Smith are gradually sinking back into history and the Bay as steadily rising waters erode more and more shoreline, much like the fate of the fictional Devon Island in James Michener's novel *Chesapeake*. Over the last 100 years, approximately 50,000 acres of shoreline have been lost to erosion.

Meanwhile, accelerated western shore development portends a steady upsurge in overall growth for the Chesapeake area. Today's regional population of approximately 12 million should exceed 16 million by the year 2020. Demand for electricity may increase tenfold, and port activity will double in bulk oil traffic. These waters and shores are also used more than ever for such recreational purposes as swimming, sport and commercial fishing, boating, hunting, camping, and, of course, vacation-home development. In essence, the Bay's multidimensional attractiveness noted by John Smith has made it popular for a whole spectrum of uses, bringing the Bay close to the edge of irreversible problems.

Hampton Roads terminal and shipyards

A Threatened Ecosystem

Today the Chesapeake is recognized as a critical American ecosystem, richly endowed but delicately balanced between nature's rhythms and the demands of an industrial society. More vulnerable than most of the world's estuaries, the Bay's western penetration brings it into the heart of the nation's megalopolis, and its ability to withstand future environmental damage will be severely tested.

For some time, there have been signs of overuse. At the turn of the century, caviar-bearing sturgeon were prevalent. Now they are essentially gone. Two fish that once spawned prolifically, the striped bass and shad, have declined, as have harvests of blue crab. Oyster catches have been diminishing since a high of over 15 million bushels a century ago in Maryland alone. Today, Maryland's oyster catch is less than one-half million bushels.

Just as alarming is the loss of wetlands, those critical refuges of waterfowl, marine life, and mammals. Since 1900, the wetlands' acreage has decreased by one-half; such a loss damages the entire ecosystem.

One need look no farther than nearby Delaware Bay for an ominous vision of what could be the Chesapeake's future. Industrial sites in Philadelphia, Trenton, and Camden have dumped into that bay an assortment of pollutants, thereby eliminating fishing and swimming. Fishing villages that once flourished along its banks are almost deserted today.

One stretch of river leading into the Chesapeake has had a brush with such extinction in recent history. In 1975, it was discovered that an insecticide called Kepone was poisoning workers at a chemical plant on the James River. It was subsequently learned that the chemical had been dumped undetected into the river for eight years, spreading through the river's whole network of marshes and tributaries. Normally a good breeding ground for oysters, the lower James had to be closed for some time to all fishing, and the long-term damage will be felt for decades.

The threats to the Chesapeake include not only chemical pollution but a range of other sources, including municipal sewage (even though treated, still a source of chemicals and organic material); various herbicides and pesticides that run off from farms; toxic metals from industry; huge amounts of sediment accumulation from soil erosion and organic solids; phosphorus and nitrogen from farm fertilizers; and growing amounts of petroleum and petrochemicals from tankers, refineries, and boats.

At the same time, federal, state, and local governments are taking significant measures to protect and revitalize the Chesapeake. A few years ago, Congress appropriated $45 million for an Environmental Protection Agency study of the Bay as a whole. Until then, the hundreds of studies undertaken were localized and fragmented. The EPA study established priorities for implementation in its Chesapeake Bay Program, giving special attention to saving submerged aquatic vegetation. These small plants inhabit the Bay's shallow margins and are a primary food source for waterfowl and some fish as well as being a critical source of food and shelter for the many small organisms upon which fish and other predators feed. They also purify the water, stabilize sediments, reduce shoreline erosion with their root systems, and trap and use dissolved phosphorus and nitrogen.

Many improvements are underway, from higher sewage-processing standards to fish-catch limitations. Bottom areas are being strewn with old oyster shells to which young spat can attach and grow. Baltimore Harbor's waters are much cleansed, aided by Bethlehem Steel's water-quality control program, so the fish and crab have returned and grasses are growing once again.

Another significant step taken to reverse the decline of the Bay's resources was the implementation of the 1987 Chesapeake Bay Agreement. The parties to this agreement are the EPA, the District of Columbia, the State of Maryland, and the Commonwealths of Virginia and Pennsylvania. By entering into this agreement, the parties involved are committed to managing the Chesapeake Bay as an integrated ecosystem and achieving the goals outlined in the agreement such as restoring and protecting the living resources of the Bay and controlling pollution. Progress will be evaluated in January 1989.

In many ways, a holding action exists as corrective measures are counterbalanced by the relentless growth of an industrial-urban society on the shores of this too-popular Bay. But the Chesapeake has proven remarkably resilient in the past, and perhaps this historic estuary can provide a lesson for the human component in better blending with the environment.

THE ATLANTIC BEACHES

In few places of the South is the relationship between human habitation and the land more delicate than along the sandy coastal strip of Atlantic beaches, which extend from Virginia Beach through North Carolina's Outer Banks to South Carolina's Grand Strand (FIGURE 5.3). The twin forces of nature and resort development are reshaping this fragile ocean fringe at an ever-accelerating pace.

The widespread attraction to this area is easy to understand. It is a strikingly scenic 500-mile stretch of sandy beaches and barrier islands laced with lagoons, bays, estuaries, and tidal marshes that provide an ideal setting for recreation. The juxtaposition of land and sea is underscored by descriptive place names: Cape Lookout, Bald Head Island, Bogue Banks, Murrells Inlet, Topsail Beach, and Southport. But the once-tranquil settings with quaint names are also becoming some of the South's most rapidly growing resort areas, overflowing with visitors and taxing a fragile environment.

There are two particularly distinctive coastal environments along these Atlantic beaches: a necklace of barrier islands ranging from Virginia Beach in the north to Little River Inlet in the south, and the Grand Strand, a 60-mile stretch of mainland beaches reaching from the North Carolina border to Georgetown. In the first environment lie the Cape Fear River estuary and the seaport city of Wilmington and surrounding beaches. The northernmost section of barrier islands includes North Carolina's Outer Banks, which extend from the Virginia border to Ocracoke Inlet.

Cape Hatteras lighthouse

The Outer Banks

The Outer Banks of North Carolina were formed in the aftermath of the last Ice Age. That period of melting is thought to have begun about 15,000 years ago, when the sea was over 400 feet below its present level and the shoreline was out beyond the continental shelf. Since then, the sea level has been rising. As the sea level rose, dune ridges on the seaward edge of the mainland became the barrier islands, and the lower areas behind these ridges were flooded, creating lagoons (FIGURE 4.8).

This chain of barrier islands is part of the longest and best-developed feature of its kind in the world. It is a special place. The barrier island is more than a beach; it is a complete system that includes beach, dunes, and marshes. Each of these environments affords the resident or visitor a different experience.

However, this environment is a sensitive and unstable one. The barrier islands are vulnerable to storm surges that could destroy an entire community and much of the island itself. Further, the islands are constantly changing as sand is taken from one place and deposited in another. No place on a barrier island is free of such erosion, although some areas are considerably safer for development than are others. Thus, all man-made structures along the shoreline should be considered temporary (FIGURE 5.4).

Settlement of these barrier islands came early but gradually, since beachheads were not easily established along this thin sliver of land. The Outer Banks were initially settled by the Algonkian Indians between A.D. 500 and 1000. When the first Europeans arrived in the sixteenth century, three distinct tribes inhabited the islands: the Poteskeet around Currituck Sound in the north, the Roanoak on Roanoke Island, and the Croatan farther south around Hatteras. Led by Sir Walter Raleigh, the English made several futile attempts to settle the Outer Banks, beginning in 1584.

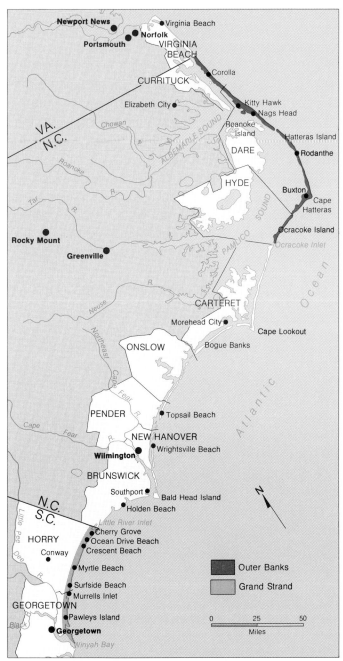

FIGURE 5.3 *Atlantic Beaches and Barrier Islands*

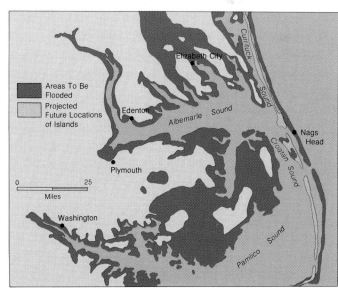

FIGURE 5.4 *Projected Upper North Carolina Coastal Zone through the Twenty-Fifth Century*

These efforts culminated in the disappearance of the Lost Colony from Roanoke, one of the most mysterious episodes in American history.

Subsequent settlement along the Outer Banks was difficult because of treacherous offshore currents and shoals, sudden ocean storms, and the lack of a good natural harbor. Dozens of shipwrecks attest to the validity of the area's epithet of "Graveyard of the Atlantic" and help explain why the North Carolina colonial area was much slower to develop than sites around the Chesapeake to the north and Charleston to the south.

The first permanent European settlers of the Outer Banks came from the Virginia colonies to the north. Enduring hurricanes and other calamities, they built their homes on the sound side of the island in wooded hammocks, which provided some protection against storms. They subsisted through stock raising, scavenging shipwrecks, fishing, and processing beached whales. Many early inhabitants clearly were there to escape the laws of society and were not model citizens.

Settlements were built in the 1700s at Hatteras, Ocracoke, and Portsmouth islands. A number of these structures stand today. In the 1830s, the first major resort community was built at Nags Head, which became a flourishing attraction by the beginning of the Civil War. Later, the area achieved historic significance when Orville and Wilbur Wright tested their new aircraft at Kill Devil Hill near Kitty Hawk in 1903.

For the most part, however, the Outer Banks remained remote and isolated. Some coastal communities developed and then disappeared entirely. Diamond City at Cape Lookout was abandoned in 1899 by its 500 inhabitants, who were discouraged over relentless hurricane damage. The townspeople of Rice Path on Bogue Banks moved away because of invading sand dunes, and Portsmouth on Portsmouth Island experienced economic demise when nearby Ocracoke Inlet was abandoned as a port of entry.

Other Outer Banks communities survived but seemed to be rooted in an earlier age. Well into the twentieth century, traces of Middle English speech could be heard among inhabitants, and to this day the citizens of Rodanthe celebrate Old Christmas on Epiphany.

When bridges from the mainland first spanned the sounds in the 1930s, commercialization began to encroach. And in the aftermath of World War II, resort expansion along the Atlantic Ocean side of the Outer Banks began in earnest, with developers seizing upon prized ocean views and beach exposure. Growth today would no doubt be much more extensive were it not for the designation of much of the Outer Banks as the Cape Hatteras and Cape Lookout National Seashores. At the same time, development that exists along the Outer Banks is highly exposed to hurricanes, as these savage storms spawned in the warm waters of the Caribbean head north each fall.

Hurricanes have pounded the Outer Banks from the islands' beginning. In June 1586, Sir Francis Drake arrived off Roanoke Inlet with a shipload of supplies for the Roanoke Island colony. Unfortunately, a hurricane arrived at the same time, blowing the supply ship out to sea and forcing residents to abandon the settlement. From that date to this, these islands have averaged a major hurricane every two to three years. Their paths are unpredictable. FIGURE 5.5 illustrates the paths of nine hurricanes of the 1950s, an especially intense period of storm activity along the Atlantic Coast.

Particularly damaging was Hurricane Hazel in 1954, which completely wiped out Holden Beach and other developing resort communities on the southern coast of North Carolina. It was that area's most devastating storm of the century. An Army Corps of Engineers report indicated that "hardly a vestige of human habitation [remained] on the Brunswick County shore following Hurricane Hazel," and noted the "absolute totality of the damage" as well as the increased potential in the future for hurricane damage when the area was rebuilt.[2]

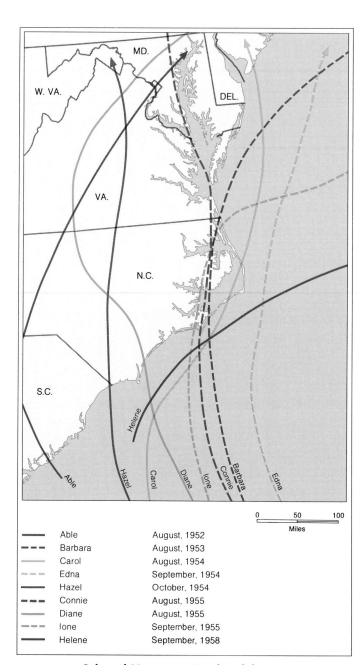

——	Able	August, 1952
– – –	Barbara	August, 1953
——	Carol	August, 1954
– – –	Edna	September, 1954
——	Hazel	October, 1954
– – –	Connie	August, 1955
——	Diane	August, 1955
– – –	Ione	September, 1955
——	Helene	September, 1958

FIGURE 5.5 *Selected Hurricane Tracks of the 1950s*

Satellite photograph of the eye of Hurricane Gloria

Hurricane Gloria—A Near Miss

With winds clocked at up to 200 miles per hour, Hurricane Gloria was billed as a Category 5 hurricane, the most dangerous. Forecasters tracked Gloria from its inception in mid-September 1985 off the coast of Africa through its tortuous 12-day path and demise in eastern Canada. "The storm is headed due north toward Cape Hatteras and the Outer Banks," said meteorologist Chris Veiden of the National Hurricane Center at Coral Gables, Florida. "But 20 or 30 miles either way could make all the difference. . . ."[3] "It's a very big, very dangerous storm," said James Munn of the Office of Emergency Management in Washington, D.C., when Gloria was reported 50 miles south of Cape Hatteras, traveling at 32 m.p.h.[4]

The governor of North Carolina ordered the evacuation of 27 coastal counties and declared a state of emergency covering approximately 100,000 people. States from Virginia through New England, encompassing 40 million people in the storm's potential path, began taking precautions ranging from a call-out of the National Guard to the closing of the World Trade Center's twin towers in New York City. Meanwhile, Hatteras Village on Hatteras Island was beginning to flood, and waves 8 to 12 feet high were breaking against the sandbags at the 114-year-old Cape Hatteras lighthouse. A tornado briefly touched down nearby. Farther along the Outer Banks, the wild ponies of Ocracoke Island were moved to higher ground by National Park Service rangers. Some individuals refused to leave, such as Nags Head Beach Postmistress Doll Gray, who said she had no plans to evacuate and would be at her small post office the next day "if the mail truck comes through from Rocky Mount."[5]

Particularly feared was a landfall from the monster storm that would coincide with high tide and maximize the dreaded destructive storm surge. However, almost imperceptively at first, Gloria shifted to the northeast in the early evening. It then curved slowly up the coast, rather than making a 90-degree run for shore. Landfall mercifully came at midnight during low tide, and the earlier slight shift in direction had a further moderating "easting" effect so that only the western edge of Gloria nicked the Hatteras shore.

After two dark days of tension, morning dawned with gentle breezes and sunshine. All along the thin sliver of barrier islands, a sense of relief prevailed. "We're just really grateful to be here today," said Norris Austin, postmaster at isolated Corolla. "There was a howl in the wind like I'd never heard before. It was a terrible, terrible sound . . . and I felt we were going to be swept away any minute. We thought this was going to be the one because we were overdue."[6]

Two port areas along this Atlantic coastline have experienced spasmodic development since their early settlement. Morehead City began in the 1850s as a resort alternative to Nags Head. Located in a more accessible and protected setting, it later experienced moderate success as a port. To the south on a narrow peninsula between the Cape Fear River and the Atlantic Ocean, a settlement variously called New Carthage, New Liverpool, and Newton began in 1730. Renamed Wilmington and incorporated in 1739, it was North Carolina's largest city and major port through the late nineteenth century. The city's status slipped substantially during the first half of the twentieth century as the state's growth concentrated farther west in the Piedmont. However, the upsurge in recent years in international trade by North Carolina and the rest of the South has revitalized Wilmington and also Morehead City to a lesser extent.

The Grand Strand

The 60-mile stretch of South Carolina coastline from the North Carolina state line at Little River to Georgetown and Winyah Bay has emerged as the recreational center of the southeastern coastal plain. Approximately nine million tourists visit this Grand Strand of beaches annually, and Myrtle Beach is the hub. The booming area of North Myrtle Beach includes a number of older beach communities: Cherry Grove, Ocean Drive, and Crescent Beach. South of Myrtle Beach there is a mixture of beaches, inlets, marshes, and towns between Surfside Beach and Winyah Bay. Among them are Murrells Inlet, a well-known fishing port and gateway to the Gulf Stream; Pawleys Island, one of the coast's oldest resort communities; and Georgetown, a historic city featuring old plantation estates.

Little in the area's past portended its present-day resort explosion. After scattered Indian settlement, Spaniards from Hispaniola landed about 50 miles north of Myrtle Beach in 1526 and established the first European settlement in the United States about 30 miles south of Myrtle Beach. Named San Miguel de Gualdape, it was abandoned the next year and the group returned to Hispaniola. The area was later settled by English landowners and eventually included several large plantations, with rice a principal crop.

However, Charleston, with its good natural harbor,

Grand Strand beachfront development

became the focus of South Carolina coastal growth. Backed by a low and swampy inland, the Grand Strand area remained remote, an ideal physical setting awaiting discovery for its recreation potential. The wide beaches of white sand stretched for miles, uninterrupted by rivers or streams. Sheltering the shore were many more trees and wooded stretches than are normally found in beach areas. And the coastline's northeast-southwest orientation provided a more southerly exposure, moderated further by the warm Gulf Stream current.

Interest in the Strand was sparked at the turn of the twentieth century when a little train named Black Maria brought passengers from Conway, 15 miles inland, to the coast. When major highway and airport links were established after World War II, the growth momentum began in earnest. Since 1950, Myrtle Beach has grown from 3,400 permanent residents to approximately 25,000 in 1985, and per capita income for the area is the highest in the state. Meanwhile, the larger Grand Strand area increased its permanent

population by over 25 percent, to 56,500 people, during the first half of the 1980s. At the height of the tourist season, over 350,000 people from the eastern United States and Canada occupy the Grand Strand.

Today the area is brimming with leisure facilities: over 40 golf courses, 150 tennis courts, 10 ocean fishing piers, 700 restaurants, and a countless array of attractions and nightclubs. There appears to be no end in sight to the Grand Strand's burgeoning popularity as one of the South's major recreational and resort areas. In fact, it is estimated that by the turn of the century, the South Carolina coastal counties as a whole will have up to 55 percent of the entire state's population.

While the Grand Strand does not have the precarious physical character of the Outer Banks, its growing population and facilities along the oceanfront do pose great potential for loss of life and prosperity in the event of a direct hit by a major hurricane. Its northeast-southwest tilt further invites a collision with a future storm.

THE SEA ISLANDS DISTRICT

South of the Grand Strand lies a fabled and enticing stretch of the Atlantic Coastal Plain. From below the Charleston area to the Saint Marys River in Florida, one encounters the Sea Islands district, rich in history and physical attractions (FIGURE 5.6).

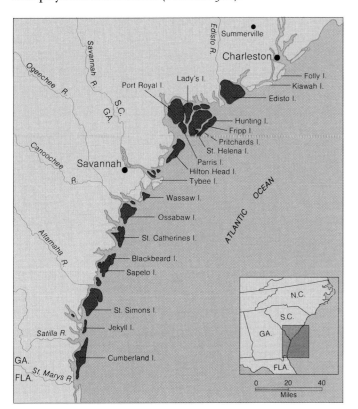

FIGURE 5.6 *Sea Islands District*

The massive forces of nature that bent the earth's crust brought land and water together here into one interconnected system. The crustal plate begins to bend downward at Charleston in an arc that does not end until it reaches Florida. This downwarping of the surface of the earth submerged parts of the coastal plain and left a fringe of islands at the new shoreline's edge. Numerous small rivers that flow eastward further mingle sea and shore by dividing the coastline and linking land, sea, and islands with watery passageways. Physically, the coast is a succession of landforms mixed in with waterways, and Southern cultures have always responded to this combination.

Nature has also made the Sea Islands a region of warmth and sun. The tepid waters of the Gulf Stream (68°F and warmer) moderate the already mild winters in South Carolina's Low Country and the Golden

Isles of Georgia. Once this favorable climate and an abundance of moisture encouraged staple crops that produced wealth and stimulated the development of major port cities such as Charleston and Savannah. Today, the same weather conditions have made the Sea Islands increasingly desirable as a resort area.

Early History

The sea helped create the Sea Islands. Its level has fluctuated over thousands of years as the polar ice caps have melted or thickened. For the last 15,000 years the sea has been rising, and these mounting waters naturally increased the effect of the downwarp of the earth's crust. As the sea invaded low spots, it surrounded rather large pieces of land that were integral parts of the coastal plain. The Sea Islands thus are remnants of the coastal plain. They are larger than the sandy, migrating barrier islands, and their central portions tend to be flat, rather high, and forested. Sizeable trees, not just bushes and scrub forests, have had time and opportunity to grow there.

The bulk and permanence of the Sea Islands have long made them useful and inviting, and people have lived and worked on them from early times. The first Europeans to explore the Sea Islands were the Spanish. Sailing from their country's colonies in the Caribbean, Spanish captains visited the Sea Islands in 1521 and 1525 and named Saint Helena Island (Punta de Santa Elena). In later years they sometimes maintained garrisons on the islands. But for a variety of reasons—problems elsewhere, resistance from the Indians, and the fact that the best route to Spain turned east from Florida—a permanent Spanish presence did not move above Florida.

Before long, Frenchmen followed the Spanish to the Sea Islands. In 1562, Jean Ribaut visited the mouth of South Carolina's Broad River with his expedition. He named Port Royal and was mightily impressed by the coastal region nearby. "We founde," he wrote, ". . . one of the goodlyest, best and frutfullest cunteres that ever was sene. . . ."[7] Misfortune and the French-Spanish rivalry, however, contributed to these islands falling eventually into the hands of English settlers.

After planters from crowded Barbados began to move to South Carolina in the latter part of the seventeenth century, the Sea Islands district kept its characteristic tie between land and water. The coast and the

islands became part of the same economy, linked by the waterways and the sheltered stretch of ocean flowing between them. Sea Islands planters loaded their crops on small boats and ferried them to nearby ports, whose businesses benefited from the resources just off the coast.

Crops

One of the first crops harvested from this region was fish. In the colonial period, fish usually were dried, salted, and sold to Caribbean sugar plantations. "Fishing Negroes," wrote one traveler, displayed a dexterity with a net that was "impossible to imagine."[8] Another water crop was rice, the mainstay of much plantation agriculture in South Carolina and Georgia. Rice cultivation requires periodic flooding of the fields, but here ocean tides naturally caused the level of drowned rivers to rise and fall. So with the construction of dikes and gates to use the fluctuating water level, conditions for rice culture were complete.

Rice plantations sprang up along coastal rivers on some of the Sea Islands throughout South Carolina and Georgia. Dominant for much of the eighteenth century, rice remained important until the latter part of the nineteenth century. Destruction brought about by the Civil War and competition from rice-growing areas of the Gulf reduced the old rice kingdom's production to only one-third of the nation's crop by 1890. Then, at the turn of the century, a succession of hurricanes destroyed dikes and floodgates and brought an end to the long era of rice cultivation.

Other crops were more important to the Sea Islands than rice. Indigo was the first major export of the islands. Well adapted to their soil, this plant supplied a blue dye that was popular in Europe. The British government awarded colonists a bounty to encourage its growth and manufacture, and planters on the Sea Islands responded to the opportunity. Despite the fact that indigo was a demanding crop to cultivate and prepare, one and a half million pounds of it per year were leaving Charleston on the eve of the Revolution.

War with England ended the British bounty, of course, but by that time another crop had emerged as a source of wealth for the islands: long-staple cotton. This was a special crop that flourished only under special conditions. Its seeds came from the Bahamas, and the unusual climate that enabled them to grow

Middleton Place near Charleston, South Carolina, reveals both the importance of coastal rivers and tides to a rice plantation and the beauty that is created there through inspired landscaping.

the 1850s, exports of Sea Island cotton averaged 8 or 9 million pounds per year. Then experimenters found that it could be grown in Florida's interior, and production increased to 15 million pounds in 1860.

The Civil War caused production of Sea Island cotton to plummet. After it had begun to rise again, a major hurricane submerged the Sea Islands in 1893, killing many people and damaging property; other major storms struck the islands in 1911 and later. But these disasters did not end the era of Sea Island cotton—the boll weevil did. From 1917 through 1919, the Mexican cotton boll weevil spread through the Sea Islands and destroyed crops (see "Spread of the Boll Weevil" on page 105).

Before it declined, however, Sea Island cotton helped establish two influential ports and two special dialects. The ports were Charleston and Savannah, sites of good harbors. Charleston early became a social haven for planters escaping from the miasmas and ague of Low Country plantations during the summer and fall. As a social center it had a festive, urban, and urbane quality that most other colonial cities in the South lacked. Over the years infusions of French planters from Haiti and other groups have kept it special, and its narrow streets, cool gardens, and side porches give it unique charm today.

Savannah, in a similar way, still gives eloquent testimony to its early history. Founded in 1733 by James Oglethorpe, the city was laid out according to a master plan. Blocks of five symmetrical lots faced onto public parks, and the wisdom of the planners is apparent today. The small squares and parks that dot this first planned city give it a remarkable feel, an elegantly human space full of welcome.

The two special related dialects were Gullah and Geechee, spoken only by blacks in the area of the Georgia and South Carolina Sea Islands. Gullah was a Sea Islands dialect; Geechee arose among blacks living near the Ogeechee River in Georgia. Both were the product of human ingenuity and an isolated history.

derived from the Gulf Stream. The Gulf Stream's warm water moderates the already mild, subtropical climate and takes the sting out of winter. Greater warmth means a longer growing season—one of the longest in the United States—and the presence of adequate moisture combined with the climate to give the Sea Islands an environment ideally suited for long-staple cotton.

Long-staple cotton had another advantage: it was a luxury product. Its soft, silky fibers measured up to two inches in length, far longer than ordinary upland cotton. This extra length, softness, and fineness made a beautiful fabric smooth to the touch. Long-staple

cotton was much in demand for making delicate European laces or scarves and the highest grades of soft, lustrous cloth. And few places could grow it.

After Georgia planters grew some Bahamian seeds in 1786, long-staple cotton spread so quickly through the district that before long it was called Sea Island cotton. In the 1820s, South Carolina's Kinsey Burden "achieved the silkiest fiber the Low Country had yet produced," and earned up to $1.25 per pound (five times the usual price) for the 18,000 pounds he produced.[9] Burden's success inspired many efforts to duplicate his accomplishments, and the state legislature vainly offered him $200,000 to reveal his secret. Until

John Blake White's painting Perspective of Broad Street *(1837) captures the bustle and concentration of human activity that the urban world of Charleston offered in the rural South.*

The slave trade had thrown black people of many West African cultures together, exposed them to Europeans, and then isolated them on a few islands. As they tried to find words with shared meanings, the isolation of the islands from the mainland caused their language to take and keep its own direction. These two dialects grew up distinct from each other and from English. Even today the unusual sounds of a true Afro-American language can sometimes be heard in the Low Country.

Gullah: The Life Cycle of a Language

The history of Gullah reminds us that languages, like people, often have a life cycle that embraces creation and decay. Gullah was a pidgin language, a new tongue created by melding basic elements of other, established languages. Such pidgin languages are always simple at first. As time passes, however, they can develop and become more complex. As early as 1734, South Carolinians were noting the existence of what they called a separate (or Black-) English. Because large numbers of pidgin-English speakers remained together on the Sea Islands, a more elaborate language began to grow through reexpansion of both structure and vocabulary.

Events in the nineteenth century tended to maintain the Gullah dialect and even encourage its elaboration. Congress closed the international slave trade in 1808, thus ensuring that there would be no dilution of the developing Afro-American dialect by new African speakers. Separate islands and even plantations began to develop their own usages.

Before 1900, however, the growth of the Gullah dialect stopped and the language began to erode. The outer world was pressing in through better transportation, communication, and cultural connections. As isolation diminished, meanings were lost, constructions disappeared, and many stopped using the language. Its life cycle became complete.

On the streets of Charleston, women sell baskets woven in a variety of traditional patterns. Some reflect the influence of African design and decoration and mark the importance of African culture in the evolution of the Low Country.

TABLE 5.1 *American Place Names and Words with African Origins*

Place Names	African Root or Origin	African Meaning
Pee Dee	mpidi (Kongo, Angola)	a species of viper
Tybee	tai bi (Hausa, North Nigeria)	fertile, low-lying farmland
Wahoo	wahu (Yoruba, South Nigeria)	"to trill the voice"
Wassaw	wasaw (Twi, Gold Coast)	name of a district, tribe, and dialect

Other Words	American Meaning	African Root
poor Joe	great blue heron	podzo - name of an African heron
cooter	type of tortoise	kuta - a similar African turtle
tackies	small wild horses found in Sea Islands	taki - African word for horse
tabby	construction material made of oyster shells, sand, and cement	tabax - African name for a house so constructed
tote	"to carry"	tota - African for "to pick up"
joggle board	seesaw	dzogal - African for "to rise"

A New Crop: Vacationers

Even before the plantation era came to a close, the spectacular sunsets and the sunlight glow of the Golden Isles had begun to attract vacationers. In fact, in the nineteenth century, the captains of a new industrial world invaded a few of the islands in numbers surpassing even today's investors.

Jekyll Island in Georgia was purchased in 1866 by a group of Northern investors who began to develop it as a club. By the turn of the century, their project probably had become the wealthiest club in the history of the world. Morgans, Vanderbilts, Rockefellers, and other leaders of the most powerful industrial, banking, and transportation concerns in the country checked into the club's inn or built summer homes on Jekyll Island. By some estimates, the members of Jekyll Island Club controlled one-sixth of the world's wealth in 1900. The members' summer cottages (actually substantial but not palatial homes) filled the central compound, where they still stand today. Although the club closed in 1942, never to reopen, the state of Georgia purchased the island in 1947 for use as a vacation retreat open to the general public.

A different fate awaited a millionaire's compound on Cumberland Island. In 1881, Thomas Carnegie, brother of the famous steel magnate Andrew Carnegie, purchased property once owned by General Nathanael Greene. He built an elegant home on the island with additional residences, a squash court, and an indoor swimming pool. Decades later, after Carnegie's wife died, the property was abandoned and began to deteriorate. Poachers set fire to some buildings, which now are either gutted ruins or sagging wrecks whose original opulence is still apparent. Since the early 1970s most of Cumberland Island, including the Carnegie ruins, has been a national seashore operated by the federal government.

Government investment in the Sea Islands pales by comparison to recent private construction, inaugurated in the 1950s by the development of Hilton Head Island. Companies, individuals, and even foreign interests have built a booming vacation and resort economy—replete with golf courses, tennis clubs, hotels, shops, and other amusements—upon the natural attractions of the Sea Islands region. Economically this new role is no less important than that of the nineteenth century's plantations.

Earthquakes

Ironically this serene and beautiful district lies in an earthquake zone, one that has been as active as most of California, except for the immediate area of the San Andreas Fault. Many of the states surrounding South Carolina are also in an earthquake zone, although at significantly lower risk (FIGURE 5.7).

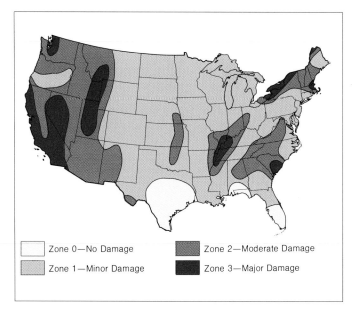

Zone 0—No Damage
Zone 1—Minor Damage
Zone 2—Moderate Damage
Zone 3—Major Damage

FIGURE 5.7 *Known Distribution of Earthquake Damage in U.S.*

In 1886, a serious quake struck Charleston. One resident, Dr. G. E. Manigault, left the following description of the evening of August 31: "As the hour of 9:50 was reached there was suddenly heard a rushing, roaring sound compared by some to a train of cars at no great distance; by others to a clatter produced by two or three omnibuses moving at a rapid rate over a paved street; by others again to an escape of steam from a boiler. It was followed immediately by a thumping and beating of the earth underneath the houses, which rocked and swayed to and fro."[10]

Frightened citizens ran into the streets and saw clouds of dust, broken chimneys, and hundreds of buildings in ruins. Sixty people died, and many more were injured. Those lucky enough to escape injury did not avoid mental scars. Dr. Manigault knew "many strong men who were completely unnerved by the events of the night, and who for weeks afterwards could not be induced to return to their houses between sunset and sunrise."[11]

The terrifying 1886 earthquake was not the only episode of seismic activity near Charleston. Historical records reveal that more than 300 earthquakes have occurred in the Charleston-Summerville region since early colonial settlement. These repeated events reinforce the experts' judgment that the region surrounding Charleston is an active earthquake zone. The epicenter or exact center of the zone is believed to be almost directly beneath the famous grounds of Middleton Place.

Although scientists have learned a great deal about South Carolina's earthquakes, their cause is still unknown. Charleston and its region are in the middle of a crustal plate, not at its edge, so explanations based on the collision of global plates do not apply. Current research is testing three theories: 1) the slow springing back of rock compressed by ancient glaciers; 2) stresses associated with the warping of the Atlantic Coastal Plain (Charleston lies at the inflection point between the portions that are rising and those that are falling); and 3) faulting and slippage in the crystalline basement rocks beneath surface sediments.

Given enough time, seismologists will surely accumulate enough data to explain the area's earthquakes. Unfortunately, given enough time, the forces at work may produce another serious earthquake. In light of man's development of the area since 1886, another major tremor could produce even more damage than its famous predecessor.

The earthquake bolts plainly visible on many Charleston buildings serve as reminders that this sunny coastal region is in the middle of an earthquake zone.

The stillness, shadows, and reflections of a coastal plain swamp make it a special environment like no other. Wildlife such as birds and alligators also abound in swamps like this one.

SWAMPS AND WETLANDS

The Lowland's swamps and wetlands are some of the wildest and most fascinating uninhabited land in the South. The poet Henry Wadsworth Longfellow recognized this fact in the nineteenth century when he wrote of trackless areas:

> Where waving mosses shroud the pine,
> And the cedar grows, and the poisonous vine
>   Is spotted like the snake.
>
> Where hardly a human foot could pass,
>   Or a human heart would dare,
> On the quaking turf of the green morass.[12]

Longfellow penned these words to describe the Great Dismal Swamp, which is on the border between North Carolina and Virginia. Ironically, he never visited the site in person. But his evocative words apply equally well to many other parts of the Atlantic Coastal Plain, for swamps, marshes, and wetlands dot this subregion (FIGURE 5.8).

Drainage is poor throughout the eastern part of the coastal plain. The gentle slope of sediments deposited by ancient oceans gives water little gradient on which to run. Moreover, marine terraces augment the effects of the minimal slope of the land (FIGURE 5.9). These ancient pools that marked the edge of a previous shoreline are nearly level, and some have even accumulated a lip of soil on their eastern edge that reduces slope and drainage still further.

The downwarping of large sections of the Atlantic Coastal Plain has increased the tendency of low-lying areas to be moist and swampy. This downwarping also lowered the beds of sluggish coastal rivers, drowning them at their mouths where they enter the ocean. The heightened barrier of ocean water increases resistance to the rivers' outward flow. The inward pressure of the ocean explains the fact that tides raise and lower river levels for miles upstream.

Poorly drained areas extend for many miles inland. As one would expect, the sections of the Atlantic Coastal Plain that are closest to the sea are the wettest; farther inland the drainage improves somewhat. There are dozens of swamps all along the edge of the Atlantic Coastal Plain.

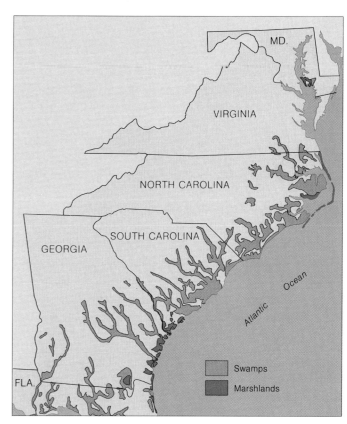

FIGURE 5.8 *Swamps and Marshlands*

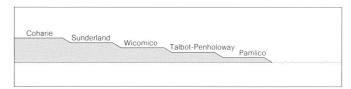

FIGURE 5.9 *Schematic Illustration of North Carolina Marine Terraces*

The Okefenokee Swamp in Georgia and the Great Dismal Swamp in North Carolina and Virginia are only the better known ones among many; others have evocative names such as Congaree Swamp, Green Swamp, Angola Swamp, and Whiteoak Swamp.

Nor are swamps the only type of wet, boggy area. The plain has an even greater number of pocosins. These watery sections found mainly in North Carolina take their name from an Indian word. The Algonkians accurately described the pocosin as a "swamp-on-a-hill." Pocosins are relatively high spots in low-lying districts, but nevertheless they are loaded with water. In addition to hundreds of pocosins, the Atlantic Coastal Plain contains numerous Carolina Bays—beautiful, elliptical lakes whose origins are shrouded in mystery.

Attitudes Toward the Swamps and Wetlands

From colonial times, swamps and wetlands have struck observers as worthless areas that must be changed to have any value. Although Indians hunted and farmed a few patches in the swamps, they changed them little. By contrast, European settlers typically desired to transform the wetlands greatly. Bit by bit over the centuries, they achieved part of their goal, and in the last twenty years the pace of modification and destruction has accelerated enormously. At the same time, the old attitude of "change the swamps to make them useful" has begun to give way to a more balanced conception. Recognition is growing that wetlands make valuable contributions to society, even in their natural, boggy state.

The desire to change the wetlands goes back at least as far as 1728, when Colonel William Byrd II of Virginia visited the Dismal Swamp. He gave the swamp its name, and also called it a "horrible desert" because its lands seemed useless to him. Byrd urged the digging of a canal through the swamp and advocated drainage. Later, several American patriots joined together to form a lumber company dedicated to draining the swamp.

When the swamps and wetlands were not being cut for timber or used as refuges by fugitives and outcasts, other people were dreaming of making them into prime farmland. The roster of those who sought to drain the wetlands in order to farm them includes the South's pioneering soil scientist, Edmund Ruffin. He took up this cause in 1837, and interest in it has continued into the present. In fact, in recent decades agribusinesses brought corporate resources to the conversion and use of swampland. Their goals included not only farming but also the extraction and processing of peat for use as a fuel.

Simultaneously, however, scientists were demonstrating that these supposedly useless areas actually play a crucial role in the ecology of the Atlantic Coastal Plain. They are vital to its water quality. The water-holding capacity of the wetlands has a crucial influence on runoff, the filtering of wastes, and the life cycles of animals in streams and estuaries. Water from swamps and pocosins moves into estuaries or marshes where shrimp, crustaceans, and other marine animals breed. The wetlands can hold heavy rains and permit a slow discharge of large amounts of fresh water that otherwise might ruin the salinity on which much sea life depends.

The wetlands must be considered endangered, since large portions of them have been destroyed in recent years. But no longer are choices being made solely on the assumption that wetlands are simply "horrible deserts." Wise decision making in the future will weigh the value to society of wetlands in their natural state against any potential benefits and costs that arise from their development. In the history of human attitudes, this marks a major change.

Pocosins

Pocosins cover large parts of the Atlantic Coastal Plain, mainly in North Carolina (FIGURE 5.10). Similar to swamps in many ways, pocosins contain peat, are acidic, hold enormous quantities of water, and are subject to periodic burning. Yet they are unlike swamps in other respects. A better way to conceive of them is as bogs; they are waterlogged areas covered by shrubs and brush much more than by forest. Pocosins need not be located on major streams.

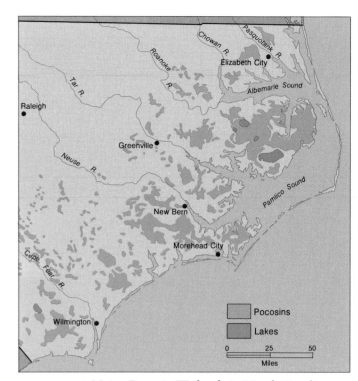

FIGURE 5.10 *Major Pocosin Wetlands in North Carolina*

In several of North Carolina's coastal counties, pocosins make up the largest single type of land area, comprising more than 50 percent of all land in some counties. But the more than two million acres of natural pocosins are rapidly disappearing. As late as 1962, no more than 10 percent of the land in pocosins had been converted to other forms and uses. By 1979, almost 750,000 acres of pocosins had been drained and ditched, their natural vegetation removed, and their soils prepared for agriculture, forestry, mining, or industry. Another 800,000 acres were in transition or partly developed. Thus, in only 17 years all but 31 percent of pocosins had been changed.

A variety of circumstances, including international events such as the OPEC (Organization of Petroleum Exporting Countries) embargo, has caused this rapid conversion of pocosin lands. Before the modern era with its technology and corporate resources, it was almost impossible to drain pocosins. Their soils conduct water hardly at all; very little will seep into a drainage ditch and flow away. Extensive ditching may lower the water table only five or six inches. Drainage is often accomplished more effectively by grading the surface to create a slight slope and thus take advantage of runoff. Because ditching and draining are

Long lines of fishing boats near Mount Pleasant, South Carolina, testify to the importance of marine life to the coastal economy of the South. Destruction of supposedly useless swamps and wetlands can have a catastrophic effect upon the reproduction of shrimp, crustaceans, shellfish, and commercially valuable fish.

expensive, little development took place before 1962. But with sufficient capital the land can be graded, ditches dug, and water levels reduced enough to allow cultivation, forestry, and other activities.

The attraction of the pocosins for large corporations is understandable. For example, the Weyerhaeuser Company has discovered that high-quality timber can be grown profitably on converted land. After engineers identify the natural outlet or drain, a rectangular grid of ditches has to be dug to feed it. Another grid of roads must be laid out one-half mile apart. Then the ground is cleared and beds are prepared for seedlings of loblolly pine. Periodic fertilization, thinning, and pruning are required, but these methods boost yields two to three times over levels of the 1950s and bring rates of return from 7 to 12 percent. Weyerhaeuser will use this high-yield forest plan to harvest much of its saw timber in the year 2000 and after.

First Colony Farms, Inc., has been prominent in the development of pocosin lands for agriculture, which requires the same extensive ditching and sloping to prepare the land, plus fertilizers and large quantities of lime to counteract the acidity of the peaty soil. But, as one study concludes, "Once developed, these wet soil types have become some of the most productive soils in North Carolina."[13] Cultivation of corn, soybeans, vegetables, and truck-farm crops can be quite profitable.

First Colony also pioneered in the extraction of peat as a source of energy for utilities and industry. The peat in 650,000 acres of pocosins in North Carolina represents an energy reserve equivalent to 20 to 30 years of use. Moreover, the peat has high heating value, low ash, and very little sulfur. Using technologies adapted from countries that burn significant amounts of peat (such as the Soviet Union, Sweden, and Finland), First Colony carried out experimental production programs in 1978 and 1979. If energy

prices soar again as they did in the 1970s, large-scale production could become economically feasible.

With the rapid development of pocosins have come environmental dangers, such as water pollution from agricultural uses. Ditching and draining have little effect on the total amount of water that flows through pocosins during a year, but they exaggerate the peaks and lows. This means that fertilizers, if combined with irrigation or heavy rains, can introduce great amounts of phosphorus into the waterways. Contamination of the Chowan River already may have occurred, but careful agricultural methods can control the problem. A simple step such as pouring seashell fragments into irrigation ditches sets up chemical reactions that bind phosphorus and remove its threat to water quality.

A far more serious problem concerns the amount of water released by developed pocosins. Runoff from coastal areas eventually reaches the brackish estuaries and marshes where commercially valuable seafoods such as shrimp develop. Even pure water from drained pocosins can kill large numbers of juvenile sea animals simply by changing the salinity of their nursery area. In one study, a natural creek maintained normal levels of salinity despite heavy rains, whereas a creek fed by developed pocosin lands showed variations of more than 100 percent within periods as short as a few hours. Such large variations kill sea life and can threaten a fishing industry that generates over $100 million in income each year. The decision of Prudential Insurance Company in 1984 to create a federal Alligator River refuge from 120,000 acres of wetland wilderness in North Carolina marks an encouraging pause in the destruction of pocosins. First Colony also has postponed its plans for energy production, thus giving society a chance to evaluate the contribution that undeveloped pocosins make to ecology and the economy.

The Great Dismal Swamp

Near the Currituck and Albemarle sounds lies the vast, irregularly shaped Great Dismal Swamp (FIGURE 5.11). The swamp's boundaries are not definite; it is roughly 10 or 11 miles wide, not counting small arms that stretch out from the central mass, and it extends 15 to 20 miles on either side of the North Carolina–Virginia border. Despite the fact that man's incursions have gradually reduced its size and changed its boundaries, the swamp remains an impressive wilderness.

Red maple, black gum, ash, sweet gum, pine, cypress, and many other trees grow there. Creepers and vines cover almost everything in some of the drier sections, and ferns and Spanish moss grow in profusion. Deer, bears, bobcats, raccoons, and various rodents make their home in the swamp.

The whole area slopes very gently from west to east, and a layer of peat generally three to five feet deep covers much of the ground. Beneath the peat lies a thick, almost impervious layer of clay. This clay acts as a seal, preventing the downward movement of water. In fact, groundwater in the area is under enough pressure to ensure that migration of water will probably be upward into the swamp rather than downward into the substrata. As a result, much of the swamp stands in water many months of the year; water levels were even higher before extensive ditching in the 1950s and 1960s. Close to the center of the swamp is Lake Drummond, a roughly circular body of water. The lake is almost three miles long but very shallow. Its maximum depth is only six or seven feet.

One of the most unusual features of Lake Drummond and the entire swamp is the water. The underlying layer of peat gives water from the Dismal Swamp very high acidity, with pH values ranging from 3.5 to

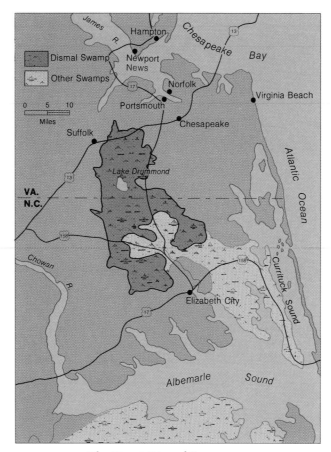

FIGURE 5.11 *The Great Dismal Swamp*

6.7. The water is also noticeably colored—brown enough to resemble bourbon and water—and has a distinct taste. People can drink it, although some find getting used to its flavor rather difficult. Ship captains used to prefer it for long ocean voyages, however, because the acidity strongly discourages the growth of micro-organisms. It is believed that Commodore Matthew Perry took Dismal Swamp water with him on his famous voyage to Japan.

Geologically speaking, the swamp is not very old (FIGURE 5.12). It probably began to form 11,000 or 12,000 years ago. The last major advance of the polar ice caps had just ended, and the climate was considerably colder than it is now. Pines, spruces, and other northern species of trees were common. Marshes existed on many of the waterways in what was to become the swamp, particularly along its eastern edge.

As the climate warmed, hardwood trees began to appear. But the major change in the swamp at this point was a slow but progressive growth in size due to

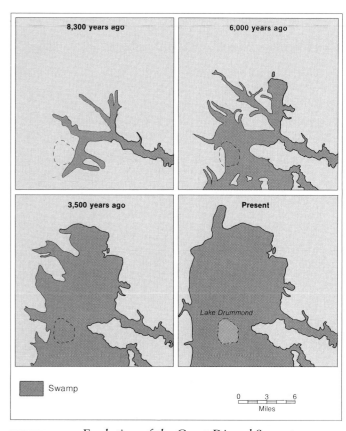

FIGURE 5.12 *Evolution of the Great Dismal Swamp*

greater moisture. As the ice caps melted, the seas rose, drowning the mouths of rivers and raising the water table. These effects were especially pronounced in low-lying areas such as the swamp, and ponding of streams for some distance inland encouraged the formation of freshwater marshes.

By about 6,000 years ago, peat covered approximately half of the swamp. Thereafter the climate continued to warm up, and it is likely that the seas rose at a slower rate. These conditions encouraged a shift from an oak-hickory forest to the kind of swamp forest familiar to us today. Ditching, logging, and periodic fires have affected the swamp in recent centuries, but its observable character has remained fairly stable. The most significant change, and the greatest threat to the swamp, has been a decrease in its size due to the drainage efforts of human beings.

Lake Drummond remains a mystery to geologists. One theory holds that the lake is a continuation of an open-water phase of the swamp, a pooling of water that had an early origin. Another popular view is that some early fire burned off a large mass of peat in the area of Lake Drummond, creating a cavity that filled with water. The lapping of water against the shore might have undermined irregular edges of peat and produced the roughly circular shoreline visible today. Recent evidence casts doubt on the first theory, but there is no conclusive proof of the validity of the second. It is also possible that ancient sediments beneath the lake may have collapsed at some earlier time.

Meanwhile, the Great Dismal Swamp survives despite many efforts at development, which began with George Washington. Washington visited the swamp seven times, beginning in 1763. On his first visit, he spent three days riding on horseback around the swamp's edge. Washington concluded that the swamp was "a glorious paradise, abounding in wild fowl and game," and his interest in its resources was powerfully stimulated.[14] He surveyed the whole region and concluded that rice could be grown there in addition to the possibilities of extracting its natural resources.

Washington's enthusiasm induced Patrick Henry and others to invest in the Dismal Swamp Land Company, also known as the "Adventurers for Draining the Dismal Swamp." This company dug two major canals and many ditches. One canal, five miles long but only four yards wide, is the oldest in use in North America. In 1830, other entrepreneurs expanded and rebuilt the Dismal Swamp Canal, and millions of juniper and cypress shingles were cut from it.

A glance at a current map shows significant changes made by human beings. Numerous drainage ditches and canals run through the swamp, especially at its southern border (FIGURE 5.13). These have siphoned off water and diminished the size of the swamp, but it is still an impressive feature of the Atlantic Coastal Plain. It is a refuge for animals, a nursery for unique plant species, and an important contributor to water quality, for just as the pocosins, it plays a vital role in filtering water and regulating runoff.

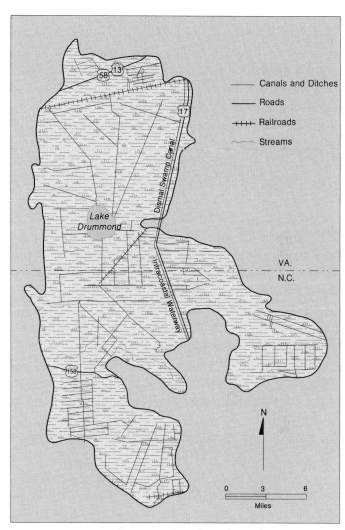

FIGURE 5.13 *Dismal Swamp Canals and Ditches*

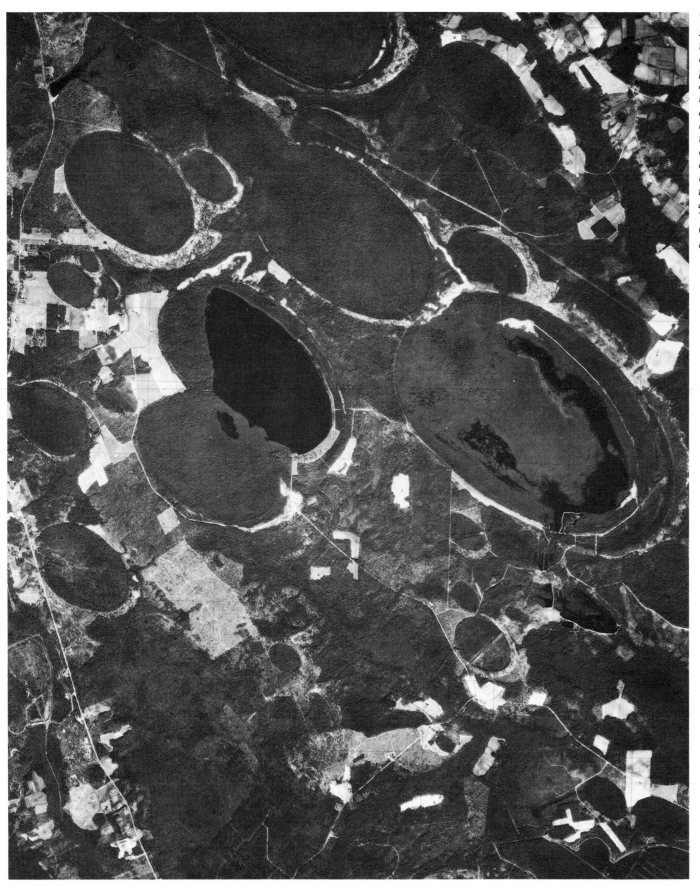

The Carolina Bays are thousands of lakes and marshes scattered through the Atlantic Coastal Plain in the two Carolinas. Elliptical in shape, they vary in size and depth. All have deposits of white sand along their rims, particularly on the southeastern side, and most are oriented along a northwest-to-southeast axis. Their name seems to have come from the bay tree that frequently grows in or around them, but their origin is unknown. One theory holds that they resulted from a major meteor shower, which would explain shape, directional orientation, and the concentration of these distinctive lakes in the Carolinas. No evidence of meteorites, however, has been found in the bays. Other theories attribute them to storm winds or to underground springs (a few do have springs), but these attempts at explanation also lack convincing support. Thus, an understanding of the geologic origin of the Carolina Bays, as of Lake Drummond, will have to await further research.

The Okefenokee Swamp

"Land of Trembling Earth," the Seminole Indians called it, and generations of later visitors have discovered how apt the name is. Much of this swamp is a floating bed of peat up to 25 feet thick, with bushes and trees growing in it. A person's movements can cause an islet to rock or quiver, and the strong stamp of one's foot may shake a tall tree.

The Okefenokee Swamp, one of the South's most famous, covers parts of five counties in southern Georgia and laps over into Florida. It had its origin when this section of the coastal plain was just emerging from the sea. A low barrier formed along the eastern edge of what is now the swamp, cutting it off from the sea and the sea's deposit of sediments. A shallow depression resulted and later filled with water. Plants that fill the swamp today soak up large quantities of water. But when the swamp's capacity is reached, the overflow runs into the Suwannee River, which winds through Florida into the Gulf of Mexico, and into the Saint Marys River, which defines the Georgia-Florida border on its way to the Atlantic.

In the Okefenokee, portions of the soggy, floating land in which cypress and bay trees root may actually break apart. A change in water level can shift weight and produce stresses that split up the mass of peat and muck. Swamp gas often has the same effect. Bacteria living in the soil manufacture tiny bubbles of methane, which expand every spring as the weather warms. These swelling bubbles exert a silent force, like ice in the cracks of a cement driveway, and they can break off a tangle of plants to form another floating island.

The Okefenokee Swamp is a refuge for some of nature's most beautiful creatures as well as a unique and fascinating environment.

The swamp is a refuge for many birds and other animals. Water moccasins abound near cypress knees and sometimes drop from low-hanging limbs of trees. Alligators frequent the eastern part of the swamp, a prairie or open marshland dotted by floating islands.

Fish gather around gator holes, apparently undeterred by the fact that some alligators here reach 15 feet in length, nearly their largest size on the continent. Black bears, bobcats, round-tailed muskrats, many species of frogs, and other animals are found here. Rare birds include the limpkin, the swallow-tailed kite, and possibly the ivory-billed woodpecker.

Among plants, larger trees dominate in western areas where the water is shallower. Longleaf pine, slash pine, live oak, tulip poplar, and other trees grow along with the cypress and bays. The fever tree, a small species with large, rose-colored sepals (the outer covering of the flower), once attracted Southerners, who made a medicine for malaria victims from its bark. A vine called the climbing heath works its way between layers of bark of the pond cypress and runs 40 feet or more up the tree. Then it sends out many flowers and branches that appear to grow straight out of the tree. Fortunately these plants and animals have considerable protection in the Okefenokee, most of which has been a national wildlife refuge since 1937.

THE INNER COASTAL PLAIN

Roughly 100 to 150 miles inland from the coast lies a belt of drier land that plays an important but often overlooked part in the life of the South: the inner coastal plain. Running from Virginia through North Carolina, South Carolina, and Georgia, this strip of land is never more than 120 miles wide and often much narrower. Bounded on the west by the Sandhills, the inner plain is quite flat, sloping only slightly toward the ocean.

Because its features are not dramatic, the inner plain brings few romantic images to mind. It lacks bustling activity and major concentrations of people, yet it is an important zone of plant resources. Southerners have tapped and felled its trees, planted it in cotton or tobacco, and today cultivate upon it a variety of crops.

Early Use

When the early settlers looked inland, they saw the deep forests of the inner plain as a storehouse of marketable resources. Timber was needed by newcomers and could be exported to other colonies in the Caribbean. Hardwoods, live oaks, and pines were used for construction, shipbuilding, and production of turpentine and naval stores. The furs of animals were another valuable resource. Before rice was grown in South Carolina, small groups of slaves moved into its forests to cut timber, while other more solitary bondsmen trapped animals or traded for pelts with the Indians.

As time went on, much of the inner plain became part of the plantation districts in which staple crops were grown. Rice could be cultivated only in the tidal zone, but cotton and tobacco spread over the inner plain. In Virginia and part of North Carolina, tobacco was the antebellum economy's linchpin. Elsewhere on the inner coastal plain, through the Carolinas and Georgia, King Cotton flourished and spread into the Piedmont.

After the Civil War, lack of credit, the crop lien, and weak prices locked many farmers into continued production of cotton. Furnish merchants, who advanced credit and furnished provisions, required cotton to be grown as the marketable commodity with which farmers would pay off their debts. But falling prices often made it impossible to pay the debts, so

---

Artesian Wells

In parts of the Atlantic Coastal Plain, people obtain water from artesian wells that flow naturally under pressure. If it were possible to cut an east-to-west cross section through the sediments of the coastal plain, the cut would reveal a number of layers piled atop each other, all sloping gently down toward the ocean. As one moves from east to west along the ground's surface, bands of these tilted sediments emerge one by one.

Rocks differ in their capacity to hold water: some are dense and impermeable, whereas others are quite permeable. Nature creates an artesian aquifer when it encloses a layer of water-porous rock between impermeable layers. Rainwater enters the porous layer where it comes to the surface in the western coastal plain or Piedmont. The water seeps down and, over time, will fill the stratum or band that is surrounded above and below by impermeable strata. When a well is drilled into one of these sloping, water-saturated layers, the water trapped within the layer higher up and to the west tries to flow down. Its weight or pressure will force water up the well. As long as the drilling site is lower than the spot where the water-bearing stratum emerges farther west, water will flow out freely.

A well-driller taps into the tilted column of water and creates an artesian well, but sometimes the forces of nature will do the job. When pressures fold and break sedimentary strata, they can free the water to rise along the plane of a fracture or at a point of slippage. This phenomenon creates an artesian spring. When conditions are right, the same forces can supply water to a stream, a marsh, or (in the desert) an oasis.

Artesian Aquifers

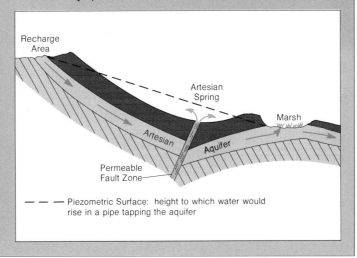

Recharge Area

Artesian Spring

Marsh

Artesian

Aquifer

Permeable Fault Zone

— — — Piezometric Surface: height to which water would rise in a pipe tapping the aquifer

---

farmers planted more cotton and hoped for better things year after year. Such circumstances kept many farmers growing cotton along the length of the inner plain for decades. From 1909 to 1949, cotton remained important for this agricultural belt, even though, as FIGURE 5.14 reveals, acreages devoted to the crop declined sharply between these years.

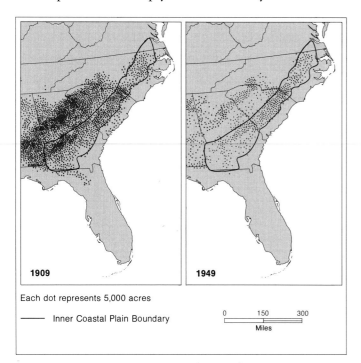

FIGURE 5.14 *Cotton Acreage in the Southeast*

Modern Crops

This record of continuity conceals as much as it makes plain, however, for King Cotton was losing its grip in the twentieth century. Production shifted toward the Gulf and Mississippi Valley and then declined. As the South's agricultural patterns changed, the farmers of the inner plain looked to new crops and methods. In many counties before 1910 (and by 1920 in most of the rest), cotton production in the inner plain had peaked and begun to decline. By the 1970s, cotton acreage here made up no more than one to two percent of total land area in most counties.

This low percentage of land in cotton is especially striking when one considers that the inner plain remains today an area of relatively intense production. It is, in fact, one of the islands of production in a region that is using less and less land for crops. Many of the South's major crops require large amounts of fertilizer (tobacco, cotton) and/or large amounts of labor (tobacco, cotton, and peanuts). Farmers try to grow these crops on the most favorable land. Better methods have increased yields so that fewer acres have to be planted to produce a given number of bushels. Thus, production tends to concentrate in certain areas and decline everywhere else. The vast majority of Southern counties now have less than one-sixth of their land under cultivation and, says one authority, "an astonishingly large number of counties had less than five percent of their land—less than one acre of every twenty—under crops."[15]

Today's inner plain produces a variety of crops: soybeans, which have replaced corn as the South's major field crop; peanuts; tobacco; and some cotton

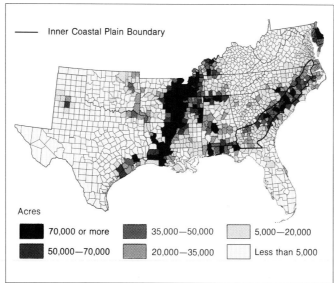

FIGURE 5.15 *Soybeans Harvested for Beans by County, 1978*

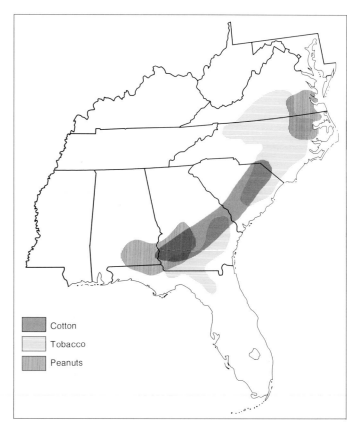

FIGURE 5.16 *Southeastern Croplands*

(FIGURES 5.15 and 5.16). Peanuts are big business at each end of the inner plain—in Virginia, North Carolina, and in the southwest corner of Georgia. Tobacco production is very heavy along an arc that is centered in eastern North Carolina. This is the heart of Southern tobacco country, although a secondary tobacco region lies in southern and eastern Georgia.

Another product of the inner plain may often be overlooked: wood, especially pulpwood (FIGURE 5.17). The modern pulpwood industry frequently harvests wood not from full-grown trees but from thickly clustered sprouts only a few years old. Giant machines can mow the young tree sprouts down, almost as a lawnmower does grass, and the roots soon send up new growth for a future harvest. Forestry experts also are experimenting with in vitro or test-tube cultivation of tree cells. The day may not be far away when scientists can clone selected tree specimens and propagate them in large numbers while developing superior varieties all the time. The nation's major source of lumber is shifting from the Northwest to the South, and forest products hold increasing importance for the South's economy.

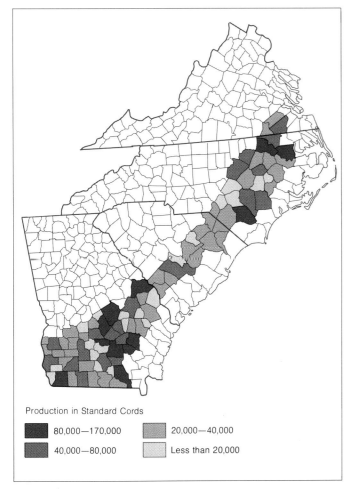

Production in Standard Cords

■ 80,000—170,000 ▨ 20,000—40,000
▨ 40,000—80,000 ▨ Less than 20,000

FIGURE 5.17 *Pulpwood Production on the Inner Coastal Plain by County, 1979*

As it was in colonial days, timber is still a major resource of the inner coastal plain. Corporate planning and management dominate the modern development of the South's forest resources, whose importance to the nation is growing.

A Revolution in Tobacco Farming

In the past, many Southerners called tobacco the 13-month crop. Raising tobacco required hard hand labor at almost every stage of its cultivation and curing, and often one crop was not entirely sold before seeds for the next crop had to be sowed. Farmers planted tobacco's tiny seeds in the winter and transplanted them in the spring. Then they suckered and topped the growing plants and harvested ripening leaves at intervals through the summer. The ripe leaves had to be looped or tied onto sticks, hung up in a barn, and cured for five to seven days while the farmer constantly monitored and adjusted the heat in the barns.

In recent years everything about this time-honored process has changed. First the leaf-sticker made it easier to sew leaf butts together for hanging on a stick, and the setter (a machine towed behind a tractor) speeded up the transplanting and watering of seedlings. But the big changes have come recently with the invention of mechanical harvesters and a new method of curing tobacco in large quantities. It seemed impossible to design a machine that could pick ripe leaves without damaging them or the rest of the plant, but such a machine was developed at North Carolina State University. Where 20 acres of tobacco was once a superhuman amount for one family to harvest, two or three times that amount now can and must be planted to justify the investment in a harvester. Metal sheds called bulk barns now cure the leaves with forced hot air in half the time that once was required.

These changes have revolutionized the tobacco business. Small family farms are giving way to larger units that are heavily capitalized and mechanized. More ominously, greater efficiency has brought greater production, so much production that surpluses threaten to destroy the entire price-support system for tobacco. Excess tobacco owned by the price-stabilization board has placed a cloud over the future as farmers compete against cheaper tobacco from Brazil and other countries.

Top: *The old mud-chinked tobacco barn, though still abundant in North Carolina, has become a symbol of an earlier, less technological era in tobacco culture.*
Center: *The mechanical harvester is one of several machines that have revolutionized the economics of tobacco growing. Change has made it almost impossible for small tobacco growers to compete, so many now rent their tobacco allotments to large-scale producers.*
Bottom: *The modern bulk barn is unsightly, but it cures a larger quantity of bright-leaf tobacco more rapidly than old tobacco barns ever could, and therefore it has become a fixture on the modern tobacco farm.*

The Sandhills

Running through North Carolina, South Carolina, and Georgia is a region known as the Sandhills (FIGURE 5.18). In the past, this region has been neither highly productive nor heavily populated, and most Southerners know less about it than about other parts of the Atlantic Coastal Plain. But its physical history is surprising and interesting.

During the Cretaceous period 65 to 136 million years ago, the oceans invaded as far inland as the present Sandhills. They are the remains of an ancient system of sand dunes. Once the border between land and sea, the Sandhills now signal a border between regions, with the Piedmont directly to their west and old shorelines and marine terraces of the Atlantic Coastal Plain to their east.

In the thousands of years that have elapsed since their formation, wind and water have eroded and transported these old dunes. But their extent was so great that the Sandhills region is everywhere an area of sandy soil. In many places the sand lies completely exposed at the surface, free of any covering of clay or humus. There are even a few spots in which the original form of the Sandhills is still visible: One can see that they are obviously huge sand dunes.

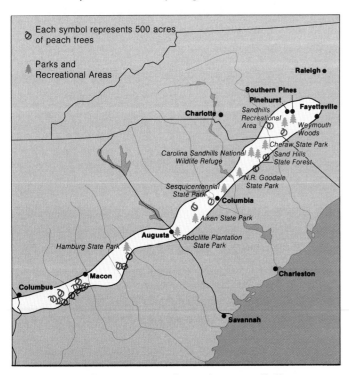

FIGURE 5.18 *The Georgia and Carolinas Sandhills*

The Sandhills are higher than the old ocean floors east of them. Rising from east to west, they have an elevation that varies roughly from 100 to about 500 feet above today's sea level. Occasional crests of dunes may be higher, but many years of weathering and erosion have created a generally flat, though slightly rolling, terrain.

The high sand content in the soil has a small but noticeable effect on climate. When exposed to sun, sand heats up more rapidly than loamy or clayey soils, and then the hot sand releases stored thermal energy into the atmosphere at night. This results in a microclimate, a pattern of weather slightly warmer than the surrounding region. The higher temperatures have their effect on both crops and people.

The soil of the Sandhills is too sandy to be highly fertile, and the combination of warm climate, abundant rainfall, and highly permeable soil prevents a thick layer of humus from building up. In antebellum days, some planters who grew large crops on rich land thought that since the Sandhills' soil was not very good, the folks who chose to live there must not be very good either. Somewhat disparaging remarks about Sandhill "tackies" can be found in famous books such as Mary Boykin Chesnut's diary.

Yet, just as Mrs. Chesnut acknowledged the fiercely independent spirit of those who lived in the Sandhills, the agriculture of the region should not be underrated. In addition to large quantities of soybeans, some cotton is grown, along with corn and other grains, sorghum, and even a little tobacco along the North Carolina edge of the region. Livestock and poultry are a part of farming there, and most of the peach industry in the Carolinas and Georgia flourishes in the Sandhills.

Recently the Sandhills have become a highly successful recreation and retirement area. Many state parks and federal facilities, like the Carolina Sandhills National Wildlife Refuge, are found there. Perhaps it was inevitable that championship golf courses would be located in the Sandhills. They possess the kind of varied, gently rolling terrain that offers an exciting challenge for expert golfers and attractive vistas for even the duffer. Pinehurst is preeminent among the several high-quality courses in the Sandhills.

Along with Southern Pines, the community of Pinehurst has also become famous as a resort and

retirement community. Many people vacation in these Sandhill areas to combine golf with dining and other recreation. Others have chosen to retire to these communities, which offer a mild and pleasant climate, attractive terrain, and an unhurried, quiet life not far from the attractions that larger cities can give. It is one of history's ironies, perhaps, that a region once scorned by Mrs. Chesnut's elite has become a popular home and playground for affluent Americans today.

A Savanna Pine Forest

When English settlers first arrived in America, tall pines soaring above an undergrowth of bushes and shrubs covered the Sandhills and other parts of the Atlantic Coastal Plain. Now the savanna pine forest has virtually disappeared. But at Weymouth Woods State Park in the North Carolina Sandhills, near Southern Pines, one example survives (see photograph on page 25).

A mature or climax forest is typically a hardwood forest. Oak, hickory, and other hardwoods crowd out pine trees because they capture more of the sky. Hardwoods spread their branches widely in a canopy that steals the sun, whereas the tall, narrow profile of pine trees allows other species to grow up beside them. Such unselfishness usually dooms the pines and permits hardwoods to take over.

How, then, did savanna pine forests arise? The secret is fire—fire that can be both a conservative and a destructive force in the forest. Blazes caused by lightning are an accidental but regular occurrence in nature. As they race along, they consume trees and destroy the undergrowth, killing the next generation of hardwoods and shrubs. But pines are relatively resistant to fire. As long as the growth tip at the top of a pine survives, it will continue to develop. Thus, repeated fires in nature gave pines the edge they needed to become dominant on the coastal plain.

At Weymouth Woods, state foresters plan and carry out controlled burns, and the visitor benefits, for a pine forest in the Sandhills creates a unique impression. The stately presence of towering trees combines with an amazing sense of openness and space. Sunlight streams down, since the pines have shed their lower branches and form no canopy. Underfoot, a trail of pure white sand stretches into the distance through slightly rolling terrain. The sensation of being in a primeval forest and also at the beach is correct, since Weymouth Woods is a forest growing on the dunes of what once was a seashore.

6 THE FLORIDA PENINSULA

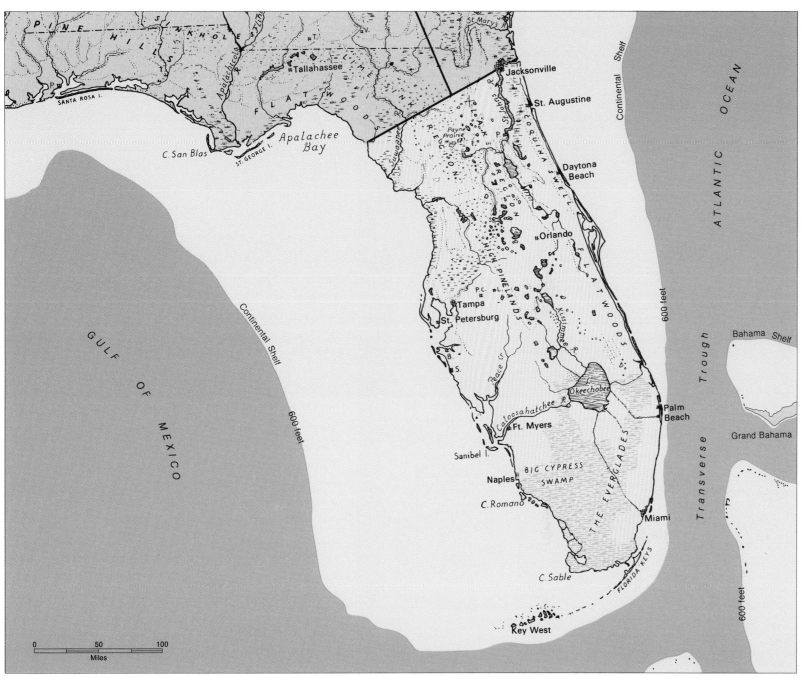

FIGURE 6.1 *The Florida Peninsula*

Among the varied environments of the South, the Florida Peninsula is one of the most distinctive (FIGURE 6.1). Other regions may be as attractive or as vivid, but none is more unusual.

Florida is preeminently the South's land of warmth and water. The southern end of the peninsula and the Florida Keys are tropical, and climate throughout the rest of the state is subtropical. But even south Florida's climate is usually pleasant rather than oppressive. Because it is a tropical wet-and-dry climate, the winters have many clear days with low humidity and cool, not cold, weather. Moreover, the ocean waters nearby improve upon Florida's natural warmth by moderating it. Sea breezes help to heat coastal areas in winter and provide refreshing and cooler breezes during summer evenings. Such warmth allows unusual tropical and subtropical vegetation.

Fresh water provides some of the amenities Floridians enjoy. In the center of the state lies the Lake Region, where scores of attractive lakes dot the earth's surface. The characteristics of limestone, which helped to form these lakes, also relate to the state's many springs. Florida has 27 of the 75 first-magnitude springs in the nation. Silver Springs, the state's biggest, discharges 500 million gallons of water per day. And because underlying limestone rocks go easily into solution and thus add little turbidity to the water, visitors enjoy crystal clear waters at springs, the Keys, and some rivers.

Salt water nearly surrounds Florida and plays a major role at many Sites within it. No state in the mainland United States has a longer tidal coastline. Counting islands, bays, sounds, and similar features, Florida has nearly 9,000 miles of detailed coastline, much of it highly desirable for recreation. On Florida's southern beaches, the tropics-warmed Gulf Stream hovers near shore and keeps water temperature in the 70s nearly year-round. Swamps, marshes, and estuaries abound near the coast. These create unique, but often endangered, environments. Indeed, the pressures of growth have made citizens increasingly aware of the vital and fragile nature of their water resources.

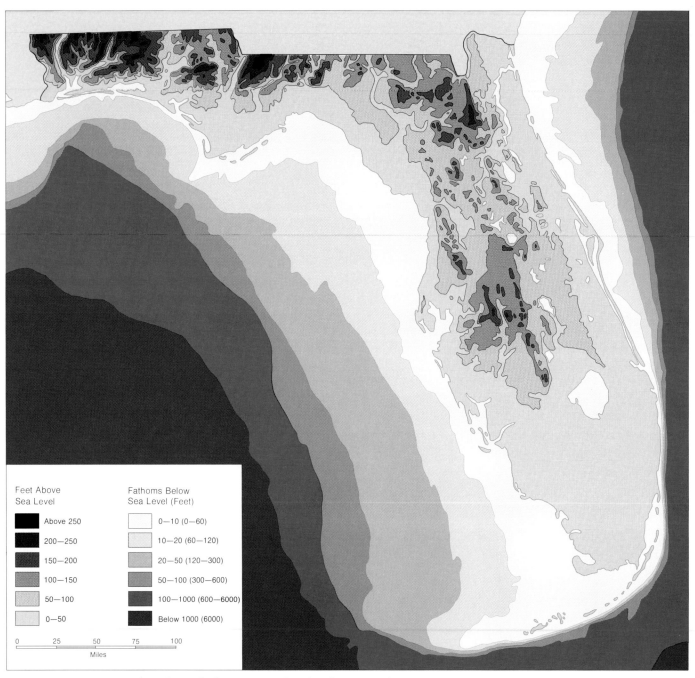

Feet Above
Sea Level

- Above 250
- 200—250
- 150—200
- 100—150
- 50—100
- 0—50

Fathoms Below
Sea Level (Feet)

- 0—10 (0—60)
- 10—20 (60—120)
- 20—50 (120—300)
- 50—100 (300—600)
- 100—1000 (600—6000)
- Below 1000 (6000)

0   25   50   75   100
Miles

FIGURE 6.2 *Ocean Depth and Land Elevation on the Florida Peninsula*

FORMATION OF THE PENINSULAR ARCH

The visible peninsula is part of a much larger rocky shelf rising upward in the ocean. This horizontal shelf lies close to the surface from the Bahamas in the southeast to the western edge of the continental shelf, which extends far into the Gulf of Mexico. The shelf is interrupted between the Bahamas and Florida, where a transverse trough (the path of the Gulf Stream) cuts through. The deep, basement rocks seem to be similar to those beneath the Piedmont. On top of them lie layers of limestone and shale known to exceed 18,000 feet in thickness.

Tremendous forces lifted up this enormous shelf of rock, which reaches its peak in north central Florida. There, at the Ocala Uplift, the limestone that lies beneath most of Florida is at or near the surface and is fully 150 feet above sea level. Surface deposits in many areas are also limestone, but more common are thin layers of sand and gravel left behind when the ocean last retreated. For 250 miles south of St. Augustine, the coastal soil contains large quantities of shells cemented together into a rock called coquina.

The surface of the peninsular arch is flat and low (FIGURE 6.2). It slopes gently from north to south and is slightly tilted on an east-west axis toward the Gulf of Mexico. Bathymetry, the measurement of ocean depths, reveals that a much larger, submerged Florida lies close to the surface, particularly to the west. At times in the distant past, when sea levels were lower, much of this part of the shelf was exposed, and bones of the mammoth and saber-toothed tiger can be found there. Changes in ocean levels could easily bring more land to the surface or, if seas were to rise, inundate much of the peninsula.

Elevation is very modest, ranging from zero to about 300 feet above sea level, but within this narrow range there is a discernible pattern of relief. The highest portions of the state are at the north end of the peninsula and in the panhandle (actually part of the Gulf Coast region), where river sand, silt, and clay washed down from the Appalachian Mountains have accumulated. A north-south ridge runs down the center of the state, extending almost as far as Lake Okeechobee. Marine terraces helped to shape the surface; geologists have identified as many as seven of them in parts of the state. Ancient seashores have left some gradients, particularly near the coasts and in the central region. South Florida, the location of Big Cypress Swamp and the Everglades, is almost completely flat. But along the eastern coast of south Florida, there is a low ridge that stretches from the Everglades National Park as far up as Lake Okeechobee. Originally a submerged barrier or bar, this ridge is no more than 50 feet high, but most settlement and development has clustered on it because it affords better drainage and helps keep residents dry during rainy seasons and violent storms.

The shoreline seems as varied as it is extensive. Extremely long barrier beaches are present, especially on the Atlantic Coast. Mangrove swamps are a key habitat along the southern shore. Saltwater marshes add to the area covered by freshwater swamps, and numerous estuaries are home to abundant sea life. In addition to sandy beaches, there are extensive islands and rocky beaches on the west coast. The Florida Keys complete a remarkably diverse shoreline. Stretching southwest in a chain that ends only 90 miles from Cuba, the Keys are actually two different types of islands. The eastern Keys were formed by living coral, left dead and dry when the oceans fell. To the west, however, these islands are limestone shoals rising up from the ocean floor.

Soil and water extend the theme of diversity. Along with many wetlands near the shore, Florida has other soils that are too well drained. Rainfall is heavy, due to the surrounding ocean; it is not uncommon for storms to dump several inches of rain, and during a hurricane in the 1950s, one town recorded 38.7 inches of rain in one 24-hour period. However, the peninsula's porous limestone carries much of the rain quickly away. In the Everglades, surprisingly, the same underlying limestone has acquired a recemented, relatively nonporous surface that contributes directly to the area's wetness. Yet this and other parts of Florida face the threat of inadequate water and degradation of water quality.

THE LAKE REGION

To explain the band of lakes that pockmark central Florida (FIGURE 6.3), one must begin with the limey sediments that settled out from the oceans. Limestone can be either a durable or soluble rock. It makes up part of the Alps and the Himalayas, where it is hard and strong, and in arid regions, it forms elevated features such as cuestas and mesas. But limestone also can be dissolved by water, especially water that is acidic.

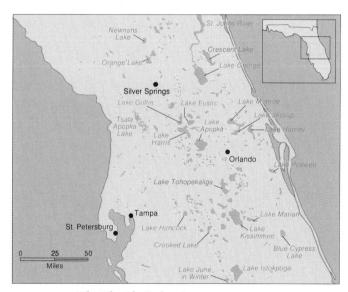

FIGURE 6.3 *The Florida Lakes Region*

Carbon dioxide in the air naturally reduces the pH of nonsaline water from a neutral value of 7.0 to a slightly acidic 5.7. Industrial wastes emitted into the air tend to reduce the pH of rainwater still further. Over the northern half of Florida, rainfall in recent years has averaged 4.7 or lower (FIGURE 6.4). In addition, groundwater picks up carbon dioxide from plant decay and organic acids released by plants. Thus, moving groundwater is slightly acidic and so is corrosive to limestone.

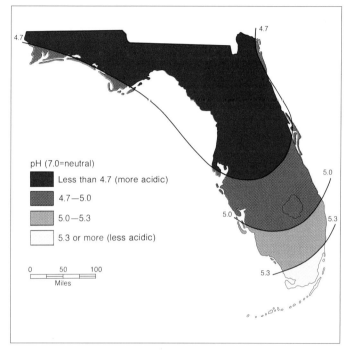

pH (7.0=neutral)

- ■ Less than 4.7 (more acidic)
- 4.7—5.0
- 5.0—5.3
- □ 5.3 or more (less acidic)

FIGURE 6.4 *pH of Rainfall in Florida*

Over time, groundwater dissolves limestone rock, especially where it encounters joints or planes around which it can circulate. Gradually carrying away part of the rock, the water creates a void, or underground cavern. Such caverns are characteristic of subsurface limestone; 44 of the 48 contiguous states have limestone caverns, and many of these are tourist attractions. Drillers have found these cavities honeycombing the rock thousands of feet beneath Florida.

KARST TOPOGRAPHY

If the formation of a cavern continues, the roof may reach the surface, or the void may undermine overlying soil so severely that it collapses into the cavern. This process produces sinks or sinkholes. Whenever the resulting hole lies deeper than the water table, a lake will form, as has happened throughout central Florida. The dissolving of limestone and the collapse of cavern roofs created Florida's Lake Region. Dry holes, which are often shallower, are also possible.

Growing demand for water can speed up the formation of sinkholes by lowering the water table and draining pockets of groundwater that lie close to the surface. This gaping hole suddenly opened in 1981 in Winter Park, Florida, near Orlando, as a result of severe drought and heavy pumping of water. As proof that it was no isolated phenomenon, seven smaller sinkholes opened up in central Florida within days of the Winter Park collapse.

The Lake Region is a prime example of *karst topography*. This term is named for the Karst region of northern Yugoslavia, where dissolving limestone shaped the land's surface and stimulated early studies of the phenomenon. Karst regions typically have many caves and springs in addition to sinkholes and sinkhole lakes. They lack well-developed surface drainage systems; in fact, streams flowing along a karst terrain frequently disappear into underground channels and caverns.

There is a natural pattern of evolution in karst regions. First, the scattered sinkholes grow until numerous craters pockmark the surface. As individual sinks enlarge and merge, much of the original surface is carried away and solution valleys are left. These are valleys resulting from the solution of underlying limestone and the subsequent collapse of the overlying surface. Eventually the dissolving action of water on limestone will lower and flatten most of the surface. Only a few knolls will remain to bear witness to the original surface (FIGURE 6.5).

FIGURE 6.5
The Evolution of Karst Topography

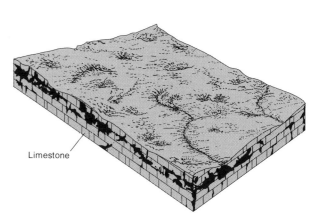

Limestone

a. Initial Stage. Scattered sinkholes dot the landscape and grow in size and number as caverns enlarge and their roofs collapse.

b. Intermediate Stage. Individual sinks enlarge and merge with those in adjacent areas to form solution valleys. Much of the original surface is destroyed. Disappearing streams and springs are common.

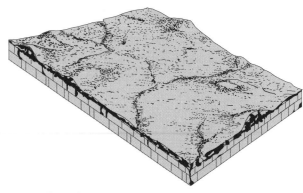

c. Late Stage. Solution activity has removed most of the limestone formation. Only isolated knolls remain as remnants of the former surface.

In Florida today the most striking area of karst topography is the central portion of the state. Limestone is not as prevalent in the northern parts of the state, and the extensive wetlands show few karst features because they tend to hold rainwater and have a very gentle slope. Although limestone underlies south Florida, the development of karst features is slight there because the rock is relatively young, and its surface may have mixed with minerals and then dried into a harder stone. In addition, south Florida's flat terrain reduces the movement of groundwater, limiting its ability to dissolve. For the Lake Region, karst topography means both natural beauty and unexpected collapses.

THE EVERGLADES

The Everglades has been called a river of grass. This name suggests both the watery character of the Everglades and the miles of saw grass that grow there (FIGURE 6.6). Saw grass, which is actually a sedge, takes its name from the sharp, sawlike edges on its leaves. But the phrase cannot convey all the unique features of this region.

The river of grass begins at Lake Okeechobee. Long ago this lake began as a depression on the ocean floor. The rising of the Peninsular Arch exposed the depression, which began to fill with fresh water. Surrounded by flat terrain, the lake had no natural outlet through channels and streams. Therefore, Lake Okeechobee filled and began to flood steadily over its southern bank, bringing water to the Everglades.

If the Everglades makes up a river, it is both a huge and a shallow one. Up to 50 miles wide, the Everglades once stretched a hundred miles from Lake Okeechobee to the Keys. Under normal conditions it is covered, except for a few islands of trees (called hammocks), with six inches of water year-round. Slowly, almost imperceptibly, this water moves seaward along the minute slope of the land—a drop as small as two inches per mile.

The Everglades region is essentially a marsh, a wetland covered by grasses, sedges, and similar aquatic vegetation. Within it, however, are both dry hammocks and swampy areas where cypress and other water-loving trees can grow. The hammocks often have a watery moat around them. This formation develops because organic acids that wash out of decaying vegetation in the hammock dissolve the limestone and soil nearby. The moat then helps to protect the hammock from fire.

Along its southern border with the sea, the Everglades supports a forest of mangrove trees. These plants, which can tolerate brackish water, use their stiltlike roots to prop their leaves up and out of the water. The mangrove forest is a unique environment and a highly productive one. Its detritus becomes food for many organisms, and the trees help protect the shore from storms. This environment also shelters many species of birds, reptiles, and mammals and is a nursery and breeding ground for numerous aquatic animals.

Not all of the Everglades has remained wet. Man's invasions of the Everglades, by draining part of the land and lowering the water table, have exposed some of the peat that lies beneath the surface. In dry years, naturally occurring fires have sometimes burned the peat right down to the limestone bedrock.

The clear waters of Florida's many springs are a mecca for divers as well as for the less ambitious vacationer. The abundance of springs, the properties of limestone, and Florida's karst topography are all aspects of the interrelation of soil and water in this environment.

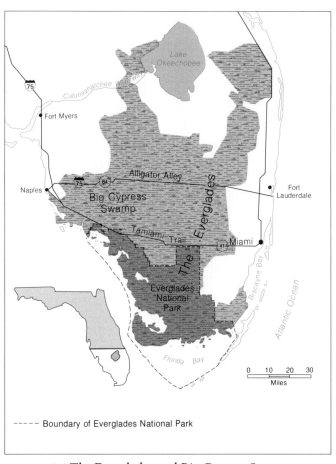

FIGURE 6.6 *The Everglades and Big Cypress Swamp*

Plants and Animals of the Everglades

As a natural region, the Everglades shelters many exotic plants and animals. The currents of the Gulf Stream and the raging winds of hurricanes carried some West Indian plants to the Everglades. Royal palm, mahogany, poisonwood, lancewood, and gumbo-limbo trees grow in some of the hammocks. So, too, does the strangler fig, an unusual tree whose root system grows down around the trunk of an already established tree. Beginning from a seed deposited by a bird on a branch or leaf, the strangler fig sends down its roots; as it grows, it gradually encircles the older tree until it constricts and kills the outermost growth layer. Then the strangler fig stands in its place.

Many air plants (epiphytes) also thrive in the Everglades. Some, called bromeliads, belong to the pineapple family. They are not parasites, though they grow on the branches of cypress, pond apple, and other trees. Like Spanish moss, they obtain nourishment from the atmosphere, and they collect water among the overlapping leaves at their base. Many varieties of ferns and vines are also found here.

Best known of all the animals is the alligator. Once threatened, this reptile now is flourishing, with individuals growing to a record 18 feet and 600 pounds. The alligator likes to create submerged pools by cleaning out muck and vegetation down to the rock. Lying in his pool, the alligator then feeds on fish that are attracted to it. In dry spells, these pools help to preserve many animals, however, by offering them water and shelter.

Another large inhabitant of the Everglades is a genuinely threatened one: the Florida panther. This powerful cat once roamed throughout every part of Florida. Now there may be no more than 100 or so, found only in the Everglades and Big Cypress Swamp. Human beings have steadily encroached upon and destroyed the panther's habitat. The state is trying to protect this impressive animal, but if the Everglades is damaged further, it may disappear entirely.

The Everglades has been severely affected by man's intrusions, but one of its sturdy denizens—the alligator—is flourishing. No longer endangered, the alligator is increasing throughout Florida and sometimes turns up in backyard swimming pools.

A profusion of birds nest in the Everglades, including the queer-looking roseate spoonbill, the tropical frigate bird, and a variety of herons, egrets, and ibis. The wood ibis or wood stork is the only true North American stork and is endangered, as are Audubon's caracara, the Cape Sable sparrow, and the Everglade kite. This kite is a highly specialized member of the hawk family; with its sharply curved beak, it feeds on the apple snail almost exclusively. The ivory-billed woodpecker, once found in the Everglades, may now be extinct.

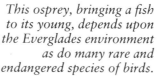
This osprey, bringing a fish to its young, depends upon the Everglades environment as do many rare and endangered species of birds.

The Florida panther has been dwindling in numbers as human activity steadily encroached on its habitat. This photograph suggests why it would be a tragedy to lose this impressive creature forever.

Costs of Development in the Everglades

The value of the Everglades once received little understanding and appreciation. As with many other Southern wetlands, people wanted to "reclaim" it, to make this supposedly useless land useful by draining and changing it. Large parts of the Everglades have been lost, perhaps as much as half of its original extent in the north, and the water table has been lowered several feet throughout.

As early as 1848, a study commissioned by the federal government concluded that the Everglades, though awesome, produced an "abiding impression" of "utter worthlessness to civilized man, in its present condition."[1] Dredging began in the 1880s, but not until the administration of Governor Napoleon Bonaparte Broward (1905–1909) did work begin in earnest. (Broward, ironically, was a reformer who inveighed against corporations for failing to undertake the drainage they had promised.) To fund the digging, Florida had to sell swamplands, but repeated scandals over highly touted, waterlogged property slowed progress. Nevertheless, by 1929 over $18 million had been spent and 440 miles of canals and levees constructed (FIGURE 6.7A).

Settlers swarmed into the northern part of the Everglades near Lake Okeechobee and began to farm on the drained muck soil. But all was not well. The canals could not prevent floods during heavy rains, and in the 1920s, fields of winter vegetables, sugarcane, and other crops were flooded for weeks and months. Hurricanes in 1926 and 1928 led to severe flooding from Lake Okeechobee, with loss of many lives. Then the 1930s and 1940s brought severe droughts that revealed the canals *over*drained the region in dry periods. Lightning started fires in the muck that burned out of control and blackened the sky over Miami. According to one account, the smoke "literally shut out the light of day."[2]

Moreover, as the organic soil was farmed, it oxidized, compacted, and subsided. Nearly a foot of soil was disappearing every 10 years. As the muck dried up, alligator holes and alligators disappeared, and salt water began to press into well fields that had once been kept fresh by the water-holding properties of the Everglades. Huge rains and floods in 1947 finally spurred modern efforts to undo part of what had been done; new projects slowed the drainage and reduced

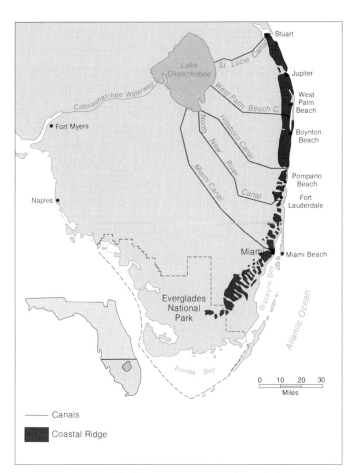

FIGURE 6.7A *Everglades Drainage Canals Built between 1907 and 1929*

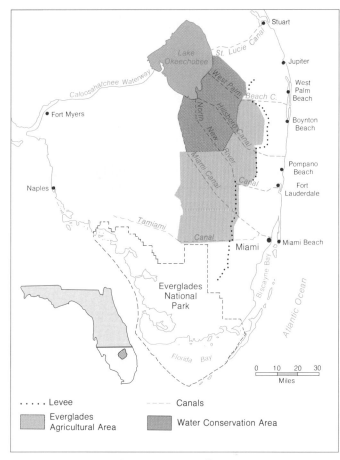

FIGURE 6.7B *Water Conservation Efforts since 1947*

the outflow of fresh water while providing more effective protection from floods (FIGURE 6.7B).

This experience helped develop a wider appreciation of the contributions that the Everglades makes to society in its natural state. In a number of ways, southeastern Florida depends on the Everglades remaining free from further serious changes.

Benefits From the Undeveloped Everglades

First, given the extremely low terrain of south Florida and its exposure to tropical rainstorms and hurricanes, the Everglades serves as a buffer to contain the worst ravages of the weather. This region in its natural state can hold enormous quantities of rainwater that would overwhelm the largest drainage projects. At the same time, the water-holding qualities of the region offer protection against the recurring droughts of Florida's climate.

This latter factor points to the second major service provided by the Everglades wilderness. Since Florida has no major rivers, it depends almost entirely upon rainfall for water for drinking, irrigation, and other human uses. The major aquifer, the Floridan Aquifer, is useful only to the northern two-thirds of the state. In south Florida, the aquifer moves deeply underground and becomes brackish. Heavily populated areas at the tip of the peninsula thus have to rely on smaller aquifers, principally the Biscayne. Its capacity is already being taxed; in dry periods, the present population begins to empty the aquifer out, and salt water invades coastal wells. Only the pressure of water moving down from the Everglades can protect and recharge this aquifer.

The recent alarming discovery that pollution of Lake Okeechobee has reached dangerous levels underlines the precariousness of Florida's water supply.

Large algae blooms show that the lake is heavily polluted by fertilizers. Excessive plant growth could quickly rob the water of its remaining oxygen and "kill" the lake, with potentially disastrous consequences for the Everglades and for all human activities dependent on it. State officials are facing the necessity of spending hundreds of millions of dollars to bring Lake Okeechobee back from the brink of collapse.

Finally, the Everglades provides more than beauty to a few million visitors each year. It also makes possible the coastal estuaries' production of marine life. This results partly from the creation of brackish estuary waters in which juvenile shrimp and other creatures grow. In addition, biologists have discovered that the inflow of fresh water aids bacteria in breaking down the cellulose in mangrove leaves. The decaying leaves become the detritus that is a primary part of the food chain for most marine animals.

BIG CYPRESS SWAMP

West of the Everglades lies the Big Cypress Swamp, a watershed of almost 2,500 square miles. Although similar to the Everglades in many respects, the Big Cypress is a different kind of wetland. It is slightly higher, has a more complex drainage system, and is wooded rather than covered with aquatic plants. Some areas of higher ground support forests of slash pine, palmetto, or oak; others with shallow marl soil feature old but stunted cypress trees. In a few finger-like strands of deeper soil, some giant ancient cypress may be found.

Most of the land in Big Cypress Swamp is flooded by rainwater at least a few months during the year. In dry seasons, however, the water in many areas will evaporate, leaving scattered ponds and sloughs. Overall, the topography is so uniform and low that drainage projects can lower the water level over a broad expanse of the swamp.

Plant and animal life in the Big Cypress are very similar to that in the Everglades. The swamp serves as a habitat for several rare and endangered species, including the Florida panther, wood stork, and Everglade kite. Bromeliads, royal palms, and the strangler fig can be found there, along with some ferns that grow 10 feet high.

Big Cypress has an important connection to

shrimp fishing on the Gulf Coast. Some of its water empties into the Ten Thousand Islands region on the southwestern tip of Florida, where many young shrimp seek food and shelter. The ability of the swampland to hold water and slowly discharge it over a period of months keeps the water in this shrimp nursery suitably brackish.

Big Cypress Swamp also recharges the shallow aquifers from which the future population of southwestern Florida will have to draw its water. Yet, in recent decades the swamp was the site of some unusually unwise development. In the 1960s, Gulf American Corporation purchased over 200 square miles of property in the swamp. Using sales tactics designed to create an atmosphere of urgency, the company sold lots on the installment plan to people all over the United States. The company was marketing Golden Gate Estates, whose plots stretch 25 miles up and down through Big Cypress (FIGURE 6.8).

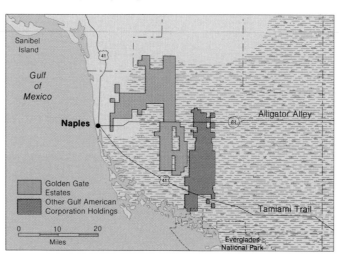

FIGURE 6.8 *Land Acquired for Florida's Golden Gate Estates Development*
County boundaries are indicated by dot-dash lines. Patterned area indicates Big Cypress Swamp.

Thousands of individuals purchased land, and sizeable profits were made. However, very few buyers ever settled on their homesites. The lots were remote and expensive to improve or even to service with telephone lines. Moreover, due to the high water table and poor drainage, conventional septic tanks could not be used. Golden Gate Estates has remained almost a ghost town.

Yet the land company honored its announced plans to dredge miles of canals and build roads. The canals,

constructed for a population that has never materialized, carry enormous quantities of scarce fresh water off to the Gulf of Mexico. In 1970, one of the canals was discharging 12½ times the amount of water then used by the nearby city of Naples. Not only did this reduce marine life in estuaries, it also created dry conditions that led to unusual forest fires.

Fortunately, public awareness of the utility of Big Cypress Swamp seems to have increased. A controversial proposal to build a major jetport in the swamp was defeated, and the state legislature contributed $40 million to the establishment of Big Cypress National Preserve. This action protected the eastern half of the swamp and essentially all of it that feeds into the Everglades National Park.

FLORIDA: A CHANGING POPULATION

Two maps suggest at a glance the vast changes that Florida's people have experienced. The first depicts place names of Indian or Spanish origin (FIGURE 6.9). In the long early history of Florida, the Indians and the Spanish played dominant roles and left their influence on later inhabitants. The second map suggests part of the explosive population growth that has affected Florida in the twentieth century (FIGURE 6.10). Florida has both a rich past and a present in which change may be occurring more rapidly than ever.

FIGURE 6.9 *Indian and Spanish Place Names*

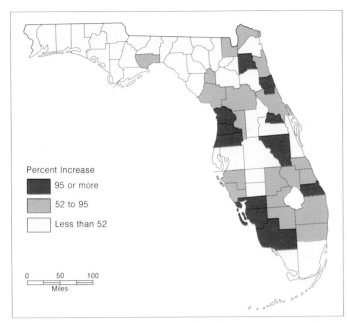

FIGURE 6.10 *Population Growth by County, 1970–1980*

The Indians and the Spanish

When the first European explorers arrived, there were probably 100,000 Indians living in Florida. The chroniclers of Hernando de Soto's expedition of 1539 were highly impressed by the Apalachees, who lived in the panhandle region. De Soto's writers described them as well organized, strong, and handsome. Descriptions also survive of the Timucua Indians, who resided in northern Florida. They lived in villages made up of round and square houses built of wattle and daub. Palisades and sentries gave them protection, and leaders of both single villages and clusters of settlements provided social direction. The Timucua tribes were destined, by their location, to have the most contact with the Spanish.

For them, and ultimately for all Florida's Indians, this contact proved fatal. Lacking immunity to European diseases, they steadily died. St. Augustine, which became the principal Spanish settlement, was founded in 1565. After little more than 100 years, most of the nearby Indians were dead. Thereafter, converted Indians brought in from the missions or tribes that migrated south from Georgia were the only Indians found near St. Augustine. In 1729, only one Timucua Indian was known to be alive. By 1763, when England gained Florida after the Seven Year's War, disease, even more than warfare, had virtually eliminated the original Indian population.

St. Augustine

From 1513 to 1763, the Spanish held onto Florida as an outpost vital to the protection of their American empire. Treasure ships from South America or the Caribbean basin sailed north to Florida before turning toward Spain. In addition, Florida gave the Spanish a foothold in North America from which they could resist the imperial ambitions of both the French and the British. Although not financially valuable in itself, Florida was essential as an outpost of empire.

This role as an outpost determined the character of St. Augustine throughout the period of Spanish control. The oldest permanent European settlement in the United States, St. Augustine was a garrison town composed of a fort, an adjacent town, and an Indian village connected with a mission (FIGURE 6.11). The surviving fort, the Castillo de San Marcos, dates from 1672. The colonial town, with its impressive city gates, was laid out in the Spanish manner around a central plaza. Officials and residents of high status lived close to the plaza, while humbler citizens had to find homes closer to the outskirts. Spanish and Creole men connected with the military lived in the city along with Creole and Indian women, other Indians, and blacks. The latter were often escaped slaves, whom the Spanish crown encouraged to run away from the English colonies of South Carolina and Georgia.

The Seminoles

During the 20 years of British rule, from 1763 to 1783, Creek Indians from Georgia and present-day Alabama began to move into Florida. Runaway slaves sometimes joined and intermarried with the Indians, becoming part of their culture. The British began to call the relocated Creeks *Seminoles,* a name derived from an Indian word meaning "wild, runaway."

With England's defeat in the American Revolution, Spain regained Florida, only to find itself too weak to derive much benefit from its old colony. American designs on Florida were apparent, and American settlers began to intervene in the Spanish territory. Repeatedly they staged raids across the border to capture escaped slaves or Seminoles who they claimed were runaway slaves. Eventually Spain recognized the inevitable and ceded Florida to the United States by treaty in 1821.

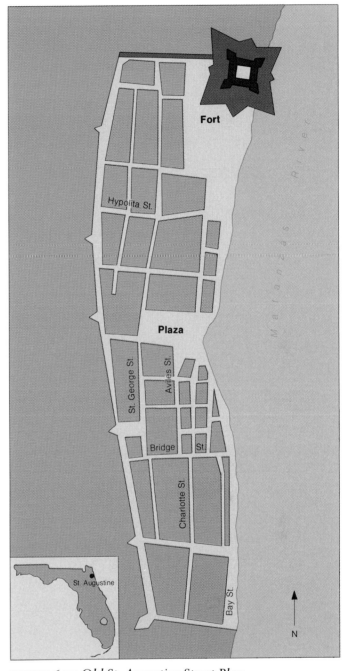

FIGURE 6.11 *Old St. Augustine Street Plan*

Even before Americans gained possession of Florida, they had begun a long series of bloody and expensive wars against the Seminoles. The first (1816–1818) began with a raid to recapture runaway slaves and featured a determined Andrew Jackson. But not even Jackson could stop slaves from running away or Seminoles from resisting white control and the capture of some of their kinsmen. In the Second Seminole War (1835–1842), Osceola led resistance to federal attempts to move the Seminoles west of the Mississippi River. The Seminoles retreated deeper into the sparsely settled peninsula and evaded the United States' attempts to capture them.

By the time fighting died away in 1842, the federal government had removed well over 1,000 Seminoles and inflicted much suffering on the remainder. But the war had cost 1,500 soldiers' lives and $20 million. In addition, a large number of Seminoles remained in the inaccessible Everglades, and their spirit of resistance was strong. Never before had the American military fought so taxing a war with so little success.

By 1858, after a third war, the Seminole population in Florida was reduced to only a few hundred. Today more than 1,000 Seminoles live in southern Florida, where there are three large and a number of small Indian reservations (FIGURE 6.12). They retain many of their traditional customs and show a renewed pride in their heritage.

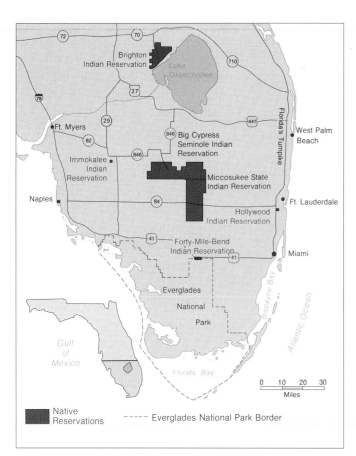

FIGURE 6.12 *Native American Reservations in Florida*

ECONOMIC DEVELOPMENT

Before the Civil War, Florida was rather thinly populated. The main thrust of trans-Appalachian settlement had gone to Alabama and Mississippi and passed the state by. In addition to cotton, some Floridians grew sugarcane, and the 1850s saw a boom in the raising of Sea Island cotton in the interior. But the Civil War slowed progress and left Florida quite undeveloped.

Modern patterns in the state's economic life began to emerge at the end of the nineteenth century. With investment from the North (which was itself a pattern), development began to tie the state more closely to the national economy. A period of railroad building created the transportation linkages necessary for growth. Following quickly upon that were a number of important trends: increased tourism, the rise of aerospace and manufacturing industries, greater production of fruit and vegetables, and more intense extraction of raw materials such as lumber and phosphate.

The Old Alcazar Hotel is one of the surviving monuments to the grandeur of Florida's early tourist developments.

In recent decades, these trends have broadened. Tourism has expanded enormously since the Second World War, and recreation and retirement now augment tourism as more people seek to enjoy Florida's sun and climate. Large pulp and paper mills and chemical factories increase the extraction of raw materials. For the first time, a diverse agricultural sector has developed a cattle industry that serves the American market. All these aspects of rapid growth bring more intensive use of the physical environment.

In the 1880s, the state government encouraged railroad development, and Northern investors responded strongly. Henry Plant and Henry Flagler were among the leaders in a feverish extension of railroad lines throughout the northern part of the state and southward into the peninsula. An effective rail network soon came into being (FIGURE 6.13). Its lines made it possible for the growers of vegetables and fruit to reach new markets in the North. Likewise, the railroads gave agriculture the opportunity to move south into parts of the state that had not yet been intensively farmed. And people outside the state now could more easily visit as well as benefit from Florida.

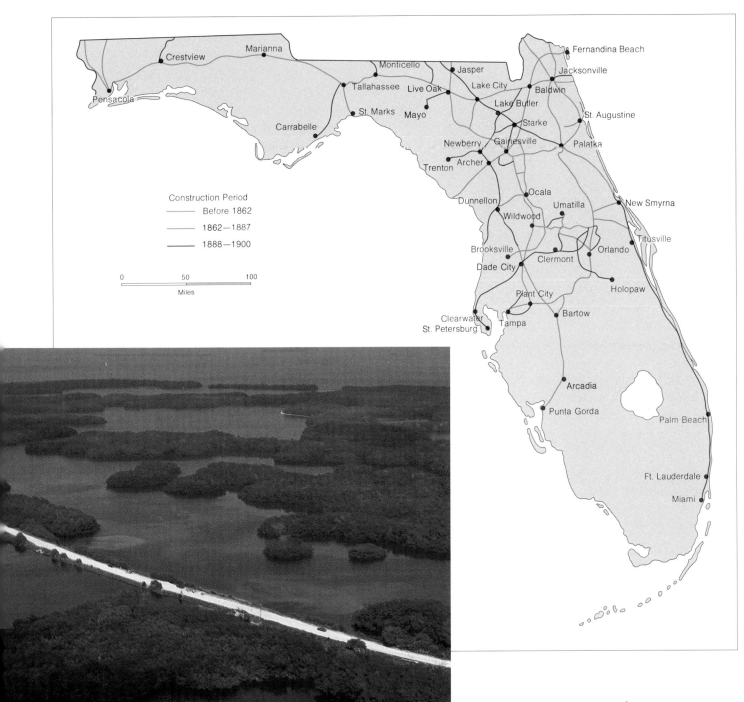

Construction Period
— Before 1862
— 1862—1887
— 1888—1900

0   50   100
Miles

Human beings are imposing their activities on a delicate environment in Florida. Land, water, and growth are inseparably related, and the effects of growth on the environment are rarely neutral.

Flagler and Plant showed considerable foresight by making tourism an integral part of their rail-building activities. They needed to encourage use of their trains, of course, but they also saw the recreational potential of Florida's tropical and subtropical climate. Each man built a number of grand hotels—Flagler on the east coast, where he hoped to create an "American Riviera," and Plant on the west coast, where his Hotel Belleview featured the first golf course provided for lodgers. Encouraging wealthy vacationers to come South and enjoy their facilities, these hotels helped to start the twentieth century's tourist boom.

In recent years, tourism has received a potent stimulus from the development of theme parks, such as Disney World, Sea World, and Circus World, in the middle of the state. From less than 3 million in 1940, the number of out-of-state vacationers has soared to approximately 40 million today. Disney World alone attracted over 22 million people in its first two years of operation. Roughly a tenth of the visitors are from foreign countries, and all of them fuel an economy heavily dependent upon tourists' dollars.

IN-MIGRATION

The natural attractions of Florida have induced many tourists to stay and escape Northern winters or to enjoy a sun-filled retirement. This influx of thousands has brought enormous change during the twentieth century. In every decade, Florida's rate of population growth has been far above the national average; in fact, since 1930 it has ranged between 280 and 420 percent of the nation's rate of growth. Such sustained population increase has meant boom, more pressure on natural resources, and cultural change.

Many commentators have questioned how "Southern" contemporary Florida is. In 1950, about 25 percent of the residents were non-natives; by 1970, that figure had climbed above 40 percent and by 1977 was nearly 66 percent. Undoubtedly, many people who have moved to Florida have adopted Southern ways, but others have given some non-Southern flavor to the state. International politics contributed significantly to the pattern of a changing population in recent decades, as large numbers of Cuban, then Haitian, and then Indochinese immigrants arrived in Florida.

AGRICULTURE AND INDUSTRY

Although much population growth has been urban, agriculture is still a large and vital part of Florida's economy. Fewer than 100,000 workers produce crops valued at more than a billion dollars.

Sunny weather and a long frost-free period help Florida prosper from intensive agriculture even though the state's soils are not particularly rich. In addition to fertilizers, irrigation is often needed, particularly in the south, because the state's heavy rains do not always occur at the right time. The tropical climate can be very changeable. During hurricanes (see pages 102–104) nearly 40 inches of rain have fallen on Florida in a single day, yet heavy rainfall can alternate with near-drought conditions. In fact, agriculture in southeastern Florida has used six times as much water as urban and industrial consumers.

Citrus production is the major success story. Despite occasional freezes and a delay of at least four years required to bring new trees into production, citrus growers have expanded production enormously over the years. They are responsible for the majority of the nation's oranges, grapefruit, limes, tangelos, and tangerines. (Lemons are one of the few citrus fruits not grown in quantity in the state.) The center of orange and grapefruit production has been in the middle of the peninsula, but in recent years urbanization has begun to push it south (FIGURE 6.14). The citrus canker of 1984 and the severe freeze of 1985 drove many growers out of business. But citrus production has always come back.

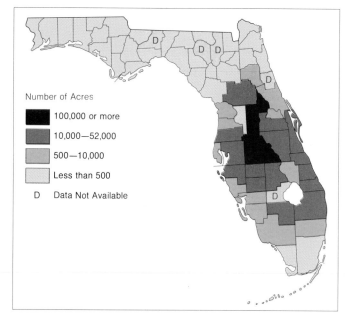

Number of Acres

■ 100,000 or more

■ 10,000–52,000

■ 500–10,000

□ Less than 500

D   Data Not Available

FIGURE 6.14 *Acres of Orange Trees in Florida by County*
There is no data for acreage between 52,000 and 100,000.

Yet citrus accounts for only 30 percent of Florida's agricultural sales. Other fruit and vegetables such as strawberries, watermelons, tomatoes, corn, and lettuce are of major importance. Since the Second World War, Florida's farmers also have developed a high-quality cattle industry, which is concentrated in the central and southern parts of the state.

Forestry, mining, and manufacturing generate large amounts of income. In the twentieth century, the invention of modern processes to turn pine into pulp has made forestry a major industry, especially for the northern part of the state, which furnishes major quantities of pulpwood and saw lumber. Corporate lumber holdings in Florida are very large: over three million acres of land, second in the South after Alabama. Phosphate mines long were important, but recently light manufacturing has clustered in the Dade County, Tampa Bay, and Orlando areas. These communities welcome the support manufacturing gives to their tourist-based economies.

Varieties of Water Pollution

Stories about toxic waste dumps lead the public to think of pollution as a problem of poisonous chemicals. In fact, pollution can result from the introduction into an environment of any contaminant, even substances not dangerous in themselves. The Florida experience highlights the variety of situations that can degrade environmental quality, especially water quality.

Many of the warm, shallow lakes in Florida's central highlands face the danger of eutrophication, which is the lowering of dissolved oxygen in the water due to the introduction of mineral and organic nutrients. As waters become eutrophic, animals die and plant life takes over, often in the form of smelly algae blooms. Urbanization can add phosphates or other algae-stimulating substances to the water supply, and the runoff from agricultural fertilization also is a problem.

Lowering of the water's oxygen content by any cause can kill fish. One by-product of residential development in Florida has been the creation of some attractive waterfront homes bordered by dead canals. By dredging 20-foot-deep canals, developers have obtained the fill on which to build houses, each equipped with a dock for pleasure boats. But the lack of circulation in the dead-end canals causes them to grow stagnant, lose their oxygen, and die.

The problem with pollution from paper mills sometimes is not chemicals but the volume of sediments or particulate matter discharged. The effluent from a paper mill includes small pieces of wood and bark, cellulose fibers, and dissolved lignin (a woody-tissue carbohydrate). Measurements at a Canadian mill once showed that a staggering 50 percent of the material consumed in making paper was being emitted as effluent into surrounding streams or rivers. These particles cloud the water, depriving plants of sunlight, and can silt up a stream, burying vegetation and overwhelming fish.

Even fresh water can degrade a saltwater environment. The dredging of a large canal for Golden Gate Estates, an ill-conceived and unsuccessful development in the Big Cypress Swamp, greatly increased the flow of fresh water into the Gulf of Mexico. As a result, marine life dependent on brackish water in Fahka Union Bay decreased markedly. The bay had been "polluted" by fresh water.

7 THE EAST GULF COASTAL PLAIN

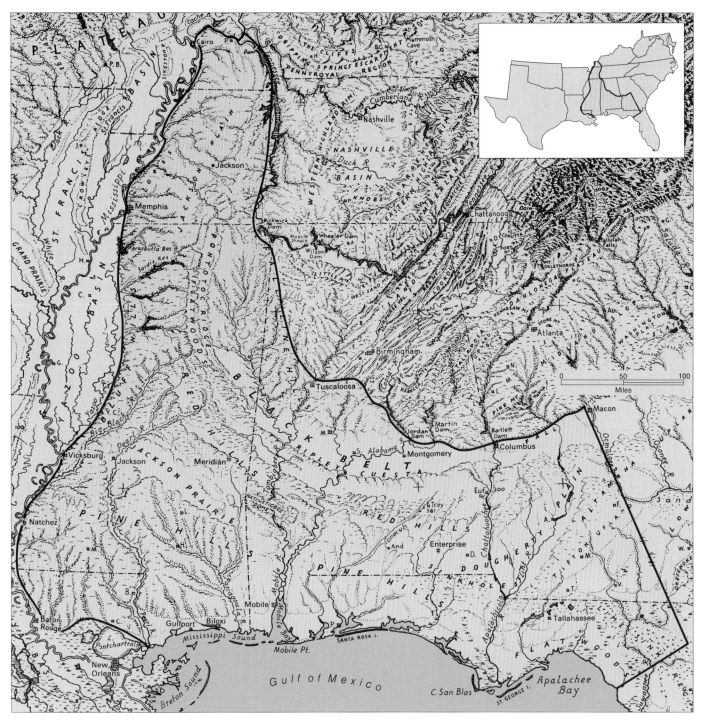

FIGURE 7.1
The East Gulf Coastal Plain

The East Gulf Coastal Plain is historic Deep South cotton country. It was here that plantation owners in the upper South moved as their original farmlands were exhausted in the rush to meet the voracious appetite of English cotton mills. The resulting southwestward frontier movement was quick and dramatic. Between 1810 and 1830, Mississippi's population increased 4-fold, but this paled in comparison with Alabama's 34-fold multiplication, from barely 9,000 to over 310,000, during the same 20-year period.

The new environment of these plantation owners and yeoman farmers was similar to but somewhat more expansive than the Atlantic Coastal Plain where many of these settlers originated. Only 200 miles wide in southwestern Georgia, the East Gulf Coastal Plain widens steadily to reach nearly 500 miles inland, where it encounters the Mississippi Valley (FIGURE 7.1). At that point, it extends well into western Tennessee and even comprises the southwestern tip of Kentucky. This widening of the plain is related to a crustal depression which allowed ancient seas to flood the interior during the Cretaceous period and Eocene epoch. This is the same depression through which the Mississippi River flows.

The early settlers encountered a shift in the direction of river drainage, from the Atlantic Ocean to the Gulf of Mexico, as they crossed onto the Gulf coastal plain. More important was the thickening of the underlying strata associated with the widening of the coastal plain. The thick seaward-sloping beds of sandstone and shale eroded more slowly than intervening layers of water-soluble limestone (called differential erosion), creating a belted topography comprised of alternating ridges and valleys roughly parallel to the coastline. As FIGURE 7.2 shows, the resistant layers formed ridges that face inland where they were exposed to the surface. These ridges, known as *cuestas,* formed escarpments that rise abruptly as much as 300 feet above the adjacent valley. In contrast to this steep escarpment, the seaward-facing side of the layer slopes gently into the valley on its backside. These escarpments form the most prominent features on an otherwise monotonous topography.

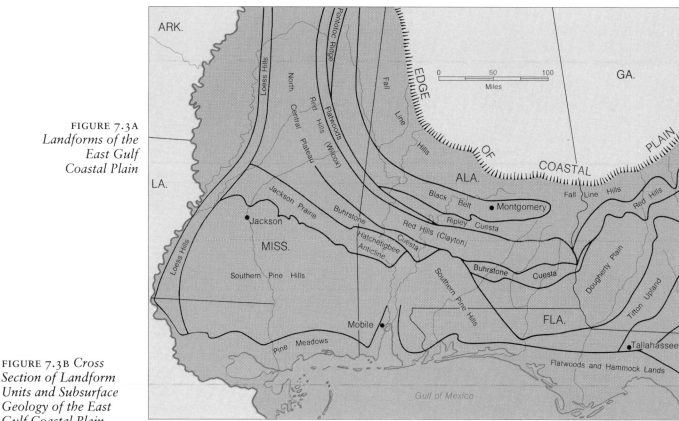

FIGURE 7.3A
Landforms of the East Gulf Coastal Plain

FIGURE 7.3B *Cross Section of Landform Units and Subsurface Geology of the East Gulf Coastal Plain*

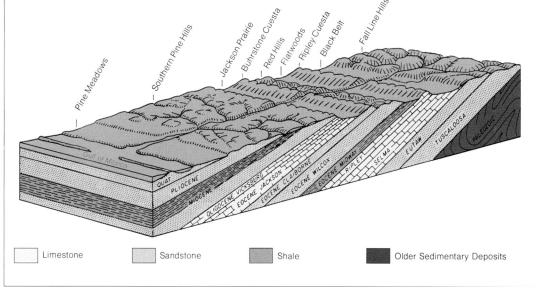

Limestone Sandstone Shale Older Sedimentary Deposits

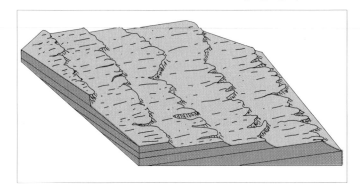

FIGURE 7.2 *Coastal Plain Cuestas*
Cuestas are long ridges that form as the gently tilted strata are eroded.

The soils in the intervening valleys, derived from the weathering of limestone, were relatively fertile and quickly attracted farmers. By contrast, the sandstone and shale ridges yielded a relatively poor soil and consequently often remained forested. Thus agriculture and settlement did not develop uniformly but in pockets, each somewhat isolated from the other. Albert E. Cowdrey noted that " . . . the enclaves of rich soil were enclosed in the usual sandy or hilly regions and pine barrens of poor to mediocre land."[1]

The belted topography of the East Gulf Coastal Plain is shown in FIGURE 7.3, which outlines the major topographic subunits. Three limestone-floored areas attracted antebellum cotton farmers and other settlers. The most notable of these was the Black Belt, a lowland 20 to 25 miles wide that runs from northwestern Mississippi into Alabama east of Montgomery. Part of this area is also known as the Black Prairie. Weathering of the organically rich Selma Chalk bed produced an unusually dark, fertile soil. In part of Mississippi, the intervening layer of sandstone is absent and the Black Belt joins the Flatwoods, a smaller but also fertile lowland area. The second of these areas, the Jackson Prairie, is more central in Mississippi and continues a short distance into Alabama. Actually, it is a lowland that contains many small, fertile black prairies.

The Black Belt near the Alabama-Mississippi state line

To the southeast of the Black Belt is the third area, the Dougherty Plain, which extends from southeastern Alabama and the panhandle of Florida eastward into Georgia. It is a nearly flat plain pocked with surface depressions that formed as groundwater dissolved some of the underlying limestone. One of the peculiarities of this area is that much of the drainage occurs underground through solution channels rather than through surface streams. The maps of cotton production in 1820 and 1850 and the 1860 population map (FIGURES 7.4 and 7.5) show clearly how settlement and farming focused strongly on these limestone lowlands of the East Gulf Coastal Plain.

The remaining topographic units of the region were much less attractive to the early settlers. The inner edge of the East Gulf Coastal Plain is marked by the fall line hills, where the coastal plain abuts on the older, harder rocks of the Valley and Ridge and Appalachian Plateau regions. These hills are as much as 250 feet above adjacent lowlands and are covered with poor soils that typically remain forested. The Tennessee River flows along the northern edge of these hills in some places. Perhaps the most substantial task in completing the Tennessee-Tombigbee Waterway project (see "The Tennessee-Tombigbee Waterway" on page 107) was cutting through these hills in order to connect the two rivers.

The two more striking cuesta-type ridges on the East Gulf Coastal Plain are the Ripley Cuesta, just south of the Black Belt, and immediately south of it the Red Hills, characterized by red-yellow soils on their forested slopes. The southern edge of the Red Hills area is known as the Buhrstone Cuesta, a name that derives from the silica rock suitable for use as mill stones (buhrstones) found there. Next to it, on the coastal side, the limestone layers of the Jackson Prairie were folded into the Hatchetigbee Anticline, and this upturning of the limestone layers through erosion produced a series of lime hills rather than a valley.

The most extensive landform area on the East Gulf Coastal Plain is the Southern Pine Hills, a series of low hills as much as 200 feet high. Red, yellow, and orange-colored soils characterize the sandy and gravelly formations of these pine-forested hills. This hilly region makes up a substantial part of the coastal plain in Mississippi, but it is more narrow in scope in

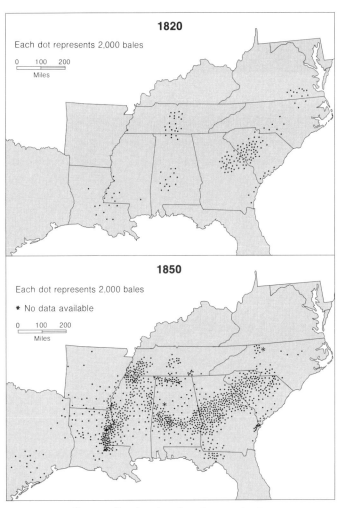

FIGURE 7.4 *Cotton Production in 1820 and 1850*

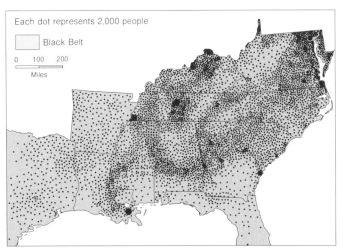

FIGURE 7.5 *Distribution of Southern Population, 1860*

Alabama and western Florida. At that point it widens somewhat and, there known as the Tifton Upland, continues into the Carolinas.

In addition to the limestone valleys of the interior, there is one other lowland area on the East Gulf Coastal Plain, a narrow strip of coastal lowland that extends eastward from Mobile Bay into Florida. It is nearly flat except for low terraces that mark earlier shorelines and form natural levees along the sluggish rivers that cut across the region. This coastal lowland averages about 20 miles in width, except near the Apalachicola River in Florida, where it widens to about 50 miles.

THE COASTAL ECOSYSTEM

The East Gulf Coast is a region of pine forests. Historically and currently they have been a major source of both timber and naval stores (turpentine and resin).

The coast here, as elsewhere, is a complex ecosystem involving several major elements. The *fringe* is the inland margin with swamps, rivers, and springs that bring fresh water to the marshes. Next is a series of *marshes* of various degrees of salinity. Plant life in the marshes varies according to the salinity level. Oystergrass thrives in the saline marshes, whereas wiregrass is more common in the less salty intermediate marshes. The marshes are essential to the life cycle of commercially valuable seafood. As on the Atlantic Coast, it is in these marshes that the larvae and young of the shrimp, blue crab, oysters and various other fishes grow to maturity before returning to the Gulf of Mexico.

Beyond the marshes are the *bays*, bodies of water usually surrounded by the marshes. Standing between the coast and the open water of the Gulf of Mexico are islands, long sandy strips that protect the marshes and bays from all but the worst storms.

The sensitivity of the ecosystem was demonstrated in the 1920s when a Chicago florist, looking for flower arrangement material, stripped the sea oats from a small island off the coast of Mississippi. The entire island and its unprotected dunes disappeared during a 1926 hurricane.

CLIMATE

The East Gulf Coastal Plain has classic Deep South climatic conditions. The average number of frost-free days exceeds 210 days per year in the northern part and 300 days along the coast. Annual precipitation ranges between 45 and 60 inches a year and is evenly distributed throughout the seasons, even though droughts are not uncommon during the growing season. Winters are mild with only occasional cold snaps, while summers are hot and humid. These conditions are ideal for growing cotton and other frost-sensitive crops.

Daily weather is influenced heavily by proximity to the Gulf of Mexico, where large warm maritime air masses generate and move inland. These air masses yield frequent thunderstorms as the unstable air in them is heated in the passage over land. Such storms provide a large part of summer precipitation.

Less common but more spectacular are the tropical storms that occasionally lash the Southern coast, including the East Gulf portion. The coasts of Alabama and the western panhandle of Florida experience the greatest number of destructive tropical storms in the United States, along with smaller areas on the southern tip of Florida and the northern coast of North Carolina (FIGURE 7.6).

FIGURE 7.6
Frequency of Destructive Tropical Storms

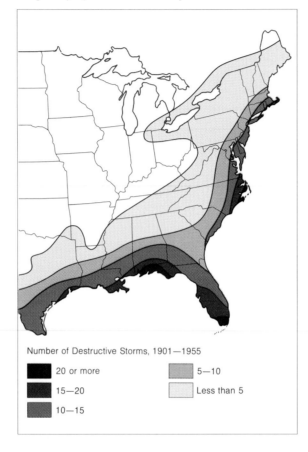

Number of Destructive Storms, 1901—1955

- ■ 20 or more
- ■ 15—20
- ■ 10—15
- ▨ 5—10
- ☐ Less than 5

Satellite photograph of Hurricane Gloria as it approached the South Atlantic coast on September 26, 1985

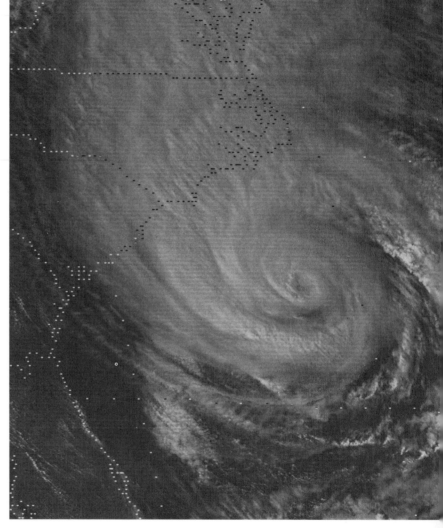

Hurricane-driven seas near Cape Hatteras, North Carolina

The most serious of these tropical storms are hurricanes, large and extremely powerful systems that usually develop over the warm waters of the Caribbean Sea. Hurricanes may be 100 to 300 miles in diameter and pack winds of 75 to 125 miles per hour. They are not unique to the Gulf Coast but are a striking feature of the weather there. Moving capriciously throughout the late summer–early autumn hurricane season (FIGURE 7.7), hurricanes sporadically attack the Atlantic and Gulf coasts of the United States.

Major Hurricanes

Hurricanes are graded on a scale of 1 to 5 according to the Saffir/Simpson Hurricane Scale. A value of 3 or higher indicates a major hurricane: least barometric pressures fall below 28.47 inches of mercury, wind speeds exceed 110 miles per hour, and the storm surge reaches at least 9 feet. Damage is usually extensive. Otherwise lower-graded storms can be classed as major if they move faster than 30 miles an hour or have unusually high storm surges.

Between 1900 and 1982, 55 major hurricanes (and 81 minor ones) hit the coast of the United States. Of these, 51 came ashore somewhere in the South. Of this group, 8 of the 10 biggest killers struck before 1940 and none since 1957. By contrast, 9 of the costliest (in terms of 1980 dollars) occurred after 1950. Only 3 of the 10 most intense storms hit after 1950. Of the total of 54 major storms to arrive in the United States between 1903 and 1982, the pattern is revealing. The 20-year average was the same for the first four decades, while it rose somewhat during the 1943–1962 period. Nine occurred during the 1950s alone. This is identical to the entire 20-year total for 1963 through 1982.

The year 1985 experienced another outbreak, with 6 hurricanes and 2 other tropical storms striking either the Gulf or Atlantic Coast, the most coastal strikes since 1916. Total damage attributed to these 1985 storms was estimated to be as high as $4 billion. That level of damage reflects the amount of commercial and residential building development that has occurred in recent years. Both the 1986 and 1987 seasons were, in contrast, unusually quiet.

TABLE 7.2
Major Hurricane Frequency in the U.S.

Years	No. of Major Hurricanes
1903–1922	14
1923–1942	14
1943–1962	17
1963–1982	9

FIGURE 7.7 *Tracks of Major Southern Hurricanes, 1969–1986*

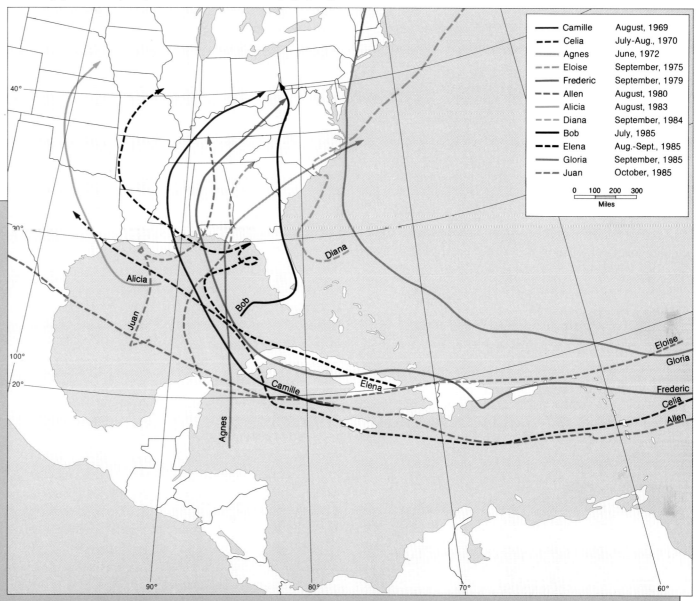

—— Camille	August, 1969	
- - - Celia	July-Aug., 1970	
—— Agnes	June, 1972	
- - - Eloise	September, 1975	
—— Frederic	September, 1979	
- - - Allen	August, 1980	
—— Alicia	August, 1983	
- - - Diana	September, 1984	
—— Bob	July, 1985	
- - - Elena	Aug.-Sept., 1985	
—— Gloria	September, 1985	
- - - Juan	October, 1985	

TABLE 7.1 *Worst U.S. Hurricanes, 1900–1986*

	DEADLIEST (number of lives lost)		COSTLIEST DAMAGE (adjusted to 1980 dollars in millions)		STRONGEST AT TIME OF LANDFALL (inches of mecury)	
1.	Galveston, Texas (1900)	6,000	*Agnes*, Northeastern U.S. (1972)	$4,700	Florida Keys (1935)	26.35
2.	Lake Okeechobee, Florida (1928)	1,836	*Betsy*, Florida/Louisiana (1965)	$4,670	*Camille*, Louisiana/Mississippi (1969)	26.84
3.	Florida Keys/Southern Texas (1919)	600–900	*Camille*, Mississippi/Louisiana (1969)	$3,810	Florida Keys/Southern Texas (1919)	27.37
4.	New England (1938)	600	*Diane*, Northeastern U.S. (1955)	$3,086	Lake Okeechobee, Florida (1928)	27.43
5.	Florida Keys (1935)	408	New England (1938)	$2,632	*Donna*, Florida/Eastern U.S. (1960)	27.46
6.	*Audrey*, Louisiana/Texas (1957)	390	*Frederic*, Alabama/Mississippi (1979)	$2,550	Galveston, Texas (1900)	27.49
7.	Northeastern U.S. (1944)	390	*Carol*, Northeastern U.S. (1954)	$1,733	Grande Isle, Louisiana (1909)	27.49
8.	Grande Isle, Louisiana (1909)	350	*Carla*, Texas (1961)	$1,412	New Orleans, Louisiana (1915)	27.49
9.	New Orleans, Louisiana (1915)	275	*Donna*, Florida/Eastern U.S. (1960)	$1,355	*Carla*, Texas (1961)	27.49
10.	Galveston, Texas (1915)	275	*Juan*, Louisiana (1985)	$1,300	Miami, Florida (1926)	27.61

The high winds and rains of these killer storms cause major destruction, but their most deadly aspect is the storm surge (FIGURE 7.8). Hurricane winds cause ocean waters to pile in front of the storm as it moves. A general rise in sea level can be experienced several hours before a hurricane arrives. The major surge occurs as the center (eye) of the hurricane reaches land, bringing with it a large mound of water that may be 15 feet above sea level and 50 to 100 miles wide. If the surge occurs in conjunction with high tide, it will be unusually large and destructive. Added to the mound of water are battering waves that break on top of it. Few man-made structures, especially if built on sand, can withstand such a powerful assault. Smaller surges may strike the shore several hours after the storm center passes. Even though these surges are smaller, they can be dangerous because they are unexpected.

In addition to damaging property and threatening lives, hurricanes have dramatic effects on the landscape. Channels are closed and opened, sand bars are shifted, and even whole islands disappear in the unstable coastal margin.

Despite their destructive tendencies, however, hurricanes also benefit the Gulf Coast and other areas. Great amounts of rainfall soak large areas, sometimes breaking the common short droughts of summer.

Improved warning systems have decreased dramatically the loss of life from hurricanes in recent years. However, the rapid development of resort communities along the Southern coast has resulted in larger increases in property damage.

EARLY SETTLEMENT

The Americans who followed the cotton frontier into the East Gulf Coastal Plain were not the first settlers to penetrate this area. In fact, the earliest European settlers on the East Gulf Coastal Plain were Spanish. In 1565, they selected St. Augustine as a port from which to provide protection for the western flank of the trade route that followed the Gulf Stream from South America back toward Spain. From that fortified city, bands of missionaries and soldiers penetrated the interior, seeking both Christian converts and gold. These efforts did not reach very far to the west until the seventeenth century, the high-water period of Spanish activity in Florida. A widely spaced series of forts and missions was completed between St. Augustine and Apalachee Bay. They were linked by a path known grandiosely as the Camino Real (Royal Road), probably an existing Indian trading path. One of the points on this trail was San Pedro, the current site of Tallahassee.

To the west of Florida the Spanish encountered the Indians of the Creek Confederacy, at that time one of the most powerful Indian nations in North America. They were too formidable for small bands of Spanish soldiers to subjugate, and they made a poor mission field for the accompanying priests. However, trade ties were established, and the Spanish purchased skins and hides from the Creeks. This scanty trade proved to be insufficient to justify the great expense of maintaining the Florida colony, and in 1763, the colony was transferred to Great Britain. Spain recovered the colony in 1783 after siding with the United States in the American Revolution. Halfhearted efforts to reoccupy the East Gulf Coast were soon overwhelmed by the flood tide of British-Americans moving in from the northeast.

In the vanguard of this early American presence were the "Kaintucks," settlers from the Ohio River area who brought their produce down the river to Natchez and New Orleans. After floating cargoes of wheat, flour, hides, furs, tobacco, hemp, and barreled pork on log rafts down the river, they found it impossible to return against the swift river currents. Instead they chose to follow an old bison and Indian trail that wound 500 miles across Mississippi and northwestern Alabama to Nashville, Tennessee. Beginning about 1785, the Natchez Trace was followed by thousands of returning "Kaintucks," many of whom squandered their money in Natchez or New Orleans or were robbed as they traveled home. Steamboats ultimately provided an easier passage home, and the Natchez Trace, never much more than a wide trail, lost most of its traffic by the 1830s. Today, tourists can travel this once arduous trail in comfort along the Natchez Trace Parkway.

Sixteenth-century Spanish explorers had penetrated far into the East Gulf Coastal Plain and even attempted to establish a colony on Mobile Bay, but it did not last. The first permanent European settlement in Alabama, in fact, was not Spanish but French. A successful colony was started by the French at Mobile Bay in 1711. French control of the coast remained in effect until 1763, when the area was ceded to Great Britain as a result of the French-and-Indian War. Mobile then became Spanish territory in 1783. In 1813, the port was seized by American forces during the War of 1812, and for the first time all of the state of Alabama was part of the United States. In the following year, Andrew Jackson defeated the Creek Indians at the Battle of Horseshoe Bend, effectively removing a major obstacle to American settlement of the interior of the East Gulf Coastal Plain. Other Indian groups were rapidly subjugated and their land opened to the invaders.

Settlement in the nineteenth century followed cotton, and cotton was grown in the rich soils of the belted coastal plain valleys and in the valleys of Mississippi River tributaries that reached into western Mississippi. The production of swine, cattle, corn, and sweet potatoes was also important in the region, despite the preoccupation with cotton.

FIGURE 7.8 *Hurricane Storm Surge*

The Boll Weevil

Southern cotton farmers from the beginning had to contend with many problems, including drought, loss of soil fertility, and fluctuating prices. But in 1894, a new evil was reported for the first time—the boll weevil. A grayish insect (*Anthonomus grandis*), it punctured the cotton bolls to lay eggs in them. The resulting larvae devoured the cotton inside the boll, thereby destroying the crop. The extreme nineteenth-century specialization in cotton made the Southern farmer especially vulnerable to this pest. As shown in the map, the boll weevil spread rapidly from Texas into the rest of the region. Losses in the early twentieth century were estimated to run as high as two million bales a year, one-third to one-quarter of the total crop.

The devastation was widespread and crippling. In one Texas county at the turn of the century, it was reported that nearly half the farms were abandoned and one-third of the stores in town were closed. Initially farmers resisted using some of the control methods for containing the pest, and they were reluctant to diversify their crops. In contrast, farmers around Enterprise, Alabama, after seeing their cotton crop wiped out, switched to soybeans, peanuts, and other crops which brought them new-found prosperity. They were so grateful that, in 1919, they erected a monument to the boll weevil bearing the inscription "In profound appreciation of the boll weevil, and what it has done as the herald of prosperity."

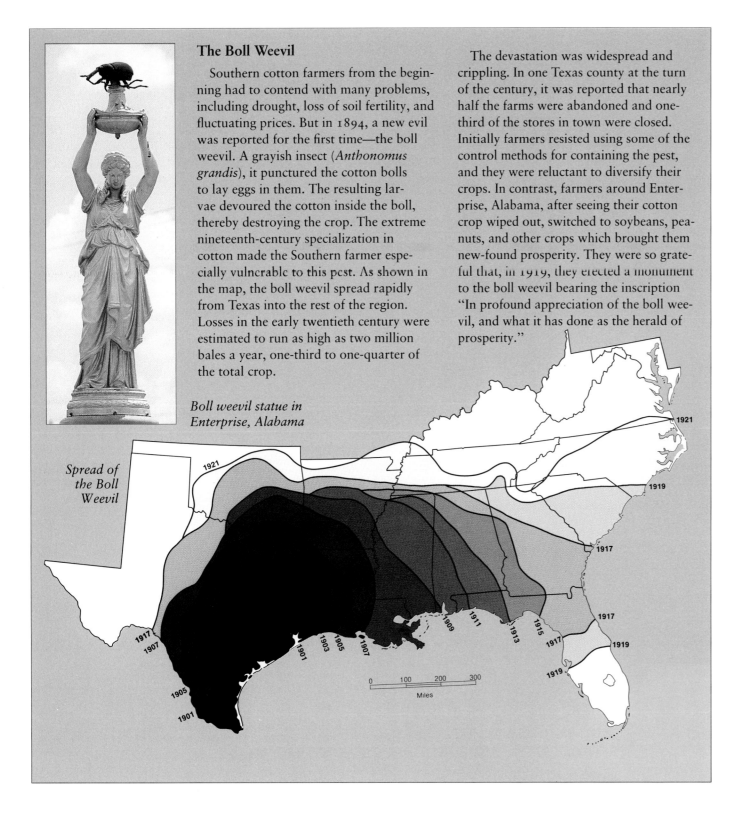

Boll weevil statue in Enterprise, Alabama

Spread of the Boll Weevil

BLACK BELT

The core of the early development pattern that persists today was the fertile Black Belt that lay between the fall line hills and the Ripley Cuesta.

Initially, footloose "farmer errants" who moved in from the Upper South avoided this valley because of hostile Indians and because they did not know how to cultivate the poorly drained, organically rich soils. Instead they sought out wooded river valleys, which were more familiar even if far less fertile. The Black Belt did not begin to fill rapidly until the 1820s, as small farmers were successful in draining the land. They were soon followed by wealthy Gulf Coast and Eastern planters who assembled large plantations on the rich Black Belt soils and drove out many of the smaller operations. Thomas Law rode through the area in the early 1830s and reported that he had "passed some fine plantations and staid this night at an old dutchman's." The host "lived in a very good house and at one of the most beautiful places I ever beheld," and as he moved through the Black Belt, Law noted that "the crops in these lands surpass anything I ever beheld."[2]

The heavy crops of cotton posed new problems for a developing territory—getting the bales to market. Prerailroad overland transportation was primitive and expensive, so the Gulf-flowing rivers became vital highways as barges and then steamboats moved the bulky bales from the Black Belt plantations down the Alabama, Tombigbee, and other rivers to Mobile. That sleepy port city became a major cotton trading and shipping center, as its hinterland was occupied by King Cotton. The only territorial consequence of the War of 1812 was that, for the first time in its history, Mobile became a United States city, a fact which greatly enhanced its emergence as a cotton port.

The Black Belt became a center of antebellum plantation agriculture, and Montgomery was the urban focus of the area. The city not only became the state capital but also served as the first capital of the Confederate States of America, earning Montgomery the title "Cradle of the Confederacy." It was then and is now a major agricultural market center.

After the Civil War, the slave-based plantation system disappeared. Cotton production was maintained by sharecroppers who worked the large tracts of land that typically belonged to former plantation owners.

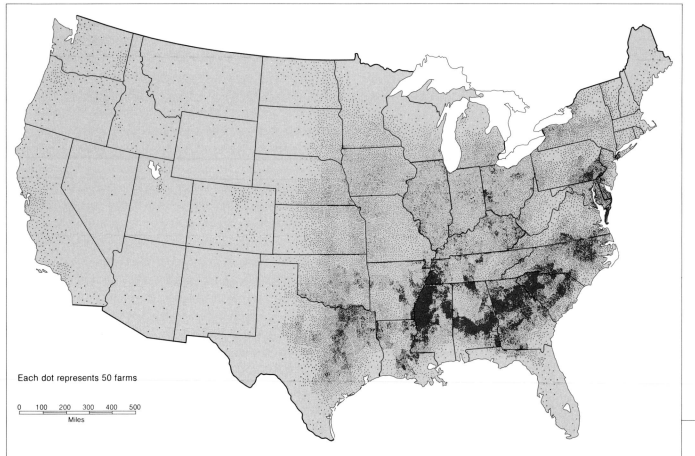

a large population of rural blacks, descendants of former slaves and sharecroppers who are trapped in a cycle of poverty. Thus, ironically, the fertile soils of the Black Belt now form the outline of an infertile crescent. Like most parts of the rural South, it has seen a strong outmigration of its underemployed populations, but until recently, it has not experienced much industrialization to provide jobs for displaced farm workers. This infertile crescent is belatedly going through the transition from a farm to an industrial economy. One example of this transition is Tuscaloosa, Alabama, on the fall line of the Black Warrior River: the Druid City (so named for the water oak trees that border its streets) is not only the home campus of the burgeoning University of Alabama but is also the focus of major industrial growth.

FIGURE 7.10
Distribution of Farms Operated by Black Tenants, 1910

FIGURE 7.9
Distribution of Tenant Farms, 1910

FIGURE 7.9, which illustrates the distribution of tenant farms in 1910, precisely outlines the Black Belt in Alabama and Mississippi. FIGURE 7.10 portrays the incidence of sharecropping by black tenants and thus suggests the extent to which the former slaves continued to be tied to the land in a new form of bondage in the Black Belt and other locales. However, by the early twentieth century, the Black Belt's preeminence as a cotton producer had waned, never to return. The boll weevil devastated the area, and the use of fertilizers elsewhere tended to offset the natural advantage that the Black Belt soils originally offered.

Even though the Black Belt retains vestiges of aristocratic old families and an Old South image, it is today a relatively poor area. Cotton production has shifted to the Mississippi Valley and Texas, and soybeans, livestock, and other crops have become more important. Coexisting with the landholding families is

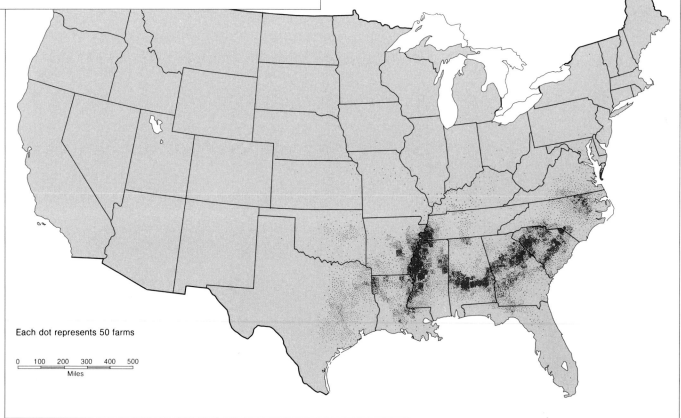

Slave-based plantation systems have been replaced on the East Gulf Coastal Plain by large mechanized farms. Economic growth has shifted from fertile agricultural valleys to urban centers such as Jackson and Montgomery and to the ports of Biloxi, Mobile, and Gulfport. Western Tennessee and northern Mississippi have experienced overflow growth from Memphis. The coastal margin itself has been impacted heavily by the exploitation of major petroleum deposits, some of which occur in southwestern Mississippi, and by the growth of nearby New Orleans.

Shipyard at Pascagoula, Mississippi

The Tennessee-Tombigbee Waterway

The most ambitious specific effort to improve the economic well-being of the East Gulf Coastal Plain area is the Tennessee-Tombigbee Waterway Project. It revives the historic roles of the Tombigbee and Alabama rivers as arteries over which cotton was taken to port at Mobile. In 1985, the Tennessee-Tombigbee Waterway project was completed after 13 years of construction at a cost of $1.8 billion. It is a 234-mile waterway that has a minimum width of 280 feet as it follows the Tombigbee River from Demopolis, Alabama, at the confluence with the Black Warrior River, northward through Mississippi. From Demopolis southward, the Tombigbee is already navigable into Mobile Bay. A massive ditch 175 feet deep was carved through the fall line hills of northern Mississippi to connect the system with the Tennessee River and thus into the entire Ohio and Mississippi river waterways. A controversial project that was almost stopped by President Jimmy Carter in 1977, the waterway is hailed by its proponents as the economic solution of the region, while opponents have attacked it as an exhorbitantly expensive environmental disaster. It may yet be the stimulus to completing the economic transition of the East Gulf Coast and removing the infertile crescent from the map, but initial levels of freight traffic on the waterway have been low.

The Tennessee-Tombigbee Waterway

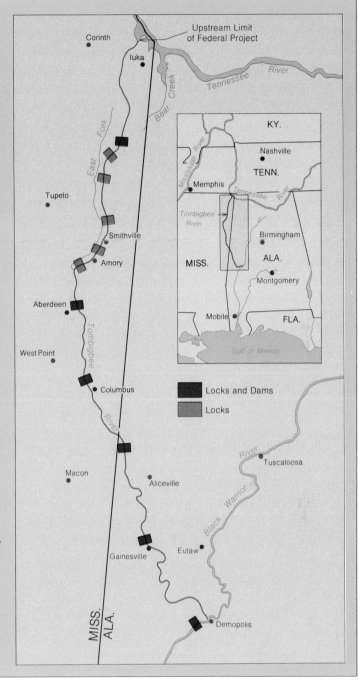

8 THE MISSISSIPPI VALLEY & DELTA

Through the middle of the Gulf Coast lowlands flows one of the great rivers of the world (FIGURE 8.1). The mighty Mississippi, itself a wonder of nature, moves heavy and full across the South to the Gulf of Mexico. For thousands of years, its waters have created and shaped this subregion. The story of the Mississippi Valley and Delta is the story of the river—a constant but changeable force.

The Mississippi River system begins far to the north, east, and west. Collecting the waters of much of the interior of the continent, its many tributaries drain 31 states and two Canadian provinces and make up the fourth-longest river system in the world. On the average, 650,000 cubic feet of water enter the lower Mississippi's channel every second, though the rate has varied from a comparative trickle of 100,000 cubic feet per second to an uncontrollable 4,000,000 cubic feet per second. Suspended in these waters is an immense load of soil carried as silt and sediment: 300 to 400 million tons per year.

The concentration of great natural forces in one river has created a distinct environment along its course. Low lying, sloping gradually toward the Gulf, the Mississippi basin is basically an alluvial floodplain with few marked changes in relief. Its climate—moist, humid, and warm—also seems uniform, and to writers and sages the river is never-changing. Yet this region also holds great contrasts: floodways that are rising, land that is building and subsiding, and terrain that is altering despite ambitious human attempts to control the process. These processes reveal both nature's bounty and its wrath, its creative forces and destructive ones.

The Mississippi Valley long has been both an oasis of great fertility and the site of repeated devastation. In the Delta, land is created at an amazingly rapid pace, yet is destroyed even more swiftly. The river itself is constantly changing, guided by human beings but seemingly contemptuous of them. Here nature's awesome power and man's short-term influence are both on display. This subregion will remain the river's

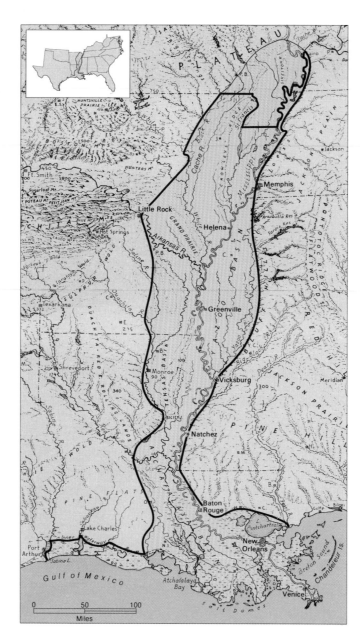

FIGURE 8.1 *The Mississippi Valley & Delta*

province, but its surface could change dramatically tomorrow.

As befits such a region, its people have been vital and varied. Nowhere else in the South did such a variety of cultures take root nor did an urban center the size of New Orleans rise to early prominence. And perhaps nowhere else have Southerners formed so complex a heritage. From its cuisine to its music, this region is recognized as a distinctive part of the South.

FORMATION OF THE REGION AND THE RIVER

The Mississippi Valley coincides with a structural trough in the earth's crust known as the Mississippi embayment. This wide depression in the earth's surface lay beneath the sea in many periods, and differing amounts of it have been exposed or submerged as the earth alternately thrust upward or subsided. Some low places on the trough's surface never became dry and turned into freshwater lakes, like Lake Pontchartrain. The river has cut channels through marine sediments and deposited immense quantities of rich soil throughout its broad alluvial floodplain.

The river system, however, did not always follow its present path to the sea. Before the last Ice Age, most of North America's rivers above the Ohio flowed northward over land or ice that covered Hudson Bay and emptied into the Arctic Ocean. The contemporary drainage pattern, which adds to the Mississippi large quantities of water from the central and northern Rockies, formed after massive glaciers began to melt and retreat. The melting of these glaciers liberated enormous quantities of water that pooled into lakes and then surged southward, carving new channels to the sea (FIGURE 8.2).

The Mississippi and its major tributaries have altered their courses many times through historic and prehistoric times. One prominent clue to earlier pathways is Crowley's Ridge in northern Arkansas and the southeastern tip of Missouri (FIGURE 8.3). Two hundred miles long, this ridge tapers from twelve to three miles in width as it descends from 250 feet to 100 feet

FIGURE 8.2

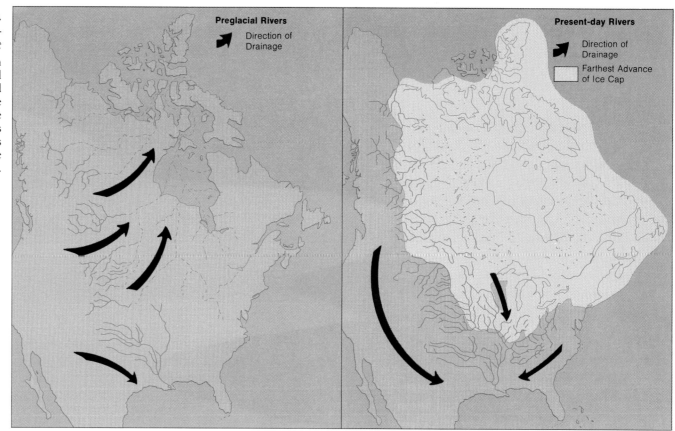

During the last great Ice Age, the drainage patterns of North America underwent a drastic change. As the map of preglacial drainage shows, major river systems flowed northward (dotted lines show earlier river courses). After crossing land or the ice shield that then covered Hudson Bay, they emptied into the Arctic Ocean. The Ice Age's glacier blocked these rivers and dammed up their waters until torrents cut new paths leading southward. The result was the pattern of drainage familiar to us today.

above the alluvial plain. Its surface was part of the uplifted trough before torrents of water, fed by melting ice, cut into the plain. The present-day valleys on each side of Crowley's Ridge are so broad that almost certainly an earlier Mississippi River scoured the passage to its west while the Ohio River cut the trough to its east.

Just as rivers can cut channels through rock or layers of sediments, they also lay down soils in their floodplains. This is what the wide, slowly moving Mississippi has been doing in recent geologic time. Steadily it has been filling up the most recent trough cut by glacial floodwaters. Alluvial deposits beneath the river's channel measure as much as 200 feet near Memphis, and deposition of soil continues. During normal spring floods, the river spreads fertile deposits widely over its floodplain.

Meanwhile, a general sinking process is also underway. The crust of the Mississippi Valley and Delta region is slowly subsiding and occasionally has shifted abruptly along a fracture zone. The famous New Madrid earthquakes of 1811–1812 would have caused tremendous fatalities had the area been densely settled. That sudden subsidence of part of the earth's crust caused many lakes to form, notably Reelfoot Lake in western Tennessee, which is 20 miles long and as deep as 20 feet.

Sinking is another major factor at the Mississippi's mouth, where new land builds up as a large portion of the river's burden of silt finally settles out (see FIGURE 8.9 on delta formation). This soft mud also compacts, however, and thus tends to sink under the weight of new deposits. The rate of sinking or building up of delta land is dependent on the river's flow and on human interventions in river processes.

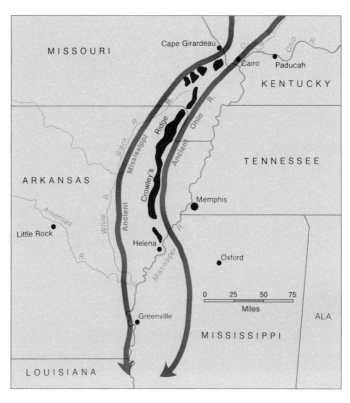

FIGURE 8.3
*Ancient Courses
of the Ohio and
Mississippi Rivers*

One other ancient feature of this subregion is an unusual one: its bluff hills (FIGURE 8.4). On the eastern side of the Mississippi and roughly adjacent to it, these bluffs are hills made of loess, which is a mealy, chalky material composed of calcium, calcium carbonate, or limestone. Rising 125 to 250 feet above the floodplain, these bluffs formed from wind-blown deposits of loess that remain 30 to 100 feet thick. The immense weight of glaciers ground stone into this fine powder, and prevailing winds deposited huge amounts of it in what is now the Mississippi River Valley.

Although these loess bluffs are not hard, water easily percolates into them, and thus they retain some very steep slopes. The locations of several major cities—Memphis, Vicksburg, Natchez, and Baton Rouge—combine the Mississippi River and a loess

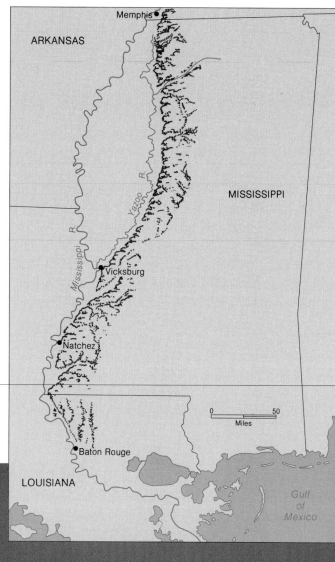

FIGURE 8.4
The Bluff (Loess) Hills

bluff in close proximity. These cities grew because they enjoyed superior transportation facilities. A rail terminus on the bluff would not be subject to flooding, yet transshipment via the river immediately below was easy.

Such advantages of location and transportation helped Memphis to develop rapidly into a major port and cotton market after its formal establishment in 1819. The disruption of cotton commerce by the Civil War and a yellow fever epidemic in 1878 greatly slowed the city's growth. But in the twentieth century, its superior transportation facilities helped Memphis regain momentum. Today it is the world's largest inland market for both cotton and lumber, as well as a city whose people made great contributions to Southern music, especially the blues.

Memphis, which grew to importance as a major river port and cotton market, has regained its vitality in the twentieth century through reliance on its fine transportation facilities.

FLOODPLAIN, BACKSWAMPS, AND BAYOUS

Except for the bluff hills, the Mississippi Valley and Delta region is a long, broad floodplain with a gradual slope and very little relief. Yet within this overall pattern, the river combines with small variations in elevation to create interesting drainage systems and habitats.

Almost 500 miles long, the Mississippi Valley varies in width from roughly 50 to 150 miles. Its widest portion is at the mouth of the river, where the Delta and the coastline merge in a long series of wetlands. The river's long valley slopes very gently toward the Gulf of Mexico—only eight inches per mile, on the average. Where the Ohio River joins the Mississippi, the elevation above sea level is 275 feet, but in northern Louisiana it has diminished to only 100 feet. From there southward the gradient is even more gradual, less than six inches per mile for the last 250 miles. If one takes into account the river's many twists, turns, and meanders, the slope is only three inches per mile or less.

This means, clearly, that the giant Mississippi tends to become ever more sluggish and slow-moving as it nears the Gulf. Some geographers have openly wondered how it manages to carry its tons of silt as far as it does. The same is true for smaller streams that join the Mississippi or eventually make their own way into the ocean. With little elevation or slope, drainage is naturally very poor. In addition to these facts, basic alluvial processes of the Mississippi magnify the problems and complicate the patterns of drainage.

Although people living near the river have been preoccupied with levees at least since the days of French control, the Mississippi actually builds its own levees. On each bank, wedge-shaped deposits of sediment build up with every flood. When the swollen river tops its banks, the current slows where water spills out onto the surrounding land. Suspended particles immediately begin to sink, and the largest and heaviest of them come to rest close to the original banks. The sediments are highest near the river, slope down away from it, and thus form a natural levee (FIGURE 8.5). In the disastrous flood of 1973, for example, floodwaters added three feet of sediment to the height of the Mississippi's levees.

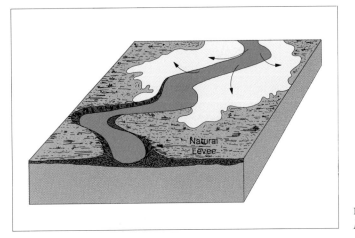

FIGURE 8.5
Formation of Natural Levees

Natural levees also grow in size and height because sediments tend to fill up the channel; then the river crests its banks and lays down another alluvial wedge, this one wider and higher than the first. In time, even without human efforts at flood control, the Mississippi would naturally flow *above* the adjacent land. In fact, almost anywhere in Mississippi and Louisiana a person looks *up* toward the river, which at high water can be flowing 15 to 20 feet above the surrounding land.

Levee building by the Mississippi complicates the drainage of nearby land. Since the whole valley is low lying and flat, smaller streams cannot carry rainwater and runoff uphill toward the Mississippi. The tendency of the great river to raise its channel and levees creates basins called *backswamps*. Water that falls in more distant parts of the valley runs into streams that move along, parallel to the Mississippi and sluggish, for miles. Only a shift in the river's course or a local zone of subsidence allows these potential tributaries to join the big river at last.

The levees on either side of the Mississippi River rise above the water and the land they protect. At times of high water, one can glimpse large boats passing well above ground level.

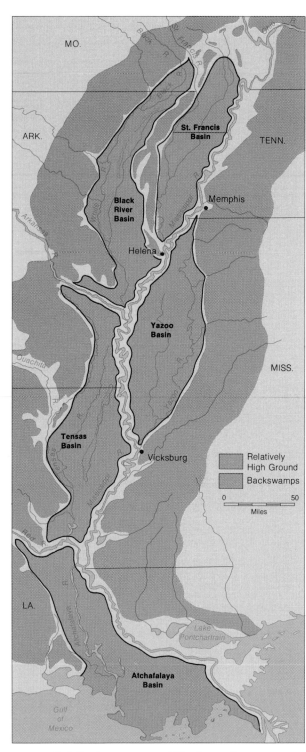

FIGURE 8.6 *Backswamps and Drainage Patterns of the Mississippi River*

Along the river's course in this region are five such backswamps (FIGURE 8.6). From south to north, they are the Atchafalaya Basin, the Tensas Basin, the Yazoo Basin, the Black River Basin, and the Saint Francis Basin. Except for the Yazoo Basin or, as it is popularly called, the Yazoo Delta, all lie on the west bank of the Mississippi. The Yazoo Basin well illustrates the complicated surface drainage patterns of backswamps.

At Memphis and at Vicksburg, the Mississippi swings eastward to the very foot of the loess bluffs. Between the Mississippi and Yazoo rivers lies the Yazoo Basin or Delta. This basin has a gentle southward slope (which is nonetheless greater than the Mississippi's due to the river's many meanders), and an even gentler eastward slope toward the Yazoo River. Streams flow southward almost parallel to the Mississippi, but they twist and turn without joining together in a purposeful way. Similarly, streams in the other basins often parallel larger rivers like the Arkansas for miles. (They are often called yazoo streams.) The Arkansas River itself probably could not have entered the Mississippi if the larger river had not swung close to Crowley's Ridge at Helena, Arkansas, and intercepted its tributary.

Well into the nineteenth century, the fertile Yazoo Basin or Delta was very sparsely settled. The same floodwaters that made its soil so rich rendered it

Miles of saltwater marsh stretch along the Louisiana coast and westward into Texas.

unsafe and undesirable for habitation. Dramatic evidence of the impact of flood control projects appeared almost immediately after 1886. In that year, engineers completed a levee system that offered reasonable protection. People moved in rapidly and established farms that joined the Mississippi Valley's leaders in cotton production. But for the disastrous 1927 flood, which inundated much of the southern part of the Yazoo Delta, people would soon have forgotten that the river had long made this area quite uninhabitable.

The term *bayou* derives from a Choctaw Indian word meaning "sluggish stream," and the word appears on maps next to many waterways in the lower Mississippi Valley. Raising the character of backswamp streams to an even higher degree of development, bayous seem not to move at all. Sometimes, near the Gulf, their waters move slowly in alternating directions, creeping southward with low tide and then reversing their lethargic flow as the pressure of the sea rises. To the casual observer, bayou waters have no pattern—they twist and turn, narrow and then widen into pools, and almost merge with water plants, muddy bars, and dense vegetation. The sluggishness of bayous is understandable; they try to flow on land that may be only a foot above sea level.

Watery bayous are not the waste areas they may seem but are extremely productive habitats. The land itself (where it is dry enough for cultivation) is astonishingly rich; its deep black soil can support three or even four crops a year. Millions of birds use the Mississippi flyway for their yearly migration and land on the Louisiana coast. It is North America's primary winter home for migratory ducks and geese; well over half a million geese, plus many other species, arrive there each November. In the spring, bayous become a breeding ground for beautiful wading birds such as the snowy egret. Sea life is even more abundant. Over a hundred species of fish spawn or live in the bayou waters; its brackish and marshy habitats nurture many commercially valuable crustaceans.

Though united by their watery character, bayous can differ considerably to the eye. In their northern reaches, Louisiana bayous are on comparatively high ground, where nonwater-loving hardwood trees grow. Farther south they feature the cypress tree with its knobby knees, profuse vegetation, and Spanish moss hanging densely from above. But near the Gulf and along the western part of Louisiana's coast, the dark shadowy cypress gives way to open vistas of salty marshes with waving grasses. Salt- and freshwater creatures mix in these coastal marshes, which are prime habitats for Louisiana's tasty crawfish and roughly 200,000 alligators.

Freshwater marshes and sluggish bayous predominate farther north and inland in Louisiana.

THE RIVER

From the northern boundary of this region to the Gulf, the river's ways have puzzled, challenged, and threatened Southerners for centuries. Though slow-moving, it is always in motion and constantly changing the land near its banks. The meandering shifts of course and delta building of the Mississippi can affect people almost as drastically as its floods.

Experiments have shown that twists and turns come naturally to rivers; even straight and smoothly flowing streams develop pools and shallow riffles with spacing related to stream width. In a laboratory, such pools and riffles eventually evolve into a series of meanders. The deepest part of a river's channel, the *thalweg*, shifts from side to side as water flows from pool to pool. Meanwhile, the flow reaches its greatest velocity on the surface directly above the thalweg, where friction from below is least. This pattern gives the river its greatest scouring power at the banks of outward bends, while sediment or alluvium builds up most in slower waters near the inner banks that lie opposite.

Once established, this pattern develops a momentum of its own that leads to a succession of meander bends, point bars, oxbow lakes, oxbow marshes, and meander scars (FIGURE 8.7). As the river cuts a deeper, rounder bend, point bars build up opposite

each eroding bank. These point bars typically have concentric ridges and depressions (called bar and swale topography) caused as the water lays down its deposits. Eventually the meander bend takes on a nearly circular shape, the oxbow. Before long, the greater volume and velocity of water in flood season shuns the long oxbow route and cuts directly across, thus forming an oxbow lake. Abandoned by the river, this lake gradually becomes a marsh, but it remains visible for a long time and may appear as a scar long after it has become dry land.

In this way, the Mississippi is constantly changing the boundary between states like Arkansas and Tennessee or Louisiana and Mississippi. Its oxbows also have lengthened navigation considerably, much to the irritation of shippers and river pilots. For a long time, engineers feared to cut across and shorten these meanders, but after the river made a large cut of this type in 1929, by itself and without disastrous consequences, the Army Corps of Engineers undertook to shorten river routes. Sixteen man-made cutoffs have been constructed between Memphis and Angola,

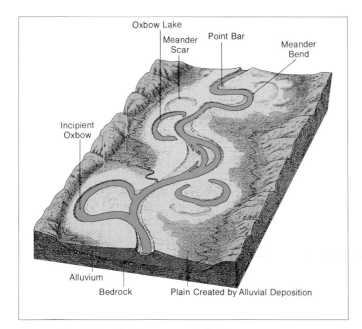

FIGURE 8.7 *Meander Features of the Lower Mississippi River*

The 1927 Flood

The 1927 flood was, said Secretary of Commerce Herbert Hoover, "the greatest disaster of peace times in our history." Beyond question it was as deep and extensive a flood as residents along the lower Mississippi ever want to see. Nearly 20,000 square miles (12.5 million acres) or two-thirds of the entire area subject to overflow was inundated. Two hundred forty-six people died, almost a million were left homeless, and property damage exceeded $400 million in valuable 1920s dollars.

As floods usually do, it came in the spring, when heavy rains coincided with the melting of northern snows. That year the effect of torrential rains was magnified by years of logging and land clearing along the river's tributaries. There was no way to stop the mountain of water. On April 21, it broke the levee, opening a crevasse at Mound Landing, 18 miles north of Greenville, Mississippi. Many workers sandbagging the levee were simply swept away. Charlie Williams, who witnessed it and survived, said that suddenly the wall of the levee "just seemed to move forward as if 100 feet of it was *pushed out* by the river."[1]

The power of the raging water was hard to comprehend. Where the water was deep it swept houses, trees, everything before it. Long after the flood had finally receded, there were blue holes near most crevasses. They were blue because they were so deep; the force of the water escaping from the river's channel dredged out depressions a hundred feet deep.

Despite the tragedy, people managed somehow to cope. Thousands lived for weeks or months in tents atop the levees. Red Cross workers labored around the clock. People prayed and sang; "Shall We Gather at the River" became a popular hymn. And after the flood, people went back to their towns and farms to begin again, as river dwellers have so often done.

The Cabin Teele Crevasse, May 3, 1927, at 5:50 P.M.

The Cabin Teele Crevasse the day after the break

Louisiana (just below the Mississippi state line), shortening river travel by almost 152 miles.

Experts and officials long have debated how best to contain and control the Mississippi's dangers while preserving its benefits. In 1718, when the Frenchman Jean Baptiste le Moyne, Sieur de Bienville, selected a site for New Orleans (the lowest, flattest, and most recently created land of any major United States city), his engineer warned that it would suffer frequent flooding. The building of levees began almost immediately and progressed up and down the river's banks as settlement increased. By the nineteenth century, under United States control, the state of Louisiana employed an official, a civil engineer, to oversee levees. After Congress passed laws encouraging reclamation of wetlands and possibly flood control, a major study of the river began in the 1850s.

Captain A. A. Humphreys and Lieutenant H. L. Abbot charted the river, established some gauge stations along its length, and examined alternative plans for river control. The two basic philosophies were dispersion and concentration—dispersing unmanageable floodwaters through other routes to the Gulf or concentrating and containing them in the Mississippi. Of these two, their report primarily favored concentration through levees, though they foresaw the possibility that the channel would build up and require steadily higher embankments. This occurred, but the levee strategy remained central as federal involvement deepened. In the twentieth century, the United States government assumed primary responsibility for financing and for flood control as well as navigation. And the 1927 flood, which overwhelmed the completed and up-to-grade levee system, forced a re-evaluation of strategies for flood control.

Virtually all the new proposals agreed that stronger levees must be supplemented by floodways, low-lying corridors designed to be flooded in a crisis. These would carry away volumes of water too great to be contained. The idea of a fuse-plug levee, a levee with a section designed to be too small and weak for emergency conditions, also made its appearance. Under the adopted plans, the federal government assumed the entire cost of a superior flood control system combining levees with three new floodways: The Bonnet Carre Floodway, the Atchafalaya Floodway, and the Boeuf Floodway—the need for which was subsequently eliminated after cutoffs for navigation lowered flood heights at Memphis and Natchez (FIGURE 8.8).

FIGURE 8.8 *The Mississippi and Atchafalaya Floodway Systems*

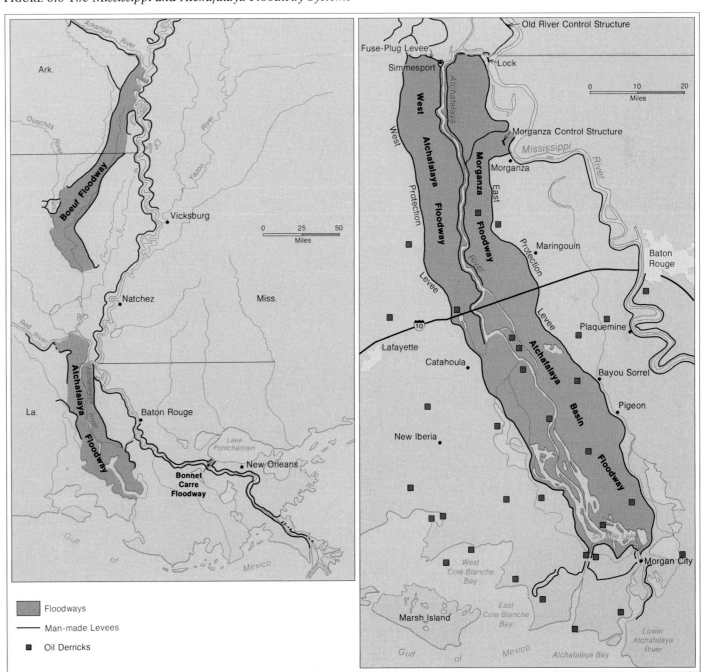

Floodways

Man-made Levees

Oil Derricks

Unfortunately, and almost inevitably, the agreement on this plan did not remove all controversy. Vigorous disagreements occur today, revolving around the effects of flood control efforts on the Mississippi Delta and on the whole Atchafalaya River Basin. Controlling the Mississippi means controlling the enormous load of suspended soil it carries and its resulting land-building activities. Today's problems relate directly to the process of *delta formation*.

Any aggrading (or soil-depositing) river has the potential to create a delta at its mouth. As the river slows and enters the sea, it drops most of its load of sediment and begins to fill its estuary. The Mississippi accomplished this long ago, and ever since, the deposits have built up, forcing the river to find new paths through an increasingly complicated, sinuous web of muddy channels. The shape of a delta varies depending on river and ocean conditions. The Mississippi forms a complex *lobate* or *bird-foot* delta.

Tides and waves have had little effect on its shape because Florida's peninsular arch juts out into the Gulf and calms its surface. Therefore, the river's sediments spill onto the shallow continental shelf and rapidly build up land—so rapidly that a multitude of small shifts of course take place and, at longer intervals, there is a major change in course for the lower river. Today's Delta is a complex of five deltas, some very ancient. It looks more like a bird's foot than a series of overlapping fans, because so much of the land is sinking due to compaction of sediment and to subsidence of the earth's floor. As this occurs, only the higher or main channels of earlier deltas remain above water. Thus, long crooked strips of land remain, similar to the toes on a bird's foot (FIGURE 8.9).

With the Delta subsiding at a rate of one to four centimeters per year, many parts of the Delta have disappeared. Among higher areas that remain are the Chandeleur Islands, lying out in the Gulf 20 miles southeast of today's shore. Once they were part of the Saint Bernard Delta, but after the river's mouth shifted, the intervening land sank. Today the islands are wind-swept, water-washed bars located just above the ocean.

Other notable islands include *cheniers,* from the French for "oak." These wooded ridges are composed of river sediments that were borne out into the Gulf and then were piled up, along with shells, by wave

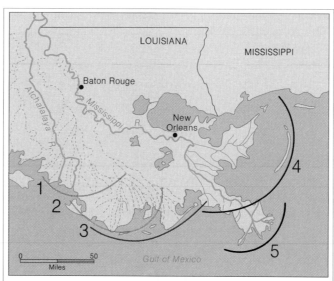

The bird-foot delta of today's Mississippi River (5 ——) is a recent creation, built up during the last 500 years. Four other deltas (1 —— , 2 —— , 3 —— , 4 ——), preceded it as the river sought and found different paths to the sea. The deltas depicted above date back approximately to the time of Christ. Note the Chandeleur Islands in delta (4 ——) which reveal its original extent despite the fact that much of the land built up by that delta has subsided beneath the waters of the Gulf. Dotted lines show earlier stream courses.

FIGURE 8.9 *Evolution of the Mississippi Delta*

action along an old shoreline. The live oaks, with their tenacious roots, got a start there and helped to anchor the soil. They maintain a precarious existence but help to dampen the power of minor storms.

Some of the other wooded hammocks in the Delta sit atop either high salt domes or low mud lumps. Both have an interesting geologic origin. There are five salt islands in the western part of the delta, all conspicuously dry and as much as 150 feet above the marsh. They appeared when salt, mobile under pressure, found a fissure in underlying rock and surged to the surface. During the Civil War, Southerners desperate for salt discovered their composition. The low mud lumps are more numerous and mysterious, but experts believe they form when highly mobile clays, under pressure from accumulating sediments, flow to the surface. Such mud lumps can be a problem for navigation.

The delta's greatest problems today, however, stem from the loss by sinking of tremendous amounts of land near the Mississippi's present mouth and the increasing sediments in the Atchafalaya Floodway. By all indications, the Mississippi is preparing for another major change of course to route most of its waters to the Gulf through the Atchafalaya. These

rivers nearly join just east of Simmesport, where the Old River Control Structure allows less than a third of the Mississippi to take the Atchafalaya's shorter, more westerly route to the ocean. The Mississippi's tendency to shift its flow and the extensive levee and floodway projects have meant less land-building sediments for a wide area around the river's current mouth and a rapidly building area to the west within the Atchafalaya Floodway.

The scale of these changes is tremendous (FIGURE 8.10). To the east, 50 square miles of wetlands are disappearing beneath the sea every year. At that rate Terrebonne, Lafourche, Saint Bernard, and most of Jefferson and Plaquemines parishes will be gone within 200 years; their compacting, sinking wetlands need new infusions of river sediment to stay above water, but the levees contain those sediments and send them out into the ocean. (There they are wasted. They fall off the continental shelf into deep water because the current delta has pushed, at a rate of 300 feet per year, to the limit of shallow water.) Oil-drilling activities, which cut channels through the marshes to accommodate rigs and pipelines, aggravate the problem. They hasten the invasion of salt water, which kills existing vegetation and spoils these brackish zones for their role as nurseries of marine life.

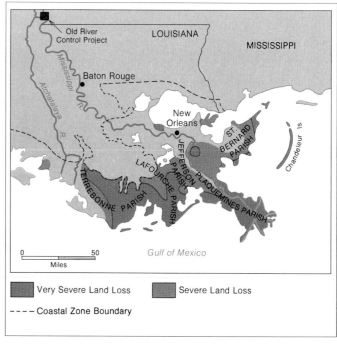

FIGURE 8.10 *Projected Loss of Land in the Mississippi Delta within the Next Two Hundred Years*

Similarly, the changes in the Atchafalaya area are startling. Designed to receive half of the worst flood possible, the Atchafalaya Floodway is already carrying much of the Mississippi and its suspended mud as the river attempts to change course. A satellite camera detected the first new land in Atchafalaya Bay in September 1973. By 1979, there were already 11 square miles of new land built up, and estimates are that 80 square miles will be added by the year 2030. Farther north along the river, the wetland along the controlled floodway is already noticeably dry and relatively high. The river's mud is filling the swamp, making it higher each year and choking its marine life. Farmers have been clearing and planting the fertile land and want to continue, but others worry that an invaluable wetland environment more productive than the Everglades is being lost.

Solutions are not easy and the stakes are high. Two million people live in the flood zones south of Baton Rouge. New Orleans, the nation's biggest port, needs a deep river and has already had its water supply threatened by the sea water creeping near its fresh-water intakes. It will be expensive to divert water onto disappearing wetlands or to try to preserve wetlands that are getting too dry or facing development. The choices are difficult, but one thing is certain: the Mississippi will continue to change and to pose challenges to the people who live near it.

Soybean fields near the Atchafalaya River reveal that this floodway is becoming higher, drier, and more valuable to commercial agricultural interests.

A new delta is emerging at the mouth of the Atchafalaya River, which already carries a large portion of the Mississippi's burden of silt. The Atchafalaya seems determined to capture more of the Mississippi's flow, despite massive human efforts to prevent this.

A RICHLY VARIED PEOPLE

A rich variety of people, undoubtedly the most varied human mixture of any place in the South, have come to the lower Mississippi. After the Indians came the French, the Spanish, and then the English. Acadians, French planters from the Caribbean, Chinese, Filipinos, Yugoslavs, Isleños, and others have also made Louisiana their home. Many came or stayed because of the river, which has always been a focus for trade and human activity. Perhaps the diversity of cultures and life-styles helped residents adapt to the changing river and exploit its fertility.

From early times, Indians used the Mississippi River and settled along it. Some of the largest mounds in North America were built by Indian cultures that grew up around the river. Hernando de Soto was probably the first European to view its wide expanse. In the seventeenth century came other European explorers: Louis Joliet and Jacques Marquette, who traveled from Minnesota to the mouth of the Arkansas in 1673; and René-Robert Cavelier, Sieur de La Salle, who floated from the Illinois River to the Mississippi's mouth in 1682. In 1718, the French founded New Orleans, which became a center for the fur trade. Long before the United States became a nation, colonists used the Ohio to reach the Mississippi and carry products to that great port city.

European powers fought over Louisiana as a rich part of the New World's bounty, and two of the earliest groups to settle Louisiana came after being caught in the middle of these great power rivalries. The Isleños, as they are called today, were Spanish. They came from the Canary Islands in 1778, along with some Iberian settlers, to try to secure Spain's brief ownership of Louisiana. Soon, however, the French reclaimed the territory, and the expanding French plantations pushed them out into the marshes. There they have remained ever since, taking a living from the land and maintaining cultural ties with Spain rediscovered by recent generations.

The Acadians were originally French settlers of Nova Scotia. Britain went to war with France, however, and expelled the Acadians from their northern home in 1755. As many as 3,000 of them made their way to France, where they were largely ignored for 30 years. Finally Spain, eager for settlers, decided to transport them to Louisiana, and thus the Acadians' long exile ended. They brought their French language, culture, and cuisine to Louisiana and have remained a dominant influence in the southern part of the state. Their descendants are called Cajuns.

Disease

Until the age of modern medicine, disease was a major drawback to settlement along the Mississippi. Malaria was endemic in the South, but the use of quinine brought some control of its symptoms. More serious in the nineteenth century were outbreaks of yellow fever. Repeatedly New Orleans suffered outbreaks that sent those who could fleeing in fear and turned public buildings into morgues. Doctors and observers had some awareness that one did not catch the disease merely by associating with a sufferer, and they suspected that some agent was carrying it to new locations. But it was not until the role of the mosquito as the disease's vector was established that drainage and other methods of mosquito control removed a major health hazard.

The major source of French influence in the nineteenth century were the Creoles, those of French background and culture who resisted the oncoming tide of English culture. Their numbers included descendants of early French settlers; more recent arrivals from Canada, France, or the French Caribbean; and considerable numbers of French-speaking free people of color. The Creoles remained loyal to their language and to the Catholic church, and many educated their sons in Canada or France. Whereas French influence in Mobile and certain Mississippi River towns became diluted as American settlers poured in, the Creoles were numerous and determined enough to

leave a permanent mark on Louisiana. The state's contemporary civil law derives partly from French codes, and people in the northern half of the state perceive the French-Catholic south as separate and different. Almost half a million people in Louisiana still speak French.

As long as European powers vied for domination in the New World, New Orleans was a great prize. The Spanish and the French had controlled it for so long that Thomas Jefferson and his ambassadors, James Monroe and Robert Livingston, were astonished when France offered to sell the entire Louisiana Territory for only $15 million. Jefferson had been concerned only about securing a duty-free outlet for American commerce. He hoped to buy no more than New Orleans and west Florida. But, suspending his strict-constructionist principles in the face of this opportunity, Jefferson leapt at a chance to double the size of the nation (FIGURE 8.11).

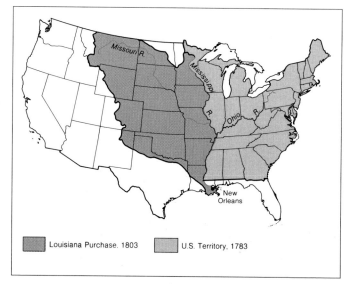

FIGURE 8.11 *Louisiana Purchase*

As Jefferson had realized, New Orleans itself was a highly desirable acquisition. It was a great port, a major city, and the most cosmopolitan of American metropolises, with its Spanish and French influences and Napoleonic law. In 1860, New Orleans was by far the largest city in the South, with 169,000 people; Charleston was a distant second at 41,000. Its dominance might have lasted far longer but for the development of a rival mode of transportation, the railroad, which was slow to connect with the great port.

Louisiana quickly became a rich and productive state. It was a fertile center for cotton production as well as commerce. With cotton plantations came a large black population, and these black people and their descendants added more than labor power and wealth. They also contributed long-lasting cultural influences in food, dance, and music, notably the blues and the rhythms and style of jazz. After French planters fled Santo Domingo in the 1790s, many of them settled in Louisiana and introduced another plantation crop, sugarcane. It was the foundation for many fortunes in the first half of the nineteenth century, and visitors today can view riverside plantation homes that cotton and sugar built.

Within the last hundred years, an amazing number of immigrants have arrived in bayou country. Chinese and Filipinos came to Barataria Bay (on the Delta below New Orleans) and built stilt villages on what was known as the Asian coast. Yugoslavs brought an Adriatic influence to many Delta fishing villages and are known as excellent oystermen. The latest arrivals are Vietnamese refugees, who are using their knowledge of the sea to make a living halfway around the globe.

Not only do these peoples sustain Louisiana's ethnic diversity, but they also contribute to a thriving coastal economy. Many trap and fish in the bayous, catching fish and trapping animals, such as the nutria, for their fur. Louisiana's fishermen bring in small fortunes in crawfish, shellfish, and shrimp. In 1982, the shrimp catch reached 91 million pounds, almost three times what it had been just 50 years before.

In southwest Louisiana's bayou country and along Texas's eastern Gulf Coast, rice is an important product. It flourishes in the wet environment of the bayous and in other areas close to the river northward. Sugarcane also grows abundantly in southern Louisiana. Farther north along the river's floodplains, soybeans, cattle, and cotton are important cash crops. They benefit from the amazing richness of alluvial soils laid down through centuries of flooding (FIGURE 8.12). In one way or another, the crops and the seafood depend on the fertile influence of the Mississippi.

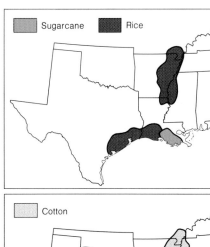

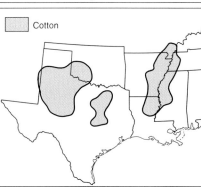

FIGURE 8.12
Major Crops of the Mississippi Valley Region and Texas

9 THE WEST GULF COASTAL PLAIN

The West Gulf Coastal Plain is the largest and most populous of Southern subregions and, incidentally, one of the last to be settled by Anglo-Americans. This rich, dynamic region encompasses much of Louisiana, portions of Arkansas, and a large part of Texas. As shown in FIGURE 9.1, it is bound by the Gulf on the south, the Mississippi Valley and Delta on the east, the Ozarks on the north, and the Balcones Escarpment on the west. Relatively flat and low-lying, the region nevertheless is full of diversity, due largely to the strong north-south variance in its underlying rocks and the considerable east-west climatic difference. Few American physiographic provinces experience such sharp contrasts in these natural features. The variation in geology and climate is particularly important because of their considerable effect on soil, topography, vegetation, and mineral resources.

As a result of a more complex settlement pattern, the cultural variety is also greater here than in many other Southern subregions. The French, Spanish, English, Lowland Southerners, and Highland Southerners converged on this coastal plain to provide a unique setting and character.

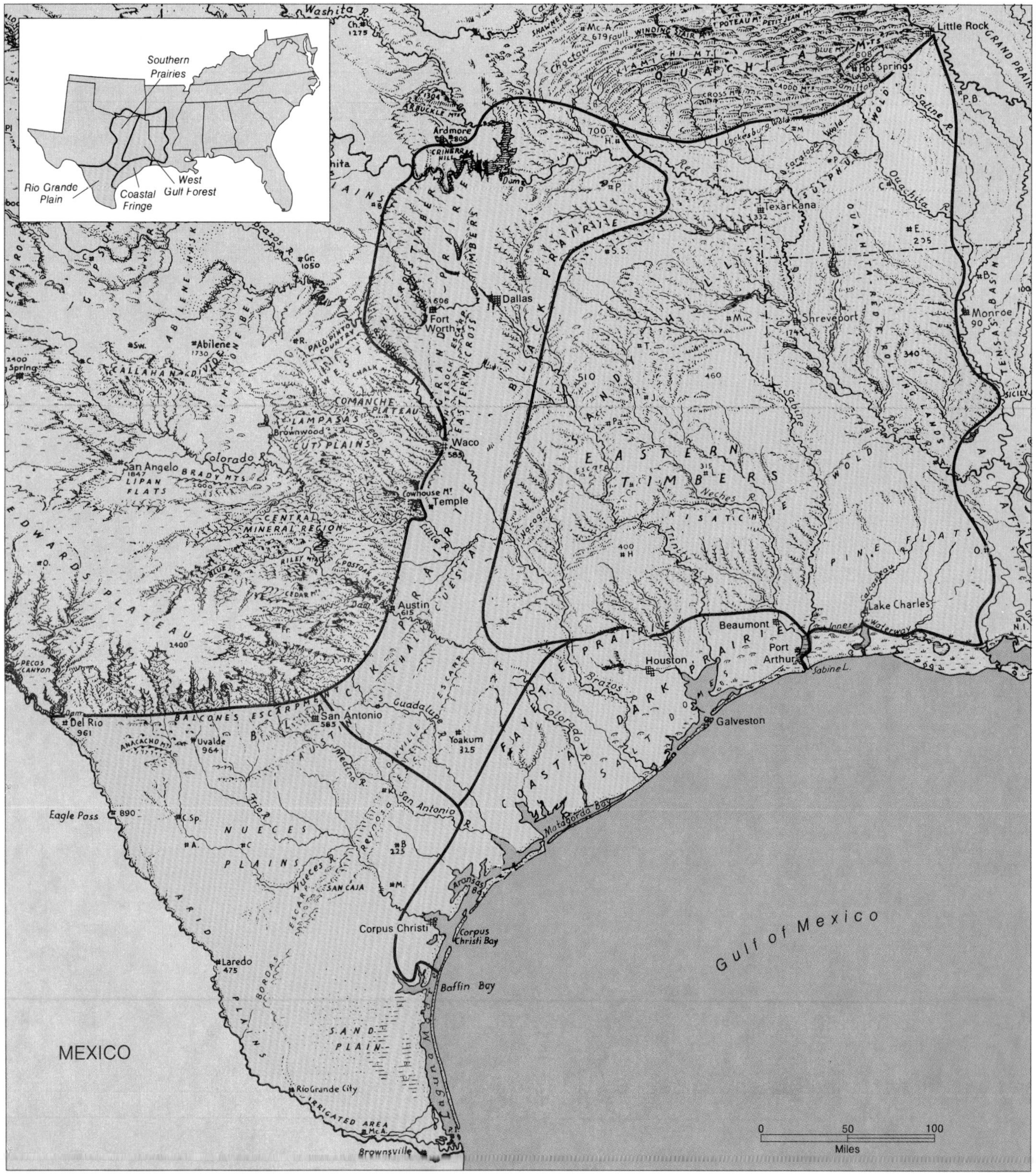

FIGURE 9.1
The West Gulf Coastal Plain

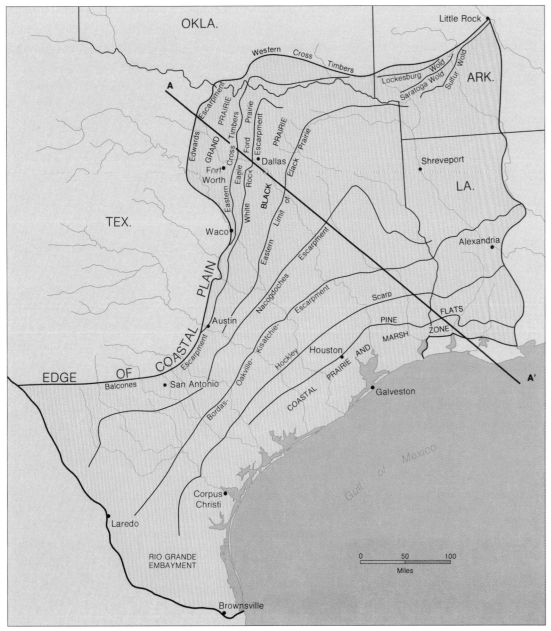

GEOLOGY

The West Gulf Coastal Plain, like the East Gulf Coastal Plain, is underlain by seaward-dipping sandstone, shale, and limestone and therefore exhibits a similar belting pattern. In fact, some of these belts extend from the Rio Grande in south Texas to Georgia. Cuestas with distinctive escarpments (also known as scarps) on the front slopes characteristically separate these belts (FIGURE 9.2). The cuestas were formed from resistant chalk or sandstone.

The underlying rock has been enormously influential in the evolution of topography and soil type. As elsewhere in the humid South, the limestone helps form deep, basic, fertile soils, and the sandstone and shale produce a more acid and less productive soil. As in the East Gulf Coastal Plain, areas underlain by limestone and shale are generally valleys and plains, while sandstone environments typically have greater relief.

FIGURE 9.2A
Landforms of the West Gulf Coastal Plain

FIGURE 9.2B
Cross Section of Landform Units and Subsurface Geology of the West Gulf Coastal Plain

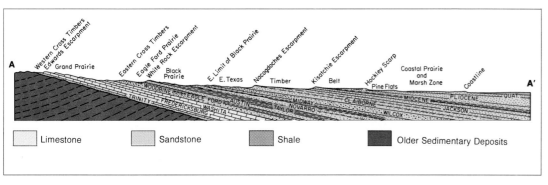

| Limestone | Sandstone | Shale | Older Sedimentary Deposits |

The structural folding and faulting of the area's underlying rocks have provided for the accumulation of oil and gas to make the West Gulf Coastal Plain one of the world's greatest oil-producing regions. The principal structural features of the region include such broad uplifts as the Sabine and Monroe uplifts and the Jackson Dome (FIGURE 9.3). Other folds form broad downwarps called synclines, or basins. Both

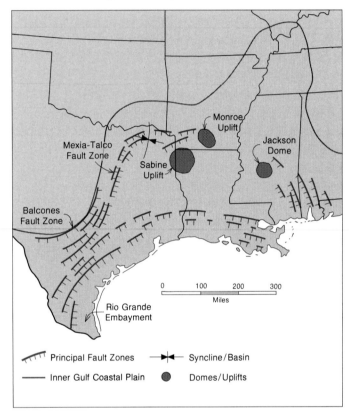

FIGURE 9.3 *Principal Structural Features of the West Gulf Coastal Plain*

uplifts and downwarps often accompany faults or breaks in the rock strata.

Associated with these major geologic structures are hundreds of domes formed by rising salt plugs. These plugs, which may be a mile or more in width, have been squeezed upwards from salt beds lying several miles beneath the surface. As they rise, they lift and drag the rock layers upward. Generally they can be located by surface examination of the topography and geologic structure. The plugs, which consist largely of rock salt, are also the major source of sulfur, salt, and gypsum for the United States. These inorganic elements, together with the area's oil and gas supply, have supported the evolution of a huge regional chemical industry.

CLIMATE AND VEGETATION

In climate, the West Gulf area is quite unlike that of the East Gulf; the transition between the humid east and the dry west found in the Dry Margin subregion also occurs here. Rainfall declines rapidly in a westward direction: from 60 inches annually along the Mississippi Valley to less than 20 inches in the Rio Grande Valley.

There is also a dramatic corresponding east-west change in vegetation. The dense forest that abounds in the east gives way first to tall grass, then to short grasses, and finally to shrubs along the western boundary (FIGURE 2.20). This variance in climate and vegetation, more than any other factor, is responsible for the differences between the eastern and western parts of the West Gulf Coastal Plain.

SETTLEMENT PATTERNS

Centuries of human development took place on the West Gulf Coastal Plain before the arrival of the Spaniards in the early sixteenth century. Sedentary Indian tribes called Caddos occupied the woodland areas of Texas, Louisiana, and Arkansas long before the Plains Indians moved into the adjacent Southwest. They are said to have been intelligent, of great integrity, and quite friendly. The many Caddoan tribes were commonly called Taysas, and the Spaniards made it *Tejas*, a Spanish term for "friend" and the word from which Texas was later derived.

However, the Caddos' numbers declined rapidly after exposure to diseases carried by the Spanish, French, and later Texans and from conflict with these groups. By 1859, when most of the remaining Caddos were transferred to a reservation in Indian Territory, their once-extensive population had been reduced to a few hundred.

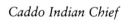

Caddo Indian Chief

Another major group of early Gulf Plains Indians was the Karankawas, who inhabited islands and coastal areas along much of Texas's coast and a thin strip of the mainland. They too were unable to withstand exposure to European and Anglo-American diseases. By 1844, disease and battle had dramatically reduced their number and the remaining few had fled to Mexico, where only six to eight survived in 1855.

Following the American Revolution, many other tribes were forced into the Gulf plain area from the eastern woodlands. They remained only a short period before they were driven farther westward.

Before the Anglo-Americans settled the area, the land had experienced a long period of European occupancy, with French settlement in Louisiana and Arkansas and Spanish settlement in Texas. Both groups were to leave a strong impression on the landscape. France's attempt to establish an empire on the Gulf

Salt dome in the West Gulf Coastal Plain

Coast began in 1682, when La Salle made a voyage down the Mississippi from Canada to the Gulf of Mexico. In 1699, the French established a colony at Old Biloxi, Mississippi. From there they governed all of the Louisiana Territory until 1762, when the French in a secret treaty ceded to Spain that portion of Louisiana west of the Mississippi.

Louisiana's settlers were never content with Spanish rule, and in 1800, Napoleon Bonaparte forced Spain to return the province to France. Thomas Jefferson, then president of the United States, feared French aggression if that country controlled the Mississippi, and that concern led to the American purchase of the Louisiana Territory. French influence remains strong in Louisiana, and this cultural impact is discussed in greater detail in chapter 8.

The Spanish era, which lasted for about 300 years, began in 1519 when Alonso Álvarez de Piñeda dropped anchor at the mouth of the muddy Rio Grande, and it continued until Mexico achieved its independence from Spain in 1821. Texas was incorporated in the new Mexican nation, but won independence from Mexico in 1836.

During this extended period, little success was achieved in establishing Spanish or Mexican settlements. By the early eighteenth century, Spanish exploration had ended with the realization that the area was without mineral wealth—in fact, with a conviction that it had little material value at all. Still, Spain claimed the vast territory of Texas and the American Southwest by right of exploration, but lacked the surplus population and capital required to settle it. For the Spaniards, the focus in North America in the eighteenth century became the diffusion of the Catholic religion. A number of missions were established, most notably at Nacogdoches (1716) and San Antonio (1718). Despite the lack of colonial development, however, Spain was jealous of intruders, and when American filibusters or traders ventured into the area, they were generally imprisoned or shot.

By the late eighteenth century, the Anglo-American frontier had reached the edge of Spanish territory, and with the purchase of the Louisiana Territory in 1803, Anglo-Americans began to flood into the West Gulf Coastal Plain. As shown in FIGURE 9.4, much of Louisiana and portions of Arkansas had been settled by 1830, and by 1850, settlers had migrated into large

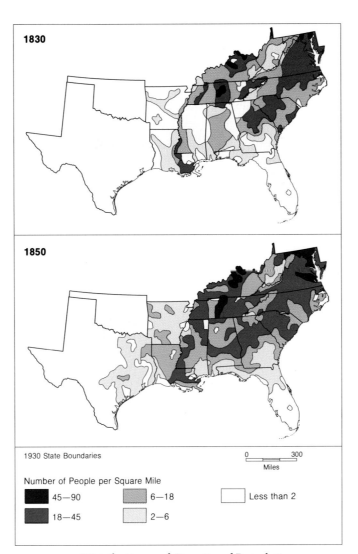

FIGURE 9.4 *Distribution and Density of Population*

portions of the Texas Gulf area. One of the earliest Anglo-American settlers into Texas was Edward Murphy, who acquired a Spanish land grant near the present-day Louisiana-Texas border in 1791. Others followed to combine their farming with wild-horse trading with the Spaniards and Indians.

However, mass movement of Anglo-Americans into Texas did not begin until after 1819, following the enactment by the Spaniards of a very liberal land law. Under its provisions, Anglo-Americans could obtain legal title to land in Texas. Stephen Austin, founder of Little Rock, Arkansas, was the first of many *empresarios* (a Spanish word for "contractor") to take advantage of this law and, by 1825, had established a colony of 1,800 persons in Texas. By the end

of 1830, 20,000 American pioneers had migrated to Texas. Without intent, the Spanish and Mexican governments had created a situation that would lead to the independence of Texas. Once they had opened the door to the aggressive Anglo-Americans, it could not be closed. Texas became independent in 1836 and on December 29, 1845, became the 28th state of an expanding United States of America.

The imprint left by the Spaniards and Mexicans is particularly strong in south Texas. Here, the cultural perspective is Western rather than Southern. Blacks are few in number, the dominant minority is a Spanish-speaking Mexican population, and there is a distinctive Spanish flavor. By 1889, Texas had experienced three other influential streams of migration: Gulf or Lowland Southerners in the east, Germans in the central Gulf plain, and Upland or Highland Southerners in the west (FIGURE 9.5).

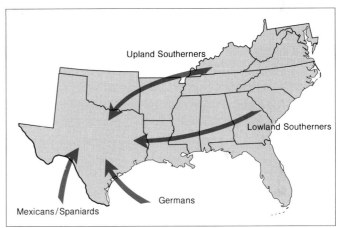

FIGURE 9.5 *Migration Streams into Texas*

Louisiana and southern Arkansas also have had a variety of settlers. Many of them came from other parts of the Deep South, bringing with them a strong rural and agricultural tradition. Additional settlers to Louisiana were of French descent; some had come earlier to the South, and others were migrant Acadians who left Nova Scotia following British domination there. This influence has given Louisiana a special flavor and charm.

The West Gulf Coast's varied climatic pattern, its geologic legacy, and its diverse cultural influences have led to the evolution of distinctive subareas: the West Gulf forest, the Southern prairies, the coastal fringe, and the Rio Grande Plain (FIGURE 9.1).

THE WEST GULF FOREST

The 1803 Louisiana Purchase brought into the United States an extensive pine-oak forest running from the Mississippi Valley floodplain throughout Louisiana and Arkansas. The forest also reaches westward into east Texas, where it is affectionately called the piney woods. Here it forms the western margin of the great Southern forest that stretches southward from Maryland.

The first Texas settlers built their homes and towns here in the piney woods of east Texas. These settlers were woodland people unaccustomed to and fearing the open plains that lay to the west, the hunting grounds of the fierce Comanches. In San Augustine, an early woodland town, several homes that were built in the period predating the Texas republic are still standing today.

Much of east Texas is in the broad timber belt that overlies alternating layers of shale and sandstone deposited during the Tertiary geologic period. Two major cuestas are conspicuous, the Nacogdoches and Kisatchie (FIGURE 9.2). The Nacogdoches Escarpment owes its origin to the high iron content of the marl and greensand from which it was formed. The Kisatchie Escarpment is the most prominent relief feature in Louisiana, where its highest elevation reaches 400 feet. It was formed from the erosion of resistant sandstone.

One of the largest groups of Indians in this area was the Caddoan tribe mentioned previously. While the public is much more familiar with the Comanche Indians who occupied the prairies to the west, the Caddos, who lived in the forested areas of Louisiana and east Texas, had a more advanced and, in many ways, a more interesting culture. The Caddos were farmers and usually grew two crops a year (squash, beans, or tobacco). They also gathered berries and fruit, hunted deer and bear, and fished from local streams. They were different from other West Gulf tribes in that the community at large fed a range of

The Cullen House in San Augustine, Texas

tribal specialists—chief, priests, and craftsmen, none of whom hunted or farmed—in return for their special skills. The rich Caddoan culture began fading by the seventeenth century.

As late as 1801, east Texas was virgin forest. Early white settlers cut the forest to harvest the timber and to make room for cotton and corn as they had in the East Gulf. The method of cultivating cotton in the antebellum South tended to exhaust the soil: lack of crop rotation and fertilizer and extensive soil erosion contributed to a decline in productivity. Consequently, the cotton planters in the south Atlantic and East Gulf states began a steady march westward for fresh soils, leaving behind deserted lands referred to as "Gone to Texas" farms. The extensive amount of abandoned land reflected the magnitude of the immigration to this east Texas forestland. By 1860, cotton had swept Louisiana and east Texas.

This growth occurred during a period of dramatic price swings. In 1801, prices reached 44 cents a pound, and here a farmer could grow a bale an acre (about 400–500 pounds). By 1811, the price had dropped to a more natural level, to 9 cents, and remained near this level for three decades. Between

1839 and 1849, prices dropped below cost, but in the decade preceding the Civil War, they rose to a quite profitable level, to 11 and 12 cents per pound. As cotton continued moving to the more productive lands in west Texas, Arizona, and California, old fields in Louisiana and east Texas were abandoned.

The forest fought back; if a farm was not regularly plowed, trees reclaimed it. By the end of World War II, most farmed land in the Eastern Timber belt had reverted to forest. Then the profitability of raising cattle was discovered, and the bulldozers came to deforest the area again, this time to establish pastureland. Today, much of the formerly forested areas of Louisiana and east Texas is now in pasture; cotton moved West and cattle came East. When fertilized, these generally acidic soils (formed from sand and clay) can carry a much higher density of cattle than can the drier traditional Western ranch country.

A place of great interest to naturalists in the West Gulf forest is Big Thicket. It stands where the eastern woodland begins to change into the western plain and has long been a hunter's paradise—the home of black bears, wolves, and panthers. And it was a significant refuge for slaves and others with reasons to hide.

The Thicket gets 55 to 60 inches of rainfall a year; with its long growing season, vegetation is prolific. The Big Thicket has eight separate plant communities. It is extremely rich in variety; for example, 40 species of wild orchids grow there. It is one of the best areas in the country in which to see forest layering. The typical forest has three layers; the Thicket has six: a top story consisting of large trees such as oaks and loblolly pines, a secondary level characterized by beech and holly trees, a third layer consisting of flowering trees like dogwood and mulberry, a fourth layer containing shrubs like swamp honeysuckle, a fifth layer of herblike plants, and a sixth layer of mosses.

In addition to the Big Thicket National Preserve, the West Gulf forest has four national forests: Sam Houston, Davy Crockett, Angelina, and Sabine (FIGURE 9.9).

THE SOUTHERN PRAIRIES

Westward of the West Gulf forest lies a series of fertile north-south prairie belts formed from underlying limestone strata. Resulting basic soils and moderate rainfall support a tall prairie grass, except in the wetter valley where woodlands grow. Separating these limestone prairie belts are thin outcrops of sand and gravel that originally supported blackjack woods and post oaks (Eastern and Western Cross Timber belts). In the nineteenth century, these belts of forest were widely used as good ground reference points, particularly where they were intersected by north-south flowing rivers. However, so much of the forested area is now in cultivation that these timber belts are often difficult to locate.

Some of the largest cities in Texas are located here—Fort Worth, Dallas, Waco, Temple, and Austin. The Dallas–Fort Worth area is the South's largest metropolitan center and serves as the subregion's political, cultural, and economic center.

Fort Worth is located in the most westward of the limestone belts, the Grand Prairie. The area is relatively dry, and much of the upland is utilized for cattle grazing, while valleys are usually farmed. This belt lies between the two thin Eastern and Western Cross Timber belts (FIGURE 9.2).

The Fort Worth area has few mineral or timber resources. It owes its development to its location; lying on a bluff overlooking the Trinity River, it became an important point on the old Chisholm Trail shown in FIGURE 9.10. From this beginning, Fort Worth has grown to become one of the largest cattle centers in the United States, still proud of its reputation as Cow Town USA. Its motto "Where the West Begins" promises cattlemen friendly greetings. But Fort Worth is also more; its economy has become quite diversified. Today it is an important center for grain storage and milling, oil, and manufacturing.

To the east of the Grand Prairie and Eastern Cross Timbers (and the small Eagle Ford Prairie and White Rock Escarpment) lies a second large prairie belt, the Black Prairie. It overlies an Upper Cretaceous limestone and marl formation. A field of black clay soil has evolved from these soft, calcareous rocks. This belt, more extensive than the Grand Prairie, extends the width of Texas from the Red River Valley to San Antonio, a distance of 400 miles. Its black, deep, rich soil is the best in Texas and one of the state's greatest natural resources. Austin, Waco, Temple, and Dallas are located within the fertile plain.

Dallas has grown from a tiny trading post established in 1841 to one of this country's major cities. It is quite different from Texas's largest city, Houston, in that it has no port and no oil—features that have played such an important role in that city's economy. It has prospered through its role as an important regional trade and commerce center for a four-state region. In contrast to Fort Worth's westward emphasis, Dallas maintains close cultural ties with the east.

The same cattle trail, the Chisholm Trail, that contributed to Fort Worth's existence also ran through Austin, which emerged where the trail crossed the Colorado River. Waco sprang up where the Shawnee Trail crossed the Brazos River.

Big Thicket National Preserve in the Texas Gulf Coast

THE COASTAL FRINGE

The Gulf of Mexico's most productive wildlife zone and its greatest concentration of industry coexist in a coastal strip that extends from eastern Louisiana to Baffin Bay, a few miles south of Corpus Christi, Texas. Here, alongside mudflats, estuaries, salt marshes, shallow lagoons, and inlets, are thousands of oil wells, hundreds of refineries, and an untold number of related industries.

Marine birds, migrating ducks and geese, and hundreds of other species of birds tolerate this intrusion; dolphin play near the many boats; and the fish continue to survive. Still, the area is heavily polluted and nature has been badly abused.

From a geologic viewpoint, the land is very young, having been shaped during the recent glacial epoch. During that time, the coastal area was repeatedly submerged, forming low, flat marine terraces. As shown in FIGURE 9.9, the coastline itself is a long arc made irregular by the estuaries and deltas of the rivers that flow into the coastal plain. The resulting ragged arc is smoothed by a series of barrier or offshore islands stretching along most of the West Gulf Coast. The islands are similar in origin, form, and use to the equally well-known barrier islands in North Carolina. Parts of both of these barrier chains are national seashores, the Outer Banks in North Carolina and Padre Island in Texas.

The saltwater marshes and estuaries that form behind these barrier islands provide the West Gulf area with one of its most valuable resources. Hundreds of species of fish and shellfish spend all or a portion of their lives in this rich and protected environment. Pollution, the dredging of bays, the filling of marshes, and artificial lakes that withhold fresh water have combined to reduce and threaten this tremendous resource. As so often is the case with resources of commons, the interest of the many is subordinated to the interest of a few.

Somewhat in reparation for this abuse, three national wildlife refuges have been established

Whooping crane

here—Aransas, Anahuac, and Laguna Atascosa. The 55,000-acre Aransas refuge is the winter home of the endangered whooping crane. Every fall these very large white birds, each with a wingspan of six and a half feet, migrate from their summer breeding grounds in Canada and fly approximately 2,600 miles to these protected mudflats and shallow bays. They are extremely rare, with an estimated world population of no more than 100. They require large areas within a diminishing habitat. Each pair of cranes will stake out a territory of several hundred acres of marshland and will not allow other cranes into that territory. It is thought that at their peak they probably numbered less than 2,000; thus, their number will probably never be very large.

The second wildlife refuge, the Anahuac, encompasses about 10,000 acres of marshland and salt water. It is a rugged area difficult to traverse. Operating chiefly as a winter feeding ground for ducks and geese, it offers protection to many other birds and animals, among them the rare yellow-tailed deer, mink, otter, alligator, and red wolf. In the early 1970s, along the coast not far from Anahuac, a Christmas bird count of 226 species was recorded within a 15-mile radius in a single day—a United States record.

A third wildlife refuge, the Laguna Atascosa, stretches over more than 46,000 acres of mud flats. While not particularly scenic, it is located where the North American central flyway narrows to funnel large numbers of birds into the refuge. An array of near-extinct birds, 30,000 geese, and 80 percent of the continent's redheaded ducks winter here.

The Karankawas adjusted to this environment in a passive way, doing little to modify or impact it. They survived and tolerated the many mosquitoes and hurricanes. The women dressed in animal skins and Spanish moss, and the men wore nothing.

The Karankawas moved about in dugout canoes, living off both the land and sea. They hunted ducks and deer, gathered berries, harvested oysters and mussels, and fish-trapped in the bay. They made portable huts and clay pots and seemed happy though their lives were hard. When the first white men, Álvar Núñez Cabeza de Vaca and his shipwreck companies, arrived in 1528, they were greeted and treated well by the Karankawas. With time, however, the Indians grew hostile to the Spaniards and reportedly, on occasion, ate their Spanish captives.

The Gulf area was farm and timber country throughout the nineteenth century. As late as 1900, 80 percent of the population of Texas lived on farms or in rural communities. Then, at 10:30 on the morning of January 10, 1901, the most prolific oil well of its time, Spindletop, erupted near Beaumont, Texas. Within a week, the well had sprayed the countryside with about 60,000 barrels of oil. Texas was never again the same, as it and the West Gulf Coast were ushered into an industrial economy that continues today. Oil was the basis for that industrial economy, the source of thousands of personal fortunes, and the catalyst for hundreds of refineries and associated industries.

Spindletop and many other oil deposits in the Gulf area owe their existence to that area's unique geology. Most have formed as a result of salt domes (FIGURE 9.6). The salt was deposited in the Jurassic period, when water of an inland sea evaporated. As the weight of 50,000 feet of overlying rocks was deposited in succeeding periods, the salt plugs squeezed upward for thousands of feet. As each plug rose, it lifted and interrupted oil-bearing sand and limestone to trap the oil and gas in a pool. There are literally hundreds of these salt domes; their distribution is shown in FIGURE 9.7.

Spindletop, Beaumont, Texas

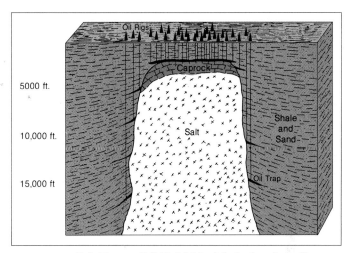

FIGURE 9.6 *Salt Dome Oil Field Modeled after Spindletop*

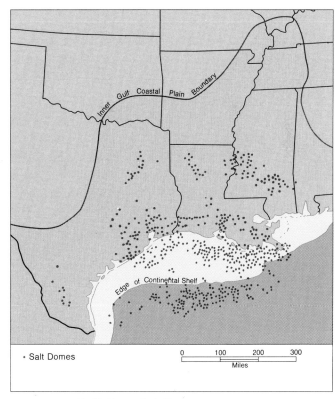

FIGURE 9.7 *Gulf Coast Salt Domes*

The industrial Texas Gulf Coast

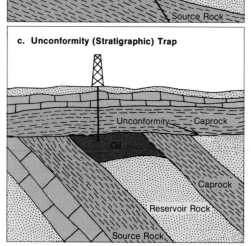

a. Anticlinal Trap

b. Fault Trap

c. Unconformity (Stratigraphic) Trap

FIGURE 9.8
Typical Oil Traps

Not all Gulf oil deposits have this origin. Some, indeed many, were formed from faults and folds not associated with salt domes (FIGURE 9.8). Along the West Gulf Coast of Texas and western Louisiana, a procession of giant oil refineries, gleaming chemical plants, and hundreds of allied industries have emerged. Various writers have labeled the strip the Golden Crescent.

Where rivers meet the ocean, cities have sprung up: Orange, Port Arthur, and Beaumont focusing on the Sabine River; Houston, Texas City, and Galveston on Galveston Bay, where the Trinity and San Jacinto rivers merge; Freeport along the Brazos; Port Lavaca along the Lavaca River and Bay; and Corpus Christi along the Nueces River and Corpus Christi Bay (FIGURE 9.9). These port cities are all connected by an intracoastal waterway protected by the array of barrier islands that flank the mainland.

The largest and most important city in the Gulf region, Houston, has emerged as a subregional center for this area as well as for the forested lands to the north and east. One out of every seven Texans lives in this city, which is some 50 miles inland from the Gulf. Early in its history, it lived under the shadow of Galveston, once the largest city and leading port in the state. However, following the destruction of Galveston by a hurricane in 1900, much of that city's surviving population and businesses moved to Houston. In 1914, the city completed the Houston Ship Canal, a 58-mile deep-sea channel to the Gulf, giving it port status. Today, Houston is one of the largest port cities in the United States.

Since the early part of this century, Houston has experienced phenomenal growth. Perhaps the famous Texan quote "Too much is not enough" originated here. This growth has been supported by a healthy chemical industry based on the large supplies of oil, gas, salt, sulfur, and lime in the Gulf Coast area. The mid-1980s decline in oil prices had a serious impact on the city's and region's economy, illustrating its dependency on the oil and gas industry. However, Houston's growth is also linked to the large cotton, rice, and cattle operation in the state.

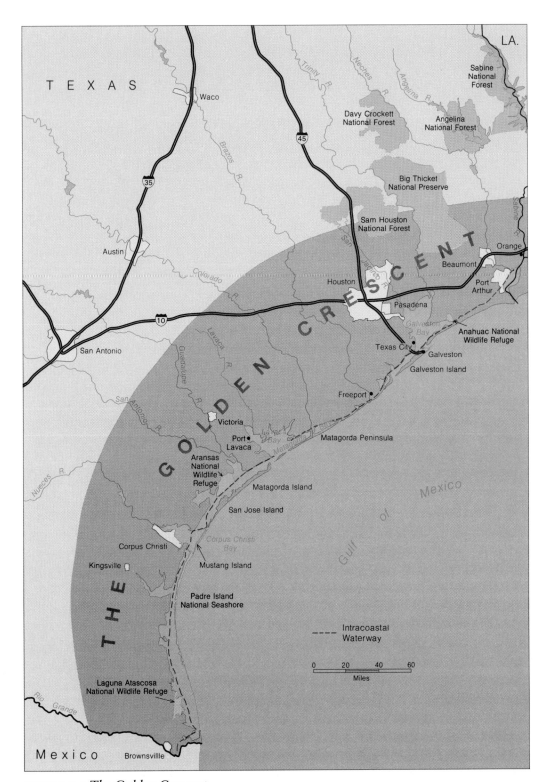

FIGURE 9.9 *The Golden Crescent*

THE RIO GRANDE PLAIN

The Rio Grande Plain has the same underlying rocks as the area to the northeast, but it is drier and the vegetation reflects that aridity. For the most part this is brush country, the land of thorns. Chief among these are mesquite, acacia, yucca, and prickly pear.

This brushy vegetation is a particular problem here. Before the white man came to the southwest, the Rio Grande Plain was a vast prairie grassland. Then the buffalo was replaced by cattle, and the overgrazing that followed killed the mature grasses and allowed the brush to spread. Today it covers much of the surface area. Fortunately for ranchers, the brush seldom forms a solid cover but leaves open areas and passages where grass grows.

Mesquite

The mesquite (*Prosopis juliflora*) is a tree that appears widely in the drier parts of Texas and Oklahoma, especially in the Dry Margin region. A phreatophyte (plant with a root system that reaches down into the groundwater table), the mesquite can develop into trees 60 feet tall with trunks several feet in diameter. More typically, however, it appears as a low, thorny shrub. It is native to this country, but it has spread due to inadvertent human encouragement. As grasslands were overgrazed by herds of cattle, the grasses disappeared and were succeeded by the hardy mesquite. Jackrabbits, competing with cattle for the grasses, flourished because they could eat the mesquite during dry spells, something the cattle could not do. Thus, in addition to the spreading of the mesquite following the overgrazing of grasslands, its existence supported a larger jackrabbit population that further denuded the grasslands. Consequently, the recovery of the grasslands became even more difficult.

The root system of the mesquite reaches 60 feet or more below the surface into the groundwater table. This steady water supply allows it to persist through the long, dry spells and makes it almost indestructible. It cannot be killed by cutting unless a growth knot several inches below the ground surface is removed.

Mesquite wood is valued for fenceposts and lumber and the bean is edible. The wood is also popular as fuel for barbecuing.

Mesquite

The brush, though, is still a serious problem for the ranchers. Not only does it take valuable land that otherwise could be in grass, but the brush's extensive root system extracts water from a wide distance, causing springs to dry up. It is also difficult to work cattle in the brush. Early south Texas riders invented the leather chaps or leggings to protect their legs.

Of all the brush, it is the mesquite that is the most bothersome. Ranchers have tried everything to rid their land of this plant. They have chopped it, dug it up, burned it, poisoned it, and more recently, root-plowed it; still the plants come back. It is generally felt that after a 50-year effort to rid the area of the brush, there is now even more mesquite than ever.

The Rio Grande Plain not only differs physically from the rest of the Gulf region but also is culturally distinct. It has a strong Spanish heritage and a very large Mexican population, so it is fitting that San Antonio is the region's cultural and economic center.

Founded by the Spaniards in 1718 (the same year the French laid out New Orleans), San Antonio is this country's classical Spanish city and a leading center of Latin American trade. Like New Orleans, it offers both resident and visitor a unique and colorful environment. The San Antonio River, which meanders throughout much of the downtown area, is particularly attractive; it passes under more than 40 bridges and is lined with scores of outdoor cafés. This little river has had an immense effect on the city, as it has given flavor and charm to an otherwise declining downtown area and is responsible for bringing millions of tourist dollars into the city annually.

The climate of the Rio Grande Plain is quite mild, and the area typically has a 330-day (or longer) growing season, permitting three crops each year. The dreaded northers that plague the Texas panhandle are only mild cold snaps by the time they reach the Rio Grande Plain, so winters are short or nonexistent. With good soils and a long growing season, almost anything will grow when water is available, and farming is important here.

Water, however, is the key. There isn't much rain, and the evaporation is high. Two major irrigated areas within the region are the Rio Grande Valley and Winter Garden. The delta and floodplain of the Rio Grande is a broad and extensive farm area irrigated from surface water carried in by the Rio Grande.

Miles and miles of vegetables, palm trees, and citrus trees fill the valley. Two hundred miles to the north lies Winter Garden, a winter vegetable farm area that is particularly well known for its spinach. Irrigation water is supplied by subsurface wells that pump water from the Carrizo Sandstones.

Cattle Drives and Cowboys

The cattle trail period, which extended from the end of the Civil War in 1865 until the late 1880s, is an important and colorful part of the Rio Grande Plain's history. It has been much romanticized by American novels, movies, and television. They typically portray a central cowboy character who represents the kind of man all young men want to be when they grow up and one all old men wish that they had been. In legend, the faults of the cowboy usually are forgotten and his virtues exaggerated. Still, the cowboy and his ranches, cattle drives, and frontier spirit transformed the plains and Southwest into a prosperous, dynamic region while influencing the philosophy and attitudes of the United States and the world.

Cattle and sheep were brought to the Americas by early English settlers, but ranching as a business was first practiced in the New World by Spanish and Mexican cattlemen in north Mexico and south Texas.

The first herds were brought into the area in the second half of the sixteenth century by the Spanish conquistadors. When the Mexican government passed large tracts of land to empresarios such as Moses Austin and Green DeWitt in the 1820s, Texas was already swarming with wild cattle. The empresarios, in turn, were responsible for introducing a specified number of settlers into their grant. Each rancher received 4,500 acres of free land, and this was the start of the American cattle era.

The Anglo-Americans first adopted the Spanish technique of working cattle from horseback here in south Texas. The Texas cowboy copied the ways of the Mexican *vaquero* with only slight modifications. The clothing was practical: The broad-brimmed sombrero shielded him from the hot sun and shaded his eyes from the glare, and the cowboy boot fitted with sharp spurs would move the horse rapidly when needed. The six-shooter pistol, however, was an American innovation allowing the Texas cowboy to match the fighting skill of both Mexicans and Comanches.

The American cowboy was also to acquire much of his ranching lingo from the vaquero: *rancho* became "ranch," *lazo* became "lasso," *chaparreras* became "chaps," and *mesteño* was changed to "mustang."

When Texas won its independence from Mexico in

Working cowboy in west Texas in the early twentieth century

1836, the Rio Grande became the boundary between the two countries. Many Mexican ranchers withdrew across the river and abandoned their cattle herds. In the unfenced country, these cattle went wild and interbred with the existing wild stock to form a rugged breed that became known as the Texas longhorn.

Until the mid-nineteenth century, Texas cattle remained a source of hides and tallow, worth no more than two or three dollars a head. As cattle drives began, prices rose. The first known cattle drives began in the 1840s. In 1842, a drive to Galveston for shipment to New Orleans was undertaken, and the first significant northern cattle drive occurred when Edward Piper drove 1,000 steers from south Texas to Cincinnati, Ohio. A few other drives to the east and several to California during the gold rush were to follow. But by the eve of the Civil War, the market for cattle in the East was quite weak. There was an oversupply of beef and prices were low.

The Civil War brought ranching to a virtual standstill. In the meantime, herds increased in size considerably; when the war ended, there were millions of wild longhorn cattle and thousands of wild mustang horses in south Texas. To the many penniless Confederate soldiers, the large cattle inventory there represented an opportunity if the men could get them to market.

During the war an important innovation, the refrigerator railcar, gave rise to the growth of the meatpacking industry and thus greatly expanded the beef market and the value of cattle. By the end of the Civil War, Northerners had acquired a taste for beef, so the Eastern market for cattle was now strong.

In 1865, enterprising veterans hired cowboys, rounded up Texan herds, and headed north. The first trails after the Civil War went to Sedalia, Missouri, the nearest railhead (FIGURE 9.10). The cowboys controlled the herd along a trail, usually with the cattle moving five or six abreast. The cook drove the chuck wagon in front of the herd; two of the men rode point, one on each side of the herd; two or more took wing behind the point position; and bringing up the rear were the drags. A wrangler, who was responsible for the horses, and a trail boss rounded out the team.

The herds typically reached railheads within three months. Steers grazed on the spring grass along the way and usually gained weight. Still, during the first years, the drives were not very successful. The early

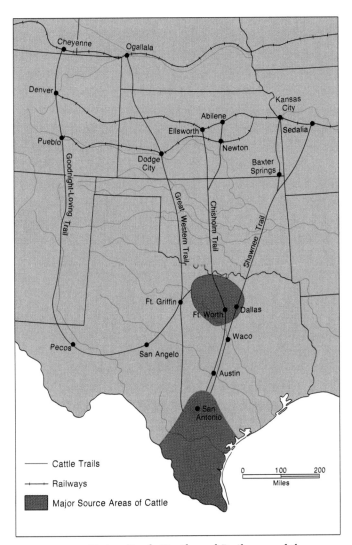

FIGURE 9.10 *Major Cattle Trails and Railways of the Southern Plains during the Trail-Driving Era, 1860s to 1880s*

trail, the Shawnee, was a troubled one; Indians demanded payment, farmers afraid of Texas fever tried to turn the herds back, and outlaw bands bushwacked the cowboys and stole their cattle.

In 1867, Joseph G. McCoy, a cattle feeder and dealer from Illinois, built a loading pen in Abilene, Kansas. McCoy confirmed the advantage of a more westward route through discussions with Jesse Chisholm, a part-Cherokee trader and former freight wagon driver. The route north to Abilene took Chisholm's name to become the famous Chisholm Trail. In the next 20 years, it was to carry five million head of cattle. When the Santa Fe Railway was extended to Ellsworth and Newton, these towns became significant railheads for Texas cattle.

Dodge City was the last of the Kansas-city cow towns and became a railhead for cattle moving up the great western trail. Among the group of rough-and-tough cow towns along the Santa Fe Railroad, Dodge was reputed to be the roughest. Its streets were lined with saloons, dance halls, whorehouses, and gambling houses. Each town hired professional gunslingers to keep law and order. Dodge City featured Bat Masterson and Wyatt Earp; Newton had Mike McCluskie and Jim Riley; Ellsworth hired Chauncey Whitney; and for Abilene, there was Wild Bill Hickok.

The cattle trails continued to move westward with the railroads. Charles Goodnight and Oliver Loving established the Goodnight-Loving Trail from San Angelo, Texas, to connect with railheads in Pueblo and Denver, Colorado, and Cheyenne, Wyoming. As the open ranch was fenced in and the railroad came to Texas, the era of the cattle drives abruptly ended as did the colorful life-style of the cowboy. By the end of the century, cowboys were penned behind barbed wire and were spending most of their time digging postholes, repairing windmills, and racking hay. The excitement of the cattle drive, the debauchery of the cow town at trail ends, gunfights with Indians and rustlers, and the fast-draw gunfighter had been left behind.

Ranching remains an important part of the Rio Grande Plain. Ranches cover much of the landscape, and many a south Texas county is named for the rancher who owns it. The largest ranch in the United States, King Ranch, is located here.

PART III

THE UPLAND SOUTH

10 INTRODUCTION—*The Upland South*

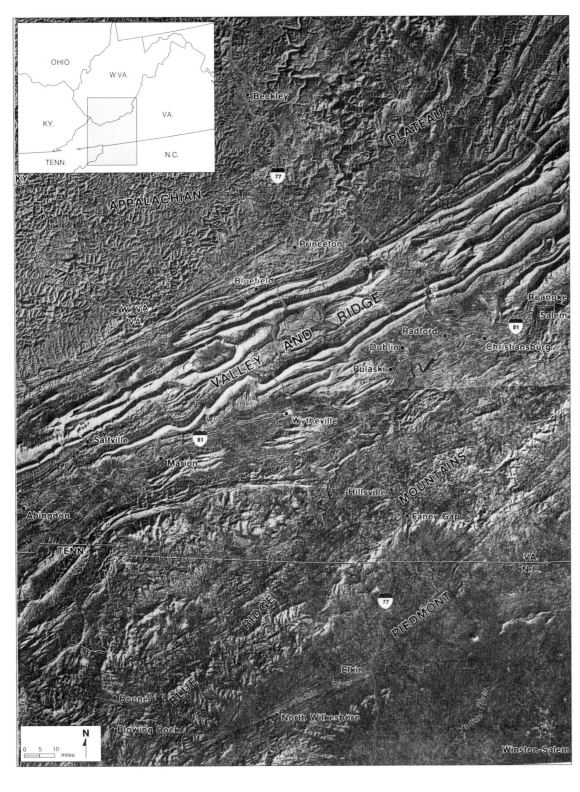

The mountains, plateaus, and high plains of the South comprise a region that is, for the most part, geologically older than the Lowland South but younger in its human history. If the Lowlands were home to the antebellum South, the Uplands served as the setting for the New South of early twentieth-century industrialization. The rolling plateaus, mist-shrouded mountains, long valleys, and grassy plains were known not so much for plantations, slaves, and cotton as for yeoman farms, textile mills, and coal mines.

Early in the history of the South, the Uplands tended either to block or to channel settlement. The Appalachian system in particular dictated that the quest for new farmlands would proceed along a southwestward axis from the upper South.

After the Civil War, it was in the Upland South that most industrialization and the growth of cities occurred. Waterpower on the rolling Piedmont promoted the emergence there of the nation's greatest concentration of the textile industry. Thick stands of hardwood trees supplied the furniture industry in North Carolina, and the Red Mountain iron ore combined with coal from the Black Warrior basin to found the great iron-and-steel district around Birmingham. The industrial might of this country is still fueled by coal from the Appalachian Plateau and oil from west Texas.

This sidelooking airborne radar photograph reveals the striking contrast between the four major components of the Appalachian system as they occur in a four-state area. Notice how the New River has incised its valley across the grain of both the Valley and Ridge and Appalachian Plateau areas after it leaves the Blue Ridge Mountains in North Carolina. This indicates that the New River is, despite its name, very old; originally it must have established its course over a more level terrain north of the Blue Ridge. Subsequent erosion of that terrain created the now-varied topography. Throughout that process, the pre-existing New River managed to carve its channel into rock units of varying hardness. General erosion, however, lowered some areas faster than others.

The Upland South can be divided into a number of subregions that are more diverse than those of the Lowland South (FIGURE 10.1). Three of these subregions, the Piedmont, Blue Ridge, and Valley and Ridge, are part of the Appalachian Mountain system. The Piedmont, a low plateau, in some respects is Lowland South, but its physical character and geologic history clearly make it a part of the Uplands. Its natural vegetation patterns, featuring mixed pine and hardwood forests, are similar to those of the Uplands. The history of development of the Piedmont also sets it apart from the Lowlands.

The Blue Ridge province shares a common geologic history and character with the Piedmont. Some differences in the makeup of the underlying rocks have caused the Blue Ridge to yield more slowly to erosion and thus remain higher. Historically, the mountains served as a barrier to westward movement, forcing the streams of migrants to move southwestward along either flank. To the west of the mountains, the elongate Valley and Ridge region gave land-hungry settlers a path around the mountains, and the long limestone valleys offered fertile soil. Beyond the bluff that marked the western edge of the Valley and Ridge lies another of the Uplands' subregions, the great Appalachian Plateau and Interior Low Plateaus of Tennessee, Kentucky, and West Virginia. There thick strata of sedimentary rocks retain much of their horizontal position, but stream erosion has carved this once-level plateau into a maze of hills and narrow valleys, rich in coal but poor in level land and hampered by isolation. Gentle uparching of the strata has exposed limestone layers to erosion, leaving broad basins floored by fertile soils. To the settlers who had struggled through the hilly plateau region, the Bluegrass Basin around Lexington, Kentucky, and the Nashville Basin seemed like the promised land.

The Blue Ridge

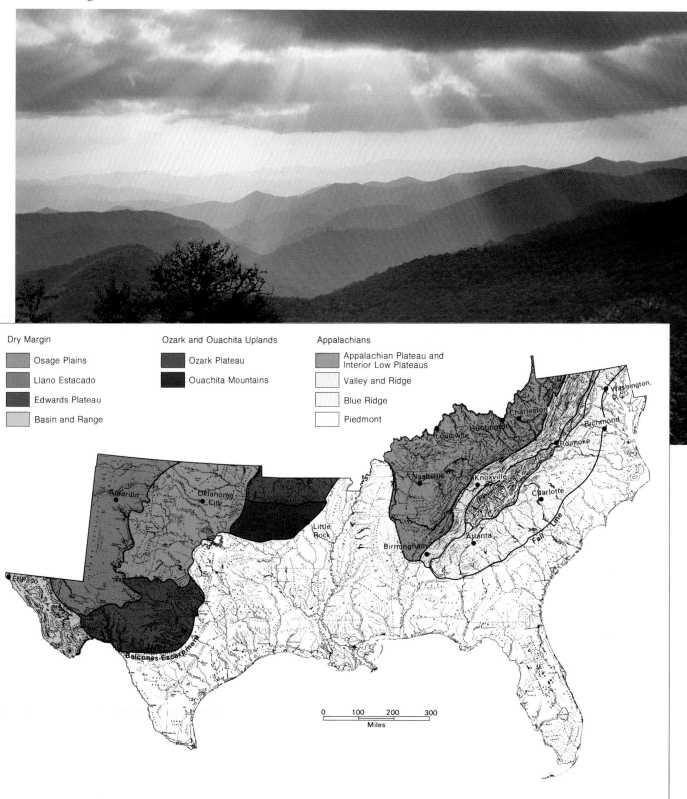

FIGURE 10.1
The Upland South

SUBREGIONS OF THE UPLAND SOUTH

The six subregions of the Upland South include the Piedmont, Blue Ridge, Valley and Ridge, Appalachian and Interior Low Plateaus, Ozark and Ouachita Uplands, and Dry Margin. They are delineated in FIGURE 10.1, and the following overview explains the major characteristics of each. Chapters 11 through 16 contain more detailed discussions of the individual subregions.

Piedmont

A long, narrow channel between the Blue Ridge Mountains and the Atlantic Coastal Plain, the Piedmont is geologically ancient. It was directly involved in the continental collision that so marked eastern North America, and its rocks are the core of an ancient mountain system. The rolling, forested topography was like an open highway to southward-moving settlers. While only peripheral to the Cotton Kingdom, the Piedmont offered gold deposits and waterpower as the first foundation for this region's emergence as a major industrial corridor.

Blue Ridge

Also a direct product of an ancient continental collision, the mountains of the Blue Ridge province are an erosional remnant of a larger mountain mass. These low mountains, never reaching 7,000 feet in elevation, pale in comparison with the height and ruggedness of other major mountain systems. But they were imposing enough for the early settlers, especially in North Carolina, where they widen into the Great Smoky Mountains. Even today they are heavily populated in only a few places, such as the Asheville Basin. The Blue Ridge uplands are major scenic and recreational attractions and are the source of many East Coast rivers.

Valley and Ridge

This narrow corridor, like the Piedmont on the other side of the Blue Ridge, also acted to funnel the flow of settlers deep into the South. Formed by some of the same forces of continental collision that contorted the entire Appalachian system, the Valley and Ridge area is composed of somewhat younger sedimentary rocks crumpled by pressure from the southeast. Subsequent erosion of these folded and faulted layers produced a region of long, parallel ridges and intervening valleys.

The latter are commonly the products of the weathering of limestone, which has left a rich and fertile soil. These productive valleys grew a large part of the food for the Confederacy during the Civil War. At its southern end, iron ore deposits in the Valley and Ridge became the basis for the Birmingham iron-and-steel complex.

Appalachian and Interior Low Plateaus

West of the Valley and Ridge, the great layers of Paleozoic sedimentary rocks were affected only slightly by the tectonic upheavals to the east. The strata remained essentially horizontal, but deep erosion by streams carved this former plain into a hilly region. Thick coal beds exposed in these valleys were exploited by absentee owners beginning in the late nineteenth century, and they continue to fuel American industry. Isolation and the lack of level land retarded the region's development, and coal mining scarred a scenic landscape. The great limestone basins around Nashville, Tennessee, and Lexington, Kentucky, offered more prosperity in their fertile limestone soils. A larger, more prosperous population developed in these oases in an otherwise impoverished land.

Ozark and Ouachita Uplands

These low mountains and hills are related geologically to the western side of the Appalachian system. They offer topographic relief to the land west of the broad, level valley of the Mississippi River. They are culturally similar to the Appalachian Plateau area, being somewhat poor and isolated.

The Dry Margin

The western fringe of the South is a varied landscape unified by the dryness of the climate. It is the transition zone between the humid South and the dry Southwest, with high grasslands and desert replacing forests. Cattle ranching spurred some early development, but more was generated in the twentieth century by the exploitation of the region's rich oil and gas deposits. The Trans Pecos area in southwestern Texas, a land of dry valleys between blocky ridges and a culture that owes much to Mexico, is the gateway to the true Southwest. Water is the critical resource, and most settlement is concentrated in the valley of the Rio Grande.

Across the broad Lowland area of the Mississippi River Valley are mountainous outliers of the Appalachian Mountain system, the Ozark and Ouachita Uplands of Arkansas and Oklahoma, which constitute another subregion. They, in turn, border an Upland subregion that is more plains than hill lands. This is the Dry Margin of the South, where the arid climate unifies a topographically varied region. Most of Oklahoma and the western third of Texas comprise the southern end of the interior Lowland of North America and the Great Plains. Grasses replace trees as the typical natural vegetation. Cotton maintains its historical importance, but cattle ranching and oil wells are more common. The lands of the Osage Plains, the Edwards Plateau, and the Llano Estacado are very different from the rest of the South. Their climate and vegetation share as much with the American Southwest as they do with the South and mark this area as a transitional zone between the two great regions. This transition is completed in the Trans Pecos region of southwestern Texas, a fragment of the great Basin and Range province and part of the American desert. The characteristics of each subregion of the Upland South are summarized in more detail in the accompanying sidebar. The subregions in turn are the subjects of chapters 11 through 16.

The Dry Margin

11 THE PIEDMONT

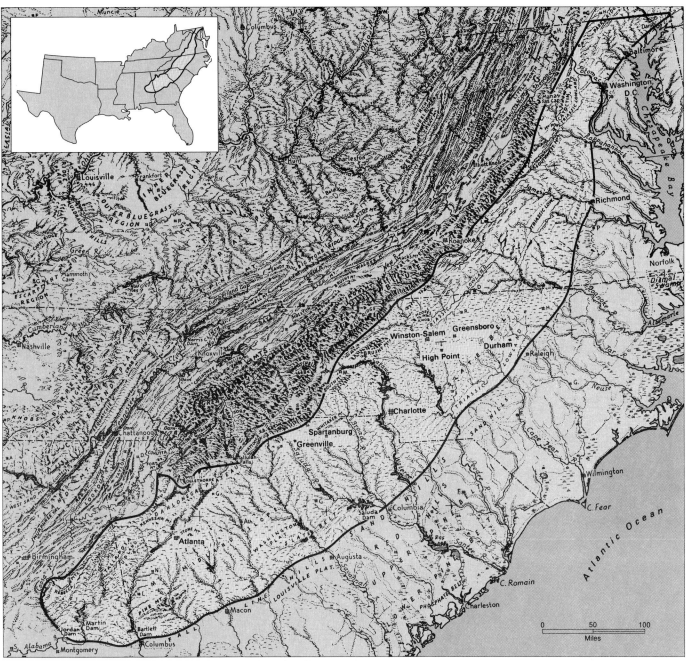

FIGURE 11.1 *The Piedmont*

Throughout its history, the Piedmont has been one of the most strategic areas in the South (FIGURE 11.1). Transitional between the Atlantic Coastal Plain and the mountains, it long served as a vital route for settlers. After the Civil War, it became the focus of industrialization as the South began to emerge from an almost purely agricultural economy. The Piedmont also became a major band of urbanization and the site of many of the South's important noncoastal cities.

The surface of the Piedmont is a rolling plateau originally covered by great stands of mixed hardwood and pine forest. It is cut by swiftly flowing rivers that follow narrow valleys on their way from the mountains to the coastal plain. Overall, the Piedmont extends 1,000 miles from New York into Alabama. It achieves its greatest width of about 125 miles in the southern portion, which is also higher, containing elevations ranging between 400 and 1,200 feet.

The Piedmont ("foot of the mountains") is bounded on the east by the fall line, where ancient, hard rocks are buried by younger, softer coastal plain sediments. To the west, the Piedmont ends where it meets the steep escarpment of the Blue Ridge Mountains. This boundary is marked by major faults, such as the Brevard Fault in western North Carolina (FIGURE 11.2). Here, in places, more recent Paleozoic rocks identical to those found in Tennessee in the Valley and Ridge province lie exposed. This indicates that the rocks of the Piedmont probably were thrust up and over the other, younger rocks. The Blue Ridge province ends in northeastern Georgia, and south of that point the Piedmont abuts directly onto those Paleozoic rocks of the Valley and Ridge area. The transition here is marked by the Cartersville Fault, a fracture zone along which the Piedmont rocks were shoved directly westward over the Valley and Ridge strata. Recent geophysical research reveals that, in fact, the entire Piedmont may have been thrust over parts of the younger rocks that are exposed at the surface in the Valley and Ridge province. This is a

The Blue Ridge Escarpment west of Greenville, South Carolina

matter of economic interest, since some of the sedimentary rocks that lie deep under the Piedmont may contain commercial quantities of petroleum.

GEOLOGY

The geology of the Piedmont is very complex, and its early history is not well understood. Apparently it was part of a suture zone that formed when a portion of the ancient Gondwanaland supercontinent was shoved up against ancestral North America and fused into it. During these cataclysmic events, sediments deposited in an offshore oceanic trough were thrust upward and westward as the continents collided. Part

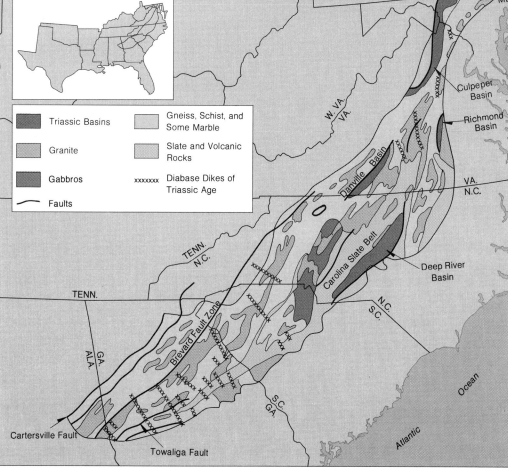

FIGURE 11.2
Geologic Structure of the Piedmont

of these maritime sediments are thought to have been overridden as the current Piedmont rocks were thrust westward. Subsequent episodes of upheaval, volcanic activity, and millions of years of erosion have given the region its contemporary character.

Most of the Piedmont is composed of rocks called *gneiss* and *schist*—metamorphic rocks that have been modified by heat and pressure, but not so much that the original nature is lost entirely. They represent shale, marl, or earlier volcanic rocks. Marble (altered limestone) and quartzite (formerly sandstone) occur less commonly. The volcanic events also left dark, low silica-content rocks called *gabbros* and *diabase*.

About 20 percent of the Piedmont is made of granite and other igneous rocks that were intruded (injected) into the subsurface and later exposed by erosion. These rocks are hard and tend to form uplands, as they erode more slowly than adjacent rocks.

Stone Mountain, Georgia

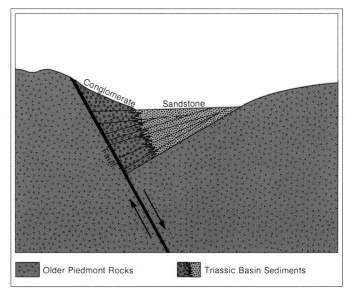

Older Piedmont Rocks   Triassic Basin Sediments

FIGURE 11.3 *Typical Triassic Basin*

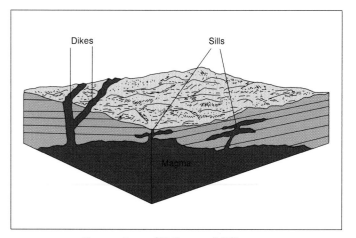

FIGURE 11.4 *Formation of Dikes and Sills*
Dikes and sills form when molten rock from the magma chamber is injected into cracks in the earth's crust.

Another 20 percent of the rocks are accounted for in the Carolina Slate Belt, in which a lower degree of metamorphism turned shale into slate. It is somewhat easier to erode; consequently, the Carolina Slate Belt tends to form low-lying areas, some of which are sites for reservoirs.

Scattered on the Piedmont, especially along its western edge, are numerous *monadnocks*. These are low mountains that have formed because their rocks are uncommonly resistant to erosion. A few of the better-known monadnocks include Stone Mountain, Georgia, and the Brushy Mountains in North Carolina. Some of these features are not large but are prominent on the otherwise low-lying surface. Stone Mountain, for example, is only one and a half miles long, but it rises 650 feet above the surface and is steep sided. Others, such as the South Mountains in North Carolina, which peak at 3,000 feet, are large and are similar in scale to the nearby Blue Ridge Mountains.

Generally the rocks of the Piedmont are either late Precambrian or early Paleozoic in age (at least 500 million years old). An exception to this is found in the Triassic basins, remnants of younger (about 200 million years ago) sedimentary deposition and faulting. These are strips on top of the Piedmont as much as 150 miles long and 5 to 20 miles wide. The basins are noted for their beds of red sandstone and other unmetamorphosed sedimentary rocks. Faulting created by a stretching of the earth's crust caused blocks to drop down below the surface. Streams flowed into these basins and filled them with sand, silt, and other materials (FIGURE 11.3).

During the same episode of stretching, other cracks were filled with molten rock that escaped from the earth's interior. Upon cooling, they formed dark layers of igneous rocks. The rocks that cut vertically through the earlier rocks are called *dikes,* and others, named *sills,* were injected in a more horizontal position (FIGURE 11.4).

FIGURE 11.2 shows the Triassic basins that are exposed at the surface. Others have been discovered under the Atlantic Coastal Plain in northern Florida, southeastern Alabama, and southwestern Georgia.

Triassic basins sometimes contain small quantities of coal and iron ore. They were used in the colonial period for local production of iron, but the deposits are too small to be of commercial interest today. In the early eighteenth century, Governor Alexander Spotswood of Virginia unsuccessfully sought to build a major iron industry based on Triassic deposits and the skill of German immigrants.

The deep weathering of Piedmont rocks over millions of years has produced *sapprolite,* a clay-rich material as much as 100 feet thick and often looking like the rock from which it derived. It is typically rich in iron, which gives it a characteristically red or orange color. It is the source of the Piedmont red clays, which make good bricks but are not especially good soil for cultivation. These red-yellow *podzolics,* or *ultisols,* are acidic and low in fertility but still capable of supporting rich forest growth. The early settlers were ecstatic when they saw the great Piedmont forests but soon learned that the cleared land would yield only a few good crops. The settlers tended to seek out oak-hickory forest stands, which they associated with a dark topsoil they called *mulatto,* in contrast with a poorer gray soil associated with the mixed growth of hardwoods and pines that covered most of the Piedmont. Overcultivation of these soils in tobacco, cotton, and other row crops not only depleted their nutrients but also made them vulnerable to devastating erosion. The application of lime-rich fertilizers made the soil productive again, but all too often erosion had removed enormous amounts of topsoil. Albert Cowdrey, commenting on erosion on the Southern Piedmont, wrote that "over the course of settlement and exploitation, but especially in the generation since the Civil War, a mass of topsoil had disappeared that has been variously estimated at six cubic miles or, more vaguely, sufficient to cover an area equal to that of Belgium."[1]

Red clay soil
on the Piedmont
of Georgia

CLIMATE

The climate of the Piedmont is classic hot-summer, mild-winter weather. The four seasons are distinct and of nearly equal length. Spring is an extended glory of dogwoods, azaleas, and hundreds of other flowering plants. Autumn is a period of crisp weather and multicolored leaves. Winter is an episode of alternating cold weather, occasional snow, and periods of weather balmy enough for tennis or golf. Summer brings enervating heat and humidity and occasional drought. Summers are not as long and hot as those in the Deep South nor are the winters as cold and long as those in the nearby mountains. The Blue Ridge uplands seem to protect the region from some of the worst effects of bitter cold air masses that sweep out of the North American interior in winter.

The major climatic problem of the Piedmont region is a relatively high occurrence of stagnating air masses, especially in the summer (FIGURE 11.5).

FIGURE 11.5
*Stagnating Anticyclones
in the Eastern U.S.,
1936–1965*

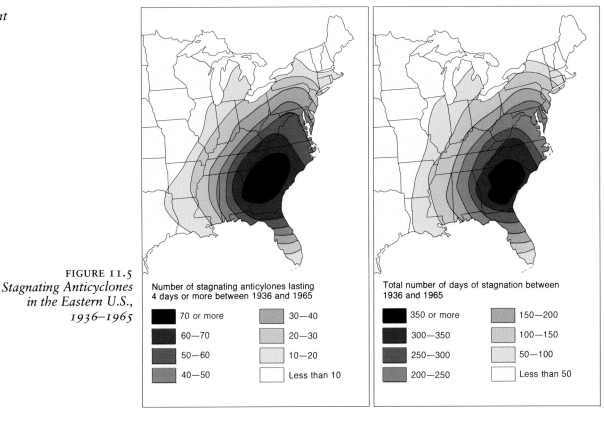

Number of stagnating anticylones lasting
4 days or more between 1936 and 1965

70 or more	30—40
60—70	20—30
50—60	10—20
40—50	Less than 10

Total number of days of stagnation between
1936 and 1965

350 or more	150—200
300—350	100—150
250—300	50—100
200—250	Less than 50

These air masses, associated with a strong maritime high-pressure cell that forms over the Caribbean, the *Bermuda High,* produce extended periods of hot, hazy, calm weather that not only yield little rain but also block other weather systems and severely restrict the dispersion of pollutants into the air. Thus pollution can be added to heat and humidity to create truly debilitating weather for Piedmont residents.

In the spring of 1986, an aberration in the jet stream caused the Bermuda High to move farther inland than usual. The result was the worst drought in the recorded meteorological history of the South. Crop losses reached into billions of dollars, and the accompanying heat was responsible for dozens of deaths. The drought affected a broad area, but its core was on the Piedmont of North and South Carolina and Georgia.

The Piedmont is crossed by a number of short, rapidly flowing rivers that carry runoff from the Blue Ridge onto the coastal plain and ultimately to the ocean. These rivers have cut relatively narrow valleys perpendicular to the axis of the Piedmont. They are filled with rapids and falls and thus navigable only in short stretches. This ends at the fall line where the rivers flow onto the weak rocks of the coastal plain and become generally navigable all the way to the coast. According to Jean Gottmann, "William Byrd II realized the advantages offered by the falls of the large rivers as sites for towns."[2] Byrd thus initiated the building of a town (Richmond) at the falls on the James River in 1737. To be sure, the presence of the fall line is of minor importance to Richmond and other fall line cities today. It was simply a nucleating factor at a time when a developing region needed towns to act as distribution, trade, and transportation centers.

The Piedmont rivers offered other advantages. Although mostly unnavigable, they were easier for southwestward-bound travelers to cross than the broad coastal plain rivers. The rolling, well-drained Piedmont was like a highway when compared with the swampy coastal plain, and the mountains to the west were an even more rugged obstacle.

What the Piedmont rivers lacked in navigability they gained in waterpower. The beginning of the textile industry after about 1880 was based in part on using the waterpower available at numerous sites on rapidly flowing Piedmont streams. In 1904, this mechanical energy became available in the form of electricity when the first hydroelectric generating station was built on the Catawba River. By 1964, there were 14 hydroelectric stations on that river alone. Today most of the electricity consumed by the textile industry is generated in coal or nuclear-powered plants, but hydropower was one of the catalysts to the development on the Piedmont of a major industrial district.

EARLY SETTLEMENT

European settlement on the Piedmont lagged initially as development naturally focused on the more accessible coast. In Virginia, the falls of the James River were referred to as world's end as late as 1704. Only a few trappers had ventured into the Piedmont, then still held by the Indians. This changed dramatically in 1716 when Governor Spotswood led his "Knights of the Golden Horseshoe" on an expedition to the Blue Ridge. This was followed in 1722 by a treaty negotiated with the Indians under which the Iroquois agreed to keep their people west of the Blue Ridge, opening the Piedmont for white settlers. A massive movement of settlers from the Tidewater followed. This migratory stream was composed of both wealthy Tidewater landowners and more humble, new immigrants who found the Tidewater occupied when they arrived. English settlers were thus joined on the Piedmont by French Huguenots, Swiss, and Palatine Germans. The Chesapeake Bay–Potomac River corridor offered the easiest access to the Piedmont in northern Virginia and the Washington area, and most inland movement into Virginia followed this route.

A different migration stream appeared in the upper reaches of the Shenandoah Valley of Virginia in 1732. These were Scotch-Irish and Germans from Pennsylvania, some newly arrived from Europe and others the children of earlier immigrants. They followed the Great Philadelphia Wagon Road through the valley system west of the Blue Ridge and then crossed over onto the Piedmont primarily through the Roanoke River gap. Others stayed in the valley or proceeded through it into Tennessee and Kentucky. The people who crossed the mountains and moved eastward dominated the settlement in the Piedmont of the Carolinas and Georgia (FIGURE 11.6).

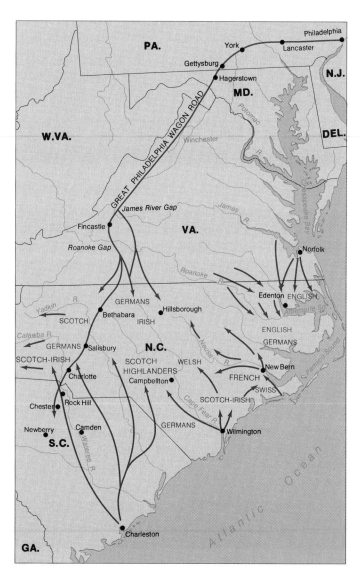

FIGURE 11.6 *Avenues of Early North Carolina Settlement*

The Scotch-Irish and Germans were hardy farmers, and they included many skilled craftsmen who operated small farms without slave labor and served as blacksmiths, carpenters, and millwrights for their neighbors. They utilized the waterpower of the Piedmont streams to operate gristmills and found it more economical to ship the higher-priced flour and meal than unprocessed grain. The English, on the other hand, opened large plantations, used slaves, and concentrated on tobacco and cotton. They were Anglicans, whereas the Scotch-Irish were staunch Presbyterians and the Germans were Lutheran. These factors led to intrastate differences in politics, economy, and general culture. The Virginia Piedmont was culturally homogeneous with the Tidewater. In the Carolinas, the Piedmont contrasted strongly with the "down east" or Atlantic Coastal Plain parts of the two states. These intrastate variations are less evident today but still exist, especially in politics. In Virginia, the contrast is between southwestern Virginia, west of the Blue Ridge, and the rest of the state. These variations became highly visible during the Civil War when part of trans-Blue Ridge Virginia refused to secede and formed the pro-Union state of West Virginia.

The Piedmont, as elsewhere, was settled initially by people looking for new farmlands. The decline of rice and indigo production along the coast, along with the escalating market for cotton, caused some principal landholders to seek new acreages on the inner coastal plain and the Piedmont. In South Carolina and Georgia, the Piedmont was a center of cotton cultivation before it spread westward into Alabama, Mississippi, and Texas. Tobacco cultivation spread from Virginia onto the northern Piedmont in North Carolina.

Sharecropping on tenant farms became the chief mode of production after the Civil War, binding thousands of black and white farmers to virtual peonage to the landowners, furnish merchants, and King Cotton. Soil depletion and erosion, overspecialization in a cash crop, unstable prices, and competition from more efficient farms along the Mississippi River and in Texas caused a steady decline in cotton production in the eastern South, including the Piedmont. Early in the 1920s, when new restrictive laws cut off the source of immigrant European labor, a massive migration to cities in the North began, fueled by sharecroppers seeking better employment opportunities.

Not until the 1960s did this outflow start to diminish, and later in the next decade, reverse, as the Southern economy underwent a major restructuring, shifting from agriculture to a more industrial service-based economy that focused on the region's cities. The resultant abandonment of thousands of Piedmont farms left great acreages to be reclaimed by weeds and the forests. Today the rural landscape contains many kudzu-covered and collapsing farm structures, and many more have disappeared. The once relatively homogenous forest vegetation has been replaced by a mixture of old forests, pastures, farms, and new vegetation on deserted farms. In many rural areas, the amount of untilled green space has actually increased.

The industrial base laid by the eighteenth-century gristmills evolved further in the nineteenth century. On the northern Piedmont of North Carolina, the skill of local craftsmen, coupled with ready access to both hardwood forests and eastern markets, led to the growth there of a major furniture industry. Similarly, large supplies of industrious labor, good waterpower sites, a strong national market for cloth, and the opening of a railroad system that followed the length of the Piedmont into Northern markets combined to trigger the rise of the cotton textile industry on the Piedmont of Virginia, the Carolinas, and Georgia.

This late-nineteenth-century episode of economic development was the fruit of the original New South movement. Leaders such as Henry Grady of Atlanta and D. A. Tompkins of Charlotte led a chorus of voices proclaiming the way out of the South's postwar economic plight was to industrialize and become more like the North. The battle cry of the New South movement was to "bring the factories to the fields," to make cloth rather than just to grow cotton. This movement was spearheaded by a group of businessmen, but it was wrapped in patriotic zeal as every town on the Piedmont sought a mill as the solution to local economic problems. This motivation, girded by high profit margins, led to a rapid spread of mills on the Piedmont. By 1903, there were over 300 mills operating within a 100-mile radius of Charlotte (FIGURE 11.7).

A second cotton mill campaign in the 1920s saw many New England companies move their mills to the South, again primarily on the Piedmont. In that same decade, hundreds of mills scattered over the Piedmont and beyond collectively surpassed the older New England district, and the South became the leading textile concentration in the United States. At about the same time, cigarettes and other tobacco products began to be manufactured in large plants in Richmond, Durham, and Winston-Salem. Otherwise, the dispersion of small textile mills onto rural and small town sites allowed the rural population to stay on the land or live in company towns rather than migrate to jobs in cities, which had been more typical in other cases of the Industrial Revolution.

High Point and Greensboro, North Carolina, rose as marketing centers for furniture and textiles, and Charlotte emerged from its gold-mining days as a marketing, distribution, and financial center for the textile industry. Atlanta, central to the entire South, became the premier distribution center for the region. However, none of these cities were initially large compared with the industrial cities of the Northeast or Midwest. In 1900, Atlanta had only 90,000 residents and Richmond counted 85,000. Ten years later Charlotte, the largest city in the Carolinas, contained just 34,000 residents.

Daniel Augustus Tompkins: industrialist, newspaper publisher, and New South spokesman

FIGURE 11.7
Distribution of the Textile Industry by County, 1913
The number of spindles in a textile mill reflects the productive capacity of the industry.

Number of Cotton Spindles
100,000—500,000
Less than 100,000

Atlanta, Georgia

FIGURE 11.8
*Southern Piedmont
Urban Regions, 1983*
Urban regions shown are Metropolitan Statistical Areas (MSAs), which are defined, named, and used by federal agencies.

THE PIEDMONT TODAY

This pattern of industrial and population dispersion that is anchored by a succession of smaller cities gave rise to the concept of a Piedmont urban crescent, most strikingly developed on the Piedmont of North and South Carolina. It is a seemingly contiguous spread of cities, towns, and industrialized countryside that appears to be coalescing as it grows (FIGURE 11.8).

Recent trends reveal that economic and population growth is focusing more on the Piedmont's urban centers. The Carolinas' Piedmont now contains five metropolitan areas of at least 400,000 residents each, including the Charlotte area, which was redefined by the United States Census Bureau in the mid-1980s to include just over one million people. Atlanta, with over two million inhabitants, anchors the southern end of the Piedmont, and Washington, with over three million people, the northern part. Richmond, Raleigh, and other significant urban areas fill out much of the rest of the Piedmont in the South.

Today as well as historically, the Piedmont is a strategic corridor through which the Deep South is connected with the Northeast. Recent growth in the South has made its location increasingly central. The rolling, well-drained, and well-watered topography will continue to foster the growth of transportation, industry, and cities.

Gold Mining

In 1799, twelve-year-old Conrad Reed made the first discovery of gold in North America in a creek in Cabarrus County, North Carolina. It weighed 17 pounds and was used as a doorstop before its true value was realized. Soon afterwards the largest nugget ever found, weighing 28 pounds, was discovered on a nearby plantation. Placer and lode mines quickly came into operation on the Carolina Slate Belt in both Carolinas. Gold mines continued to operate in downtown Charlotte in the early twentieth century, and the Haile gold mine in Lancaster, South Carolina, operated until 1942. It was reopened on a trial basis in 1985.

The gold-mining activity around Charlotte led to the opening there in 1837 of a branch of the United States Mint, which operated until 1861. That early start in the gold business is credited with laying the foundation for Charlotte's emergence as a major financial center today. The discovery of gold in 1828 in Dahlonega (from the Cherokee Indian word *taulonica,* which means yellow metal), Georgia, led to another gold rush and the establishment there of an additional branch of the mint. These Piedmont gold mines accounted for the entire United States' production of the precious metal until gold was discovered in California in 1848.

Areas of Known Gold Deposits in the Piedmont

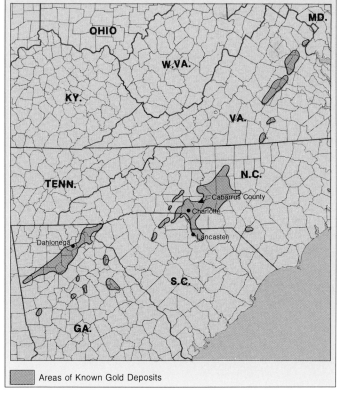

Areas of Known Gold Deposits

12 | THE BLUE RIDGE

The Cherokee Indians called them the "unending mountains." European settlers who made a new home amid the tumbled peaks would say it is a place where "you have to lie down and look up to see out."

The Blue Ridge always seems to cast an almost hypnotic spell over those who enter its province, whether it be the first Indian inhabitant, the pioneering mountaineer, or the modern-day traveler. The complex interplay of physical features provides a sense of the mysterious and the unexpected. There is a labyrinth of steep inclines plunging into remote hollows, sharp ridges rising unexpectedly, and serpentine streams winding their way into the distance. There are successive waves of hills in profile, receding into the mist and far horizon. And there is a sense of the grandeur of high places. With 46 mountain peaks above 6,000 feet in elevation, the region is indeed the rooftop of eastern North America. Their names reflect their Cherokee and Scotch-Irish dwellers: Unaka, Cheoah, Unicoi, and Wayah; Rough Butt Bald, Parson Bald, Hell Ridge, and Pumpkin Patch Mountain.

The bond has always been special between the mountain people and their blue-hazed sentinels. For a long time this was a world unto itself, a cultural isolation as total as that which existed on the eastern sea-reaching barrier islands. Therefore, it is not surprising that the mountaineers developed a sixth sense about their physical environment, living entirely from its resources, talking and singing about it, and possessing a degree of feeling for it uncommon to most people for a region.

Evidence of this traditional and self-contained lifestyle is still found throughout the Blue Ridge: split-rail fences, patchwork quilts, gourd dippers, log cabins, raw cider, and fiddles. Although efforts persist to preserve the old customs and settings, if not the life-style itself, the forces of change have worked their way into this mountain outpost; the signs include resort land development promotions, ski lodges, golf courses, and belated growth of some of the villages and towns.

Blue Ridge Mountains

Cades Cove, Great Smoky Mountains National Park

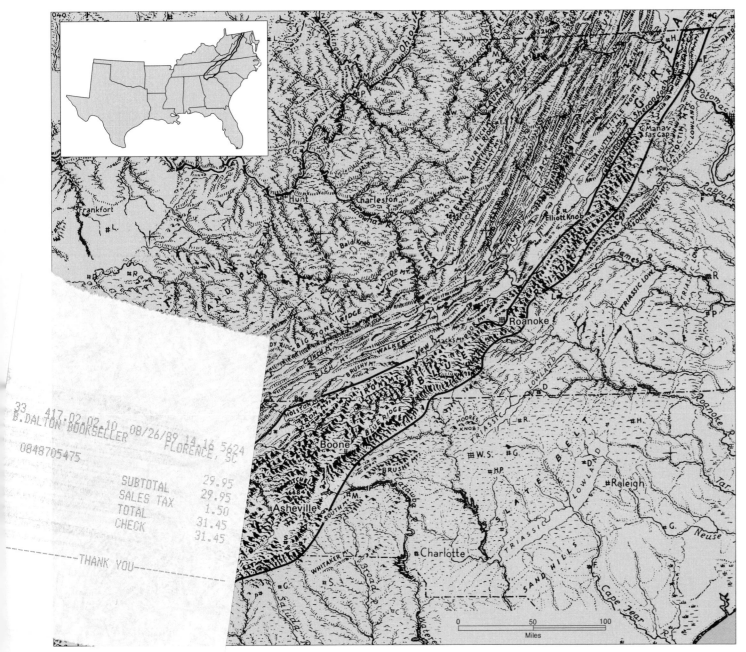

FIGURE 12.1 *The Blue ...*

33 417·02·02·10 08/26/89 14.16 5624
B.DALTON BOOKSELLER   FLORENCE, SC
0848705475

SUBTOTAL   29.95
SALES TAX   29.95
TOTAL   1.50
CHECK   31.45
                31.45

----THANK YOU----

THE NATURE OF THE BLUE RIDGE

Quite abruptly, to the west of the Piedmont plateau above the urban, industrialized midlands, rises the ragged escarpment of the Blue Ridge Mountains (FIGURE 12.1). It is a great wall, the boundary of another world.

The Blue Ridge is the mountainous core of the Appalachian system that separates the Piedmont from the Valley and Ridge areas. Extending from northern Georgia almost to Harrisburg, Pennsylvania, this upland consists of two main regions, northern and southern, with the dividing line at Roanoke, Virginia. North of the Roanoke Valley, the Blue Ridge Mountains narrow to about 12 to 14 miles in width. Elevations are modest, the highest peaks barely exceeding 4,000 feet—Hawksbill at 4,049 feet, for example. The chain is broken by a number of gaps that were created when the Potomac, James, and Roanoke rivers cut through the uplands. Other more elevated passes mark places where past streams carved channels through the uplands before their basins were intercepted by the advances of other streams. These *wind gaps* joined the water gaps in providing easy access through the mountains.

South of Roanoke the scene changes markedly. The mountains are wide—up to 70 miles—and more rugged and higher. Two hundred and eighty-eight peaks reach 5,000 feet, with Mount Mitchell the tallest mountain in the eastern United States at 6,684 feet. These more massive uplands are not broken by any one valley or river. They presented an almost impenetrable barrier for early westward-moving settlers.

The southern Blue Ridge is actually a system composed of several subunits. The name Blue Ridge is also applied to one of them as well as to the overall system. The Blue Ridge Mountains proper form the eastern edge of the system, continuing southward from Virginia into Georgia. The western portion of the Blue Ridge system is known as the Unaka Mountains, and it includes a number of mountain ranges, most notably the Great Smoky Mountains.

A good part of the Blue Ridge Mountains is truly hilly, especially around Blowing Rock, North Carolina, and nearby Grandfather Mountain, the highest peak in the Blue Ridge Mountains proper at 5,964 feet. In other areas, particularly around Hillsville, Virginia, near the North Carolina line, and on the Pisgah Plateau, along the North Carolina–South Carolina line, the upper surface consists of a fairly level plateau. In both cases, the mountains form steep escarpments that rise sharply above the Piedmont floor. At Fancy Gap Mountain, Virginia, the escarpment ascends 1,500 feet over one mile from the North Carolina Piedmont to the Hillsville Plateau. And at Caesar's Head, South Carolina, the Pisgah Plateau soars 1,900 feet over a similarly short distance. Dramatic views of these escarpments are available from interstate highways, Fancy Gap on Interstate 77 and Caesar's Head on Interstate 26.

The Blue Ridge Mountains form an important drainage divide, with streams on the southeastern flanks flowing into the Atlantic Ocean and those on the southwest entering the Tennessee-Ohio River system. This is true only in the southern Blue Ridge Mountains; in the northern part, the drainage is entirely southeastward into the Atlantic.

The Great Smoky Mountains of the Unakas is the most massive mountain system in the eastern United States, with many peaks reaching 6,000 feet in an almost unbroken chain. The highest point is on Clingmans Dome, at 6,643 feet. Other ranges in the Unakas include the Cohutta Mountains in north Georgia, the southern end of the Blue Ridge Mountains proper, and the Black Mountains of North Carolina, dominated by Mount Mitchell.

Craggy Gardens rhododendron on the Blue Ridge Parkway

The topography of the Blue Ridge uplands lacks the angularity so common in western mountains. Summits are rounded, often dome shaped, and crags and bare cliffs are uncommon. The greatest slopes are on valley sides rather than on the upper slopes. The region is largely forested, even after decades of lumbering. Some peaks are grass-covered balds, possibly the result of past cooler climates, earlier soil or drainage conditions, or Indian burnings of the forest. Their precise cause is still subject to much speculation.

Not all of the Blue Ridge area is mountainous. The Asheville Basin is part of the valley of the French Broad River, a major source of the Tennessee River. Near Mount Mitchell, this basin is 10 to 12 miles wide and winds irregularly through the mountains for nearly 40 miles. Surrounded by the peaks of the Black and Pisgah mountains, the valley floor averages a little more than 2,000 feet in elevation.

Especially distinctive is the Ducktown Basin on the Georgia–North Carolina–Tennessee lines. It is a rolling plain at an elevation of around 1,600 feet that is 10 miles wide and 20 miles long. Drained by the Ocoee River, it presents a striking landscape. It is underlain by major deposits of sulfide minerals that are copper ore and minor amounts of precious metals. At the turn of the century, the ores were roasted in open furnaces to extract the copper. The by-product of sulfur fumes combined with moisture in the air to form weak acids that denuded the vegetation over a 25-square-mile area, leaving a virtual desert. Open-air roasting was discontinued decades ago when it became more profitable to extract the sulfuric acid as well as copper from the ore. Despite efforts at replanting, the plateau remains today a barren land on which the sporadic vegetation does not come close to covering the red, gullied surface.

View from Water Rock Knob on the Blue Ridge Parkway

The distinctive climate of the Blue Ridge Mountains not only influenced the look of the land but also has been a constant source of discussion, folklore, and conjecture on the part of mountain people. The contrasts brought about through elevation and sun exposure are endless. The climate of this mountainous region is understandably cooler and more humid than the lower-lying topography next to it. On a hot summer day, the temperature may be 10 to 15 degrees lower on Clingmans Dome than it is on the valley floor in Tennessee. Precipitation generally averages 40 or more inches annually, exceeding 50 inches in the upper parts of the Unakas. The western heights of the Great Smoky Mountains receive over 80 inches a year, making it the wettest area in the eastern United States. The mountains are *orographic* barriers: They cause the winds blowing in from the west to rise as they encounter the western slopes (FIGURE 12.2). The air cools as it ascends, causing it to yield much of its moisture on the windward side. The air descends as it reaches the eastern side of the mountains, and this descent causes the air to heat up again. This effect has created an *isothermal belt* at the foot of the mountains, where temperatures tend to be slightly higher than in areas to the east.

THE SHAPING OF THE BLUE RIDGE

These mountains, which developed more than 125 million years before the Rockies were formed, are among the oldest in the world. They tell a story of alternating periods of deposition, upheaval, and erosion over hundreds of millions of years.

The mostly Precambrian (600 to 800 million years old) rocks of the Blue Ridge system are granite and gneiss that originated in the floor of a great trough that once formed along the coast of the ancient North American continent. In the Unakas, the Ocoee series of rocks contain 20,000 feet of metamorphosed siltstone, sandstone, and conglomerate, sedimentary rocks that span the late Precambrian and early Cambrian ages. Although significantly modified by subsequent heat and pressure, the original sedimentary character of these strata is plainly visible, and they are less altered than are the metamorphic rocks of the Piedmont. The Virginia section of the Blue Ridge contains Precambrian volcanic rocks that were later metamorphosed.

The heat and pressure that modified the Blue Ridge rocks tended to toughen them and make them more uniformly resistant to erosion. This and their great thicknesses, especially in the Unakas, account for their high elevations even after many millions of years of erosion.

The contours of the Blue Ridge and its blanket of forest have been greatly affected by the sculpturing agents of water and air temperature and their influence on the luxuriant plant life. The persistent agent of erosion has gentled the jagged edges and rounded the peaks as it flowed, froze, and thawed its way into every crack and depression. Throughout recent ages, the mountain landscape has been formed and re-formed by the natural forces of floods, windstorms, landslides, and forest fires.

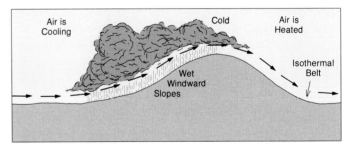

FIGURE 12.2 *Orographic Precipitation*

Heavy rainstorms periodically cause severe flooding and damage in the narrow stream valleys that dissect these mountains. The most dramatic demonstration of this in recent years came in 1972 with Hurricane Agnes, which drifted from the Gulf of Mexico and through the Southeastern states. It dumped close to 10 inches of rain in a 24-hour period in some areas. The massive flooding, landslides, and associated winds made Agnes one of the most destructive hurricanes in the nation's history. In great part, this was not because it was a particularly intense storm but because it dropped so much rain on a hilly terrain, the river channels of which carried the heavy waters out onto densely populated lowlands.

The ridges, slopes, and coves of the Blue Ridge are covered by an abundance of plant life equaled in few other parts of the world. For example, the Great Smokies alone are the home of more than 130 tree species, or about 45 more than exist in all of Western Europe.

The vertical changes in temperature and moisture in the mountains have caused a layering of the forest vegetation. The higher elevations of the Great Smoky Mountains are covered by a spruce-fir forest that is more typical of higher latitudes. In addition to spruce and fir, species include white pine, hemlock, birch, maple, beech, and cherry trees. Below that forest is a zone of northeastern hardwood forest, a more varied array of species: birch, beech, maple, hemlock, white pine, elm, red oak, and basswood. The lower slopes are covered by the oak-pine forest that also covers the Piedmont. Species include a number of oaks, shortleaf pines, pignut, and hickory trees.

The great diversity of vegetation is also the result of other factors, including the last Ice Age. The ancient trees survived on the southern edge of the ice sheet and spread through the cool summits of the southern Appalachians. Ample moisture and sunny, south-facing slopes also encourage a wide variety of plant species. The seasonally changing abundance of blooms, flowering plants, and foliage color is a major part of the area's beauty.

One important species is missing today—the once-prolific American chestnut, revered by early settlers for its many uses due to its durable wood and substantial nut crop. These magnificent trees were totally destroyed by a blight early in this century, a reminder of nature's fragility.

Common soils on the lower slopes are the red-yellow podzolics (ultisols-udults) that are typical of the Piedmont. They are thin, acidic soils that have developed under the warm, humid climate and make an excellent growth medium for great stands of forest. The higher elevations are covered by mountain soils, which are also acidic but even thinner and more poorly developed in the cooler environment.

Cherokee Indian, North Carolina

SETTLING THE SLOPES AND HOLLOWS

Evidence of prehistoric occupation of these mountains dates back 10,000 years, when the mountains were used by Indians as hunting grounds and travel routes. The Cherokee tribe, which derived from the Iroquois to the north, was born in the valleys of the Tellico and Little Tennessee rivers and settled throughout the Southern Appalachian chain and over what is today an eight-state region. One of North America's major tribes, the Cherokee possessed a rich culture, including an advanced system of democratic government, a complete alphabet, and mud-and-log cabin homes—all well before the introduction of European customs.

Throughout the Blue Ridge, a good system of trails existed for hunting, trading, and war (FIGURE 12.3). A major trail, the Great Trading Path, followed the Great Valley, with major forks at Big Lick, the present site of Roanoke, Virginia, and Wolf Hills, among others. One route continued southwestward through the Great Valley and to the Cherokee homeland base along the Tennessee River tributaries. The other cut east through the Roanoke River Gap and then south into the Piedmont and what is today Catawba County. The European pioneers followed these same paths when they came into the area.

The coming of the Europeans led eventually to the tragic demise of the great Cherokee nation in one of the country's most unfortunate episodes. The quest for land and gold brought pressures for Cherokee land, and by 1829, numerous state laws had been passed to declare their constitution null and void and to authorize the division of their lands. The Indian Removal Act of 1830 gave President Andrew Jackson the power to order all Southeastern tribes to relocate in Oklahoma, and the tragedy of the Trail of Tears began (see FIGURE 3.13 on page 48). Of about 20,000 Cherokee who were marched overland through one bitter winter, nearly a quarter died along the way.

Several hundred Cherokee refused to leave and fled deep into the mountains where they remained undetected. A few years later, the government allowed them a much smaller piece of land in their mountains, and they are there today on the Qualla Reservation, their diminished corner of the Blue Ridge.

The first European through the area was the Spanish conquistador Hernando de Soto, who ventured across the southern end of the Blue Ridge in 1540 seeking gold. The first colonists did not begin trickling into the mountains until about 1730. Tales of fertile lands and majestic mountains began filtering back to the Scotch-Irish in the mid-Atlantic states, the Germans in Pennsylvania, and the restless English settlers in the coastal areas. Consequently, many followed the Indian trails leading down the Great Valley and westward along river valleys (FIGURE 12.3). They came in small groups and single families, seeking freedom and their own plot of land. The first settlers located along the more fertile river bottoms, while those who followed often had to seek land higher up the slopes, along creek branches and steeper hillsides. Isolation was the rule, because the coves and hollows could not support large numbers; sometimes the nearest neighbors were five miles away.

Almost everything had to be handmade—shoes, clothing, quilts, baskets, tools, and moonshine. The settlers immediately established a close partnership with the land upon which they depended for their survival. Folkways abounded and music often was the form of entertainment and expression. Drawing upon a rich heritage of Scottish, Irish, and English folk songs, mountain people chose the fiddle and the mournful ballad as the basis for Appalachian music, which later spread to the Ozarks and Texas and eventually farther west (FIGURE 12.4).

With only slight changes, this was the pattern of life in the Blue Ridge for almost two centuries. It was a life of isolation and hard work. Old age came early to these highland dwellers, but they had their independence and their own land in their beloved mountains.

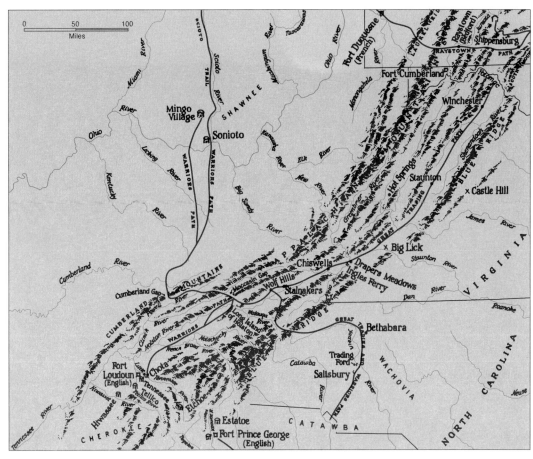

FIGURE 12.3
Major Indian Trails and European Settlement Routes in the Blue Ridge

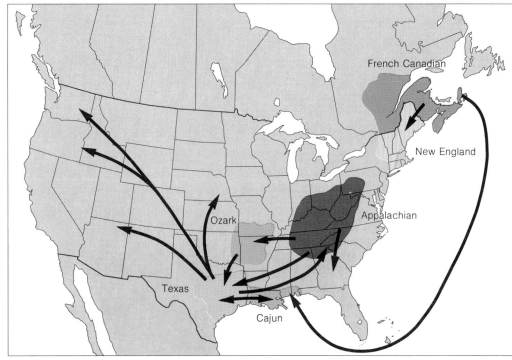

FIGURE 12.4
Spread of Fiddle Music

Appalachian Music

The setting is ideal for music, as are so many places throughout the Blue Ridge. It is a clear, cool summer evening at the foot of Mount Jefferson in Ashe County, North Carolina, where the annual West Jefferson Fiddlers Convention is underway. On the stage, at the base of a grassy slope, old-time fiddler Ralph Blizard and his band play an Appalachian fiddle tune that contains strains of melodies dating back to Ireland and Scotland.

The scene continues late into the night and is repeated many times during the spring, summer, and fall throughout the Blue Ridge Mountains. Each year the music festivals seem to proliferate as musicians from all over the country and the British Isles are drawn to the hills seeking the opportunity to play the old tunes.

The early British settlers brought the original melodies, and as they made their way into the remote coves and hollows of the Blue Ridge, the music was exposed to an Appalachian interpretation that spawned new tunes or variations. The Appalachian songs have a special force and ethereal intensity; many traditional Appalachian singers sing unaccompanied in high lonesome voice, not unlike the fiddle sound. Their unadorned style draws upon the deeply felt sentiments of mountain people in haunting modal melodies, lonely ballads, and hopeful hymns. Life was hard in those early years, bound to the seasons and the land. Music was often the form of release and a means of community. To the strains of the fiddle, then banjo, and later guitar and dulcimer, they danced or sang through the night.

There was a time when it seemed that the old-time Appalachian music was dying out, as younger generations turned toward textile jobs in the flatlands and away from the old customs. But folklorists such as Cecil Sharpe, renowned English song collector, and Bascom Lamar Lunsford, master fiddler from North Carolina's Buncombe County, collected and preserved the songs, often going deep into the Appalachians to trace the sources. Consequently, when a recent generation of musicians rediscovered the richness of the Appalachian music heritage, the tunes were there for the playing. Today Ralph Blizard and others play them with a new virtuosity, but with special care to preserve a form of expression that belongs to many others back through time and the mountains.

Sounds of the Appalachians: traditional music instruments, Carroll County, Virginia

TRANSFORMATION OF THE BLUE RIDGE

Change from the outside world came first with the lumbering industry. The first two decades of the twentieth century saw tremendous amounts of board-foot lumber produced, especially in the vicinity of the Smokies. Railroads were built, sawmills dotted the mountains, and towns emerged. The alteration in the land and the life-style was substantial as mountain people were employed to cut the trees, saw the timber, and lay the roads. Many sold their small tracts of land to the lumber companies. Forests that had stood for centuries were leveled, often leading to heavy erosion. Fires ravaged many mountain slopes.

Next came better roads, rural electrification in the 1930s, and TVA. As the outside world came into the Blue Ridge, the younger generation began discovering better economic opportunity in textile mills of the Piedmont and factories of the North. In some cases, whole families of "millbillies" were recruited by company agents. Seeking work for the entire family, they showed up at the mills in wagons containing all of their worldly goods. Catherine Marshall refers to this in her classic novel, *Christy*, which is based on her mother's experiences as a young schoolteacher in the Smoky Mountains in the early twentieth century. In the prologue, she writes of visiting the area with her mother after the Second World War. The floor of the deserted mountain cabin where her mother lived was littered with pieces of paper; they were receipts of many weeks of pay from a South Carolina textile mill. She looked at the dates and said, "They're so many years back. The children must have left the mountains to work in a mill. And they sent most of their pay home."[1] The strong family bonds that produced this unselfish sharing overcame distance for a while until the old folks died. Few of the children have returned to live in the mountains.

People in the wider valleys and basins established a more prosperous life, and their isolation, never as great, was broken by the opening of roads and railways that permitted their towns to become railway and market hubs. Asheville became a recreational and trade center for this mountain kingdom, the Land of Sky. The forests, minerals, and water of the area support a significant industrial base as well.

As improved roads made the Blue Ridge much

Mabry Mill on the Blue Ridge Parkway

Cades Cove,
Great Smoky Mountains
National Park

more accessible, the final wave of outside forces of change came to the mountains in the form of tourism and resort development. In fact, the Blue Ridge has become one of the nation's major recreational resources. The Great Smoky Mountains National Park contains approximately 516,000 acres, and it receives over 10 million campers, hikers, and sightseers every year. It has spawned commercial developments on its margins, especially in Gatlinburg, Tennessee, the focus of a major ski area. The park includes a particularly unique Blue Ridge environment in Cades Cove, an isolated lowland area surrounded by the western edge of the mountains. Geologists call this a *fenster* (German for "window"), an area in which a break in the general rock reveals underlying strata. In this case, the underlying rock is Paleozoic limestone belonging to the layers that make up the valleys in the adjacent Valley and Ridge province. The same overthrusting that occurred in the Piedmont was responsible for this phenomenon as well. The limestone strata typically produced a fertile soil that attracted settlers as early as 1818. Today the descendants of early settlers operate a few farms under arrangements with the United States Park Service.

Wind Gaps

In any uplands area, the passes through the hills and mountains were critically important to early travelers. Often the major passes are valleys cut by descending rivers, and three (Potomac, James, and Roanoke) cut through the northern half of the Blue Ridge Mountains. However, there are many more passes in the Blue Ridge Mountains through which no rivers flow today. These are called "wind gaps," and they have an interesting geologic history.

Wind gaps are products of *stream piracy*, a process through which one stream enlarges its headwaters faster than other streams and thereby captures part of the other headwaters. The intercepted stream disappears, leaving behind its channel. The Shenandoah Valley has classic examples of this phenomenon.

At one time erosion virtually leveled the area, with the current Blue Ridge Mountains comprising only a string of small hills. The young Shenandoah River and other streams drained the area, cutting right across the young Blue Ridge Mountains. Major earth movements caused the area to be uplifted, and erosion began

wearing the surface down as the streams cut down more vigorously in response to the increased gradient. The Shenandoah River, flowing across the relatively easily eroded limestone floor of the Shenandoah Valley, quickly enlarged its headwaters. Meanwhile, the crystalline rocks of the Blue Ridge Mountains resisted the renewed erosion, and the streams that crossed them became divided into two parts. The northwestern portions were captured by the advancing Shenandoah River, while the shorter southeastern segments continued to flow across the Piedmont. Eventually, all of the streams that previously cut across the Blue Ridge Mountains were captured in this way by the Shenandoah River. The former stream valleys were left high and dry as today's wind gaps. These passes (most notably Cumberland Gap, the historic pass that Daniel Boone followed from Virginia into Kentucky) occur throughout the Southern Uplands.

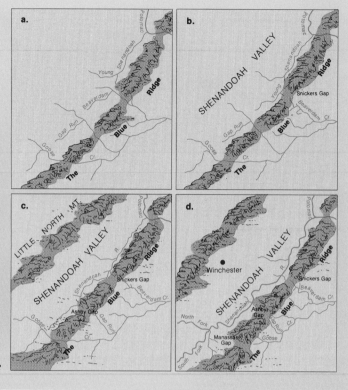

Wind Gaps of the Blue Ridge

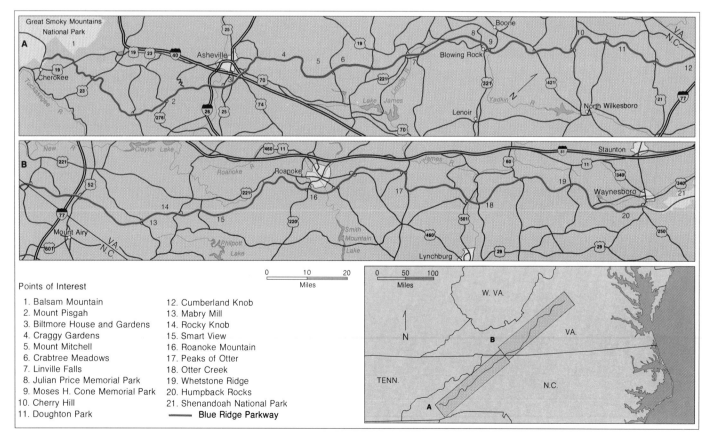

Points of Interest

1. Balsam Mountain
2. Mount Pisgah
3. Biltmore House and Gardens
4. Craggy Gardens
5. Mount Mitchell
6. Crabtree Meadows
7. Linville Falls
8. Julian Price Memorial Park
9. Moses H. Cone Memorial Park
10. Cherry Hill
11. Doughton Park
12. Cumberland Knob
13. Mabry Mill
14. Rocky Knob
15. Smart View
16. Roanoke Mountain
17. Peaks of Otter
18. Otter Creek
19. Whetstone Ridge
20. Humpback Rocks
21. Shenandoah National Park
—— Blue Ridge Parkway

The Shenandoah National Park covers approximately 195,000 acres of the Blue Ridge Mountains in Virginia, between Front Royal and Waynesboro. It attracts several million visitors annually and is the northern terminus of the Blue Ridge Parkway (FIGURE 12.5), a ridgetop road that winds 469 miles through the Blue Ridge until it ends at the Great Smoky Mountains National Park, near Cherokee, North Carolina. Begun in 1935, this scenic highway, which affords a simultaneous view in Virginia of the Shenandoah Valley and the Piedmont, reached final completion in September 1987 with the construction of the Linn Cove Viaduct around Grandfather Mountain. Attracting over 17 million visitors a year, the Blue Ridge Parkway is one of the most beautiful drives in America as it winds around mountain folds, cutting gracefully through a blaze of rhododendron in spring or the foliage of fall. It is the most visited federal parkland area east of California.

FIGURE 12.5
The Blue Ridge Parkway

In the 1960s, the Appalachian highlands, especially in the Blue Ridge, began to experience a major episode of recreational development. Overbuilding of condominiums and amusement centers threaten to destroy, in places, the prized environment that people were seeking to enjoy. One of the attractions that also drew people into the region was the emergence of a ski industry. Twenty or more ski centers were opened in the Blue Ridge, with the largest cluster operating around the Boone–Blowing Rock area in North Carolina. Snow-making machines supplement the erratic natural snowfall of the mountains.

A subtle but perhaps more pervasive threat than overdevelopment to the Blue Ridge is acid rain. This form of air pollution appears to be killing thousands of trees here. Acid rain is responsible for current acute levels of destruction in European countries, and left unchecked, it could denude these lovely mountains, subjecting their slopes to massive erosion.

Although the transformation of the Blue Ridge has had some negative consequences for the land and culture, there are positive aspects as well. With the outside influences have come better economic well-being and improved educational opportunity for the people. And, in recent years, there has been a resurgence of interest in preserving Appalachian folkways, music, and crafts. An Appalachian consortium of universities and agencies has been created for just such a purpose. Land-use regulations and planning have helped control some of the extremes of resort over-development. Cities such as Asheville and Roanoke are revitalizing their downtowns and restoring a rich historical legacy.

A renewed sense of community and of the land is continuously observed. In places throughout the Blue Ridge, get-togethers and celebrations of all sorts go on: street festivals, apple festivals, craft fairs, dance contests, and fiddlers' conventions. Often music seems to be a common bond of the strong sentiments about the mountains. These high places are not only becoming a new home to those discovering the lure of the hills, they are now beginning to hold onto their own and welcome back those who have left for a while.

*Ski slopes in
North Carolina mountains*

Blue Ridge Parkway

13 THE VALLEY & RIDGE

The Shenandoah Valley, land of green meadows, mist-shrouded valleys, limestone caverns, Civil War battle-fields, and historic towns, is one of America's premier scenic areas. It is also the best-known part of the long Great Valley system that runs for hundreds of miles from Pennsylvania into central Alabama. Actually, the name Great Valley is something of a misnomer, because the Valley and Ridge province of which it is a part is really a long corridor of narrow, sometimes zigzag ridges alternating with valleys. The entire complex is about 65 miles wide in Virginia but narrows to only 40 miles in east Tennessee and in central Alabama, where it ends by abutting the East Gulf Coastal Plain (FIGURE 13.1).

GEOLOGY

The topographic variety of the Valley and Ridge is a direct product of the regional geology, but it is a complex situation. The same collision of landmasses and later tectonic events that transformed the Pied-mont and the Blue Ridge highlands bent and fractured beds of sedimentary rocks laid down during the Pa-leozoic era in the continental interior. The heat and pressure of this trauma were less here, however, and the original limestone, shale, and sandstone were only slightly changed or metamorphosed.

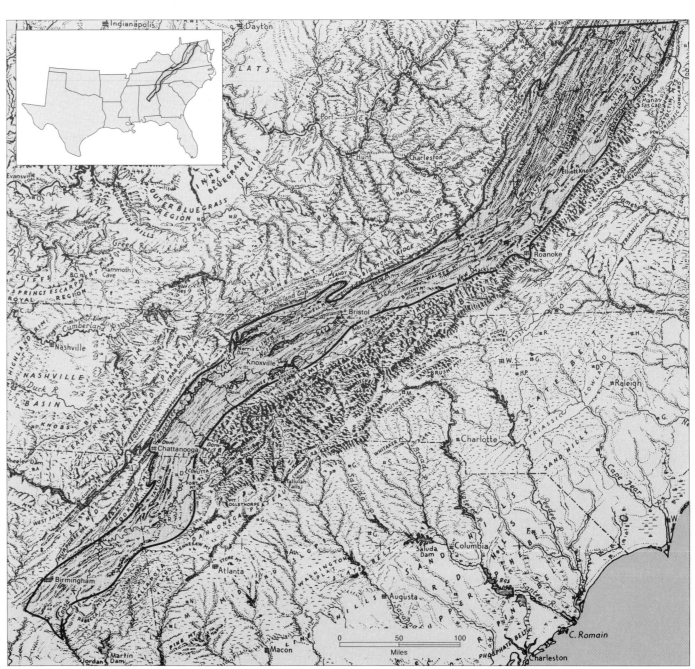

FIGURE 13.1
The Valley & Ridge

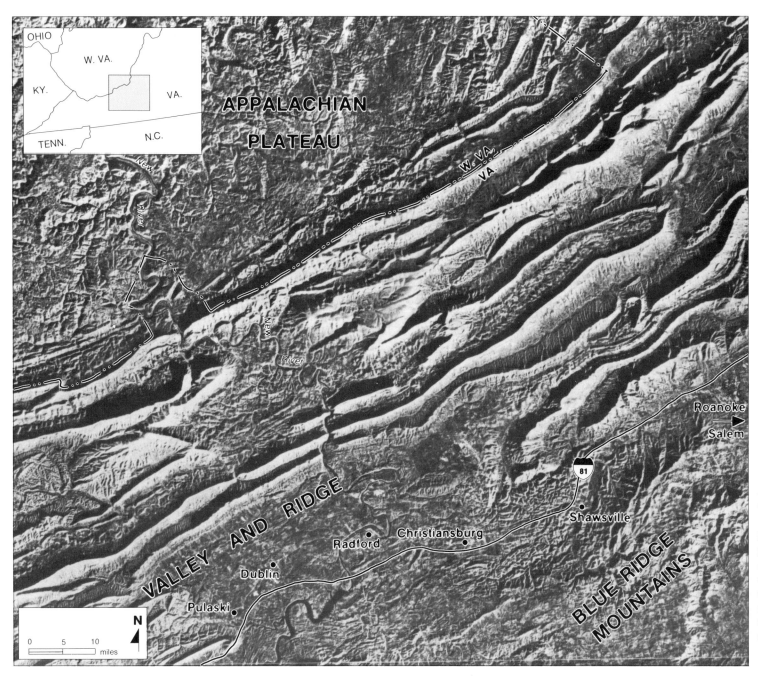

OHIO

W. VA.

KY.

VA.

TENN.

N.C.

APPALACHIAN

PLATEAU

New River

W. VA. VA.

New River

VALLEY AND RIDGE

Roanoke

Salem

81

Shawsville

Christiansburg

Radford

Dublin

Pulaski

BLUE RIDGE MOUNTAINS

N

0   5   10   miles

Radar photograph of a segment of the Valley and Ridge in Virginia. The Great Valley portion is the more level portion followed by Interstate 81. Paralleling it to the northwest are the characteristic elongated ridges that run up against the edge of the Appalachian Plateau, near the Virginia–West Virginia state line.

The pressure from the southeast not only changed the internal character of these rocks but also bent them to produce fold features known as *synclines* and *anticlines* (FIGURE 13.2). The former are structural valleys and the latter are structural hills, the up-and-down parts of folding. In the southern part of the Valley and Ridge, the pressure was so severe that some folds were pushed over on their sides and even faulted, causing broken folds to slide over each other (*thrust faults*). However, the creation of anticlines and synclines through folding and faulting did not immediately create the contemporary topography. In fact, the work of erosion has reversed the earlier landscape (FIGURE 13.3). In the millions of years that have transpired since the last episode of folding, erosion has removed the less-resistant rocks more rapidly than some others. Typically, limestone (which is highly soluble in the warm, humid climate) has been removed most rapidly. Shale, weak but not as soluble as limestone, was denuded more slowly. Sandstone, composed of virtually insoluble silica sands, proved to be far more resistant to the destructive powers of wind, water, heat, and cold. Consequently, today the long, more or less parallel ridges do not necessarily occur where anticlines were created but where strong beds

of sandstone are found. Conversely, the valleys tend to be underlain by the weak limestone. It is common for topographic ridges to form from the bottoms of ancient synclines where layers of sandstone were hardened by the compression that accompanied folding. The uparching that formed anticlines stretched the outer layers of rock, causing them to crack. These cracks accelerated the penetration of underlying limestone beds by groundwater, resulting in their dissolution and removal. Thus the former hill now is a valley and the former valley is a ridgetop.

The relationship between topography and rock composition has been a fortuitous one for the Valley and Ridge area. The sandstone-capped ridges tend to produce a relatively poor soil, but the limestone valleys are blessed with rich soil. This is not universal throughout the valleys, since in some areas the valley is floored with shale, a source of clayey, acidic soil.

The tendency of the valley floors to have good soil combined with the expanses of rolling land and proximity to rivers to make the valleys of this region a highly prized environment to the original settlers and their descendants. The scenic beauty of the terrain enhances its economic viability.

FIGURE 13.2
Formation of Anticlines, Synclines, and Thrust Faults

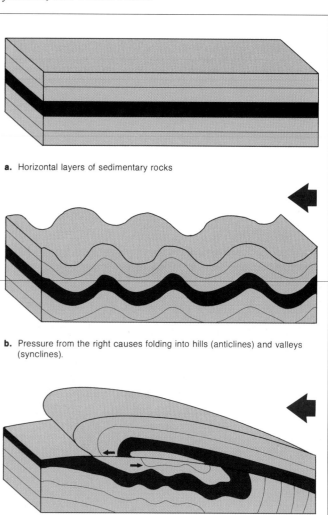

a. Horizontal layers of sedimentary rocks

b. Pressure from the right causes folding into hills (anticlines) and valleys (synclines).

c. Continued pressure causes the folds to fracture, forming thrust faults along which the folded layers slide over each other.

The Shenandoah Valley of Virginia

FIGURE 13.3 *Inverted Topography*

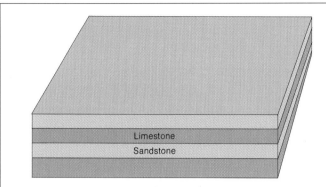

a. Horizontal layers of sedimentary rocks

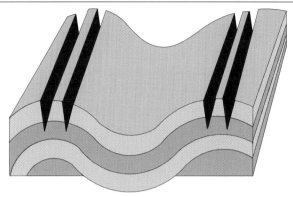

b. Compression causes the layers to fold. Stretching along the ridge top cracks the strata, allowing water to seep into and dissolve the underlying limestone. The sandstone in the valley floor is compressed and resists erosion.

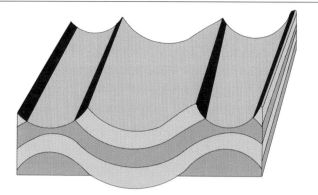

c. Continued erosion creates valleys under the former ridge, while the sandstone remnant now tops a ridge. Thus the original topography is inverted.

Four geologic features in Tennessee:

Horizontally layered sedimentary rocks

Small syncline

Small anticline

Faulting. Diagonal layer is the fault zone. Folded layers in the upper right appear to have moved up over those in the lower left.

From a cultural perspective, the Valley and Ridge area is defined primarily by the major valleys and the river systems that drain them. The Great Valley is a string of valleys on the eastern side of the Valley and Ridge province. On the western side, especially in Maryland, West Virginia, and Virginia, the ridges are closer together, and consequently, the valley floors are much more narrow. The Shenandoah Valley is the widest expanse of the Great Valley. It runs northward from about Buchanan (locally pronounced "Buck-hanan"), Virginia, into Pennsylvania. The valley is drained by the Potomac River, most particularly its tributary, the Shenandoah, and by the James River. The Potomac breaches the Blue Ridge at historic Harpers Ferry, West Virginia. In its central extent, south of Winchester, Virginia, the Shenandoah Valley is split by Massanutten Mountain, a synclinal ridge topped by the Clinch sandstone, a formation that protects many a ridgetop in the Great Valley from erosion. The Shenandoah River splits into north and south forks as it goes around Massanutten Mountain.

Drainage Patterns

The pattern formed by the network of streams that carry water over a landscape is a vital aspect of its topography. There are three basic types of such patterns, and all occur in the Valley and Ridge province.

Solitary, rounded peaks have streams that flow down in a *radial* pattern from the center of the mountain. This pattern develops most clearly on the flanks of large volcanic cones, but it is evident occasionally on hills in the Valley and Ridge province.

With *trellis* drainage, streams flow straight down the ridge into the master streams moving through the adjacent valley floor. The looping valleys of the dendritic pattern are missing, at least among the tributary streams.

On generally level surfaces of homogeneous character, a branchlike or *dendritic* pattern forms. Small streams carve winding valleys that lead into progressively larger streams, typically forming a master stream that carries the entire runoff into the ocean. A mature dendritic system will carve the originally level surface into a deeply dissected terrain of valleys and intervening hills that separate one stream from another.

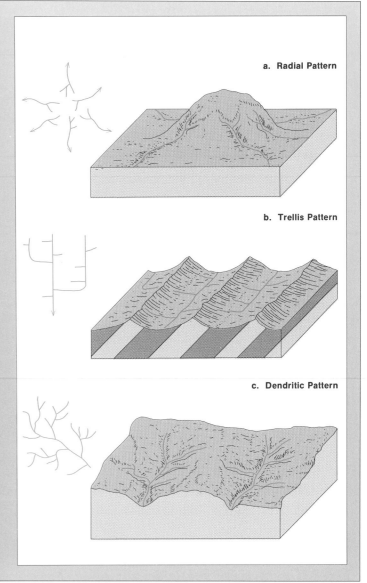

a. Radial Pattern

b. Trellis Pattern

c. Dendritic Pattern

The Blue Ridge Mountains to the east contain numerous wind gaps that were important passes through the mountains onto the Piedmont. However, the next river south of the Potomac that cuts through the mountains is the James, more than 150 miles distant. There also the Shenandoah Valley pinches out. Smaller valley areas continue through Fincastle and into the Roanoke Valley, site of another river through the mountains. Here, 40 miles south of the James, the Roanoke River flows out of the Great Valley on its journey to Albemarle Sound in North Carolina.

The Potomac River at Harpers Ferry, West Virginia

These three river gaps (Potomac, James, and Roanoke) have been important transportation corridors since the beginning of European settlement (FIGURE 13.4). They were improved by canals before the railroad era; the Chesapeake and Ohio Canal (now a national historic park) was completed along the Potomac all the way from Washington to Cumberland, Maryland, in 1850.

The next year the James River Canal was finished as far west as Buchanan and beyond, connecting valley towns with Richmond and eventually Norfolk. Very soon afterwards the canals were superseded by the rail network that was flung across the United States in the latter half of the nineteenth century. The Baltimore and Ohio Railway followed the Potomac Valley, and the James River Valley was chosen by the Chesapeake and Ohio Railway. The latter line and the Norfolk and Western, which followed the Roanoke Valley, extended rail lines into the Appalachian coal fields of Virginia, Kentucky, and West Virginia. Soon after the turn of the century, the Virginian Railway paralleled the Norfolk and Western in carrying great coal trains out of the mountains to the ports at Hampton Roads. The Virginian was later absorbed into the Norfolk and Western, which in turn merged with the Southern to form the Norfolk-Southern Railway.

FIGURE 13.4
Rivers, Early Railroads, and Canals in the Valley of Northern Virginia
Railroad names changed a number of times during the nineteenth century and since that time. The following major railroad names, which were in use by the late nineteenth century, are abbreviated on this map: Baltimore and Ohio, Chesapeake and Ohio, and Norfolk and Western.

Locks on the old James River Canal

The floor of the Great Valley stands at about 600 to 800 feet above sea level in northern Virginia and West Virginia (FIGURE 13.1). It rises steadily until it reaches an elevation of 2,500 feet at the divide between the drainage basins of the Shenandoah and James rivers near Staunton. It descends again to about 1,200 feet in the James River Valley and then rises again slightly to the southwest at the divide between the James and Roanoke river basins. Another valley has been cut by the Roanoke River, which goes on to follow its valley eastward through the Blue Ridge Mountains. To the southwest of Roanoke, the Great Valley is blocked by hills, such as Christiansburg Mountain, which rise to 2,200 feet in elevation. These hills were an effective barrier to many early settlers, who, instead of trying to climb them, turned eastward through the Roanoke River gap and issued out onto the Piedmont. Thus, they followed the Piedmont into the Carolinas and Georgia. Those who continued down the valley by climbing the blocking hills tended to travel nearly 200 miles to the next valley through the Appalachian Plateau or the Cumberland Gap in Kentucky, or they followed the Great Valley into Tennessee.

Ascent of Christiansburg Mountain and the other hills brings one onto a more elevated valley floor that also contains the drainage divide between the Roanoke and New rivers. Here is something of a continental divide in that the waters of the New River ultimately flow into the Gulf of Mexico via the Ohio River, whereas the Roanoke drains into the Atlantic Ocean. The hilly valley floor around Wytheville, Virginia, rises to about 2,500 feet, where the drainage divide between the New and the Tennessee river basins occurs. The Great Valley southwestward into Tennessee and Alabama is more of a continuous valley, although it narrows overall to 30 or 40 miles. Surface elevations in Tennessee are lower and drop steadily to about 400 feet where the Valley and Ridge meets the East Gulf Coastal Plain south of Birmingham, Alabama. The Tennessee River drains the broad valley in east Tennessee until it enters its meandering gorge through the Appalachian Plateau at Chattanooga. The southernmost section of the Valley and Ridge is drained by the Coosa River, which rises in the Blue Ridge in northern Georgia and flows down the length of the Great Valley until it leaves it just north of Montgomery, Alabama.

EARLY SETTLEMENT

The Valley and Ridge area, most particularly the Great Valley, was settled (as noted earlier) from the north southward as Scotch-Irish and Germans poured into the valley from Pennsylvania beginning around 1732.

Not only did these people represent one of the most important population groups that settled the South, but their movements clearly demonstrated the strong relationship between topography and early settlement. This relationship is illustrated vividly in the maps of FIGURE 13.5, which portray the spread of Presbyterianism, the denomination of Scots and Scotch-Irish, in the eighteenth century. Strong controls in the beginning on the evolution of these patterns were the Valley and Ridge corridor that opened up into Pennsylvania and the ports of entry along the Delaware Bay.

The 1750 map shows this movement being deflected southwestward into the Valley and Ridge as the settlers sought to avoid the wall of the escarpment that marks the beginning of the Appalachian Plateau. Had the topography been more open at this point, presumably the Scotch-Irish would have headed straight westward into Ohio. The 1776 pattern is more fully developed in the Shenandoah Valley, and some of the Presbyterians had moved westward into Pittsburgh and the upper Ohio Valley. However, the main event in the South was the deflection once again of the flow of Presbyterians by the topography. The closing of the Shenandoah Valley around the James River gap near Fincastle and the blockage of the valley by hills south of the Roanoke River gap caused the Presbyterians to move through these gaps and onto the Piedmont. They then moved over the more open terrain southwestward all the way into South Carolina.

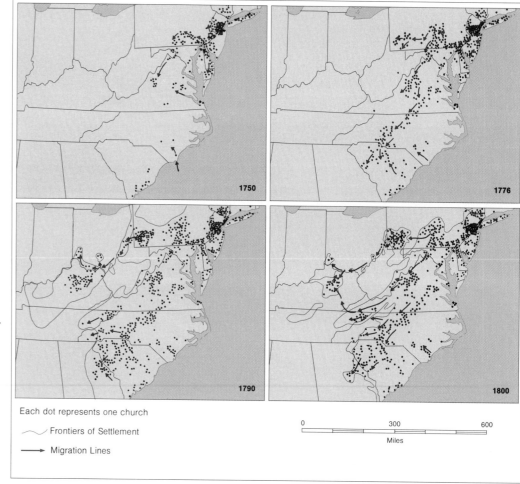

FIGURE 13.5
*Spread of
Presbyterian Churches*

Each dot represents one church

〰 Frontiers of Settlement

→ Migration Lines

0   300   600

Miles

By 1790, the invasion of the Ohio Valley via Pittsburgh into Louisville and the Cincinnati area was well developed. In the South, some of the Presbyterians pushed into southwestern Virginia and eastern Tennessee or followed the Cumberland Gap into the Lexington Basin. There that migration stream coalesced with the one in the Ohio Valley. On the Piedmont, the pattern was more diffuse, extending into Georgia and, following river valleys, into the Blue Ridge. By 1800, the earlier pattern had become more extensive on its edges, especially in the Blue Ridge and in Georgia. Outside the Lexington Basin, however, the Presbyterians almost totally avoided the Appalachian Plateau country of West Virginia, Kentucky, and Tennessee.

These maps also make clear the pivotal role that the Valley and Ridge topography played in peopling the South. It acted as an inverted funnel through which thousands of settlers were directed to their new home sites throughout the South. Those who stayed in the Shenandoah Valley established a region of farms similar to those to the north. Wheat, other grains, cattle, and horses were characteristic features. Cotton was not grown, slaveholding was minimal, and mules were seldom used. This area became the granary of the Confederacy during the Civil War. It was a strategic corridor into Union areas from the South, but to the Union, the valley led away from Richmond and other more strategic targets. Robert E. Lee's armies moved into the valley west of Frederick through a wind gap before being stopped at Sharpsburg, Maryland, in the battle of Antietam Creek. Earlier, Thomas J. "Stonewall" Jackson used the topography of the valley around Massanutten Mountain to shield his small force from a larger Union army. Late in the war, Union armies ravaged the valley in order to deny its food to the Confederacy.

General farming was the tendency in the southern part of the Great Valley, although some cotton was grown in the Alabama portion. Slaves were not numerous in this stretch of the valley. East Tennessee was a major source of hogs, mules, and horses in the antebellum period. Large herds were driven up the French Broad River near Asheville and out onto the Piedmont, where they were purchased by the cotton plantations.

The different settlement history and agricultural practices in the Great Valley were the basis for political and cultural differences with the Lowland South that still persist. They were even stronger before and after the Civil War. Secession ardor was generally modest, and some counties sent as many troops to the Union as to the Confederacy; east Tennessee became a Republican stronghold. After the Civil War, federal legislation established land grant universities, and as one of these, the University of Tennessee was located in Knoxville rather than in middle or west Tennessee, which were more populous parts of the state but also more loyal to the defeated Confederacy. This hampered support for the university from Democratically controlled legislatures until well into the twentieth century. The university's emergence as a national football power did as much as anything to generate the legislative support that later helped make it into one of the South's largest universities. The university was a major factor in Knoxville's emergence as the regional capital of east Tennessee.

The Virginia Military Institute in Lexington, Virginia

Jackson's Valley Campaign

A famous student of Valley and Ridge topography was Thomas J. ("Stonewall") Jackson, brilliant Confederate general and pioneer advocate of tactical mobility. In the spring of 1862, he was given orders to keep Union armies under Generals Nathaniel P. Banks and Irvin McDowell from reinforcing General George B. McClellan in the latter's planned attack on Richmond. Stationed in Winchester, Virginia, Jackson used the topography of the Shenandoah Valley, especially Massanutten Mountain, which runs down its middle, to shield his armies from the confused Union forces. Between March 12 and June 9, 1862, his army, numbering between 6,000 and 15,000 troops, marched up and down the valley either seeking battle or avoiding it when conditions were unfavorable. In one 15-day period, his "marching cavalry" covered 215 miles, nearly 15 miles a day, fighting four battles or heavy skirmishes in the process. In so doing, Jackson tied up over 50,000 Union troops and twice caused President Abraham Lincoln to cancel orders for the Richmond assaults.

James T. Sowder, a soldier in Jackson's army, gave a vivid account of the heart of the campaign—the surprise attack on Front Royal and the subsequent advance on Winchester—in a letter written near Winchester on May 26, 1862. After marching 37 miles in two days, Jackson's forces surprised the small Union garrison at the critical railroad station in Front Royal and then marched another 22 miles toward Winchester to fight again. The day after the Front Royal battle, Sowder wrote that "we advanced that night until about an hour before day. We then lay down beside the road until daylight. We were then within two miles of Winchester." After describing the rout of Banks' forces at Winchester and the capture of much-needed supplies, Sowder wrote, "It has been one of our greatest victories, I think, we have ever won, for we have lost so few men and accomplished so much. There has been a good deal of grumbling at General Jackson about marching us so much, but this tune has changed now, and they think he is one of the greatest men that have ever lived. For my part, I don't think

the least hard of him for anything that we have to do." Sowder never returned to his Shawsville, Virginia, home.

(The observations of James Sowder were taken from a letter belonging to one of his descendants, Mary Louise Stuart. James was the older brother of her grandmother, Louisa Sowder Bell.)

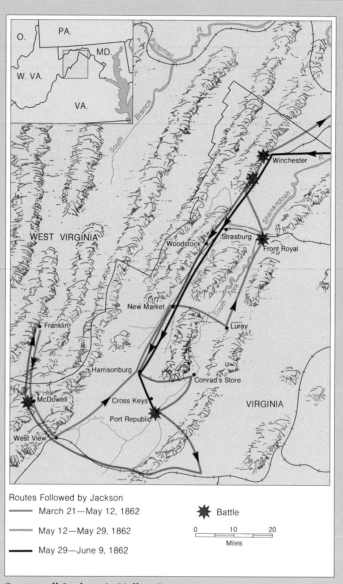

Routes Followed by Jackson
— March 21—May 12, 1862
— May 12—May 29, 1862
— May 29—June 9, 1862

✳ Battle

0   10   20
Miles

Stonewall Jackson's Valley Campaign

THE ENVIRONMENT TODAY

Mineral resources have been vital in the development of the Valley and Ridge area. The Paleozoic rock formations carry beds of salt, some of which reach the surface in the form of brine as groundwater dissolves the salt and brings it upwards. Saltville, in southwest Virginia, was an important source of salt for the early settlers and a major salt source for the Confederacy. Gypsum is mined in the area, with one shaft reaching 1,900 feet below the surface before it was closed. Today, after 150 years of salt mining, some shafts are collapsing, causing the surface to subside. Other salt springs attracted wild game, and they became important hunting sites for Indians and Europeans.

Roanoke, Virginia, is built on a salt lick, the reason for its original name of Big Lick. This was changed to the present name in the 1880s after Philadelphia investors made Roanoke the intersection between a rail line being built down the Great Valley and another line extending across the state from Norfolk to Bristol. This intersection and the location in Roanoke of the new Norfolk and Western's office and shops triggered such explosive growth that the new city took as its nickname the "Magic City." The railroad prospered as it hauled huge tonnages of high-grade bituminous coal out of the Appalachian fields to Norfolk. From there it was shipped up the coast to northeastern industrial areas and to overseas markets.

Small quantities of coal also were delivered to sites up and down the valley where it was combined with local iron ore and limestone to make iron and, less commonly, steel. Blast furnaces mostly produced pig iron that was shipped northward to steel mills. These merchant pig-iron mills were important industrial employers in the Valley and Ridge, initially undergirding the growth of Roanoke and other towns (FIGURE 13.6). After 1920, the national market for steel temporarily collapsed, and virtually every blast furnace in the Valley and Ridge went out of business and never reopened. When the national industry recovered, the big steel companies found it more economical to produce pig iron near the steel mills, so they moved coal to the big, integrated steel mills of Pennsylvania and the Great Lakes area. Fortunately, by this time the towns that were built, in part, around an ironworks had grown to add other industries to their economic bases.

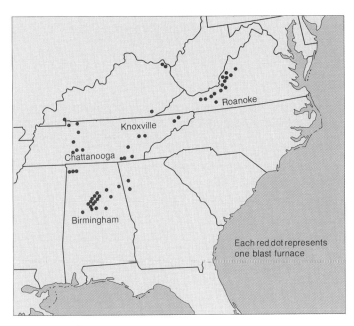

FIGURE 13.6
*Location of Blast Furnaces
in the Southeast, 1900*

More enduring was the iron-and-steel complex that developed around Birmingham. Red Mountain, which is near the city, contains a seam of hematite ore that extends for 25 miles with a thickness of 15 to 22 feet. It also is interspersed with layers of limestone, which makes the ore self-fluxing, an unusual advantage. Nearby in the Appalachian Plateau are several coal-fields, including those in the Black Warrior basin.

Coal from that field is of coking quality, the form of coal essential in making iron. This proximity of basic resources initially offset the low quality of the iron ore deposits. Iron production around Birmingham was crucial to the Confederacy, but the advantages of raw materials in such close proximity were not recognized and exploited on a major scale until about 1880. An intense rivalry with earlier production

The Tennessee Valley Authority

The Tennessee River, which rises in the Appalachian highlands and drains parts of the Valley and Ridge and Appalachian Plateau regions, has been notorious for the violent floods that periodically devastated its valley.

After the First World War, Henry Ford sought to purchase, at a bargain price, the Muscle Shoals Dam complex on the river in Alabama. It had been built by the federal government to provide hydroelectricity used in extracting nitrates from the air for gunpowder. Senator George William Norris of Kansas opposed this

virtual giveaway, and Mr. Ford withdrew his offer in the mid-1920s. Soon after, President Franklin D. Roosevelt saw in this poverty-stricken, flood-ravaged valley an opportunity to develop regional planning as a tool for dealing with the depression and the chronic poverty of the South.

The Tenneseee Valley Authority was established to be the "silver yardstick" of river-basin planning and development. It would involve power generation, navigation, flood control, recreational development, and overall land-use planning. Despite charges of socialism and other ideological objections (which persist to this day), the TVA opened the first facility it built, Norris Dam, in 1936.

Today the Tennessee Valley Authority operates over 40 dams that create a host of reservoirs and generate large amounts of hydroelectricity, and the Tennessee River has a minimum nine-foot channel throughout its entire course from the Kentucky Dam to Knoxville. Currently, about 80 percent of the energy produced by the TVA is generated in coal-burning or nuclear plants; this federal agency purchases over 50 million tons of coal a year. In 1933, only 3 percent of the farms in the TVA area had electricity, but by 1954, this was raised to 93 percent.

The navigable waterway and large supplies of electricity were important factors in the economic development of the region. Heavy energy users, such as the Alcoa Aluminum Refinery near Knoxville, were attracted to the area. The most unusual development was the Oak Ridge National Laboratory, built in isolated valleys near Knoxville during the Second World War to produce plutonium for atomic bombs. It still consumes huge quantities of electricity, and it has attracted so many scientists and engineers that the Knoxville metropolitan area has one of the largest concentrations of Ph.D.'s in the country.

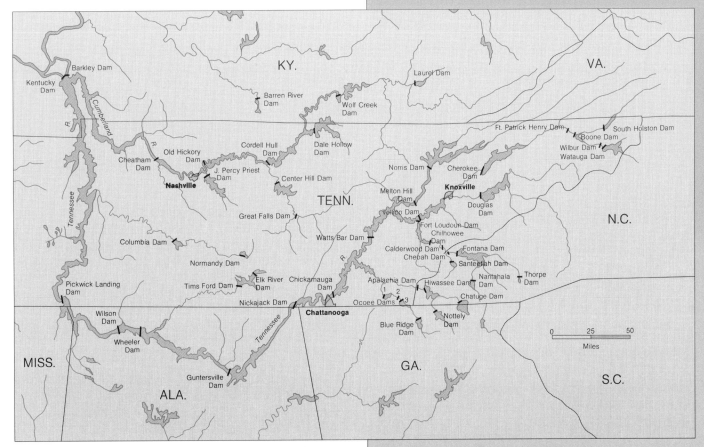

The Tennessee Valley Authority Region

centers in Pennsylvania ensued as the Birmingham district developed into one of the world's leading iron-producing districts in the late nineteenth century. In 1907, the United States Steel Corporation gained control of the Tennessee Coal and Iron Company, owner of a substantial part of the iron-and-steel production facilities in Birmingham. Discriminatory pricing policies established by the major steel companies, including United States Steel, helped to keep the Birmingham district from realizing its potential. The closeness of the iron-making mineral deposits as an advantage was canceled by the difficulties associated with extracting the coal and iron ore. This, coupled with increasing labor costs, further retarded the industry's future growth. High mining costs were reduced after World War II, when iron ore from new Venezuelan deposits was brought into Mobile and shipped up the canalized Black Warrior River to a point near Birmingham. However, in the 1980s, the Birmingham iron-and-steel industry contracted sharply and perhaps permanently as the United States steel industry generally declined. Meanwhile, the city has grown beyond its initial dependence on the steel industry and has emerged as a major Southern commercial center.

The Valley and Ridge is one of the South's most inviting regions. In addition to its scenic beauty and historic interest, it contains some of the world's most picturesque caverns. These formed from the solution of the extensive limestone beds in the valleys. Limestone caverns are common throughout the region, but the best known are around Front Royal, Luray, and New Market, Virginia.

Today, the influence of topography on life in the Valley and Ridge is not nearly so obvious as it was in the eighteenth century. Highways and rail lines mostly follow the valleys, which are also where the people live. At the same time, some roads, especially interstate highways such as Interstate 77, cut right across the grain of the land. They allow the motorist to ignore the topography except, of course, when heavy rains trigger landslides that temporarily close the roads.

However, now as in the past, the Valley and Ridge derives much of its significance from being a scenic corridor connecting the northeast with the Deep South. This will be true in the future as well.

The Spas of Virginia and West Virginia

In the Valley and Ridge and Appalachian Plateau areas of Virginia and West Virginia, a number of springs bring mineralized waters to the surface. The waters carry various salts, sulfur dioxide, iron, and other minerals. Additionally, there are thermal springs in which the waters have temperatures as high as 106°F. All of these waters have long been thought to have curative powers, and people were attracted to them. Beginning in the late 1700s, hotels were built around several of these springs, and as many as 75 spas (some located on the map) attracted visitors from the entire eastern United States.

Before and after the Civil War, whole families would come to the spas in the summer to escape the heat of the Lowlands and to take the waters. The spas also became famous gathering places for politicians.

The spas declined in the twentieth century, and most of them closed. Today the Homestead in Hot Springs, Virginia, and the Greenbrier in White Sulphur Springs, West Virginia, continue the tradition of gracious resorts, but the rest of the spas are gone. A few remnants are visible, such as the gazebo made of tree limbs at the site of the Alleghany Springs Spa near Shawsville, Virginia, but typically only the springs themselves remain.

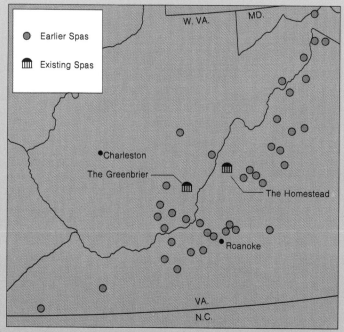

Historic Spas of Virginia and West Virginia

14 THE APPALACHIAN PLATEAU & INTERIOR LOW PLATEAUS

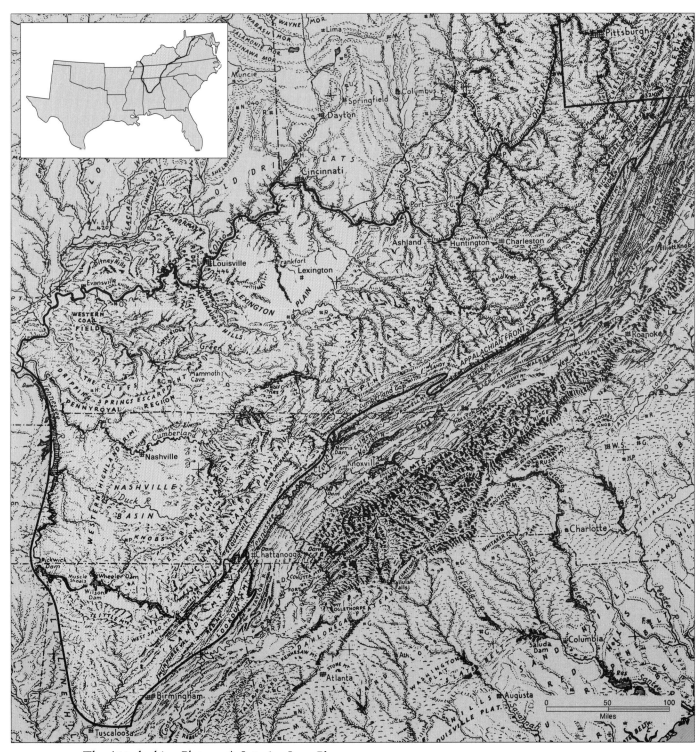

FIGURE 14.1 *The Appalachian Plateau & Interior Low Plateaus*

West of the Valley and Ridge province lies a region of startling variation. The contrasts within it are as dramatic as any in the South. Here, in the Appalachian Plateau and Interior Low Plateaus, one finds very rich soils and extremely poor ones, gently rolling bluegrass pastures and steep, rugged terrain (FIGURE 14.1). Two prosperous areas, the Lexington Plain and the Nashville Basin, seem worlds apart from the isolated and impoverished coal counties that surround them. In the eastern part of this region, numerous streams have eroded and cut the surface into a sharply pitched jumble, whereas parts of the west feature karst topography with its sinkholes, dry solution valleys, and disappearing streams. Natural forces, especially water acting on various types of strata, have created great differences across these plateaus.

The Appalachian Plateau and Interior Low Plateaus have much in common structurally. Both consist of layer upon layer of sedimentary rocks that have experienced a great deal of erosion through time. The differences within the region spring from the types of rocks that have been exposed. Sandstone and shale have been the basis for poor soils and certain kinds of surface features; limestone, under the influence of erosive forces, has produced very different environments.

The varied nature of this region's land testifies to the connection between ancient geologic history and the conditions of modern life. Rich lands in this region are associated with affluent communities; poorer lands seem linked to poor people. Perhaps nowhere else is the influence of the land on its people more clear. Some blame the land directly for problems of poverty in Appalachia, a charge that may be overly simple. But if basic features of the Appalachian Plateau have not caused poverty, they certainly have made good transportation, economic development, and affluence difficult to attain there. Conversely, prosperous areas within the interior plateaus have always been fertile and productive, attractive to settlers, and, consequently, centers of wealth.

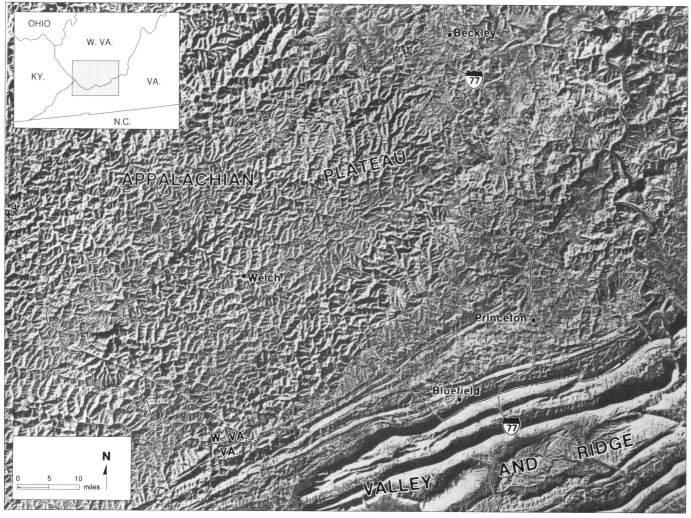

A radar photograph taken by the U.S. Geological Survey in May 1984. Most of the photograph illustrates the dissection by streams of a portion of the Appalachian Plateau into a hilly terrain. Notice the strong contrast with the elongate ridges and valleys in the lower right corner.

Some development has occurred along Interstate 77, which includes a major segment of the West Virginia Turnpike, but otherwise, this plateau area is sparsely populated. Several tunnels carry Interstate 77 through mountains in Virginia before the highway climbs onto the Appalachian Plateau.

Whether rich or poor, the residents of the Appalachian Plateau and Interior Low Plateaus have shown a characteristic devotion to their region. It has been home to rich and poor, and it continues to evoke symbols tied strongly to the South. Kentucky racehorses, Kentucky bourbon, Harlan County coal miners, country music, and Nashville's Grand Ole Opry—where could one find a set of images more closely connected with Southern life?

FORMATION OF THE LAND

The Appalachian Plateau and Interior Low Plateaus are bordered on the east by a long escarpment and on the north and west by the Ohio River. These two boundaries point toward the influence of distant geologic events: the collision of continental plates and (much more recently) the Ice Age (FIGURE 14.2).

When the prehistoric continents collided, the effect was like a battering ram pushing in from the southeast, folding and thrusting up rock layers to form the Blue Ridge and the Valley and Ridge provinces. As noted earlier, the area farther inland was too remote from the collision to be turned into mountains, but a long ridge appeared on its eastern edge. This escarpment, the Appalachian Front (also called the Allegheny Front to the north and the Cumberland Front farther south), lies at the hinge where land was bent upward or downward. Along part of its length faulting or slippage of rock layers occurred.

Though more easily crossed today, the Appalachian Front was a formidable barrier to westward migration. It ran all the way from Alabama to Pennsylvania, a distance of 700 miles. This escarpment presented an apparently solid wall several hundred feet high to pioneers, who previously had been able to zigzag their way west through the Valley and Ridge region. Thus, the Appalachian Front dammed up the westward flow of migration, forcing a pause in the onrushing stream of American settlement. Rediscovery of the Cumberland Gap released a torrent of frontiersmen and farmers eager to see the lands of Kentucky. Though Daniel Boone was not the first to find the Gap—Indians and some Europeans had traveled it earlier—he was the first to map out a road through it. Quickly settlers poured into the Appalachian and Interior Low Plateaus.

The Ohio River marks both a northern boundary for this region and, in the southern part, the approximate limit of earlier glaciation. Heavy glaciers had ground their way southward during the Ice Age, stopping just short of the Interior Low Plateaus. In fact,

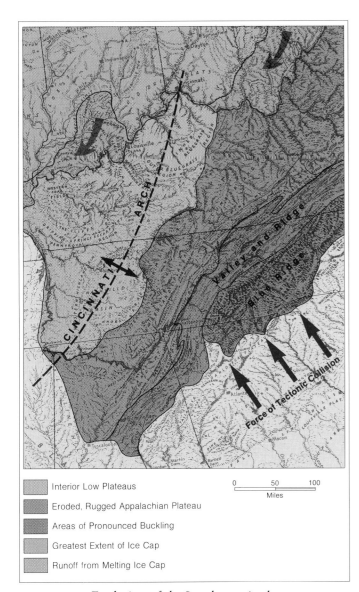

FIGURE 14.2 *Evolution of the Landscape in the Appalachians*

Along the southern border of the Appalachian and Interior Low Plateaus, the compressive forces caused by the collision of massive tectonic plates buckled the land and pushed up mountain ridges. Along the region's northern border, the melting of vast sheets of ice unleashed torrents of water that helped to carve the channel of today's Ohio River.

Interior Low Plateaus

Eroded, Rugged Appalachian Plateau

Areas of Pronounced Buckling

Greatest Extent of Ice Cap

Runoff from Melting Ice Cap

their melting waters produced the torrential flow that reversed the direction of river systems and carved the modern-day channel of the Ohio River. Wherever glaciers crawled across the land to the north, they scraped and tore at it, changing its surface and depositing *till* (a mixture of boulders, gravel, sand, and clay that glaciers carry along). The interior plateaus remained free from these effects. Other natural forces, mainly erosion, determined its surface features.

The key to understanding the Appalachian Plateau and Interior Low Plateaus lies in the pattern of sediments that were laid down and later exposed. Before the collision of the continental plates, this region had been covered intermittently by the seas. Layers of

sediment that accumulated on the ocean floor eventually became the strata of limestone, shale, and sandstone that appear today. Interspersed among them are layers of coal, reflecting interludes when the land was raised above the sea and coursed by tropical swamps and forests.

When the climate was tropical, lush, and swampy, trees and green plants flourished. Later, as they decayed and came under pressure from other sediments, the plants tended to turn into layers of coal. In a similar manner (according to theories favored by petroleum geologists), the decay of vegetation has also produced some oil and gas deposits that are trapped in shallow fields between layers of sedimentary rock.

Teays—The Lost River

Today the New River rises in the mountains of northwestern North Carolina and flows across southwest Virginia into West Virginia. There it empties into the Kanawha River, which flows past Charleston, West Virginia, and on into the Ohio River at Point Pleasant, West Virginia/Gallipolis, Ohio.

Before the Ice Age glaciers invaded North America, however, these Southern mountain rivers were tributary to another mighty river, the Teays. The New and Kanawha rivers were the upper part of that river, which flowed northwestward across central Ohio and entered central Indiana to the northeast of Indianapolis. From there it turned to flow toward the Gulf of Mexico.

The invasion of continental glaciers occurred less than two million years ago, reaching as far south as Cincinnati along a line that approximates the present course of the Ohio River. The glaciers buried much of the channel of the Teays River in Ohio and beyond. A new river channel was established along the edge of the melting glacier. This new channel took over the work of draining a large part of surface waters from a region that stretched across western Pennsylvania, Ohio, Kentucky, and Indiana. The ancient Teays is gone except for its original source areas in the mountains of West Virginia, Virginia, and North Carolina.

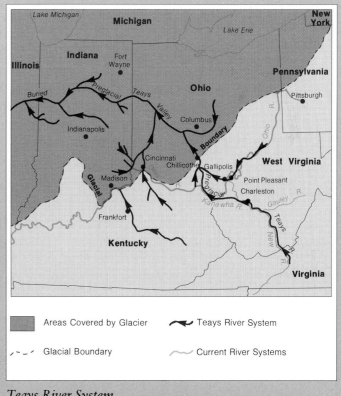

Teays River System

Areas Covered by Glacier

Glacial Boundary

Teays River System

Current River Systems

The wells that operate in the region are small ones, but together they account for a fairly significant production. The region's deposits of coal, on the other hand, have long been recognized as some of the richest in the nation.

The layers of sandstone, shale, limestone, and coal lie atop each other in horizontal belts that are named according to their geologic period or age (see TABLE 2.1, *Geologic Time Scale,* on page 8). The Permian, Pennsylvanian, Mississippian, and Devonian layers are higher up because they are younger. They consist of sandstone and shale, alternating at times with deposits of coal. The Silurian and Ordovician layers, on the other hand, are older limestone containing large amounts of organic material.

The characteristics of these rocks determine both their fertility and their durability. Sandstone and shale are rather infertile and make poor soils. They also tend to be soft and erode easily once streams or rivers break through the surface or caprock and begin to scour at lower strata. Limestone almost everywhere makes a more fertile soil, and this is especially true in the Appalachian and Interior Low Plateaus. The limestone deposits here are full of phosphates that help enrich the soil. And rather than eroding, limestone tends to go into solution with water. This can produce the sinks and caves of karst topography, but it also means that rain can make the organic materials and phosphates of the underlying soil available to plants and crops.

Roughly the same amount of surface material has been worn away all across the Appalachian and Interior Low Plateaus, yet different strata appear on the surface in the east compared to the west. The infertile sandstone and shale dominate in the Appalachian Plateau, whereas productive phosphatic limestone lies at the surface in the Interior Low Plateaus, particularly its Lexington Plain and Nashville Basin (FIGURE

14.3). How did these richer, older, and generally deeper limestone soils come to be found at the surface?

The answer is a slight upward bowing or bending of strata called the Cincinnati Arch. This arch is another result of the collision of the continental plates. The compression that folded layers of rock into mountains in the Appalachians and raised the Allegheny Front caused a gentle but significant upward bending farther west in the middle of the Appalachian and Interior Low Plateaus region. FIGURE 14.4 shows a generalized cross section of the earth's surface of this region.

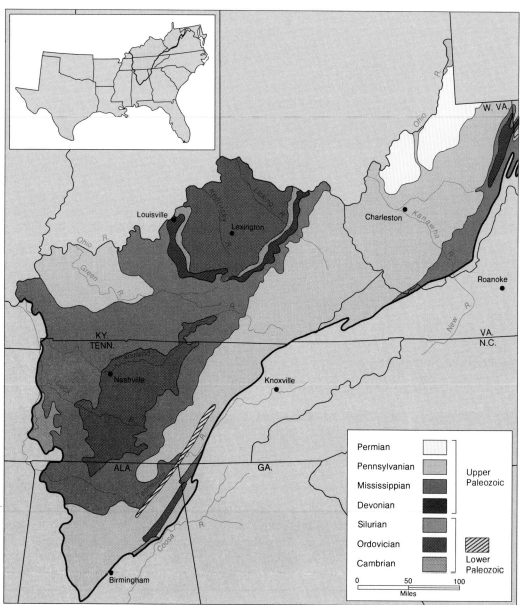

FIGURE 14.3
*Paleozoic Strata in the
Appalachian Plateau &
Interior Low Plateaus*
The area containing
strata from all three periods is
indicated as Lower Paleozoic.

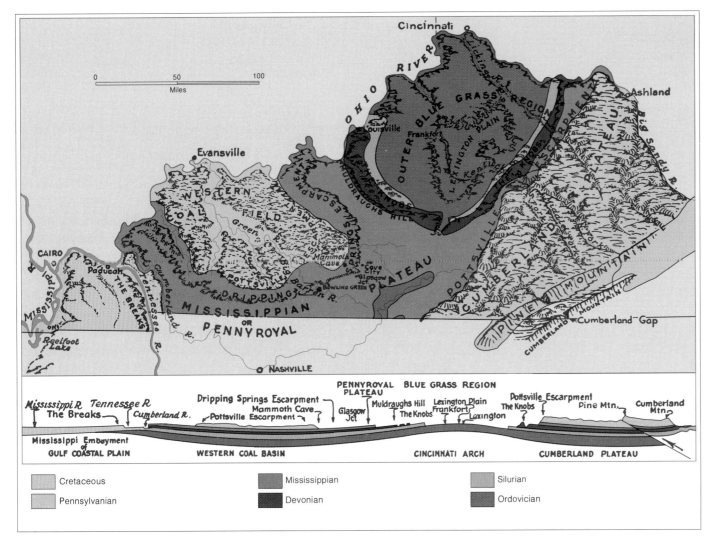

FIGURE 14.4 *Landform Regions of Kentucky and Underlying Geology*

Two other surface features deserve mention in the Appalachian and Interior Low Plateaus: the Knobs on the outskirts of the Lexington Plain, and the caves and solution valleys that exist farther west and south (FIGURE 14.4). The Knobs are prominent, low hills that were left after erosion carried away most of the sandstone and shale near them. Over time, they weathered into their present rounded shape. The karst topography (see FIGURE 6.5 on page 90) of western Kentucky and middle Tennessee long has been a famous feature of the region, and in many counties, caves have been a revenue-generating, tourist attraction for over a hundred years. Mammoth Cave is one of the more spectacular results of the solution of underground limestone. Another is the rolling, rounded surface produced by many small sinks. In the Mammoth Cave region, small sinks grew together to produce solution valleys and an occasional flat ridge. This process is illustrated in FIGURE 14.5.

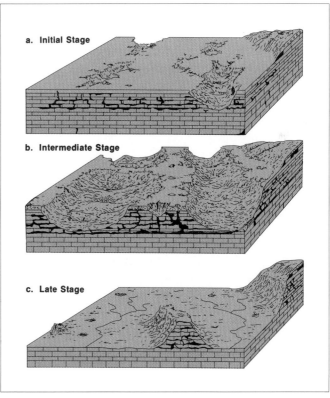

FIGURE 14.5 *Formation of a Solution Valley*

The Cincinnati Arch brought limestone strata closer to the surface and caused the covering layers of sandstone and shale to crack as they were bent convexly. Through erosion, a rich bottom layer became the top as infertile covering layers were carried away, and the bottom was covered by rich, limestone-derived soil.

A similar amount of erosion has occurred in the eastern part of the region, in the Appalachian Plateau. But there is a crucial difference: because the bending of the Cincinnati Arch was very slight so far to the east, the covering layers remained lower and are still found on the surface today. Rich phosphatic limestone that was exposed in the Lexington Plain and Nashville Basin lies buried in the Appalachian Plateau beneath sandstone and shale that account for its infertile soils.

Moreover, the sandstone and shale were so easily cut by streams that they permitted the creation of an incredibly steep and rugged terrain. No region of the United States, not even the Rocky Mountains, has a generally steeper gradient or slope. The eroded hillsides often seem straight up and down, on an angle of 45 degrees or more. For any resident, the plateau here seems mountainous, with demanding hills to climb and scarcely a level spot in many places.

Dendritic drainage caused the Appalachian Plateau's steep slopes. A branching network of watercourses is the most efficient means for collecting rainfall and runoff on a fairly level surface, so a dendritic pattern evolved on the Appalachian Plateau. Radial and trellis drainage patterns also occur occasionally (see chapter 13, "Drainage Patterns," page 158).

LAND AND PEOPLE

The influence of the land on human activity is strikingly apparent in the Appalachian Plateau. Offering both opportunities and constraints, the land has influenced where people live, how they earn a living, and the quality of their lives.

Through much of the plateau there is little, if any, flat land. Most development seems to be on a hillside or along river valleys (and these are much more narrow and winding than the broad valleys of the Valley and Ridge province). Accordingly, farming and settlement have taken place in those valleys, and most of the remaining acreage is wooded. Population density in the valleys can exceed 100 people per square mile, whereas ridgetops are very sparsely settled (FIGURE 14.6). Though the narrow river valleys are the only logical place to settle and can be picturesque, they hold a predictable danger: flooding. Repeatedly, especially before the TVA brought some improvement, Appalachian towns found themselves under water when heavy rains flowed down from the hills.

FIGURE 14.6
River Valley Settlement Patterns

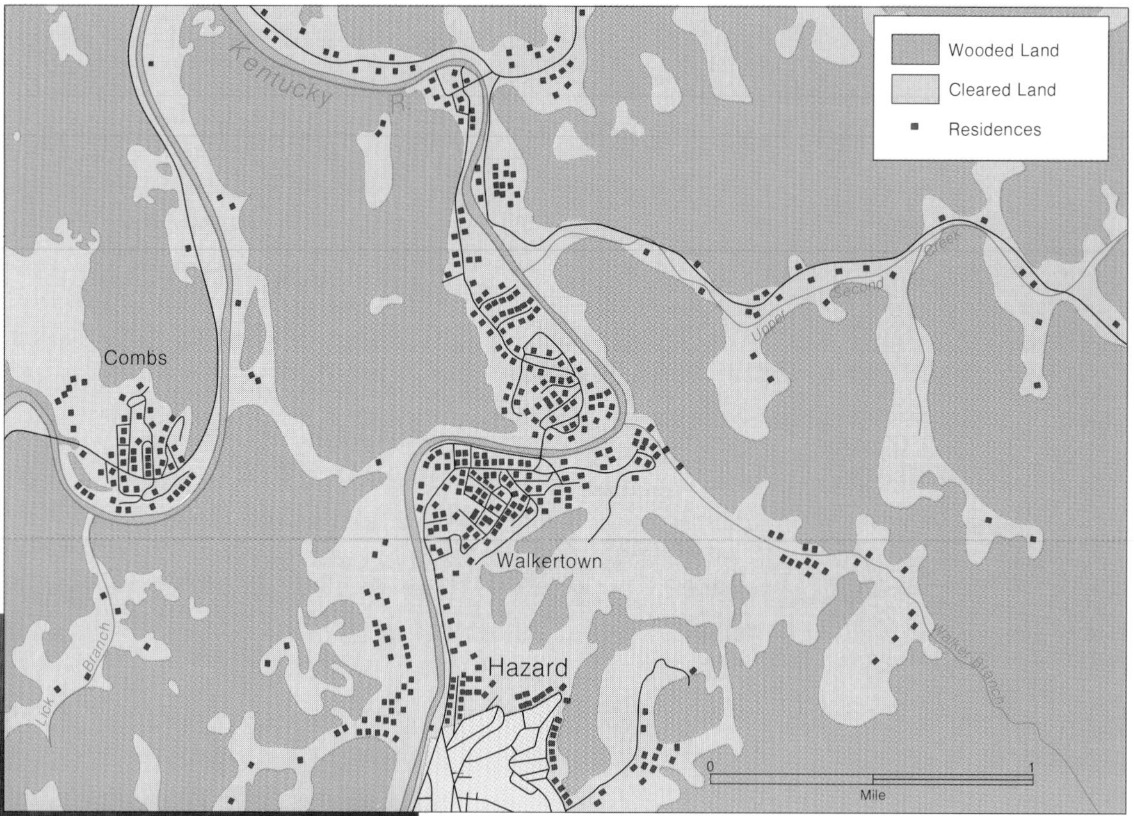

Isolation was another traditional enemy of Appalachian residents. Because the terrain was so rugged and dissected, both economic activity and the flow of information suffered. Only a few decades ago, more than three-quarters of the residents in some portions of Appalachia received no daily paper; more than half received no weekly paper. Many farmed without the benefit of modern machinery in a region that was often called "The Land of Do Without." Federal road-building projects have done something to break down this isolation, but the difficult terrain continues to have a large impact.

The narrow Appalachian valleys have long been the locus of human settlement. Unfortunately, as this photograph reveals, the valleys are also extremely vulnerable to floods.

Many of the important cities of the eastern plateau grew up in major river valleys. The coincidence of river valleys, commerce, and the principal cities of the region is striking. Charleston and Huntington, West Virginia, for example, as well as Ashland, Kentucky, are all located in river valleys. The broad alluvial land provided room for growth, and the river itself served as a transportation corridor. Some manufacturing also has developed in these cities, particularly along the Kanawha River near Charleston, West Virginia. The river provides the large amounts of water needed for industrial processes.

In general, the thoroughly dissected surface of the Appalachian Plateau and the difficulties of transportation have discouraged manufacturing. Most industrial plants need fairly extensive amounts of level surface on which to locate. Like settlement, manufacturing tended to cluster in the few river valleys when it came to the Appalachian Plateau at all. One of the region's major areas of manufacturing today centers on the Kanawha River. Glass, rubber, and ferroalloy manufacturing are prominent in the economy of Charleston, West Virginia. Large chemical plants operate there, some of them tapping the brine that can be found deep beneath the surface and put to use in the manufacture of alkalies.

Historically, the principal industries of the region have been extractive. Limited by the terrain in what they could do, people tried to survive by using what the land had to offer. It offered timber and coal in great abundance, and timber was one of the first products taken from the hills. As the nation's industry developed, coal mining became a major industry and a principal source of employment for many who lived up in the hills and valleys.

One of the nation's great concentrations of bituminous coal lies beneath or near the surface of the Appalachian Plateau (FIGURE 14.7). In the past, much of this coal proved well suited for coking operations, and it enjoys the advantage today of being low in sulfur, a pollutant. (Coalfields farther west in

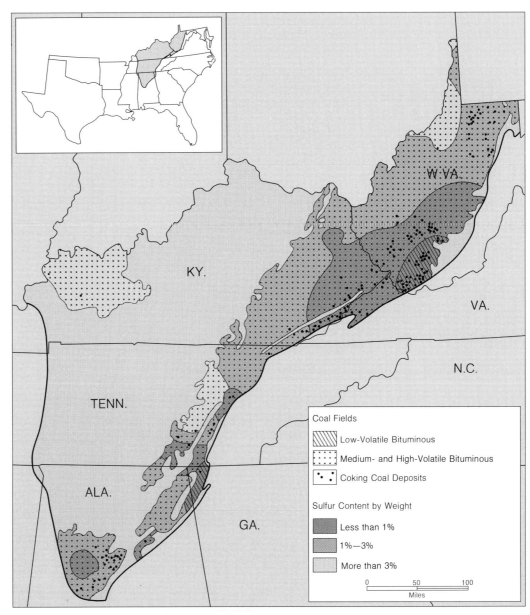

FIGURE 14.7
Distribution of Coal Deposits in the Appalachian Plateau & Interior Low Plateaus

Kentucky, by contrast, contain a higher amount of sulfur.) The sharp dissection of the ground's surface naturally has carried much coal away, but it also has exposed seams for miners to work. These seams are eight to ten feet thick in some places. Virtually all types of mining go on in the region—some coal mines dig horizontally into the face of an exposed seam; others sink shafts; and, where large amounts of coal are close to the topsoil, strip mining tears off the covering layer of earth to get to the coal.

Whereas the coalfields of Pennsylvania and eastern Ohio helped spur the industrialization and

urbanization of the Great Lakes area, the same benefits did not accrue farther south. Without major cities and factories, the Appalachian Plateau has seen most of its coal exported by companies whose ownership lies outside the region. Moreover, the once vigorous coal industry has become relatively sick today. By the 1950s, coal's cost had become high relative to other sources of energy. Management and organized labor decided to mechanize extraction in order to lower costs. This strategy has helped to keep up production, but the market has remained unfavorable and the number of jobs has declined.

On the Interior Low Plateaus, the strong influence of the land on its population's activity is similarly apparent. Two of the major centers of population coincide with the location of notably rich soils. The Lexington Plain and the Nashville Basin boast fertile, phosphatic limestone and have been famous for their richness since first settlement by Europeans. The beauty and fertility of the land, which evoked the enthusiasm of early settlers, are still apparent to today's visitor riding on an interstate highway. Large and prosperous-looking farms dominate the approaches to Lexington and Nashville.

The rich soils of the Lexington Plain support the bluegrass that is justly famous as pastureland for horses and livestock. Since the founding of the nation, the Bluegrass country and horses have thrived together. Calumet Farms and other famous stables present a beautiful view around the growing city of Lexington today, and elsewhere herds of sheep represent a valuable investment in livestock. In Kentucky, burley tobacco remains the most important crop. Wheat, oats, and some corn are also grown in Kentucky and Tennessee.

Nashville and Lexington have grown far beyond their early importance as centers of a rich agricultural region. Today they offer business the expertise of major universities and the services important to a modern economy. Nashville grew up as a port city on the Cumberland River and as the northern terminus of the Natchez Trace. Railroads continued its reputation for outstanding transportation, and today it manufactures airplane parts, fertilizer, boats, barges, and bridges, with automobile production nearby. And, of course, Nashville is without peer in the country-music recording industry.

Kentucky Horse Country

The beauty of the Kentucky horse country is hard to duplicate. Gently rolling meadows covered with lush bluegrass and neat wooden fences have a peaceful charm, and the horses that are raised in the area certainly seem contented as they graze quietly or run about at play. But behind the calm beauty lies a booming business.

There are approximately 100,000 horses in Kentucky. Most of them are pleasure horses such as Saddlebreds, Tennessee Walking Horses, quarter horses, and Appaloosas. Thoroughbreds and Standardbreds, which make the region famous for racing, comprise no more than a fifth of the horse population. But interest in racehorses as an investment has been skyrocketing.

When Keeneland Sales first auctioned select yearlings in 1944, the average price was about $5,000. Twenty years later, that figure had quadrupled, and in the 1970s, it surpassed $500,000. By the 1980s, individual racehorses with outstanding records often brought over $10 million, and their stud fees approached a million dollars, even without guarantee that a live foal would result.

Yet horse racing remains an unpredictable and risky business, which surely is part of its enduring attraction. Some of the best-blooded horses, purchased at enormous prices, have proved unable to run, while unpromising yearlings occasionally develop into champions. Seattle Slew, for example, had a crooked leg and a mediocre pedigree. As a yearling he brought only $17,500, but he went on to win $1.2 million and earn far more for his owners at stud. Such is the stuff of which dreams are made, but Brownell Combs II, president of Spendthrift Farm, warns investors that the risks are huge: "If a horse's leg shatters, that's it. The end of the line is a can of Alpo. I tell them the horse may ultimately be worth about nine cents a pound."

The rich and gently rolling land of Kentucky's Bluegrass country (the Lexington Plain) supports rich farms and the beautiful horse farms so important to racing.

Lexington had early prominence as both a tobacco center and a center of education, the home since 1780 of Transylvania University. Today it is best known for the University of Kentucky, but it also has a variety of manufacturing enterprises and large professional and legal communities. Like Nashville, Louisville also benefited from its location on a river (a system of locks around the falls of the Ohio is found there). By the 1850s, the railroads had made the city Kentucky's leading commercial center. Today it is a major producer of tobacco products and bourbon, but with several colleges and universities, it boasts a diversified economy. Louisville is also renowned for its achievements in drama, and its skyline includes some of the most renowned post-Modernist architecture in America.

The Humana Building in Louisville, Kentucky, is one of the two or three most acclaimed examples of post-Modernist architecture in the United States.

STRONG ATTACHMENTS

It is not difficult to see why cities like Nashville, Louisville, or Lexington are growing or why their residents speak proudly about their attractions. But many other people in the Appalachian and Interior Low Plateaus fondly call this region home, even where the economy has not been healthy or where growth is not occurring. Loyalties here have deep historic and cultural roots.

In the twentieth century, considerable parts of the Appalachian Plateau have been among the poorest counties in America. A variety of government programs have attempted to overcome nature's barriers to transportation by building roads. There have been improvements, to be sure, but no dramatic turnaround was achieved. Poverty still remains, and perhaps the natural endowment is simply too scant here to support a vastly more successful economy.

For generations, a high birth rate accompanied (and contributed to) the region's poverty. Large numbers of people migrated out of the Appalachian Plateau to find jobs and opportunities elsewhere. The industrial cities of the upper Midwest, such as Detroit and Cleveland, claimed many former mountaineers and depended on their labor. But numerous folk songs and stories testify to the continuing hold of the Appalachian region on the migrants' thoughts, and tens of thousands of residents stay there today, stubborn in their attachments to home and kin.

The Appalachian Plateau may be as good a representative as any of the locally defined culture for which Southerners show a preference. Farther west, too, in the Interior Low Plateaus, the affection for home ties and a familiar, face-to-face social universe prevails. The writer Calvin Trillin has told *New Yorker* audiences about Kentucky's pan-fried chicken and talented local storytellers. In communities with names like Horse Cave or Chicken Bristle, everyone knows his neighbor's family tree, and in Kentucky politics, many successful careers rose from a foundation of wide local acquaintance. Tennessee, too, is famous among political scientists for the importance of some of its local machines and the persistence of loyalties founded during the Civil War.

Modern times have changed many things, especially things the traveler sees along roads and highways. But the character of the people is durable. It adapts rather than changes completely. Communications technology fosters fervent devotion to the Kentucky Wildcats or the Tennessee Volunteers as well as, or even in place of, the local high school. But the loyalty remains immediate and personalized in the way of farm folk and small-town people. Just as Alabama has its famous folk hero Bear Bryant, Kentucky has Adolf Rupp and Eddie Sutton, and Tennessee has Johnny Majors. People on the Appalachian and Interior Low Plateaus may be far from Spanish moss and close to the Ohio, but they remain firmly within the South.

15 THE OZARK & OUACHITA UPLANDS

One of the South's most attractive regions covers most of northern Arkansas and parts of eastern Oklahoma (FIGURE 15.1). The Ozark and Ouachita Uplands contain steep, wooded mountain ridges, narrow valleys, and rolling plateaus. Morning mists follow splendid sunsets; rivulets trickle through forests to become clear, cool streams and lakes; and in the evening, the sounds of birds and bullfrogs, katydids and crickets fill the air. Since major highways run nearby but do not intrude upon the higher elevations, a growing number of visitors and residents can savor its natural beauty.

Not long ago this beauty was threatened. The forests were being cut down or blackened from fire, and the streams were cloudy and turbid with erosion from the hillsides' thin topsoil. The Ozark and Ouachita region appeared to be excluded from the benefits of modern civilization, its people trapped in time and forgotten by the world.

For these reasons, the changes during recent generations are especially welcome. Geologically and physically, the Ozark and Ouachita Uplands are similar to the Appalachian Mountains and to the Appalachian Plateau and Interior Low Plateaus. But until recently, they seemed to share none of the eastern region's prosperity, only its social and economic problems, such as a colonial economy, isolation, and poverty. Improvement of the natural and economic environments promises a brighter future, one that is consistent with the region's beautiful but limited natural endowment.

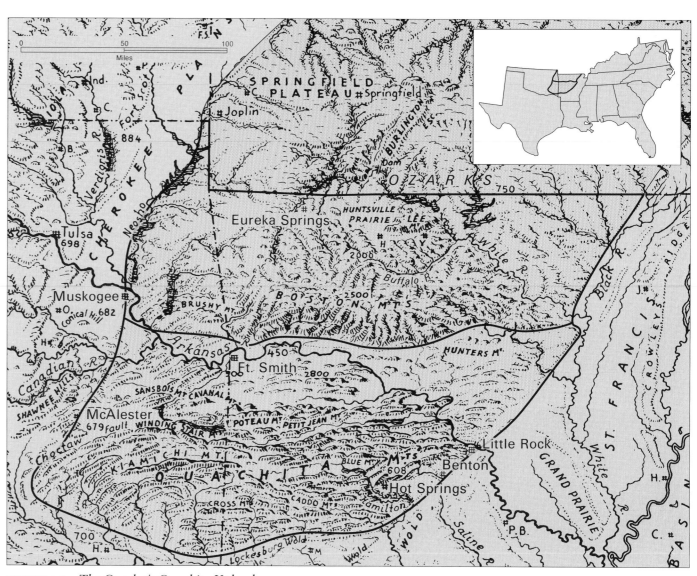

FIGURE 15.1 *The Ozark & Ouachita Uplands*

THE LAND AND ITS HISTORY

Three hundred miles separate the Ozark and Ouachita Uplands from the Appalachian chain and the Appalachian Plateau and Interior Low Plateaus. Yet, despite the fact that two Lowland areas—the Mississippi Valley and Delta and the East Gulf Coastal Plain—intervene between these uplands, they share the same structural history. Similarities of topography, sediments, and natural features abound, most of

them deriving from a common geologic formation.

In comparing these eastern and western upland regions, one needs to keep in mind that the Ozark and Ouachita region has a similar amount of geologic history as the Appalachian and Interior Low Plateaus, but it is crunched into a smaller space. Thus, although the Ozark and Ouachita region contains features of the Valley and Ridge province as well as the

Appalachian Plateau and Interior Low Plateaus, it tends to be less fertile than either.

The collision of continental plates in the distant past shaped all these upland regions. Enormous compressive forces accompanied that collision, forces that reduced the Ouachita area to half its original width. Such compression caused the folding, bending, and faulting that threw up mountains—the Appalachians

The Ozarks in Arkansas have become a recreational haven for urban visitors and offer great natural beauty year-round.

and the Ouachitas—now greatly eroded. (see FIGURE 2.5B). In the millions of years since that collision, the earth's crust subsided between the two regions, creating the lowlands that separate them. But in all probability, a section of folded, compressed rocks that would have filled in the gap between the Ouachitas and the Appalachians lies buried beneath the surface of the Mississippi Valley and the coastal plain.

Within each upland area there are also broad similarities of surface features. The Ouachita Mountains are folded, sometimes faulted mountains that have been worn down through time. Hence they correspond to the Appalachian Mountains and particularly to the Valley and Ridge province; they exhibit the same pattern of parallel ridges alternating with valleys, except that the Ouachitas are more compact. As

a result, valleys of the Ouachita Mountains are quite narrow. And just as in the Appalachian Mountains and Appalachian Plateau, beds of valuable coal lie between layers of sedimentary sandstone and shale in the Ouachitas.

As one moves from the southern edge into the interior of each of these regions, richer and more fertile areas appear. Whereas the eastern uplands have two such areas, the Lexington Plain and the Nashville Basin, the Ozark and Ouachita Uplands have only one: the fairly narrow valley of the Arkansas River. Beyond these fertile zones in both regions the upland plateau resumes, marked here in the west by the Boston Mountains and the Ozarks. Part of the plateau is highly dissected in both regions; in this respect, the Boston Mountains correspond to the Appalachian Plateau.

The Ouachita Mountains are not as high as the Appalachians, and the Ozarks are not quite as low as the Interior Low Plateaus. At the eastern and western extremes of the chain, the Ouachitas are only 500 or 750 feet above sea level and about 250 feet above the nearby plain. They rise toward a peak near the boundary of Oklahoma and Arkansas, where they reach 2,600 feet in elevation, 1,500 feet above the valley floors. The dissected plateau known as the Boston Mountains reaches a maximum elevation of 2,250 feet in its middle third, where it rises 700 to 1,000 feet above nearby river valleys. The rolling uplands of the Ozarks are generally 1,000 feet above sea level.

The agricultural potential of the Ouachitas is similar to the Appalachian Plateau with its jumbled, rugged surface. Farming in the Ouachitas has always been small-scale, subsistence cultivation. The Arkansas River Valley was the only site for large farms or plantations, and historically it could be considered part of the Cotton Belt.

The western part of the Boston Mountains forms a low arch roughly analogous to the Cincinnati Arch, though there is more folding and breaking of layers in this western region than is true east of the Mississippi.

Another similarity of the two upland areas is the presence of limestone in the interior of both the Ozarks/Ouachita and Appalachian regions, with the sinks and caves that typically accompany this water-soluble stone. Arkansas boasts many well-known springs as a result of the prevalence of limestone.

Structurally and geologically, the Ozarks differ in one notable way from the Interior Low Plateaus. Beneath layers of sandstone, shale, and limestone rises a dome of igneous rocks, mainly granite and porphyry. This dome of harder rock, which pushed up the sediments in the Ozarks, extends well into Missouri. It has its peak at the Saint Francois Mountains in the southeastern part of that state, only 50 miles from the Mississippi River. The layers of Mississippian-era shale and limestone in the Ozarks are much thicker in southeastern Oklahoma and adjoining parts of Arkansas than they are farther north. Beds that are 16,000 feet thick taper northward to a comparatively thin shelf less than 1,000 feet in width.

The limestone soils of the Ozark and Ouachita Uplands tend to be less fertile than those of the Appalachian Plateaus and Interior Low Plateaus. They contain substantial amounts of chert, a crystalline silica that is similar to flint or to the rocks used to cover many driveways. These flinty rocks are insoluble, so they tend to accumulate at the surface as the limestone weathers away. Even with moderate surface relief, much of the better soil is carried off, leaving the chert. Only in the valleys is there much soil lying above it; therefore, most farms must be located there.

Another rock, whose origin is debated but which may be a form of chert, adds a unique feature to the Ouachitas. Novaculite is an exceedingly dense and very fine-grained rock composed of almost pure silica. Though very abundant in the Ouachita Mountains, it is almost unknown in the rest of the world. To households, it is very familiar as the typical oilstone or whetstone used to sharpen knives. Along with sandstone, it comprises an important part of the Ouachitas (FIGURE 15.2).

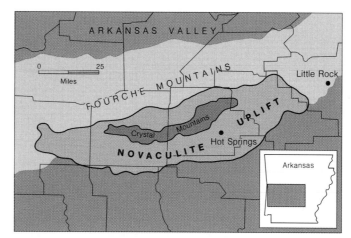

FIGURE 15.2 *The Novaculite Uplift*

Two special features in the Ozark and Ouachita Uplands deserve mention, and both are connected with water. One is that this is a great region for springs. Some springs are so large that they are referred to as rivers or even used for waterpower. Other springs have become famous as resorts. The Eureka Springs in Arkansas pour forth water that has descended through chert and emerged at the top of a layer of shale. The Hot Springs in Arkansas have been famous since prehistoric times; Indians honored the area as neutral, holy ground and lay in its soothing, hot water and mud to regain their health. By 1820, a resort hotel was in operation, and 1,000 acres were set aside as a national park in 1921. The waters that

FIGURE 15.3 *Hot Springs, Arkansas*

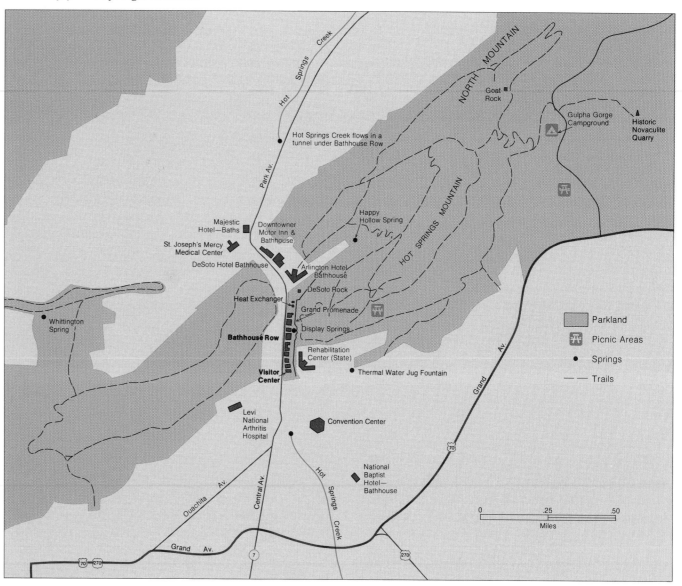

issue from 47 mineral springs within the park are heated geothermally to temperatures ranging from 95°F to 143°F. Their daily flow measures almost a million gallons (FIGURE 15.3).

The rivers of the Ozark Plateau are the other special feature, and they have occasioned a good deal of research and study among geographers. Many of them present an apparent contradiction. Their courses twist and turn in the meanders characteristic of the sluggish Mississippi. Yet their torturous flow runs through layers of rock, not soft soil or alluvial muck, and steep walls on either side of the stream often show that it has cut deeply down through the rock. For example, along much of the river's path in the Buffalo River National Park in northern Arkansas, sheer bluffs of sandstone and limestone rise as high as 525 feet above the water on each side.

How could rivers with power enough to cut sharply down into their rock beds flow along the twisting, meandering paths characteristic of mature, slow-moving waterways? The basic answer lies in the sequence of geologic events that occurred far back in time. When the Ozark region had been thoroughly eroded and worn down to a plain, rivers developed the winding, twisting course characteristic of that stage of maturity of a river valley. Then, however, the whole plain in which these rivers meandered was thrust upward, thereby gaining much greater gradient or slope. The rivers in turn gained speed and erosive power and carved much more deeply into their channels. Downcutting thus came after meanders had developed and was a result of uplift.

Geographers call these *entrenched* or *incised* meanders, because they literally have trenched or cut their way downward without changing shape. Along a few rivers, such as the Black, the steep canyon wall rises only on one side of the river, the outward side of its twists and bends. Land on the inner, or concave, side of the river's curves slants down to the water along a gradual slip-off slope. Often such a slope is littered with stream gravel, which shows that the water was shallower and moving more slowly there. In such cases, it seems clear that the river shifted its channel laterally as it cut downward. The experts speak of one other special kind of meander: the *ingrown* meander. This occurs if the rapidly moving water cuts horizontally into its gorge and creates an overhang, but these meanders are not as common in the Ozarks as are the twisting gorges whose walls rise steeply on each side.

The Buffalo River is a challenge and thrill for boaters and a source of interest for geologists and geographers, who note the way its meandering bends have cut down through hundreds of feet of rock.

THE PEOPLE LEFT BEHIND

The people who settled the Ozark and Ouachita Uplands were primarily small, independent farmers. Called yeomen, such people were the pioneer settlers in virtually every region of the South. They came mostly from the British Isles, particularly from the Celtic fringe of Scotland, Ireland, and Wales, and raised livestock and practiced a form of agriculture based on corn. After clearing small amounts of land, the yeoman farmers would sow a corn crop and allow their animals (mostly hogs) to roam in the woods and fatten themselves on mast (nuts) and plants from the forest floor. Hunting brought additional food to these farmers' tables.

The yeoman farmer's style of life put a premium on independence and involved a considerable degree of isolation. Many of these rugged individuals liked being off to themselves at the edge of settlement. They often moved on because they didn't like to hear the sound of another man's axe or feel crowded. Others committed themselves just as surely to a frontier life-style through their dependence on livestock. Though small acreages supported the yeoman's corn and vegetables, 100 to 200 acres of open range were needed to supply mast for the hogs and game for hunting. Thus, more intensive forms of agriculture or economic development clashed with the yeoman's way of life.

When these settlers came to Arkansas early in the nineteenth century, their counterparts could be found in many areas of the South. Though never as well-to-do as slaveholding planters, yeomen enjoyed a standard of living that compared favorably at that time with the rest of the world and was not deficient relative to most small farmers throughout the United States. But time seemed to stop for them in the Ozark and Ouachita mountains.

The rugged terrain and small amounts of level, fertile soil kept population increase low and blocked most kinds of economic development in the region. Physically isolated and involved in their traditional ways of life, most of the region's people began to be "left behind" in the eyes of others. A Kansas City reporter and photographer named Charles Phelps Cushing came to the region in 1910 and found Americans who seemed to have been forgotten by time and progress. They were, he noted, largely English and Scotch-Irish, "a people of pure quill American stock." They said *buss* for 'kiss' and *hit* for 'it' and used other expressions that dated back to seventeenth-century England. In Cushing's opinion, they showed "sublime indifference concerning matters of geography . . . a few even took pride in the fact that they never had journeyed farther from home than the nearest county seat town or the ridge-tops at the horizon line."[1]

Like other observers, Cushing felt that these uplands people were being excluded from modern progress, and in quantifiable ways, they were. While economic development pushed income upward and transformed ways of life in the countryside, towns, and cities of other regions, things stayed the same for residents of the Ozarks and Ouachitas. Their economy became backward by comparison, their means of transportation and communication remained rudimentary, and rates of illiteracy and infant mortality were high. By 1950, per capita income in the area averaged only $300, and the region's population was shrinking. Despite the rugged beauty of the hills and plateaus, they offered only a hard life.

This was true despite a kind of development that had come to the Ozark and Ouachita Uplands. Like many parts of the Appalachian Mountains and Plateau, most industry was extractive industry. It made use of the rich but limited resources in the area, taking them out of the ground or from the hillsides

The "people left behind." Charles Phelps Cushing photographed these mountaineers in 1910 and was impressed by their cultural isolation and the difficulty of their daily lives.

and sending resources elsewhere with a minimum of processing. Since such industries were often owned by people outside the region, they generated comparatively little prosperity in the uplands and fit the pattern of a colonial economy—that is, they fueled the prosperity of the areas that used the resources but had little benefit for the area supplying the resources.

First to come were large timber companies from the East. Having cut much of the best wood from the northern lakes area, these businesses turned to the interior highlands for new supplies of lumber. In roughly 40 years, from about 1880 to 1920, they cut first the pine and then the hardwoods for flooring, structural timbers, and crossties. Arkansas's cedar became very popular around 1900 for use in pencils. But the reserve of standing timber soon thinned, and the oak-hickory climax forest would need generations to return. Recent decades have seen smaller-scale cutting of the remaining oaks for whiskey-barrel staves and harvesting of trash trees for cheap pallet lumber. But basically, the forest-products boom was over quickly.

Mining enterprises soon followed. Around 1900, companies began to uncover the region's mineral resources, principally lead and zinc. The largest deposits of lead are in the northern Ozarks, in Missouri, but zinc predominates in the so-called Tri-State District at the borders of Missouri, Oklahoma, and Arkansas. Long the nation's leading producer of zinc, this area now has lost its leadership position, leaving a pockmarked expanse of strip-mined land. Only bauxite remains a major source of mineral wealth today in the South's Ozark and Ouachita Uplands. Virtually all of the nation's domestic ore comes from an area in the eastern Ouachitas. Near Benton, Arkansas, opencut mines remove and ship ore from which aluminum is extracted.

These enterprises were insufficient to bring prosperity to the region, and other industrial activities involving wood products, synthetic yarns, brickmaking, and coal mining have been on a small scale only. Agriculture had to generate the money for most of the improvements that were going to occur. Unfortunately, agriculture was not healthy, even outside the subsistence-farming regions.

Commercial agriculture and the trade that it generates flourished most in the valley of the Arkansas River. There were the best and broadest expanses of alluvial land, and there grew the largest cities of the region: Little Rock and Fort Smith, where marketing and trading of various types took place. But cotton production in the Arkansas Valley suffered, just as it did elsewhere, from overproduction, sharecropping, slow growth in demand for the fiber, and attendant problems. The region's prosperity could not be built on cotton.

Through much of the hilly sections of the region, the land was actually growing poorer in the early decades of the twentieth century. Destruction of the oak-hickory forest exposed the forest floor, and less desirable trees and brush began to sprout. Natives called the thick, almost impassable tangle of new growth "redbrush," and they thought they knew what to do with it. They burned it off, following a practice that may have ancient roots among Celtic cultures on the other side of the Atlantic. Burning the woods was a fairly common practice in other parts of the South, but here its results were disastrous.

Men who set the fires believed that they were clearing the useless underbrush and killing off ticks and other insect pests. But in the rugged, hilly uplands, covered originally with no more than a thin layer of mediocre soil, the fires exposed the ground to rains and hastened erosion. Each shower muddied the streams and left the land poorer. Before long, farmers were commenting, with a stoic sort of humor, that the soil was "so worthless the only way you could grow a crop would be to tie two rocks together around a seed."

Such humor helped many people stay in the region, despite hard times, but others began to leave. Blacks and younger whites, especially, concluded that the limited opportunities of the Arkansas Valley and the picturesque hills and mountains were narrowing still further, so they left to seek a better life elsewhere. From the 1920s into the 1950s, an immense outmigration occurred. It has been estimated that almost 800,000 people left the farm economy in Arkansas in 30 years. This outward tide along with other, more hopeful changes coincided with the Great Depression of the 1930s.

MODERN RENAISSANCE
THROUGH RECREATION

The depression deepened people's suffering, but it also inaugurated change. Government programs began to alter the situation by taking land out of production, fostering conservation, and damming up rivers to create recreational lakes. In the thirties, forties, and fifties, the United States Soil Conservation Service established several land-planning projects involving from 15,000 acres to 100,000 acres. Often such programs met local opposition as the poor but proud residents sought to keep control over their affairs. But conservation and recreation efforts continued.

The results have been striking. Coupled with the out-migration of many farm workers, conservation laid the basis for improvement in agriculture. Whereas too many people had tried to work deteriorating land, by the late 1950s, a more modest number of farmers were at work on larger and better cultivated farms. On the average, these were 50 percent larger in 1957 than they had been in 1939, and investment per farm had multiplied by four. Intensive patterns of growing row crops were giving way to livestock raising and dairy farming. Agriculture was beginning to find its way out of the past and into a brighter future.

Large-scale conservation projects and the creation of lakes and recreation areas also brought progress. They enhanced the natural beauty of the region and added a major new element to the economy: recreation and tourism. Today an unusually large portion of the Ozark and Ouachita Uplands is devoted to parks and recreational areas where visitors can relax

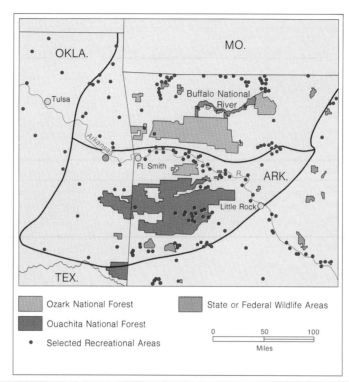

FIGURE 15.4 *National Forest and State Recreational Areas in the Ozark & Ouachita Uplands*

and escape an urban world. The Ozark National Forest and the Ouachita National Forest, for example, each encompass around a million and a half acres. And these do not begin to exhaust the area's recreational opportunities (FIGURE 15.4).

Augmenting the region's original waterways, newly created lakes help to make this area a virtual fisherman's paradise. Bull Shoals, Blue Mountain Lake, Nimrod Reservoir, Lake Hamilton, and other bodies of water are well known to midwestern anglers. They also tempt tourists unfamiliar with the area and offer boating and other recreational uses to those who choose not to fish. Modern technology has added a land of lakes to the handsomeness of the area's mountains.

These developments are stopping the loss of the region's scarce resources and capitalizing on some of

its best assets. Always rugged and attractive, the Ozark and Ouachita Uplands can conserve natural beauty that an urban nation needs. They also are elevated above the hot, surrounding plains or lowlands and therefore are refreshingly cooler in the summer. Though not served internally by major transportation arteries, Interstate 40 and other major highways run nearby. These easily convey visitors to the edge of a region that remains internally undeveloped and unspoiled.

Having arrived at his destination, the traveler can appreciate a series of hairpin turns on beautiful mountain roads. Vacationers relish the region's cool mountainsides, sweeping vistas, relaxed pace, and numerous sources of water for fishing, boating, or swimming. Along with Arkansas's springs, such natural assets have caused both the vacation and retirement industries to boom. Today prosperity is increasing, and the region's population is growing with new arrivals—as well as with some who once left to earn a better living but now are returning home.

16 | THE DRY MARGIN

Climate rules life on the Dry Margin of the South (FIGURE 16.1). Robert Caro, speaking of the Texas Hill Country on the eastern edge of the Edwards Plateau, called this land a trap baited with water and grass. A lush grass cover, "stirrup high," had slowly developed on the limestone-derived soils of the area, but it had taken centuries to evolve. Early settlers in the 1850s marveled at it, but they failed to notice that the trees were miniature versions of their species in the humid East and cacti were scattered in the grass—telltale signs of a dry climate. Each step west of the 98th meridian took them into progressively drier country. But they ignored the warning signs and quickly began to till the dark soils for cotton or to raise cattle on the lush grasses. Soon wind and occasional rainstorms removed the millenia's thicknesses of soil no longer protected by the thick sod, and the land was ruined. So were the farmers and ranchers who had invested their early profits in more land, slaves, and houses. The trap of a marginal, semiarid climate had been sprung.

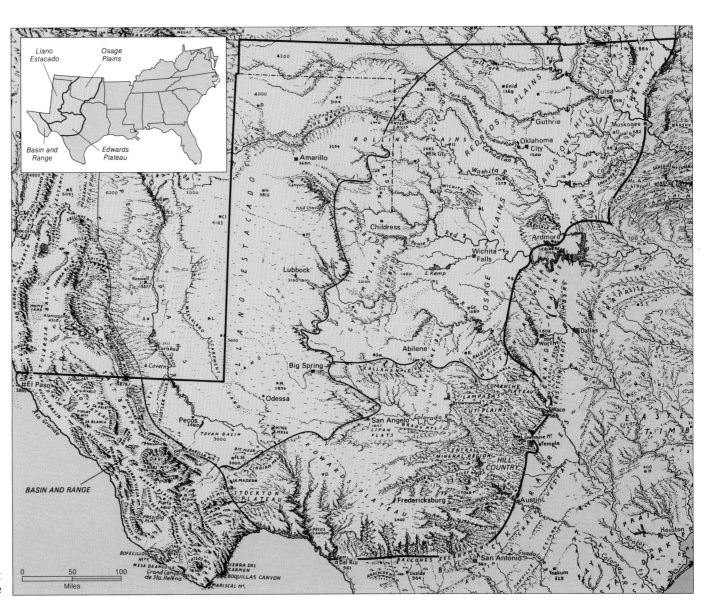

FIGURE 16.1
The Dry Margin

DRYNESS AND HIGH LANDS

The Dry Margin does not lack topographic variety, however. Coinciding roughly with the 98th meridian is the Balcones Escarpment, a bluff several hundred feet above the West Gulf Coastal Plain. It was created by faulting as the great weight of sediments on the coastal plain caused the surface to collapse. Thus, west of the Balcones Escarpment the land rose sharply in elevation just as the climate became too dry to support many typical humid-South crops, such as corn, and many trees.

Dryness and elevation both increase to the northwest of the Balcones Escarpment. In the High Plains Country, the natural landscape was sterile compared with the grasslands in the Texas Hill Country. Randolph Marcy recognized this during his explorations of the Red River Country in 1852–1854. Upon reaching the High Plains, he noted that " . . . the entire face of the country, as if by the wand of a magician, suddenly changes its character."[1] He further observed a land so dry that " . . . even the savage does not venture to cross it except at two or three places where they know water can be found."[2] Later, windmills were used to bring subterranean waters to the surface to turn parts of this environment into productive farming regions, but water still remains the critical resource in this area.

The *Edwards Plateau* is the southern end of the Great Plains, the high level land that extends north into Canada and covers the interior of North America right up to the foothills of the Rocky Mountains. Nothing in the East or in their European heritage had prepared the American settlers for the strange environment of this high, semiarid, vast grassland.

In western Texas, the Edwards Plateau gives way to the even higher *Llano Estacado*, or "staked plains," that extend through the panhandle of Texas and Oklahoma. They were so named because the early Spanish travelers found the country so flat and barren that they drove stakes into the ground periodically to mark their trails. To the north of the Edwards Plateau, in north central Texas and much of Oklahoma, are the *Osage Plains*. They are the southern end of the lower interior lowland of North America that covers a large part of the American Middle West, east of the Great Plains.

A small portion of the *Basin and Range*, an even drier and geologically different part of the state, is in the extreme southwestern part of Texas. To Texans, this is the greater part of the Trans-Pecos country.

WATER: THE CRITICAL RESOURCE

The aridity of this region stems from several factors. The most basic is that it lies deep in the continental interior of North America. The prevailing westerly winds cannot bring moisture-bearing air masses from the Pacific across the mountains into this area. Most of the precipitation that is received comes from maritime air masses that move northwestward from the Gulf of Mexico. Many of these systems turn to the east before reaching west Texas; consequently, precipitation levels decrease steadily from east to west. Finally, the latitude of the area is such that it receives high levels of solar radiation. Evaporation is high, thereby reducing the effectiveness of the already low precipitation levels.

On the eastern edge of the region, precipitation averages about 25 inches a year and declines westward to less than 10 inches. Because of the combination of interior location and high elevation, summer temperatures average about 5 degrees higher and winter temperatures 10 degrees lower than at comparable latitudes in the humid South. However, lower

The Trans Pecos region near El Paso, Texas

Fleeing a dust storm, Cimarron County, Oklahoma, 1936

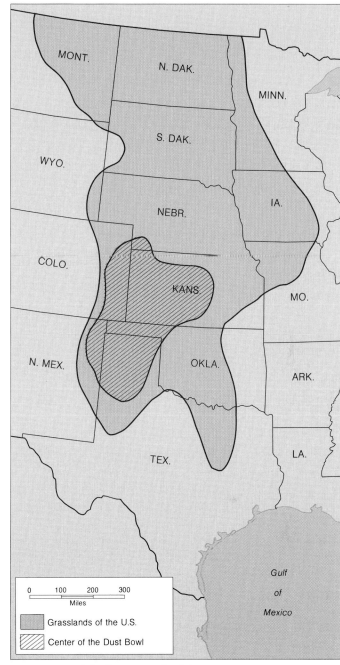

FIGURE 16.2 *The Dust Bowl of the 1930s*

humidity levels tend to make the summer heat less oppressive than it might otherwise be.

The climate of the Dry Margin was a trap to the early settlers not only because of the dryness and fragile grasslands but also because the rainfall there tends to be unreliable. In areas where precipitation is low, there is a general tendency for rainfall to vary more from year to year than it does in humid regions.

Furthermore, wet years tend to run together, to be followed by droughts lasting several years. Farmers have tended to overextend cultivated areas during wet cycles, making them very vulnerable to the inevitable return of dryness.

Analysis of tree rings confirms that there has been a long-term tendency, dating back at least to the sixteenth century, for droughts to occur in the Dry

Margin about every 20 years and to last for a number of years each time. Strong droughts occurred in the 1890s, 1910s, 1930s, and 1950s. The 1950s drought extended through most of the decade, and a great deal of topsoil was lost during that time to wind erosion. However, the most famous episode produced the Dust Bowl of the 1930s (FIGURE 16.2). High demand for wheat during and after World War I coincided with a humid period. Vast areas of grasslands were plowed under to cash in on the high wheat prices. Then in the mid-1920s, the market dropped and recession set in for wheat farmers. They began to abandon the new wheat farms, and the general depression of the 1930s began. The drought led to the wind picking up the exposed topsoil and forming great dust clouds that choked the sky. Dunes up to 10 feet high were built from the drifting topsoil. Some of this dust showed up as far away as the East Coast. Thousands of ruined families piled their scanty possessions into trucks and headed for the "promised land" of California.

Government crop control programs, the introduction of better farming practices to help retain soil moisture, and the planting of thousands of trees to serve as windbreaks have diminished the impact of later droughts. Drought was experienced on schedule in the 1970s, but it was less severe on the Great Plains than earlier episodes. The combination of reduced severity and improved water conservation practices minimized the overall effect of this period of dryness.

In the late nineteenth century, a popular theory held that rain could be induced by setting off loud explosions. The United States Congress was persuaded to appropriate $14,000 for a test of this theory, and Major R. G. Dyrenforth was put in charge. Heavy charges of dynamite were exploded at frequent intervals, and explosives-bearing kites and balloons were detonated in the atmosphere. These experiments were conducted near Midland and San Antonio, Texas, with inconclusive results. The major soon acquired the name of Major Dryhenceforth.

A factor that drew wheat farmers to the prairies was the richness of the soils. In this dry climate, the scanty precipitation does not remove the water-soluble basic components, in contrast to their rapid leaching in the humid South. The prevailing grass vegetation gives the soil a high level of organic matter, which decays slowly in the semiarid environment. The dense root systems of the grass also produce a desirable soil structure. The resulting prairie or chestnut soils (ustolls and ustalfs) are among the most naturally fertile in the world. However, it seems that nature has played a joke on humankind by creating them in environments that are very risky for cultivation. Nikita Kruschev felt the brunt of this irony in the 1950s when similar cultivation of "virgin lands" in the USSR first succeeded and then failed as the rainfall diminished.

Long grasses predominated originally in the more humid parts of the region, interspersed with trees in well-watered sites. Natural grasses were shorter in the dryer areas, and mesquite and scrub vegetation also became more common. The initial destruction of grasslands through overgrazing and cultivation appears to be permanent, and broad areas are now covered sparsely by scrub plants.

Typically, much of the precipitation in this region occurs in brief but heavy summer rainstorms. The dry ground cannot absorb the water very readily, so large amounts have little benefit for vegetation. Thus, even the marginal annual amounts of precipitation are exaggerated in terms of their effectiveness. And the heavy rains falling on this dry surface produce dangerous flash floods. They arise suddenly and rush through dry stream beds almost without warning miles away from the storm.

More spectacular and certainly more deadly than the summer thunderstorm with which it is often associated is the tornado, a strong wind funnel in which velocities may reach 200 miles per hour. Although very compact storms, tornadoes are a scourge in this area. Texas and Oklahoma are part of "Tornado Alley," where tornadoes are more common than anywhere else in the world (FIGURE 16.3). The intense heating of the dry surface and the openness of the terrain seem to encourage their formation and virtually unrestricted movement.

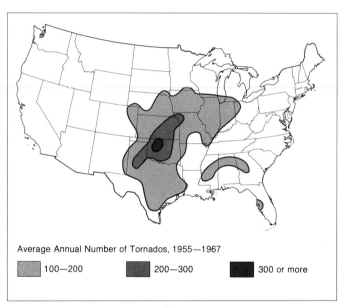

Average Annual Number of Tornados, 1955—1967

☐ 100—200   ☐ 200—300   ■ 300 or more

FIGURE 16.3 *Average Annual Tornado Frequency in the U.S.*

GEOLOGY, OIL, AND THE HIGH COUNTRY

The underlying geology of western Texas and Oklahoma is dominated by sedimentary rock formations of Paleozoic age, products of oceanic invasions of the continental interior. Great strata of limestone, shale, and sandstone occur here as well as in parts of the Appalachians to the east. During the latter part of the Paleozoic era, in the Permian period, shallow, warm seas left similar deposits, but beds of gypsum and other salts were laid down also as part of the sea evaporated. Subsequently, in the humid east, layers of such water-soluble materials were easily eroded, but in the dry west, limestone and gypsum became important ridge builders. They are resistant to wind erosion, a more important process on a sparsely vegetated, dry landscape. Conversely, sandstone, which is composed of discrete particles of silica sand, can resist the water-based weathering processes in the east, but it is vulnerable to removal by the wind.

The various strata of sedimentary rocks, the environments in which they formed, and the following episodes of folding and faulting to which they were subjected have created in these strata some of the world's great oil and gas deposits. The folding and faulting, along with internal variations in the composition of some layers, created traps that stopped the liquid-gaseous petroleum from moving farther through permeable rock layers (see FIGURE 9.8). Pools of "Texas Gold" accumulated in these traps.

There are four major oil- and gas-producing areas within the Dry Margin region: (1) the flanks of the Wichita and Arbuckle mountains in south-central Oklahoma and on into eastern Oklahoma; (2) the Wichita-Amarillo fields in southern Oklahoma, north central Texas, and in the Texas-Oklahoma panhandles; (3) the Bend Arch region of north central Texas; and (4) the Permian Basin of west Texas and eastern New Mexico (FIGURE 16.4).

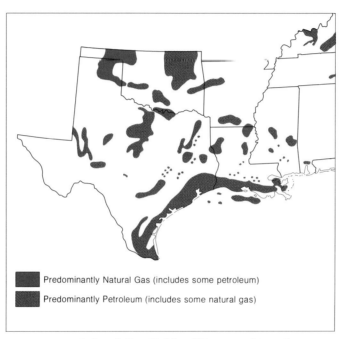

Predominantly Natural Gas (includes some petroleum)

Predominantly Petroleum (includes some natural gas)

FIGURE 16.4 *Oil and Gas Fields of Texas and Nearby Southern States*

The physical regions of the Dry Margin are closely related to its geologic history. The Osage Plains have strata that are slightly inclined, mostly to the west, because of past shifts in the earth's crust. The harder layers tend to form cuesta-type ridges whose steepest sides face to the east. In eastern Oklahoma, they form ridges 300 to 400 feet high in a 50- to 60-mile-wide belt called the Sandstone Hills. To the west are the Red Hills Plains, a smooth lowland 50 to 150 miles wide with a characteristically red soil on the surface. Western Oklahoma is noted for the Gypsum Hills, where the gypsum-capped ridges were sometimes eroded into low hills. These are the most striking examples of the calcium sulfate salt deposits (gypsum) that were left behind by the evaporating Permian seas.

The Osage Plains are cut by eastward-flowing rivers, notably the Arkansas and Red rivers and their tributaries. In some areas, especially along the Red River in southeastern Oklahoma, the alluvial soils of the floodplains support very productive farms.

In southern Oklahoma, the Osage Plains are broken by several upland areas. In the southeast, the Arbuckle Upland rises 300 to 400 feet above the surrounding plains. An uparching of the Paleozoic sedimentary rocks, this upland forms a plateau that is about 65 miles long and 30 miles wide.

To the west are the higher Wichita Mountains, an uplift in which granite and other igneous rocks are exposed. These mountains rise as much as 1,500 feet above the plains and cover an area similar in extent to that of the Arbuckle Mountains.

The large part of the Osage Plains in Oklahoma that is comprised of the Red Hills Plains extends southward into northern Texas. In the southern part, the characteristic cuesta ridges, low and rounded in Oklahoma, are somewhat more rugged in Texas, and the red soil coloring fades out. One of these ridges, composed of limestone, marks both the southeastern and southern edges of the Osage Plains as it swings westward toward Big Spring, Texas.

Some of the formations on the Osage Plains are fossil bearing. A notable example is near Glen Rose, Texas, in the Dinosaur Valley State Park. Remnants of dinosaurs are found here, including footprints in limestone along the Paluxy River. This was a coastal tidal flat 100 million years ago.

The Texas part of the Osage Plains is drained by the Brazos River. As the land rose in the past, the river cut a 3- to 4-mile-wide valley that in some places is 500 feet below the surrounding surface.

South of the Osage Plains, the Edwards Plateau is underlain predominantly by Cretaceous limestone deposited when the ocean invaded the area from the southeast. These hard, horizontal strata of limestone are cut here and there by streams, providing most of the relief on an otherwise monotonous surface.

Northwest of Austin, in the Central Mineral Region, the Llano-Burnet Uplift occurred. The sedimentary rock layers were arched up gently, to the point that in the center of the arch, older igneous and metamorphic rocks were exposed to the surface.

Along the eastern edge of the Edwards Plateau, just west of Austin, is the Texas Hill Country. This area encompasses erosional hills that were carved out of the horizontal limestone beds when streams cut into them as they flowed off the plateau onto the West Gulf Coastal Plain. It was here, in the 1850s, that the ancestors of President Lyndon B. Johnson and others walked into the trap set by the rich grasslands of the semiarid environment.

To the west of both the Osage Plains and the Edwards Plateau, sharp bluffs mark the beginning of the Llano Estacado. Here the surface rises from an elevation of 2,500 feet, on its eastern edge, to over 5,500 feet toward New Mexico. In contrast, typical elevations on the Edwards Plateau range from 1,200 to 1,800 feet. The bluff that bounds the Llano Estacado is not a cuesta but the end of a thick layer of sand, gravel, and clay that was laid down during the late Tertiary period, less than 10 million years ago. It represents an episode of massive erosion of the newly formed Rocky Mountains to the west. Streams carried millions of tons of rocks into Texas and Oklahoma, burying the rocks now exposed on the surface of the Edwards Plateau. Subsequent erosion of these layers removed some of this blanket, which once extended even farther east than it does today. In northern Texas and Oklahoma, where the bluff is as much as 250 feet high, the scarp is known as either the Break of Plains or the Caprock Escarpment.

The Llano Estacado is underlain at great depth by the central basin platform, a feature that has been pushing upward slowly for perhaps 500 million years (FIGURE 16.5). Occasionally the thick layers of rock that flank this platform slip, causing an earthquake like the mild one that occurred in June 1978 under Odessa, Texas. Another feature on the Llano Estacado lies south of Amarillo where the Prairie Dog Town Fork of the Red River has cut the spectacular gorge of the Palo Duro Canyon. It is a great gash 800 feet deep in the otherwise flat plain (FIGURE 16.6).

Much of the Llano Estacado north and west of Lubbock is a landscape of cotton farms, oil wells, and huge cattle feedlots. The cotton and feedlots depend on water brought up from subsurface aquifers. Originally pumped by windmills, the aquifers are now drained by great diesel pumps scattered among the fields. The southern part of the Llano Estacado down to Big Spring remains a flat, barren land not unlike that first viewed by the Spanish.

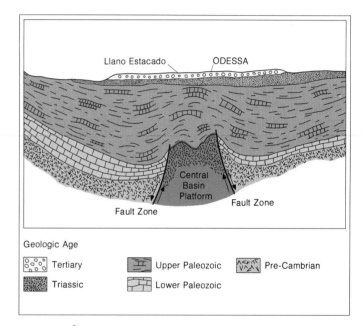

Geologic Age

Tertiary · Upper Paleozoic · Pre-Cambrian

Triassic · Lower Paleozoic

FIGURE 16.5
The Central Basin Platform

FIGURE 16.6
*The Palo Duro
Canyon*

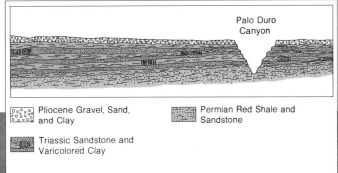

*Palo Duro Canyon,
Texas*

*Irrigation rig
in a cotton field
on the Llano Estacado
west of Lubbock, Texas*

The Ogallala Aquifer

Agriculture on parts of the Llano Estacado is made possible only by huge quantities of water that are pumped out of the Ogallala Aquifer. A sandstone-gravel layer no more than 300 feet thick, the Ogallala was laid down for several hundred miles east of the Rocky Mountains as erosion tore those great hills down even as they were being thrust high above the western Great Plains. Melting snow and rain from the mountains entered the permeable Ogallala formation over thousands of years, creating a veritable underground lake.

This subterranean aquifer was mined slowly at first. In 1930, there were only 170 windmill-driven irrigation wells on the Llano Estacado, but by 1957, this number multiplied to 42,225, most powered by diesel pumps. Today nearly two billion gallons of water are pumped annually out of the Ogallala, making it possible for the Texas High Plains area to produce about one-quarter of the nation's cotton and grain sorghum as well as 15 percent of all United States feed cattle.

Unfortunately, the water is being mined faster than it is being replenished. Only 60 million gallons of the annual withdrawal is being returned to the ground, just over three percent of the original total removal. The chief instrument of this loss is the center-pivot irrigation rig. It is comprised of wheeled lines that turn slowly from a center point spraying the water from the length of the moving line. The resulting circles are up to a mile in diameter, forming great green circles on an otherwise brown land—a striking feature when seen from the air. These rigs draw 900 gallons of water a minute from an average depth of 1,000 feet. They can consume 50 gallons of diesel fuel per acre in applying 22 inches of water per year. The Ogallala is running out of water, and serious attention is being given to returning more of the liquid for recycling rather than discharging it into rivers.

In Lubbock, Texas, the effluent from the city's waste-water treatment plant has been used for farming since the 1930s. Because more water was available than needed, the land was over-irrigated, which resulted over the years in a 50-foot rise in the groundwater table. The recycled water, now essentially pure after being filtered through the ground, is pumped back into Lubbock to supply lakes and streams in a 1,450-acre park. Major research is now being conducted in the area to develop the techniques for recycling used water in order to stave off the ruinous possibility of completely depleting the Ogallala Aquifer.

German Pioneers in Texas

The first permanent European settlers on the plains west of the Balcones Escarpment were not Indian-fighting pioneers but German immigrants. In 1842, idealistic German nobles formed the Society for the Protection of German Immigrants in Texas, or the *Adelsverein*. They wanted to transplant German culture to America as an outlet for oppressed peasants and to develop new markets for German goods. Texas was chosen because of reports of its salubrious environment (which was believed to be everywhere the same as eastern Texas), the availability of land, and the lack of restrictive controls under the Republic of Texas. In what turned out to be a fraudulent deal, the Adelsverein purchased a large tract on the Edwards Plateau, an area uninhabited at the time by the Texans.

During 1844–1846, the Adelsverein brought 7,380 Germans into Texas. By this time, the Society was virtually bankrupt and ill equipped to accommodate the immigrants, let alone live up to promises of housing, crop financing, and public services. Despite great hardships, the German immigrants succeeded, and at one time Texas had the largest percentage of German-born people of any state, including Wisconsin.

Some of the Germans founded New Braunfels and other towns along the inner West Gulf Coastal Plain. Another group landed at Indianola, a small port on the coast near Victoria. The wagons they expected to hire had been rented instead to the United States Army for use in the fighting against Mexico. Hundreds of men, women, and children were stranded on the disease-ridden coast. They walked several hundred miles, crossing rain-swollen streams in their journey up onto the Edwards Plateau, at that time the domain of the Comanche Indians. The trail was littered with the graves of those who succumbed to the rigors of this harrowing trip. The survivors built the town of Fredericksburg, near the Pedernales River in the Texas Hill Country. The Comanche tolerated these intruders because they were led to believe that the Germans were a different tribe from the hated Mexicans and Texans. Fredericksburg today is a charming town of almost 6,500 people that is noted for its wide main street (built wide enough to allow an oxen team and wagon to turn around), German names, and stone houses.

The most famous descendant of these courageous German immigrants was Chester W. Nimitz, Fleet Admiral and commander of the United States Pacific Fleet during the Second World War. His grandfather was an original immigrant who opened a hotel in Fredericksburg. The hotel now is part of the Admiral Nimitz State Historical Center, which focuses on the admiral's life and career and includes exhibits of the Pacific Theater of World War II.

EARLY SETTLEMENT

Settlement in this High Plains region proceeded slowly after initial sporadic penetrations by the Spanish. Though windmills became available in 1873, early attempts to drill deepwater wells were unsuccessful. This country remained virtually uninhabited until about 1910, when the discovery of oil near Amarillo triggered a modest wave of interest.

The entire Dry Margin region was not penetrated easily by the American settlers. Not only were they unprepared for the dry climate, but they were also ill equipped to deal with the fierce Apache, Penetaka, and Comanche Indians and the Mexicans. The Indians were accustomed to fighting on horseback and used spears and bow and arrows with devastating effect against the unwanted intruders. They also terrified the settlers because of their tendency to cruelly torture their captives. The Americans were armed with the bore-loading rifle, deadly accurate but cumbersome from horseback, and the single-shot pistol. It was the invention of the six-shooter revolver by Samuel Colt that first gave the Texans the upper hand. This rapid-fire gun became available in the 1840s. The Texas Rangers were formed as a mobile striking force that, armed with this new weapon, began to clear the region of hostile Indians and Mexicans.

Fredericksburg: a German town in the Hill Country of Texas

The heavy steel plow was another technological innovation that made possible cultivation of the grasslands. It was necessary in order to penetrate the heavy root network of the prairie grass. Water was always the most precious resource. It was said that one had to "dig for wood and climb for water," a reference to digging up the buried roots for wood and climbing windmill towers to repair them.

The discovery and exploitation of oil and gas resources in the twentieth century brought more people and development to the region than did the raising of cattle or wheat. But even today, it is still a thinly populated area. As in the past, its future may depend more heavily on water than petroleum, reflecting the transitional nature of the climate.

The settlement of Oklahoma was a unique episode in American history. This empty land initially was the destination of Indian tribes that were forced out of the eastern South between 1820 and 1842. The Oklahoma Territory became the western end of the Trail of Tears, and all of eastern Oklahoma was given over to the Indian immigrants. Five Indian nations settled there under the protection of treaties with the United States government. The natives were to own these lands "as long as grass shall grow and rivers run." However, growing American outposts on the eastern

border and cattle drives from Texas across Oklahoma to Kansas soon led to pressure to open the lands for settlement. Participation in the Civil War on the Confederate side by some tribes weakened Congressional support for the Indians, leading to the loss of access to hunting lands in western Oklahoma. Land-hungry people called Boomers urged Congress to buy land from the tribes, and in 1889, over three million acres were so purchased. At noon, April 22, 1889, nearly 1.9 million of these acres were opened for claim by Americans. In the ensuing race, 50,000 people moved into the area before nightfall. The towns of Guthrie and Oklahoma City had 10,000 citizens each by the end of the day. "Sooners" sneaked in ahead of the legal settlers and claimed some of the best land. Another 6.5 million acres were opened in the Cherokee Outlet on September 16, 1893, during which another 50,000 people rushed in to claim more former Indian lands. By 1890, Oklahoma's 169,500 native Americans made up less than six percent of Oklahoma's population. However, this was the largest concentration of Indians in any state in the United States except for California. Lands under the jurisdiction of the United States Bureau of Indian Affairs totaled 19.5 million acres in Oklahoma in 1920, an amount that shrunk to 1.2 million acres in 1980.

THE BASIN AND RANGE

The southwest corner of Texas, the Trans Pecos, is a strikingly different geologic environment. Most of it is in the Basin and Range, a landform unit that cuts across parts of California, Nevada, Oregon, Idaho, and Utah. It is characterized by long, block-faulted ridges separated by broad, level valleys (FIGURE 16.7). The strata are quite varied. Paleozoic sedimentary rocks are widespread, and in many areas, they are covered by other sediments of Cretaceous age. Intermingled in them are volcanic intrusions of the Tertiary period. Erosion in a few places has revealed ancient (Precambrian) crystalline rocks.

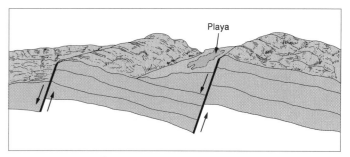

FIGURE 16.7 *Fault Blocks*

Fault blocks are characteristic of the Basin and Range region. Faulting has lifted great blocks that form the ranges. The downfaulted areas form the intervening valleys, or basins, that are partially filled with rock that has eroded from the adjacent ranges. Typically the basins are covered in part by playas (temporary lakes).

A large part of the Basin and Range is drained by the Rio Grande, but in the desert climate, many valleys have no drainage outlets. In a humid climate, water would eventually accumulate sufficiently to overflow the basin. Here the water evaporates rather than accumulates. Intermittent lakes or *playas* form, which leave behind the salt that was dissolved in the water. These salt flats are indeed some of the flattest areas on the earth.

The Rio Grande is a classic *exotic* river, one that rises in the more humid highlands and has sufficient volume to flow through a desert despite the intense evaporation to which it is subjected in its journey. The Rio Grande loses half its volume in its travels from Albuquerque to El Paso, for example. A result of this severe evaporation is that the salt content of the river rises steadily in what amounts to a process of natural distillation. This has been measured at 180 parts per million (ppm) at Santa Fe and 780 ppm at El Paso. The level reaches 2,380 ppm where the Rio Grande is joined by the Pecos River, partly because the latter flows over salt beds before it reaches the Rio Grande. Water with a salinity of 4,000 ppm is not desirable for crops or livestock.

Surface elevations in the Texas portion of the Basin and Range usually are above 3,000 feet, and the mountains reach 8,000 feet. The highest point in Texas (8,751 feet) is Guadalupe Peak in the Guadalupe Mountains, east of El Paso on the New Mexico border. These mountains also include El Capitan Peak, a remnant of an enormous Permian-age coral reef comparable in magnitude with the Great Barrier Reef near Australia.

In the Basin and Range, the topography is structurally controlled. The ridges are blocks that were thrust up by faulting on their sides, and the valleys are areas that dropped between the ridges. This is in contrast with some highlands areas in eastern North America where the topography was controlled primarily by erosion. What mattered most in the humid east was how erosion-resistant a rock layer was rather than whether it was thrust above other layers. Furthermore, in most highland areas in the east, the structural features are old, meaning that erosion has had ample time to wear them down. In the Basin and Range, erosion by water is slow and the structural features are relatively young. In fact, they are still developing, as indicated by periodic movement along the fault lines. Thus, the resulting topography strongly reflects the structural history rather than being a product of erosion.

Another factor in the shaping of this dry landscape is the sparseness of vegetation. The wind almost constantly sweeps across the exposed surface, carrying sand particles with it to literally sandblast the rocks. The result is a sharply angular, sculptured topography that contrasts strongly with the green, gently rounded highlands of the eastern South.

In the southwestern corner of Texas, where the Rio Grande swings northward briefly before resuming its southward journey, is Big Bend National Park (FIGURE 16.8). It is a desert area of over 700,000 acres that is the core of the complex geology of the Big Bend region. Indian legend has it that when the Great Creator finished making the land and had placed stars in the heavens, birds in the air, and fish in the sea, there remained here and there bits of unused rock. He collected them in one great pile and out of it made the Big Bend. The rocks are mixed, strata stand on end or are lopsided, and mountains are out of place. Great canyons open out onto the river, and mountain peaks jut abruptly out of the plains. Water is scarce, more so than in the past, giving the impression that when streams had finished cutting the canyons, the Great Creator also turned off the water. The presence of many fossils, including coral, dinosaurs, and ancestors of the modern horse, also points to a more humid past.

Precipitation in the Basin and Range part of Texas averages about 10 inches a year or less, except in the Guadalupe Mountains, where it reaches 20 inches. The effectiveness of this modest rainfall is diminished by the high rate of evaporation, especially in summer when most of the rain falls. This limits settlement to the valley of the Rio Grande and a few other places where water is available.

In the dry lowlands of the region, the creosote bush and succulent cacti are the predominant vegetation, along with clumps of desert grass. Upper elevations support piñon and juniper forests and, occasionally, yellow pine and Douglas fir.

Soils are thin and mostly of the red desert type. They are limey (basic) even at the surface, and the organic content is low. *Caliche* forms when the calcium carbonate that is dissolved by occasional rain is deposited just below the surface or as it is drawn back near the dry surface by capillary action and then evaporates. The caliche forms a hard layer that is difficult to break. Along the rivers, alluvial deposits make excellent soils that can be very productive when irrigated and properly drained so as to prevent salinization or the formation of caliche.

The Rio Grande Valley was the site of the earliest European settlement in Texas. In the early seventeenth century, the area became the headquarters for Spanish explorations and the establishment of missions out of Mexico. The first mission near the present site of El Paso was built in 1682. Spanish efforts to colonize the West Gulf Coast, including San Antonio, were organized from the Rio Grande Valley.

American interest in the Rio Grande area developed only in the late nineteenth century. The public debate in the 1850s over choosing a transcontinental railway route included one that passed to the south through El Paso. Although this was later to become the course followed by the Southern Pacific, the Civil War finally decided the debate over the route to be used for the first transcontinental railroad in favor of the North.

El Paso, a city of over 425,000 people, has emerged as the region's capital and trade center. It is the focus of two major agricultural regions, one of the few places where the valuable long-staple cotton is still grown. Much of El Paso's contemporary significance derives from its position on a major transportation corridor that connects the Gulf Coast with Southern California. The city is also a major point of contact with Mexico through its sister city, Ciudad Juárez. This strong international flavor and the region's sunny, dry climate make El Paso a popular winter resort city.

FIGURE 16.8
*Big Bend
National Park*

The Big Bend region, Texas

PART IV

THE LAND & THE FUTURE

17

To conserve what was once a pristine land . . . the people of the South must declare their interdependence— not only with one another but with the natural world.

DORIS BETTS
1986 Report of the Southern Growth Policies Board's
Commission on the Future of the South

The South is one of the most distinctive regions of the United States. It has been so for centuries, and most Southerners want their home to remain characteristically Southern. They are loyal to the South, they care about their region, and they do not welcome the thought of it being swallowed up by megalopolises or homogenized past recognition in a mass culture. Their attachment to place runs too deep to permit an easy loss of the South's uniqueness.

Yet, it is undeniable that the South is changing, changing in manifold ways and with a breadth and rapidity that are without precedent. Although it touches many areas, a sure sign of the profound nature of change is its effect on both the people and the land. Alterations in ways of life can be striking and highly visible, but in the end, they may be less permanent than alterations in the South's physical environment. People and their ways are only part of Southern distinctiveness; the land also bears an intimate connection to the essence of the region's identity.

Some of these changes win warm applause within the region. One of the ironies in the history of this proud people is that certain things that made the South unique were neither sought nor desirable. For much of its history, relative to the rest of the United States, the South was poor, less educated, and less healthy. When the South lost the Civil War, it had to live with a dominant society's judgment against a loser. Slavery and segregation also produced singular but negative images of the region that its residents did not welcome. These unpleasant facts undeniably were part of the South's character in the eyes of the world.

Therefore, it is not surprising that Southerners have been happy to leave many of these circumstances behind. They have embraced prosperity with enthusiasm, because it is simply better to be prosperous than to be poor. They are pursuing advanced education and improved health because these too are indisputable elements of a better life.

However, it is a source of serious concern to Southern leaders that these advances are not uniform across the region. As urban centers surge ahead, too many rural areas are being left behind with weakened agricultural economies and a tax base too small to support education, industrial development, and other crucial forms of public investment.

Two recent studies have highlighted the seriousness of this widening gap between the "two Souths." In its 1986 report of the Commission on the Future of the South, the Southern Growth Policies Board noted that "the sunshine on the Sunbelt has proved to be a narrow beam of light, brightening futures along the Atlantic Seaboard, and in large cities, but skipping over many small towns and rural areas."[1] A Ford Foundation-funded panel on rural economic development struck a similar theme in its much-quoted "Shadows in the Sunbelt" report, observing that "this explosive urban growth has masked the growing difficulties of the rural South. After two decades of reasonably solid growth, many rural communities now find themselves in serious trouble, faced with a serious decline in manufacturing and agriculture. In short, while we live in the Sunbelt, there is a dark cloud hanging over many of our rural neighbors."[2] Both reports emphasized that a major challenge facing the South in the 1990s will be how to rescue those Southerners left behind.

Marked progress has been made in the South's most fundamental historic conflict—race relations. Measurably ahead of Northern communities in integration, Southerners are happy to see long-established and unflattering stereotypes of their region fading from the media. Scenes of violence from the 1950s and 1960s have given way to notable examples of progress and harmony. Perhaps in the matter of race, more than anything else, the change in Southern ways has been truly dramatic.

Recently a distinguished historian, a native who continues to live in the South, raised some questions about race and racial attitudes. After analyzing the long history of racism among white Southerners, this scholar declared that the surrender of racism threatened the white Southerner with "loss of his sense of self."[3] Racism, he insisted, had been a vital part of the region's culture, and individuals had relied on racism "to make themselves whole . . . to smooth over the crudely sewn seams of their lives."[4] He concluded: "A very large part of the race problem in the South resolves itself into the question of how one takes the racism . . . out of the Southern mind without killing the Southerner. How does one excise an integral and functioning part of the body and yet preserve the life of the patient?"[5]

Yet many Southerners (and many historians) would disagree with this point of view. There are millions of Southerners, a new generation, who have not experienced the grim realities about which this scholar wrote. A few years ago, when three of the authors of this book asked their classes to discuss what was distinctive about the South, not one student mentioned the matter of race relations. It had no special significance for them, despite its long influence on the South's past.

Change in matters of race has been enormous, and it shows clear signs of becoming persistent. Although much remains to be accomplished, the South is ahead of the nation in many respects, and the region's dynamic economic centers seem determined to have positive race relations. As journalist and Southerner Fred

Powledge observed, "We have already taken away what we once considered the region's most important identifying characteristic, its institutionalized racism, and it remains the South."[6]

Opinion surveys suggest that most Southerners, white and black, agree with Powledge. Black Southerners are no longer leaving but returning to the South, and they are far more likely to describe themselves as highly satisfied with life than other black Americans. As for whites and their racial attitudes, 98 percent of white Southerners favored absolute segregation of public schools in 1942. By 1980, not only were Southern schools more integrated than schools in the rest of the nation, but only 5 percent of white Southerners disapproved of the situation (the same percentage as for whites elsewhere). Moreover, survey data show there are other identifiably Southern attitudes and that these are persisting.

John Shelton Reed, who has analyzed opinion polls over many decades, finds three areas in which Southerners' thoughts and values are different. One is localism, or attachment to a particular place. Repeatedly and by large margins, Southerners are far more likely than other Americans to name their community or state as the most desirable or to identify a local individual as the person they most admire. Like Southern novelists, Reed sees affection for one's home place as a Southern trait. He also found differences in attitudes toward the use of force or violence (with Southerners more approving) and attitudes toward religion. Southerners are more Protestant, and they seem more religious and more inclined to accept traditional tenets of faith.

Responses to opinion polls change over time, but Professor Reed has been tabulating and tracking the changes. He finds not only that the regional distinctions have persisted, but also that other parts of the country are conforming their attitudes more closely to those of the South. As American culture has moved in various directions, Southern positions have become more in vogue. Partly in jest, Reed has asked whether the *enduring* South might not be on its way to the status of *prevailing* South.

In the short run, Reed argues, change is almost certain to stimulate Southerners' sense of regional identity, at least for a while. Over many generations, fundamental changes in the Southern economy, political system, and social system have the capacity to alter the Southern character. But in the years immediately ahead, Southerners will be thrown into more frequent contact with non-Southerners, and the experience will make each more aware of his dissimilarities. Some people who may have given it little thought will find that they are different, that they are uniquely Southern.

Most of us would be quick to add other items to John Shelton Reed's list of Southern characteristics. Certainly cuisine, habits of speech, and preferences in music or sports or recreation come quickly to mind. But there is another factor that is crucial, and again Fred Powledge said it well: "The South's future is its environment. Take away the other qualities that people usually list when they try to define the South—its food, its way of talking, its slower pace, even its manners—and you'd still have something that you can pretty much call *The South* . . . But take away the environment of the South and you might as well have New Jersey."[7]

The land of the South is an irreplaceable part of Southern distinctiveness and has been an enduring force in its history. For many generations it has been a constant factor, a presence that made its influence felt and became a part of the experience of the region and its people.

There have been changes, to be sure, for no group of inhabitants left the land unchanged. Even the Indians cleared small patches of ground, and the pace of alteration quickened as European settlement advanced. With the expansion of the Cotton South, Southerners began to comment upon the problem of soil erosion, which was washing away once-fertile land and encouraging discouraged farmers to move farther west. At the end of the nineteenth century, the large-scale exploitation of Southern forest resources began, as whole mountains were stripped of massive oaks and chestnuts that have not returned even today. The mining of mineral wealth also left some areas stripped, denuded, and apparently ruined during the twentieth century.

Slowly, however, earlier generations of Southerners became aware of these dangers and began to respond to them. Probably the greatest turnabout has occurred in agriculture. With new crops such as soybeans, cattle, and poultry; with new practices that emphasize soil conservation; and with technology, Southern agriculture has been transformed. No longer labor intensive and chronically depressed, Southern agriculture has become much more varied and productive and is far better suited to the soil and the terrain. The forests, too, have returned, although outside of national preserves, trees grow in ordered uniformity under corporate management. The tree farms of

Weyerhaeuser, Georgia Pacific, and other corporate giants promise to make the South an even larger producer of lumber in the future than the Northwest. And, thanks to federal legislation, the mining industry is no longer devastating the horizon but replanting after coal and other minerals have been removed.

Nevertheless, today's risks are pervasive and greater than ever before. Both the technology that has brought so much progress and the economic growth that is so welcome involve danger on a new order of magnitude. If Southerners are not careful, they could despoil or permanently ruin major parts of the environment. Some areas are essential to both ecological processes and commercial activities but are not widely recognized as valuable.

Perhaps the best examples of future environmental dangers involve water. If there is one essential resource that the Sunbelt South does not possess in abundance, perhaps that resource is water. Many communities have already experienced serious problems with water supplies or water quality. Overuse or long-term pollution of groundwater has recently become a serious concern, and developmental pressures threaten many special wetland environments that play a vital role in the region's water supply.

On the South's dry western margin on the High Plains in Texas, the exhaustion of groundwater that accumulated slowly over centuries threatens the future. Commercial agriculture has thrived for decades in this region, but it is entirely irrigated agriculture. The sparse and variable rains of the region will not support significant farming, so farm operators have relied on wells to supply the long assemblies of pipes and sprayers that lumber across growing fields on soft rubber wheels. But signs of serious trouble have begun to appear. On farm after farm, wells have run dry, and even the sinking of deeper shafts does not always suffice to locate the falling water table. Residents hope to find some way out of their dilemma, but the possibility is real that exhaustion of groundwater in that habitually dry region will end the profitable commercial farming that never existed before irrigation.

From Texas eastward to Florida and north to Virginia, the poisoning of the environment, and sometimes the groundwater, by toxins presents another danger. Heavy industrialization along the Gulf of Mexico has sometimes damaged the ocean waters. Commercial and sport fishermen have noticed severe declines in more than one kind of fish, and state authorities have had to limit the catch to give species a chance to replenish. While researching this book, the authors stopped at one seafood restaurant on Texas's Gulf Coast, amid the "spaghetti alley" of petrochemical pipelines. When they asked what was fresh and good that day, an embarrassed and saddened proprietress had to confess that all her fish were frozen and shipped in. Environmental damage had made seafood from the Gulf, which she once vowed to serve exclusively, unavailable.

Chemical pollution from agriculture has also been a serious problem. As was the case elsewhere, problems arose first with DDT. This compound, and other chlorinated hydrocarbons, once seemed the answer to many insect pests. A heavy boll weevil infestation in 1949 led cotton growers in the lower Mississippi Valley to spread DDT massively by airplane. But by 1954, weevils that were resistant to the new insecticides began to appear, first in Louisiana, then in the Yazoo Delta, the Red River Valley, and the Ouachita Valley. These were, as one authority noted, "precisely where farmers carried out the most intensive control programs."[8] Then other toxins were used, but shortly they began to have lethal effects on Florida's eagles and other birds. The chemicals were entering the environment and the food chain.

More recently a new danger arose from Temik, a popular pesticide that seemed to promise victory over the troublesome nematode, a worm that bleeds away the nutrients of many crops. Temik was once described by the senior toxologist of the Environmental Protection Agency as perhaps "the most acutely toxic chemical currently registered in the United States" for use on farms. In 1979, dangerously high levels of this chemical began to show up in the wells of potato growers in New York State. After investigation, the manufacturer pointed to the flat terrain, sandy, porous soil, and high water table (characteristics Florida has in common with New York) as important factors in the problem. Somehow, no one connected these factors to Florida's agriculture, but soon contamination was detected there. Use of Temik on citrus was banned by state officials by the end of 1983.

Officials and residents hope that this has ended the problem, but wherever serious contamination of groundwater occurs, the population faces a long-term problem that requires monitoring. There is nothing like the circulation of the large amounts of water trapped in porous strata deep below the ground. Except in unusual conditions, groundwater moves slowly, so an area whose wells are poisoned may have to avoid using the water for decades. Even after the contamination has left the original site, the movement of the pollutant has to be tracked so that other communities do not unknowingly inherit the problem. Sources as commonplace as leaking gasoline tanks have caused serious problems in several states.

Statistics from Florida give some sense of the dimensions of the problem. In a recent inventory, officials logged 92 known cases of contamination of groundwater. Almost two-thirds of these affected or threatened water supplies. In addition to chemical runoff from agriculture and waste products from manufacturing, a frequent problem was saltwater intrusion. This intrusion is tied to development. As residential and business development occurred in Florida, it often and necessarily brought along with it measures to increase drainage. Unfortunately, such drainage lowers the water table and allows a wedge of denser salt water to move inland or up waterways. The accompanying maps illustrate the fact that, despite modern control measures, saltwater intrusion has continued to grow in southern Florida (FIGURE 17.1).

As earlier chapters of this book have pointed out, uninhabited marshes, swamps, and other wetlands play a very important role in filtering water and in maintaining the productivity of many commercially valuable types of sea life. Yet these wetlands have often been the least appreciated and most endangered kinds of Southern environments. They appear to have no value to man, so frequently they have been drained and destroyed. Since the arrival of Europeans, Florida's wetlands have shrunk enormously (FIGURES 17.2, 17.3), and much of that state remains vulnerable to careless development (FIGURE 17.4). In general, the coastal regions of other Southern states are similar to Florida in their sensitivity to development, and most of the South is relatively vulnerable to the environmental damage of acid rain (FIGURE 17.5).

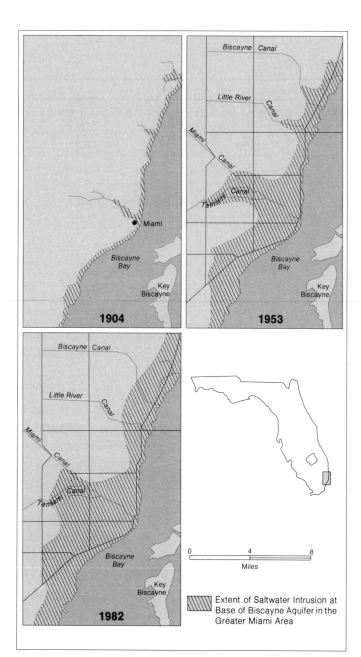

FIGURE 17.1 *Saltwater Intrusion*

FIGURE 17.2
Estimated Original Extent of Florida Wetlands

FIGURE 17.3 *Florida Wetlands, 1972–1974*

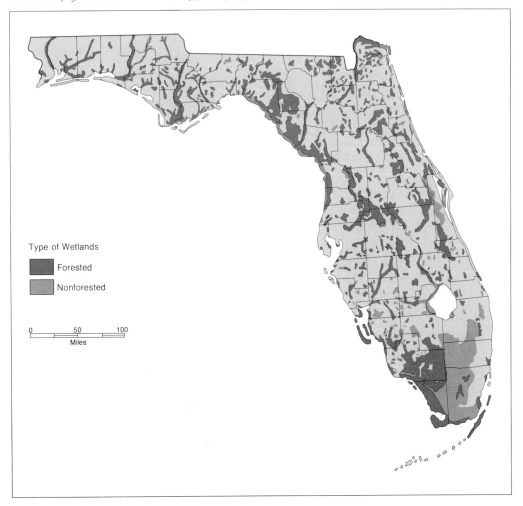

Type of Wetlands

Forested

Nonforested

0 50 100
Miles

FIGURE 17.4
*Development
Tolerance*

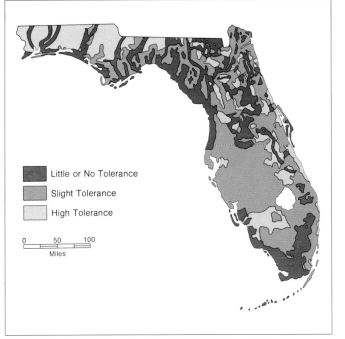

Little or No Tolerance

Slight Tolerance

High Tolerance

0 50 100
Miles

FIGURE 17.5
*Areas Sensitive
to Acid Rain*

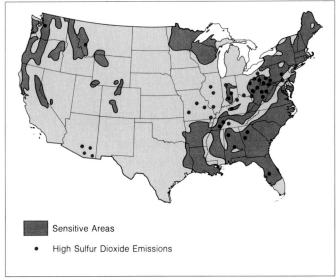

Sensitive Areas

• High Sulfur Dioxide Emissions

NOTES

PREFACE

1. Excerpt from Adlai Stevenson's last speech, made on 9 July 1965, to the 39th session of the Economic and Social Council in Geneva, Switzerland.

Chapter 1. INTRODUCTION

1. John Lawson, *A New Voyage to Carolina* (London: 1709; reprint, Chapel Hill: University of North Carolina Press, 1967), 86.

Chapter 2. LAND OF THE SOUTH

1. Lawson, *Voyage to Carolina*, 33.

Chapter 3. PEOPLE FOR THE LAND

1. J. Leitch Wright, Jr., *Only Land They Knew* (New York: Free Press, 1981), 14.
2. Frederick W. Hodge, ed., *Original Narratives of Early American History: Spanish Explorers in the Southern United States, 1528–1543*, reprint (New York: Barnes & Noble, Inc., 1953), 30.
3. Carl Bridenbaugh, *Myths and Realities*, rev. ed. (New York: Atheneum, 1980), 130.
4. Everett Dick, *The Dixie Frontier: A Social History of the Southern Frontier from the First Transmontane Beginnings to the Civil War*, rev. ed. (New York: Capricorn Books, 1964), 4.
5. Ibid., 15.
6. Ibid., 17–18.
7. Ibid., 18.
8. Grant Foreman, *Indian Removal*, rev. ed. (Norman: University of Oklahoma Press, 1972), 91.
9. Mary Beth Norton et al., *A People and A Nation: A History of the United States*, 2d ed. (Boston: Houghton Mifflin Co., 1987), 289.
10. Malcolm J. Rohrbough, *The Trans-Appalachian Frontier: People, Societies, and Institutions, 1775–1850* (New York: Oxford University Press, 1978), 192.
11. Dick, *Dixie Frontier*, 3.
12. Rohrbough, *Trans-Appalachian Frontier*, 202.
13. Ibid., 196.
14. James Oakes, *The Ruling Race: A History of American Slaveholders* (New York: Alfred A. Knopf, Inc., 1982), 75.
15. Dick, *Dixie Frontier*, 59.
16. Clement Eaton, *The Growth of Southern Civilization, 1790–1860* (New York: Harper & Row Pub. Inc., 1961), 31–32.
17. Ibid., 33.
18. Ibid., 34.
19. Ibid.
20. Ibid.
21. Ibid., 35.
22. Catherine Clinton, *The Plantation Mistress* (New York: Pantheon, 1982), 167.
23. Eaton, *Civilization*, 38–39.
24. Ibid., 39.

Chapter 4. INTRODUCTION

None

Chapter 5. THE ATLANTIC COASTAL PLAIN

1. Philip L. Barbour, ed., *The Complete Works of Captain John Smith (1580–1631)*, vol. 1 (Chapel Hill: University of North Carolina Press, 1986), 144.
2. Orrin H. Pilkey, Jr., William J. Neal, Orrin H. Pilkey, Sr., and Stanley R. Riggs, *From Currituck to Calabash: Living with North Carolina's Barrier Islands*, 2d ed. (Research Triangle Park: North Carolina Science and Technology Research Center, 1980), 9.
3. *Charlotte Observer*, 27 September 1985.
4. Ibid.
5. Ibid.
6. *Charlotte Observer*, 28 September 1985.
7. *The Whole & True Discoverye of Terra Florida* (London: 1563; reprint: Florida State Historical Society, 1927), 91.
8. Peter H. Wood, *Black Majority: Negroes in Colonial South Carolina from 1670 through the Stono Rebellion* (New York: W. W. Norton & Co., 1974), 201.
9. William H. Freehling, *Prelude to the Civil War* (New York: Harper & Row Pub. Inc., 1965), 31–32.
10. G. E. Manigault, "The Earthquake at Charleston," reprint in "Out of the Past," *Earth Science* (Winter 1983), 24–26.
11. Ibid.
12. Henry Wadsworth Longfellow, "The Slave in the Dismal Swamp" from *The Poems of Henry Wadsworth Longfellow*, The Modern Library, Bennett A. Cerf, Donald S. Klopfer, and Robert K. Haas, eds. (New York: Random House, n.d.), 463.
13. Curtis J. Richardson et al., eds., *Pocosin Wetlands: An Integrated Analysis of Coastal Plain Freshwater Bogs in North Carolina* (Stroudsburg, Penn.: Hutchinson Ross Pub. Co., 1981), 225.
14. Hubert J. Davis, *The Great Dismal Swamp: Its History, Folklore and Science*, rev. ed. (Richmond: Cavalier Press, 1962), 49.
15. John Fraser Hart, "Cropland Concentration in the South," *Annals of the Association of American Geographers* (December 1978), 508.

Chapter 6. THE FLORIDA PENINSULA

1. Luther J. Carter, *The Florida Experience: Land and Water Policy in a Growth State* (Baltimore: Johns Hopkins University Press, 1974), 62.
2. Ibid., 85.

Chapter 7. THE EAST GULF COASTAL PLAIN

1. Albert E. Cowdrey, *This Land, This South: An Environmental History* (Lexington: University Press of Kentucky, 1983), 79.
2. Rohrbough, *Trans-Appalachian Frontier*, 402.

Chapter 8. THE MISSISSIPPI VALLEY & DELTA

1. Pete Daniel, *Deep'n As It Come: The 1927 Mississippi River Flood* (New York: Oxford University Press, 1977), 14.

Chapter 9. THE WEST GULF COASTAL PLAIN

None

Chapter 10. INTRODUCTION

None

Chapter 11. THE PIEDMONT

1. Cowdrey, *This South*, 29.
2. Jean Gottmann, *Virginia in Our Century* (Charlottesville: University Press of Virginia, 1969), 80–82.

Chapter 12. THE BLUE RIDGE

1. Catherine Marshall, *Christy* (New York: McGraw-Hill Book Co., 1967), 16.

Chapter 13. THE VALLEY & RIDGE

None

Chapter 14. THE APPALACHIAN PLATEAU & INTERIOR LOW PLATEAUS

None

Chapter 15. THE OZARK & OUACHITA UPLANDS

1. "A Step Back in Time," *American Heritage* 27, no. 4 (June 1976), 38.

Chapter 16. THE DRY MARGIN

1. Ralph H. Brown, *Historical Geography of the United States* (New York: Harcourt, Brace & World, 1948), 440.
2. Ibid., 442.

Chapter 17. THE LAND & THE FUTURE

1. Southern Growth Policies Board, *Halfway Home and a Long Way To Go* (Research Triangle Park, N.C.: Report of the 1986 Commission on the Future of the South, 1986).
2. MDC, Inc., *Shadows in the Sunbelt: Developing the Rural South in an Era of Economic Change* (Chapel Hill: MDC, Inc., 1986).
3. Joel Williamson, *The Crucible of Race* (New York: Oxford University Press, 1984), 499.
4. Ibid.
5. Ibid.
6. Fred Powledge, *Journeys Through the South* (New York: Vanguard Press, Inc., 1979), 238–239.
7. Ibid.
8. Joyce Egginton, "Temik Troubles Move South: Contamination of Groundwater in Florida," *Audubon* 85 (May 1983), 34.

SELECT BIBLIOGRAPHY

Adams, James T., and Coleman, R. V., eds. *Atlas of American History*. New York: Charles Scribner's Sons, 1977.

Atwood, Wallace W. *The Physiographic Provinces of North America*. Waltham, Mass.: Blaisdell Pub. Co., division of Ginn & Co., 1940.

Ayers, H. Brandt, and Naylor, Thomas H. *You Can't Eat Magnolias*. New York: McGraw-Hill Book Co., 1972

Baarslag, Karl. "Island Besieged." *Oceans* (November 1975): 34–37.

Basile, Robert M. *A Geography of Soils*. Dubuque, Iowa: William C. Brown Co. Pub., 1971.

Bass, Jack, and De Vries, Walter. *Transformation of Southern Politics: Social Change and Political Consequences Since 1945*. New York: Basic Books, Inc., 1976.

Billington, Ray Allen. *Westward Expansion: A History of the American Frontier*. 3d ed. New York: Macmillan Co., 1967.

Birdsall, Stephen S., and Florin, John W. *Regional Landscapes of the United States and Canada*. New York: John Wiley & Sons, Inc., 1981.

Bridenbaugh, Carl. *Myths and Realities*. Rev. ed. New York: Atheneum, 1980.

Brown, Ralph H. *Historical Geography of the United States*. New York: Harcourt, Brace & World, 1948.

Camp, Cordelia. *The Influence of Geography upon Early North Carolina*. Raleigh: Carolina Charter Tercentenary Commission, 1963.

Cantú, Rita. *Great Smoky Mountains*. Las Vegas, Nev.: KC Publications, 1979.

Caro, Robert A. *The Years of Lyndon Johnson: The Path to Power*. New York: Alfred A. Knopf, Inc., 1983.

Carter, Luther J. *The Florida Experience: Land and Water Policy in a Growth State*. Baltimore: Johns Hopkins University Press, 1974.

Cash, Wilbur Joseph. *The Mind of the South*. New York: Alfred A. Knopf, Inc., 1941.

Citizen's Program for the Chesapeake Bay. *Chesapeake Citizen's Report* 3, nos. 1–3 (January–April 1981). Annapolis: Chesapeake Bay Program, 1981.

Clark, Thomas H., and Stearn, Colin W. *The Geological Evolution of North America: A Regional Approach to Historical Geology*. New York: Ronald Press Co., 1960.

Clay, James W.; Orr, Douglas M., Jr.; and Stuart, Alfred W. *North Carolina Atlas: Portrait of a Changing Southern State*. Chapel Hill: University of North Carolina Press, 1975.

Clinton, Catherine. *The Plantation Mistress*. New York: Pantheon, 1982.

Cobb, James C. *Industrialization and Southern Society, 1877–1984*. Lexington: University Press of Kentucky, 1984.

Cohen, Stan B. *Historic Springs of the Virginias: A Pictorial History*. Charleston, W. Va.: Pictorial Histories Pub. Co., 1981.

Cook, Earl. *Man, Energy, and Society*. San Francisco: W. H. Freeman & Co., 1976.

Cowdrey, Albert E. *This Land, This South: An Environmental History*. Lexington: University Press of Kentucky, 1983.

Daniel, Pete. *Deep'n As It Come: The 1927 Mississippi River Flood*. New York: Oxford University Press, 1977.

Davis, Hubert J. *The Great Dismal Swamp: Its History, Folklore and Science.* Rev. ed. Richmond: Cavalier Press, 1962.

Davis, William Morris. *The Coral Reef Problem.* 1928. Reprint. New York: AMS Press, Inc., 1969.

Deagan, Kathleen. *Spanish St. Augustine: The Archaeology of a Colonial Creole Community.* New York: Academic Press, 1983.

Dick, Everett. *The Dixie Frontier: A Social History of the Southern Frontier from the First Transmontane Beginnings to the Civil War.* Rev. ed. New York: Capricórn Books, 1964.

Dobyns, Henry F. *Their Number Become Thinned.* Knoxville: University of Tennessee Press, 1983.

Driver, Harold E. *Indians of North America.* Chicago: University of Chicago Press, 1969.

Dunne, Thomas, and Leopold, Luna B. *Water in Environmental Planning.* San Francisco: W. H. Freeman & Co., 1978.

Eaton, Clement. *The Growth of Southern Civilization, 1790–1860.* New York: Harper & Row Pub. Inc., 1961.

Ellis, Ray, and Cronkite, Walter. *South By Southeast.* Birmingham, Ala.: Oxmoor House, Inc., 1983.

Esposito, Colonel Vincent J. *The West Point Atlas of American Wars, 1689–1900.* Vol. 1. New York: Frederick A. Praeger Pub., 1959.

Farb, Peter. *Face of North America.* New York: Harper & Row Pub. Inc., 1963.

Feibleman, Peter S., and editors of TIME-LIFE Books. *The Bayous.* Vol. 13, *The American Wilderness,* edited by Charles Osborne. New York: TIME-LIFE Books, 1973.

Fenneman, Nevin M. *Physiography of Eastern United States.* New York: McGraw-Hill Book Co., 1938.

Fernald, Edward A., ed. *Atlas of Florida.* Tallahassee: Florida State University Foundation, Inc., 1981.

Fernald, Edward A., and Patton, Donald J., eds. *Water Resources Atlas of Florida.* Tallahassee: Florida State University Foundation, Inc., 1984.

Fisher, A. C., Jr. "My Chesapeake—Queen of Bays." *National Geographic* 158 (October 1980): 428–467.

Foreman, Grant. *Indian Removal.* Rev. ed. Norman: University of Oklahoma Press, 1972.

Foth, Henry D., and Schafer, John W. *Soil Geography and Land Use.* New York: John Wiley & Sons, Inc., 1980.

Freehling, William H. *Prelude to the Civil War.* New York: Harper & Row Pub. Inc., 1965.

Friis, H. R. "A Series of Population Maps of the Colonies and the U.S., 1625–1790." *The Geographical Review* 30 (1940): 463–470.

Frome, Michael. *Strangers in High Places.* Knoxville: University of Tennessee Press, 1980.

Garbarino, Merwyn S. *Native American Heritage.* Boston: Little, Brown & Co., 1976.

Geraghty, James J.; Miller, David W.; Van der Leeden, Frits; and Troise, Fred L. *Water Atlas of the United States.* Port Washington, N.Y.: Water Information Center, Inc., 1973.

Gottmann, Jean. *Virginia in Our Century.* Charlottesville: University of Virginia Press, 1969.

Hamblin, W. Kenneth. *The Earth's Dynamic Systems: A Textbook in Physical Geology.* Minneapolis: Burgess Pub. Co., 1978.

Hart, John Fraser. *The Southeastern United States.* New York: Van Nostrand Reinhold, 1967.

Hilliard, Sam Bowers. *Atlas of Antebellum Southern Agriculture.* Baton Rouge: Louisiana State University Press, 1984.

Hollon, W. Eugene. *The Southwest: Old and New.* Lincoln: University of Nebraska Press, 1973.

Hudson, Charles. *The Southeastern Indians.* Knoxville: University of Tennessee Press, 1976.

Hunt, Charles B. *Natural Regions of the United States and Canada.* San Francisco: W. H. Freeman & Co., 1974.

Johnson, Guion Griffis. *A Social History of the Sea Islands with Special Reference to St. Helena Island, South Carolina.* New York: Negro Universities Press, 1969.

Johnson, Guy Benton. *Folk Culture of St. Helena Island.* Hatboro, Pa.: Folklore Association, 1968.

Jones, Katharine M. *Port Royal Under Six Flags.* New York: Bobbs-Merrill, 1960.

Jordan, Terry G. "The Imprint of the Upper and Lower South on Mid-Nineteenth Century Texas." Association of American Geographers, *Annals* 57 (1967): 667–690.

Josephy, Alvin M., Jr., ed. *The American Heritage Book of Indians.* New York: American Heritage Pub. Co., 1961.

Keller, Edward A. *Environmental Geology.* Columbus, Ohio: Charles E. Merrill Pub. Co., 1982.

Kirby, Jack Temple. *Media Made Dixie.* Baton Rouge: Louisiana State University Press, 1978.

Kirk, Paul W., Jr., ed. *The Great Dismal Swamp.* Charlottesville: University Press of Virginia, 1979.

Kuchler, A. W. *Potential Natural Vegetation of the Conterminous United States.* New York: American Geographical Society, Special Publication 36, 1964.

Kuralt, Charles. *Southerners: Portrait of a People.* Birmingham, Ala.: Oxmoor House, Inc., 1986.

Larson, Lewis H. *Aboriginal Subsistence Technology on the Southeastern Coastal Plain During the Late Prehistoric Period.* Gainesville: University Presses of Florida, 1980.

Leuchtenburg, William E. *New Deal and Global War, 1933–1945.* Vol. 11 of TIME-LIFE *History of the United States.* New York: Time Inc., n.d.

Lippson, Alice Jane and Robert L. *Life in the Chesapeake Bay.* Baltimore: Johns Hopkins University Press, 1984.

MDC, Inc. *Shadows in the Sunbelt: Developing the Rural South in an Era of Economic Change.* Chapel Hill: MDC, Inc., 1986.

Martin, Sandra O. "Last Chance for Chesapeake Bay." *Planning* (June 1986): 12–19.

Mason, Herbert Molloy, Jr. *Missions of Texas.* Birmingham, Ala.: Oxmoor House, Inc., 1974.

Morton, Richard L. *Colonial Virginia.* Chapel Hill: University of North Carolina Press, 1960.

Norton, Mary Beth; Katzman, David M.; Escott, Paul D.; Chudacoff, Howard P.; Paterson, Thomas G.; and Tuttle, William M., Jr. *A People and A Nation:*

A History of the United States. 2d ed. Boston: Houghton Mifflin Co., 1987.

Oakes, James. *The Ruling Race: A History of American Slaveholders.* New York: Alfred A. Knopf, Inc., 1982.

Odum, Howard. *Southern Regions.* Chapel Hill: University of North Carolina Press, 1936.

Parkins, A. E. *The South: Its Economic-Geographic Development.* New York: John Wiley & Sons, Inc., 1938.

Phelan, Richard. *Texas Wild: The Land, Plants, and Animals of the Lone Star State.* New York: Excalibur Books/E. P. Dutton & Co., Inc., 1976.

Peirce, Neal R., and Hagstrom, Jerry. *The Book of America: Inside Fifty States Today.* New York: W. W. Norton & Co., 1983.

Pilkey, Orrin H., Jr.; Neal, William J.; Pilkey, Orrin H., Sr.; and Riggs, Stanley R. *From Currituck to Calabash: Living with North Carolina's Barrier Islands.* 2d ed. Research Triangle Park: North Carolina Science and Technology Research Center, 1980.

Powledge, Fred. *Journeys Through the South.* New York: Vanguard Press, Inc., 1979.

Reed, John Shelton. *The Enduring South: Subcultural Persistence in Mass Society.* Lexington, Mass.: Lexington Books/Heath, 1972.

Rhyne, Nancy. *The Grand Strand.* Charlotte, N.C.: Fast & McMillan Pub. Inc., 1985.

Richardson, Curtis J.; Matthews, Mary L.; and Anderson, Stephen A., eds. *Pocosin Wetlands: An Integrated Analysis of Coastal Plain Freshwater Bogs in North Carolina.* Stroudsburg, Pa.: Hutchinson Ross Pub. Co., 1981.

Rohrbough, Malcolm J. *The Trans-Appalachian Frontier: People, Societies, and Institutions, 1775–1850.* New York: Oxford University Press, 1978.

Roland, Charles P. *The Improbable Era: The South Since World War II.* Lexington: University Press of Kentucky, 1975.

Roller, David C., and Twyman, Robert W., eds. *The Encyclopedia of Southern History.* Baton Rouge: Louisiana State University Press, 1979.

Rooney, John F., Jr.; Zelinsky, Wilbur; and Louder, Dean R., eds. *This Remarkable Continent.* College Station: Texas A & M University Press, 1982.

Ruffner, James A., and Blair, Frank E., eds. *The Weather Almanac.* Detroit: Gale Research Co., 1984.

Sale, Kirkpatrick. *Power Shift: The Rise of the Southern Rim and Its Challenge to the Eastern Establishment.* New York: Random House, 1975.

Seyfert, C. K., and Sirkin, L. A. *Earth History and Plate Tectonics: An Introduction to Historical Geology.* New York: Harper & Row Pub. Inc., 1979.

Sheldon, Robert A. *Roadside Geology of Texas.* Missoula, Mont.: Mountain Press Pub. Co., 1982.

Shelford, Victor E. *The Ecology of North America.* Urbana: University of Illinois Press, 1963.

Silverburg, Robert. *Mound Builders of Ancient America: The Archaeology of a Myth.* Greenwich, Conn.: New York Graphic Society Ltd., 1968.

Smith, Robert Leo. *Ecology and Field Biology.* New York: Harper & Row Pub. Inc., 1974.

Southern Growth Policies Board. *Halfway Home and a Long Way To Go.* Research Triangle Park, N.C.: Report of the 1986 Commission on the Future of the South, 1986.

Steila, Donald. "Potential Evapotranspiration and Life Zones in the United States." Paper presented at the annual meeting of the Association of American Geographers, San Antonio, April 1982.

Strahler, Arthur N. *Introduction to Physical Geography.* New York: John Wiley & Sons, Inc., 1973.

Stuart, George E. and Gene S. *Discovering Man's Past in the Americas.* Washington, D.C.: National Geographic Society, 1969.

Thornbury, William D. *Regional Geomorphology of the United States.* New York: John Wiley & Sons, Inc., 1965.

Tindall, George B. *The Emergence of the New South 1913–1945.* Baton Rouge: Louisiana State University Press, 1967.

Twelve Southerners. *I'll Take My Stand: The South and the Agrarian Tradition.* New York: Harper Brothers, 1930.

U.S. Department of Commerce. Bureau of the Census. *Statistical Atlas of the United States.* Washington, D.C.: 1914.

U.S. Department of Commerce. Hebert, Paul J., and Taylor, Glenn. *The Deadliest, Costliest, and Most Intense United States Hurricanes of the Century (and Other Frequently Requested Hurricane Facts).* Miami: National Hurricane Center, NOAA Technical Memorandum NW NHC 18, June 1985.

U.S. Department of the Interior, Geological Survey. *The National Atlas of the United States of America.* Washington, D.C.: Government Printing Office, 1970.

Vandiver, Frank E., ed. *The Idea of the South.* Chicago: University of Chicago Press, 1964.

Visher, Stephen Sargent. *Climatic Atlas of the United States.* Cambridge, Mass.: Harvard University Press, 1954.

Walton, Susan. "Chesapeake Bay: Threats to Ecological Stability." *Bioscience* 32, no. 11 (December 1982): 843–844.

Weather of U.S. Cities. 2 vols. Detroit: Gale Research Co., 1981.

White, L. Langdon; Foscue, Edwin J.; and McKnight, Tom L. *Regional Geography of Anglo-America.* Englewood Cliffs, N.J.: Prentice Hall, Inc., 1974.

Williamson, Joel. *The Crucible of Race.* New York: Oxford University Press, 1984.

Wood, Peter H. *Black Majority: Negroes in Colonial South Carolina from 1670 through the Stono Rebellion.* New York: W. W. Norton & Co., 1974.

Woodward, C. Vann. *Origins of the New South: 1877–1913.* Baton Rouge: Louisiana State University Press, 1951.

———. *The Burden of Southern History.* New York: Vintage, 1961.

Wright, J. Leitch, Jr. *Only Land They Knew.* New York: Free Press, 1981.

Zelinsky, Wilbur. *The Cultural Geography of the United States.* Englewood Cliffs, N.J.: Prentice Hall, Inc., 1973.

FIGURE SOURCES

CHAPTER 1

FIGURE 1.1B: Wilbur Zelinsky, THE CULTURAL GEOGRAPHY OF THE UNITED STATES, © 1973, pp. 118–119. Reprinted by permission of Prentice Hall, Englewood Cliffs, New Jersey.

CHAPTER 2

FIGURE 2.1: Modified from C. K. Seyfert and L. A. Sirkin, *Earth History and Plate Tectonics: An Introduction to Historical Geology* (New York: Harper & Row Pub. Inc., 1979), 183.

FIGURE 2.2: Modified from C. K. Seyfert and L. A. Sirkin, *Earth History and Plate Tectonics: An Introduction to Historical Geology* (New York: Harper & Row Pub. Inc., 1979), 248, 310, 311, 372.

FIGURE 2.3: Modified from "Continents Adrift," *Readings from Scientific American* (San Francisco: W. H. Freeman & Co., 1970), 130.

FIGURE 2.4: Modified from Charles B. Hunt, *Natural Regions of the United States and Canada* (San Francisco: W. H. Freeman & Co., 1974), 218.

FIGURE 2.5A: U.S. Department of the Interior, Geological Survey, *The National Atlas of the United States of America* (Washington, D.C.: Government Printing Office, 1970), 74–75.

FIGURE 2.5B: From *The Physiographic Provinces of North America* by Wallace W. Atwood, Copyright, 1940, by Ginn and Company. Used by permission of Silver, Burdett & Ginn Inc.

FIGURE 2.9: Modified from Stephen Sargent Visher, *Climatic Atlas of the United States* (Cambridge, Mass.: Harvard University Press, 1954), 23.

FIGURE 2.10: Modified from James J. Geraghty, David W. Miller, Frits Van der Leeden, and Fred L. Troise, *Water Atlas of the United States* (Port Washington, N.Y.: Water Information Center, Inc., 1973), plate 2.

FIGURE 2.11: Modified from James J. Geraghty, David W. Miller, Frits Van der Leeden, and Fred L. Troise, *Water Atlas of the United States* (Port Washington, N.Y.: Water Information Center, Inc., 1973), plate 11.

FIGURE 2.12: Modified from James J. Geraghty, David W. Miller, Frits Van der Leeden, and Fred L. Troise, *Water Atlas of the United States* (Port Washington, N.Y.: Water Information Center, Inc., 1973), plate 4.

FIGURE 2.13: Modified from James J. Geraghty, David W. Miller, Frits Van der Leeden, and Fred L. Troise, *Water Atlas of the United States* (Port Washington, N.Y.: Water Information Center, Inc., 1973), plate 2.

FIGURE 2.14: Compiled from *Weather of U.S. Cities*, vols. 1–2 (Detroit: Gale Research Co., 1981), 4, 5, 116, 117, 136, 137, 204, 205, 224, 225, 268, 269, 272, 273, 280, 281, 308, 309, 328, 329, 368, 369, 448, 449, 464, 465, 480, 481, 712, 713, 732, 733,

740, 741, 928, 929, 956, 957, 968, 969, 984, 985, 1008, 1009, 1016, 1017, 1020, 1021, 1036, 1037, 1076, 1077, 1080, 1081, 1096, 1097, 1120, 1121, 1132, 1133; James A. Ruffner and Frank E. Blair, eds., *The Weather Almanac* (Detroit: Gale Research Co., 1984), 380, 381, 412, 413, 420, 421, 476, 477, 620, 621, 764, 765.

FIGURE 2.15: Compiled from *Weather of U.S. Cities*, vols. 1–2 (Detroit: Gale Research Co., 1981), 4, 5, 116, 117, 136, 137, 204, 205, 224, 225, 268, 269, 272, 273, 280, 281, 308, 309, 328, 329, 368, 369, 448, 449, 464, 465, 480, 481, 712, 713, 732, 733, 740, 741, 928, 929, 956, 957, 968, 969, 984, 985, 1008, 1009, 1016, 1017, 1020, 1021, 1036, 1037, 1076, 1077, 1080, 1081, 1096, 1097, 1120, 1121, 1132, 1133; James A. Ruffner and Frank E. Blair, eds., *The Weather Almanac*, (Detroit: Gale Research Co., 1984), 380, 381, 412, 413, 420, 421, 476, 477, 620, 621, 764, 765.

FIGURE 2.16: Compiled from *Weather of U.S. Cities*, vols. 1–2, (Detroit: Gale Research Co., 1981), 380, 381, 412, 413, 420, 421, 476, 477, 620, 621, 764, 765.

FIGURE 2.17: Reprinted with permission from Donald Steila, "Potential Evapotranspiration and Life Zones in the United States," paper presented at the annual meeting of the Association of American Geographers, San Antonio, April 1982.

TABLE 2.2: Compiled from *Weather of U.S. Cities*, vols. 1–2 (Detroit: Gale Research Co., 1981), 4, 5, 116, 117, 136, 137, 204, 205, 224, 225, 268, 269, 272, 273, 280, 281, 308, 309, 328, 329, 368, 369, 448, 449, 464, 465, 480, 481, 712, 713, 732, 733, 740, 741, 928, 929, 956, 957, 968, 969, 984, 985, 1008, 1009, 1016, 1017, 1020, 1021, 1036, 1037, 1076, 1077, 1080, 1081, 1096, 1097, 1120, 1121, 1132, 1133.

FIGURE 2.19: Compiled from U.S. Department of the Interior, Geological Survey, "Existing Major Waterways and Ports of the United States" (Reston, Va.: 1981), map no. 1; "Tenn-Tom: Lose a Billion or Keep Digging," *U.S. News & World Report*, 15 June 1981, 12.

FIGURE 2.20: Modified from U.S. Department of the Interior, Geological Survey, *The National Atlas of the United States of America* (Washington, D.C.: Government Printing Office, 1970), 85–88; Robert M. Basile, *A Geography of Soils* (Dubuque, Iowa: William C. Brown Co. Pub., 1971), 74–75; Henry D. Foth and John W. Schafer, *Soil Geography and Land Use* (New York: John Wiley & Sons, Inc., 1980), 38, 39, 40, 41.

FIGURE 2.21: Modified from U.S. Department of the Interior, Geological Survey, *The National Atlas of the United States of America* (Washington, D.C.: Government Printing Office, 1970), 90–91; Robert G. Bailey, *Description of the Ecoregions of the United States* (Ogden, Utah: Forest Service, U.S. Department of Agriculture, May 1978), accompanying map.

CHAPTER 3

FIGURE 3.1: Modified from Merwyn S. Garbarino, *Native American Heritage* (Boston: Little, Brown & Co., 1976), 7; Alvin M. Josephy, Jr., ed., *The Ameri-*

can Heritage Book of Indians (New York: American Heritage Pub. Co., 1961), 11.

FIGURE 3.2: Modified from Robert Silverburg, *Mound Builders of Ancient America: The Archaeology of a Myth* (Greenwich, Conn.: New York Graphic Society Ltd., 1968), 243, 265, 298; George E. and Gene S. Stuart, *Discovering Man's Past in the Americas* (Washington, D.C.: National Geographic Society, 1969), 134.

FIGURE 3.3: Modified from Charles Hudson, *The Southeastern Indians* (Knoxville: University of Tennessee Press, 1976), 92.

FIGURE 3.4: U.S. Department of the Interior, Geological Survey, *The National Atlas of the United States of America* (Washington, D.C.: Government Printing Office, 1970), 130–131.

FIGURE 3.5: Modified from Harold E. Driver, *Indians of North America*, (Chicago: University of Chicago Press, 1969), map 3; Lewis H. Larson, *Aboriginal Subsistence Technology on the Southeastern Coastal Plain During the Late Prehistoric Period* (Gainesville: University Presses of Florida, 1980), 5.

SIDEBAR *Routes of Early Spanish Explorers in the South:* Modified from Ray Allen Billington, *Westward Expansion: A History of the American Frontier*, 3d ed. (New York: Macmillan Co., 1967), 19, 424.

FIGURE 3.6: Modified from Richard L. Morton, *Colonial Virginia* (Chapel Hill: University of North Carolina Press, 1960), 64.

FIGURE 3.7A: Compiled from H. R. Friis, "A Series of Population Maps of the Colonies and the U.S., 1625–1790," *The Geographical Review* 30 (1940): 463–470.

FIGURE 3.7B: Compiled from H. R. Friis, "A Series of Population Maps of the Colonies and the U.S., 1625–1790," *The Geographical Review* 30 (1940): 463–470.

FIGURE 3.8: Modified from U.S. Department of the Interior, Geological Survey, *The National Atlas of the United States of America* (Washington, D.C.: Government Printing Office, 1970), 137.

FIGURE 3.9: Reprinted with permission of Macmillan Publishing Company from page 170 of WESTWARD EXPANSION: A HISTORY OF THE AMERICAN FRONTIER, 3d ed., by Ray Allen Billington. Copyright © 1967 by Macmillan Publishing Company.

FIGURE 3.10: U.S. Department of Commerce, Bureau of the Census, *Statistical Atlas of the United States* (Washington, D.C.: 1914), plate 3.

FIGURE 3.11: U.S. Department of Commerce, Bureau of the Census, *Statistical Atlas of the United States* (Washington, D.C.: 1914), plate 7.

FIGURE 3.12: U.S. Department of Commerce, Bureau of the Census, *Statistical Atlas of the United States* (Washington, D.C.: 1914), plate 10.

FIGURE 3.13: Modified from Charles Hudson, *The Southeastern Indians* (Knoxville: University of Tennessee Press, 1976), 458.

SIDEBAR *Spanish Missions:* Modified from Ray Allen Billington, *Westward Expansion: A History of the American Frontier*, 3d ed. (New York: Macmillan Co., 1967), 27; Herbert Molloy Mason, Jr., *Missions of Texas* (Birmingham, Ala.: Oxmoor House, Inc., 1974), 32–33.

FIGURE 3.14: Reproduced by permission from the *Annals*, Association of American Geographers. Terry G. Jordan, "The Imprint of the Upper and Lower South on Mid-Nineteenth Century Texas," *Annals* 57 (1967): 667–690.

FIGURE 3.15: Reproduced by permission from the *Annals*, Association of American Geographers. Terry G. Jordan, "The Imprint of the Upper and Lower South on Mid-Nineteenth Century Texas," *Annals* 57 (1967): 667–690.

FIGURE 3.16: Modified from Sam Bowers Hilliard, *Atlas of Antebellum Southern Agriculture* (Baton Rouge: Louisiana State University Press, 1984), 71, 76, 77.

CHAPTER 4

FIGURE 4.3: Modified from Robert A. Muller, *Physical Geography Today: A Portrait of a Planet* (Del Mar, Calif.: CRM Books, division of Ziff-Davis Pub. Co., 1974), 212.

FIGURE 4.4: Modified from Charles B. Hunt, *Natural Regions of the United States and Canada* (San Francisco: W. H. Freeman & Co., 1974), 247.

FIGURE 4.5: Modified from Charles B. Hunt, *Natural Regions of the United States and Canada* (San Francisco: W. H. Freeman & Co., 1974), 213.

FIGURE 4.6: Modified from Charles B. Hunt, *Natural Regions of the United States and Canada* (San Francisco: W. H. Freeman & Co., 1974), 213.

BARRIER ISLAND ENVIRONMENT: Modified from Paul J. Godfrey, "Barrier Beaches of the East Coast," *Oceanus* 19 (1976): 29; art by Caroline Wellesley.

FIGURE 4.7: Modified from Orrin H. Pilkey, Jr., William J. Neal, Orrin H. Pilkey, Sr., and Stanley R. Riggs, *From Currituck to Calabash: Living with North Carolina's Barrier Islands*, 2d ed. (Research Triangle Park: North Carolina Science and Technology Research Center, 1980), 20.

FIGURE 4.8: Modified from Curtis J. Richardson et al., eds., *Pocosin Wetlands: An Integrated Analysis of Coastal Plain Freshwater Bogs in North Carolina* (Stroudsburg, Pa.: Hutchinson Ross Pub. Co., 1981), 246.

FIGURE 4.9: Reprinted from William Morris Davis, *The Coral Reef Problem*, American Geographical Society Special Publication no. 9 (1928; reprint, New York: AMS Press, Inc., 1977). © 1977 by AMS Press, Inc. Used with permission.

TABLE 4.1: Reprinted with permission from John H. Ryther, "Photosynthesis and Fish Production in the Sea," *Science* 166 (1969): 72–76. Copyright 1969 by the American Association for the Advancement of Science.

FIGURE 4.11: Modified from Erwin Raisz, "Landforms of the United States," to accompany Wallace W. Atwood, *The Physiographic Provinces of North America* (Waltham, Mass.: Blaisdell Pub. Co., division of Ginn & Co., 1940).

CHAPTER 5

FIGURE 5.1: Modified from Erwin Raisz, "Landforms of the United States," to accompany Wallace W. Atwood, *The Physiographic Provinces of North America* (Waltham, Mass.: Blaisdell Pub. Co., division of Ginn & Co., 1940).

FIGURE 5.2: Modified from Alice Jane and Robert L. Lippson, *Life in the Chesapeake Bay* (Baltimore: Johns Hopkins University Press, 1984), 6.

FIGURE 5.4: Modified from Orrin H. Pilkey, Jr., William J. Neal, Orrin H. Pilkey, Sr., and Stanley R. Riggs, *From Currituck to Calabash: Living with North Carolina's Barrier Islands*, 2d ed. (Research Triangle Park: North Carolina Science and Technology Research Center, 1980), endsheet.

FIGURE 5.5: Modified from Orrin H. Pilkey, Jr., William J. Neal, Orrin H. Pilkey, Sr., and Stanley R. Riggs, *From Currituck to Calabash: Living with North Carolina's Barrier Islands*, 2d ed. (Research Triangle Park: North Carolina Science and Technology Research Center, 1980), 12.

SIDEBAR *Hurricane Gloria:* Modified from the *Charlotte Observer*, 27 September 1985, 10A.

TABLE 5.1: Modified from Peter H. Wood, *Black Majority: Negroes in Colonial South Carolina from 1670 through the Stono Rebellion* (New York: W. W. Norton & Co., 1974), 184.

FIGURE 5.7: Modified from Howard Kunreuther, R. Ginsberg, L. Miller, P. Sagi, P. Slovic, B. Borkan, and N. Katz, *Disaster Insurance Protection: Public Policy Lessons* (New York: Wiley-Interscience, 1978), 22.

FIGURE 5.8: Modified from U.S. Department of the Interior, Geological Survey, *The National Atlas of the United States of America* (Washington, D.C.: Government Printing Office, 1970), 159.

FIGURE 5.9: Reprinted with permission from James W. Clay, Douglas M. Orr, Jr., and Alfred W. Stuart, *North Carolina Atlas: Portrait of a Changing Southern State* (Chapel Hill: University of North Carolina Press, 1975), 113.

FIGURE 5.10: Modified from Curtis J. Richardson et al., eds., *Pocosin Wetlands: An Integrated Analysis of Coastal Plain Freshwater Bogs in North Carolina* (Stroudsburg, Pa.: Hutchinson Ross Pub. Co., 1981), 7.

FIGURE 5.11: Modified from Paul W. Kirk, Jr., ed., *The Great Dismal Swamp* (Charlottesville: University Press of Virginia, 1979), 2, 3.

FIGURE 5.12: Modified from Paul W. Kirk, Jr., ed., *The Great Dismal Swamp* (Charlottesville: University Press of Virginia, 1979), 34, 35, 37.

FIGURE 5.13: Modified from Paul W. Kirk, Jr., ed., *The Great Dismal Swamp* (Charlottesville: University Press of Virginia, 1979), 83, 141, 157.

SIDEBAR *Artesian Aquifers:* Modified from Thomas Dunne and Luna B. Leopold, *Water in Environmental Planning* (San Francisco: W. H. Freeman & Co., 1978), 197.

FIGURE 5.14: Modified from John Fraser Hart, "The Demise of King Cotton," *Annals of the Association of American Geographers* (September 1977): 312, 313.

FIGURE 5.15: Compiled from U.S. Department of Commerce, Bureau of the Census, 1978 Census of Agriculture (Washington, D.C.: Government Printing Office, 1982), 147.

FIGURE 5.16: Modified from John Fraser Hart, "Cropland Concentrations in the South," *Annals of the Association of American Geographers* (December 1978): 507.

FIGURE 5.17: Compiled from Thomas R. Bellamy and Cecil C. Hutchins, Jr., *Southern Pulpwood Production, 1979*, U.S. Department of Agriculture, Forest Service Resource Bulletin SE-57, April 1981.

CHAPTER 6

FIGURE 6.1: Modified from Erwin Raisz, "Landforms of the United States," to accompany Wallace W. Atwood, *The Physiographic Provinces of North America* (Waltham, Mass.: Blaisdell Pub. Co., division of Ginn & Co., 1940).

FIGURE 6.2: Modified from Edward A. Fernald, ed., *Atlas of Florida* (Tallahassee: Florida State University Foundation, Inc., 1981), 16.

FIGURE 6.3: Modified from Edward A. Fernald, ed., *Atlas of Florida* (Tallahassee: Florida State University Foundation, Inc., 1981), 7.

FIGURE 6.4: Modified from Edward A. Fernald, ed., *Atlas of Florida* (Tallahassee: Florida State University Foundation, Inc., 1981), 53.

FIGURE 6.5: Modified from W. Kenneth Hamblin, *The Earth's Dynamic Systems: A Textbook in Physical Geology* (Minneapolis: Burgess Pub. Co., 1978), 204.

FIGURE 6.6: Modified from Luther J. Carter, *The Florida Experience: Land and Water Policy in a Growth State* (Baltimore: Johns Hopkins University Press, 1974), 230.

FIGURE 6.7A: Modified from Luther J. Carter, *The Florida Experience: Land and Water Policy in a Growth State* (Baltimore: Johns Hopkins University Press, 1974), 72.

FIGURE 6.7B: Modified from Luther J. Carter, *The Florida Experience: Land and Water Policy in a Growth State* (Baltimore: Johns Hopkins University Press, 1974), 93.

FIGURE 6.8: Modified from Luther J. Carter, *The Florida Experience: Land and Water Policy in a Growth State* (Baltimore: Johns Hopkins University Press, 1974), 234.

FIGURE 6.9: Modified from Edward A. Fernald, ed., *Atlas of Florida* (Tallahassee: Florida State University Foundation, Inc., 1981), 151.

FIGURE 6.10: Modified from Edward A. Fernald, ed., *Atlas of Florida* (Tallahassee: Florida State University Foundation, Inc., 1981), 82.

FIGURE 6.11: Modified from Kathleen Deagan, *Spanish St. Augustine: The Archaeology of a Colonial Creole Community* (New York: Academic Press, 1983), 12.

FIGURE 6.12: Modified from Edward A. Fernald, ed., *Atlas of Florida* (Tallahassee: Florida State University Foundation, Inc., 1981), 100.

FIGURE 6.13: Modified from Edward A. Fernald, ed., *Atlas of Florida* (Tallahassee: Florida State University Foundation, Inc., 1981), 135.

FIGURE 6.14: Compiled from U.S. Department of Commerce, Bureau of the Census, 1982 Census of Agriculture, County Data (Washington, D.C.: Government Printing Office, 1984), 344.

CHAPTER 7

FIGURE 7.1: Modified from Erwin Raisz, "Landforms of the United States," to accompany Wallace W. Atwood, *The Physiographic Provinces of North America* (Waltham, Mass.: Blaisdell Pub. Co., division of Ginn & Co., 1940).

FIGURE 7.3A: Modified from Nevin M. Fenneman, *Physiography of Eastern United States* (New York: McGraw-Hill Book Co., 1938), 68–69.

FIGURE 7.3B: Modified from Nevin M. Fenneman, *Physiography of Eastern United States* (New York: McGraw-Hill Book Co., 1938), 68–69.

FIGURE 7.4: Modified from Sam Bowers Hilliard, *Atlas of Antebellum Southern Agriculture* (Baton Rouge: Louisiana State University Press, 1984), 67, 70.

FIGURE 7.5: Modified from Sam Bowers Hilliard, *Atlas of Antebellum Southern Agriculture* (Baton Rouge: Louisiana State University Press, 1984), 26.

FIGURE 7.6: Modified from James W. Clay, Douglas M. Orr, Jr., and Alfred W. Stuart, *North Carolina Atlas: Portrait of a Changing Southern State* (Chapel Hill: University of North Carolina Press, 1975), 106.

FIGURE 7.7: Compiled from National Hurricane Center data.

TABLE 7.1: U.S. Department of Commerce, Paul J. Hebert and Glenn Taylor, *The Deadliest, Costliest, and Most Intense United States Hurricanes of the Century (and Other Frequently Requested Hurricane Facts)* (Miami: National Hurricane Center, NOAA Technical Memorandum NW NHC 18, June 1985).

TABLE 7.2: U.S. Department of Commerce, Paul J. Hebert and Glenn Taylor, *The Deadliest, Costliest, and Most Intense United States Hurricanes of the Century (and Other Frequently Requested Hurricane Facts)* (Miami: National Hurricane Center, NOAA Technical Memorandum NW NHC 18, June 1985).

SIDEBAR *Spread of the Boll Weevil:* Modified from John Fraser Hart, "The Demise of King Cotton," *Annals of the Association of American Geographers* (September 1977): 319.

FIGURE 7.9: Modified from U.S. Department of Commerce, Bureau of the Census, *Statistical Atlas of the United States* (Washington, D.C.: 1914), plate 317.

FIGURE 7.10: Modified from U.S. Department of Commerce, Bureau of the Census, *Statistical Atlas of the United States* (Washington, D.C.: 1914), plate 330.

CHAPTER 8

FIGURE 8.1: Modified from Erwin Raisz, "Landforms of the United States," to accompany Wallace W. Atwood, *The Physiographic Provinces of North America* (Waltham, Mass: Blaisdell Pub. Co., division of Ginn & Co., 1940).

FIGURE 8.2: Modified from W. Kenneth Hamblin, *The Earth's Dynamic Systems: A Textbook in Physical Geology* (Minneapolis: Burgess Pub. Co., 1978), 233; Thomas H. Clark and Colin W. Stearn, *The Geological Evolution of North America: A Regional Approach to Historical Geology* (New York: Ronald Press Co., 1960), 277.

FIGURE 8.3: Modified from William D. Thornbury, *Regional Geomorphology of the United States* (New York: John Wiley & Sons, Inc., 1965), 58.

FIGURE 8.5: Modified from W. Kenneth Hamblin, *The Earth's Dynamic Systems: A Textbook in Physical Geology* (Minneapolis: Burgess Pub. Co., 1978), 169.

FIGURE 8.6: Modified from Nevin M. Fenneman, *Physiography of Eastern United States* (New York: McGraw-Hill Book Co., 1938), 92.

FIGURE 8.7: Modified from Robert A. Muller, *Physical Geography Today: A Portrait of a Planet* (Del Mar, Calif.: CRM Books, division of Ziff-Davis Pub. Co., 1974), 303.

FIGURE 8.8: Modified from Nevin M. Fenneman, *Physiography of Eastern United States* (New York: McGraw-Hill Book Co., 1938), 92; Jack and Anne Rudloe, "Trouble in Bayou Country," *National Geographic* (September 1979): 385.

FIGURE 8.9: Modified from W. Kenneth Hamblin, *The Earth's Dynamic Systems: A Textbook in Physical Geology* (Minneapolis: Burgess Pub. Co., 1978), 175.

FIGURE 8.10: Modified from "Setting the Mississippi Free," *Newsweek*, 20 September 1982, 100.

FIGURE 8.11: Modified from Mary Beth Norton et al., *A People and a Nation: A History of the United States*, 2d ed. (Boston: Houghton Mifflin Co., 1987), 215.

FIGURE 8.12: Modified from U.S. Department of Commerce, Bureau of the Census, 1978 Census of Agriculture (Washington, D.C.: Government Printing Office, 1982).

CHAPTER 9

FIGURE 9.1: Modified from Erwin Raisz, "Landforms of the United States," to accompany Wallace W. Atwood, *The Physiographic Provinces of North America* (Waltham, Mass.: Blaisdell Pub. Co., division of Ginn & Co., 1940).

FIGURE 9.2A: Modified from Nevin M. Fenneman, *Physiography of Eastern United States* (New York: McGraw-Hill Book Co., 1938), 102–103.

FIGURE 9.2B: Modified from Nevin M. Fenneman, *Physiography of Eastern United States* (New York: McGraw-Hill Book Co., 1938), 102–103.

FIGURE 9.3: Modified from Charles B. Hunt, *Natural Regions of the United States and Canada* (San Francisco: W. H. Freeman & Co., 1974), 231.

FIGURE 9.4: Modified from A. E. Parkins, *The South: Its Economic-Geographic Development* (New York: John Wiley & Sons, Inc., 1938), 110, 112.

FIGURE 9.6: Modified from Robert A. Sheldon, *Roadside Geology of Texas* (Missoula, Mont.: Mountain Press Pub. Co., 1982), 161.

FIGURE 9.7: Modified from William D. Thornbury, *Regional Geomorphology of the United States* (New York: John Wiley & Sons, Inc., 1965), 66.

FIGURE 9.8: Modified from Edward A. Keller, *Environmental Geology* (Columbus, Ohio: Charles E. Merrill Pub. Co., 1982), 386.

FIGURE 9.10: Modified from L. Langdon White, Edwin J. Foscue, and Tom L. McKnight, *Regional Geography of Anglo-America* (Englewood Cliffs, N.J.: Prentice Hall, Inc., 1974), 354.

CHAPTER 10

FIGURE 10.1: Modified from Erwin Raisz, "Landforms of the United States," to accompany Wallace W. Atwood, *The Physiographic Provinces of North America* (Waltham, Mass.: Blaisdell Pub. Co., division of Ginn & Co., 1940).

CHAPTER 11

FIGURE 11.1: Modified from Erwin Raisz, "Landforms of the United States," to accompany Wallace W. Atwood, *The Physiographic Provinces of North America* (Waltham, Mass.: Blaisdell Pub. Co., division of Ginn & Co., 1940).

FIGURE 11.2 Modified from Charles B. Hunt, *Natural Regions of the United States and Canada* (San Francisco: W. H. Freeman & Co., 1974), 259.

FIGURE 11.5: Modified from James W. Clay, Douglas M. Orr, Jr., and Alfred W. Stuart, *North Carolina Atlas: Portrait of a Changing Southern State* (Chapel Hill: University of North Carolina Press, 1975), 10.

FIGURE 11.6: Modified from Cordelia Camp, *The Influence of Geography upon Early North Carolina* (Raleigh: Carolina Charter Tercentenary Commission, 1963), 1.

FIGURE 11.7: Modified from U.S. Department of Commerce, Bureau of the Census, *Statistical Atlas of the United States* (Washington, D.C.: 1914), plate 469.

FIGURE 11.8: Compiled from 1983 data from the U.S. Department of Commerce, Bureau of the Census.

SIDEBAR *Areas of Known Gold Deposits in the Piedmont:* Compiled from U.S. Department of the Interior, Geological Survey, *Gold Deposits of the Southern Piedmont* (Washington, D.C.: Government Printing Office, 1948).

CHAPTER 12

FIGURE 12.1: Modified from Erwin Raisz, "Landforms of the United States," to accompany Wallace W. Atwood, *The Physiographic Provinces of North America* (Waltham, Mass.: Blaisdell Pub. Co., division of Ginn & Co., 1940).

FIGURE 12.3: Reprinted with permission of Charles Scribner's Sons, an imprint of Macmillan Publishing Company, from ATLAS OF AMERICAN HISTORY, edited by James Truslow Adams and R. V. Coleman. Copyright 1943 by Charles Scribner's Sons, renewed 1977, plate 52.

FIGURE 12.4: Modified from John F. Rooney, Jr., Wilbur Zelinsky, and Dean R. Louder, eds., *This Remarkable Continent* (College Station: Texas A & M University Press, 1982), 239.

CHAPTER 13

FIGURE 13.1: Modified from Erwin Raisz, "Landforms of the United States," to accompany Wallace W. Atwood, *The Physiographic Provinces of North America* (Waltham, Mass.: Blaisdell Pub. Co., division of Ginn & Co., 1940).

FIGURE 13.5: Modified from Robert D. Mitchell, "The Presbyterian Church as an Indicator of Westward Expansion in Eighteenth Century America," *The Professional Geographer* (September 1966): 295–298.

FIGURE 13.6: Modified from U.S. Department of Commerce, Bureau of the Census, *Statistical Atlas of the United States* (Washington, D.C.: 1914), plate 428.

SIDEBAR *Stonewall Jackson's Valley Campaign:* Compiled from Colonel Vincent J. Esposito, *The West Point Atlas of American Wars, 1689–1900,* vol. 1 (New York: Frederick A. Praeger Pub., 1959), 49–53.

SIDEBAR *The Tennessee Valley Authority Region:* Compiled from Stephen S. Birdsall and John W. Florin, *Regional Landscapes of the United States and Canada* (New York: John Wiley & Sons, Inc., 1981), 187; "Facts About TVA Dams and Steam Plants," TVA, May 1984.

SIDEBAR *Historic Spas of Virginia and West Virginia:* Compiled from Stan B. Cohen, *Historic Springs of the Virginias: A Pictorial History* (Charleston, W. Va.: Pictorial Histories Pub. Co., 1981).

CHAPTER 14

FIGURE 14.1: Modified from Erwin Raisz, "Landforms of the United States," to accompany Wallace W. Atwood, *The Physiographic Provinces of North America* (Waltham, Mass.: Blaisdell Pub. Co., division of Ginn & Co., 1940).

FIGURE 14.2: Modified from Erwin Raisz, "Landforms of the United States," to accompany Wallace W. Atwood, *The Physiographic Provinces of North America* (Waltham, Mass.: Blaisdell Pub. Co., division of Ginn & Co., 1940).

SIDEBAR *Teays River System:* Modified from William D. Thornbury, *Regional Geomorphology of the United States* (New York: John Wiley & Sons, Inc., 1965), 207.

FIGURE 14.3: Modified from A. K. Lobeck, *Geologic Map of the United States* (New York: Columbia University, Geographical Press, 1941).

FIGURE 14.4: Modified from A. K. Lobeck, *Physiographic Diagram of Kentucky* (Maplewood, N. J.: C. S. Hammond & Co., 1932).

FIGURE 14.5: Modified from Nevin M. Fenneman, *Physiography of Eastern United States* (New York: McGraw-Hill Book Co., 1938), 422.

FIGURE 14.6: Modified from Stephen S. Birdsall and John W. Florin, *Regional Landscapes of the United States and Canada* (New York: John Wiley & Sons, Inc., 1981), 173.

FIGURE 14.7: Modified from U.S. Department of the Interior, Geological Survey, "Coal Resources, Production and Distribution: 1974" (Washington, D.C.: Government Printing Office, 1980).

CHAPTER 15

FIGURE 15.1: Modified from Erwin Raisz, "Landforms of the United States," to accompany Wallace W. Atwood, *The Physiographic Provinces of North America* (Waltham, Mass.: Blaisdell Pub. Co., division of Ginn & Co., 1940).

FIGURE 15.2: Modified from Nevin M. Fenneman, *Physiography of Eastern United States* (New York: McGraw-Hill Book Co., 1938), 677.

FIGURE 15.3: Modified from U.S. Department of the Interior, National Park Service, "Hot Springs" (Washington, D.C.: Government Printing Office, 1980).

CHAPTER 16

FIGURE 16.1: Modified from Erwin Raisz, "Landforms of the United States," to accompany Wallace W. Atwood, *The Physiographic Provinces of North America* (Waltham, Mass.: Blaisdell Pub. Co., division of Ginn & Co., 1940).

FIGURE 16.2: Modified from William E. Leuchtenburg, *New Deal and Global War, 1933–1945,* vol. 11 of TIME-LIFE History of the United States (New York: Time Inc., n.d.), 34.

FIGURE 16.3: Modified from Stephen S. Birdsall and John W. Florin, *Regional Landscapes of the United States and Canada* (New York: John Wiley & Sons, Inc., 1981), 309.

FIGURE 16.4: Modified from Earl Cook, *Man, Energy, and Society* (San Francisco: W. H. Freeman & Co., 1976), 298.

FIGURE 16.5: Modified from Robert A. Sheldon, *Roadside Geology of Texas* (Missoula, Mont.: Mountain Press Pub. Co., 1982), 125.

FIGURE 16.6: Modified from Robert A. Sheldon, *Roadside Geology of Texas* (Missoula, Mont.: Mountain Press Pub. Co., 1982), 133.

CHAPTER 17

FIGURE 17.1: Modified from Edward A. Fernald and Donald J. Patton, eds., *Water Resources Atlas of Florida* (Tallahassee: Florida State University Foundation, Inc., 1984), 149.

FIGURE 17.2: Modified from Edward A. Fernald and Donald J. Patton, eds., *Water Resources Atlas of Florida* (Tallahassee: Florida State University Foundation, Inc., 1984), 63.

FIGURE 17.3: Modified from Edward A. Fernald and Donald J. Patton, eds., *Water Resources Atlas of Florida* (Tallahassee: Florida State University Foundation, Inc., 1984), 64.

FIGURE 17.4: Modified from Edward A. Fernald and Donald J. Patton, eds., *Water Resources Atlas of Florida* (Tallahassee: Florida State University Foundation, Inc., 1984), 123.

FIGURE 17.5: Modified from Canadian Embassy, *Fact Sheet on Acid Rain* (Washington, D.C.: Government Printing Office, January 1984).

PHOTOGRAPHY CREDITS

Photographers' names for *Southern Living®* magazine are in parentheses.

Page i, left: *Southern Living* (Beth Maynor)
  right: ©Bruce Roberts
Page iii, left: *Southern Living* (Bruce Roberts)
  right: *Southern Living*
Page iv, left: ©Bruce Roberts
  right: *Southern Living* (Mike Clemmer)
Page v: ©Bruce Roberts
Page vi: ©Bruce Roberts
Page viii: Everglades National Park Service
Page x: *Southern Living* (Mike Clemmer)
Page 2: *Southern Living*
Page 3, clockwise from top left: *Southern Living* (Bruce Roberts); ©Bruce Roberts; *Southern Living* (Mike Clemmer); Tourist Division of the Georgia Department of Industry and Trade; *Southern Living* (Frederica Georgia)
Page 16: ©Bruce Roberts
Page 22, left: James W. Clay
  right: Reproduced from the Marbut Memorial Slide Set, 1968, by permission of the Soil Science Society of America
Page 23, left: Reproduced from the Marbut Memorial Slide Set, 1968, by permission of the Soil Science Society of America
  right: ©Bruce Roberts
Page 24, left: Reproduced from the Marbut Memorial Slide Set, 1968, by permission of the Soil Science Society of America
  right: *Southern Living* (Mike Clemmer)
Page 25, left: Weymouth Woods–Sandhills Nature Preserve
  right: *Southern Living* (Mike Clemmer)
Page 26, left and right: Reproduced from the Marbut Memorial Slide Set, 1968, by permission of the Soil Science Society of America
Page 28, top and bottom: Everglades National Park Service
Page 29, top and bottom: ©Bruce Roberts
Page 30: Walter E. Martin
Page 31, top: *Southern Living* (Bruce Roberts)
  bottom: *Southern Living* (Frederica Georgia)
Page 32: *Southern Living* (Beth Maynor)
Page 33, left: James W. Clay
  right: *Southern Living* (Frederica Georgia)
Page 35: *Southern Living*
Page 37, left and right: From *America 1585: The Complete Drawings of John White,* edited by Paul Hulton. ©1984 University of North Carolina Press. Drawings, ©1964 Trustees of the British Museum. Used with permission of the publisher.
Page 40: From *America 1585: Complete Drawings of John White,* edited by Paul Hulton. ©1984 University of North Carolina Press. Drawings, ©1964 Trustees of the British Museum. Used with permission of the publisher.
Page 42: Middleton Place, Charleston, South Carolina
Page 44: *Southern Living* (Mike Clemmer)
Page 50: *Southern Living* (Mike Clemmer)
Page 52: Walter E. Martin
Page 54: *Southern Living* (Mike Clemmer)
Page 55: ©Bruce Roberts
Page 56: Walter E. Martin
Page 57: *Southern Living* (Sylvia Martin)
Page 64: ©Bruce Roberts
Page 66: ©Bruce Roberts
Page 67: Courtesy of Norshipco
Page 69: ©Bruce Roberts
Page 71: U.S. Department of Commerce, NOAA National Environmental Satellite, Data, and Information Service
Page 72: Courtesy Myrtle Beach Area Chamber of Commerce
Page 74: Middleton Place, Charleston, South Carolina
Page 75, left: Collection of City Hall, Charleston, South Carolina. Artist John Black White, *Perspective of Broad Street* (1837)
  right: *Southern Living* (Bruce Roberts)
Page 76: ©Bruce Roberts
Page 77: *Southern Living* (Beth Maynor)
Page 79: ©Bruce Roberts
Page 82: U.S. Department of the Interior, Geological Survey, North Carolina Department of Natural Resources and Community Development

Page 83: *Southern Living*

Page 85, left: ©Bruce Roberts
top right: ©Bruce Roberts
middle right: ©Bruce Roberts
bottom right: ©Bill Norment

Page 90: Southern Growth Policies Board

Page 91: ©Wes C. Skiles

Page 92, left: *Southern Living* (Mike Clemmer)
top right: *Southern Living* (Mike Clemmer)
bottom right: Florida Game and Fresh Water Fish Commission

Page 96: St. Augustine and St. Johns County Chamber of Commerce. Alcazar Hotel built by Henry Flagler.

Page 97: *Southern Living*

Page 100: Alfred W. Stuart

Page 102, left: ©Bruce Roberts
right: U.S. Department of Commerce, NOAA National Environmental Satellite, Data, and Information Service

Page 105: ©Bruce Roberts

Page 107: ©Bruce Roberts

Page 110: ©Bruce Roberts

Page 111: ©Kelly W. Culpepper

Page 112: *Southern Living* (Beth Maynor)

Page 113: *Southern Living* (Beth Maynor)

Page 114, top: Corps of Engineers, Vicksburg
bottom: Corps of Engineers, Vicksburg

Page 117, top: U.S. Department of Commerce, NOAA National Environmental Satellite, Data, and Information Service
bottom: ©C. C. Lockwood, 1983

Page 122, left: ©John S. Shelton
right: Courtesy Institute of Texan Cultures at San Antonio

Page 124: Courtesy San Augustine Chamber of Commerce

Page 125: Texas Parks & Wildlife Department

Page 126: *Southern Living* (Mike Clemmer)

Page 127: *Southern Living* (Frederica Georgia)

Page 128: James W. Clay

Page 129: James W. Clay

Page 130: Courtesy of North Fort Worth Historical Society

Page 133: U.S. Department of the Interior, Geological Survey, SLAR, Southern Appalachian Project Area 4, Bluefield and Winston-Salem, May 1984

Page 134: *Southern Living* (Bruce Roberts)

Page 135: *Southern Living*

Page 137: ©Bruce Roberts

Page 138: *Southern Living*

Page 139: ©Bruce Roberts

Page 141: ©Bruce Roberts

Page 142: Public Library of Charlotte and Mecklenburg County, Carolina Room

Page 143: ©Bruce Roberts

Page 144, left: ©Bruce Roberts
right: *Southern Living* (Bruce Roberts)

Page 146: ©Bruce Roberts

Page 147: ©Bruce Roberts

Page 148: ©Bruce Roberts

Page 150: Douglas M. Orr, Jr.

Page 151, left: *Southern Living* (Bruce Roberts)
right: ©Bruce Roberts

Page 153, left: *Southern Living* (Bruce Roberts)
right: ©Bruce Roberts

Page 155: U.S. Department of the Interior, Geological Survey, SLAR, Southern Appalachian Area 4, Bluefield, May 1984

Page 156: *Southern Living* (Bruce Roberts)

Page 157, all: Alfred W. Stuart

Page 158: *Southern Living* (Mac Jamieson)

Page 159: ©Bruce Roberts

Page 161: *Southern Living* (Bruce Roberts)

Page 166: U.S. Department of the Interior, Geological Survey, SLAR, Southern Appalachian Project Area 4, Bluefield, May 7, 1984

Page 170: Reprinted with permission from *The Courier-Journal & Times*

Page 172: *Southern Living* (Geoff Gilbert)

Page 173: Louisville Chamber of Commerce

Page 175: *Southern Living* (Bruce Roberts)

Page 177: *Southern Living* (Beth Maynor)

Page 178: Charles Phelps Cushing/H. Armstrong Roberts

Page 182: *Southern Living*

Page 183: From the collections of the Library of Congress. Arthur Rothstein, photographer

Page 187, top: *Southern Living* (Mike Clemmer)
bottom: Alfred W. Stuart

Page 188: Alfred W. Stuart

Page 191: *Southern Living* (Frederica Georgia)

Page 192: *Southern Living* (Beth Maynor)

Page 199: *Southern Living* (Mike Clemmer)

FIGURE INDEX

GENERAL INDEX

DESIGN
Earl Freedle

TEXT TYPE
Sabon

TYPESETTING
Media Services, Inc.
Birmingham, Alabama

COLOR SEPARATIONS
Capitol Engraving Company
Nashville, Tennessee

MANUFACTURER
Arcata Graphics
Kingsport, Tennessee

TEXT SHEETS
Patina
by S. D. Warren Company
Boston, Massachusetts

ENDLEAVES
Rainbow Colonial
by Ecological Fibers, Inc.
Lunenburg, Massachusetts

COVER MATERIAL
Arrestox B
by IGC, Inc.
Kingsport, Tennessee